The Genius of Science

The Genius of Science

A Portrait Gallery

ABRAHAM PAIS

Rockefeller University, New York

OXFORD

UNIVERSITY PRESS

OXFORD
UNIVERSITY PRESS

Great Clarendon Street, Oxford OX2 6DP

Oxford New York
Athens Auckland Bangkok Bogota Bombay Buenos Aires
Calcutta Cape Town Dar es Salaam Delhi Florence Hong Kong
Istanbul Karachi Kuala Lumpur Madras Madrid Melbourne
Mexico City Nairobi Paris Singapore Taipei Tokyo Toronto

and associated companies in
Berlin Ibadan

Oxford is a trade mark of Oxford University Press

Published in the United States
by Oxford University Press Inc., New York

A catalogue record for this book is available from the British Library

Library of Congress Cataloging in Publication Data

Pais, Abraham, 1918–
The genius of science: a portrait gallery / Abraham Pais.
Includes bibliographical references and index.
1. Scientists–Biography.   2. Science–History–20th century.   I. Title.
Q141.P29 2000   509.2'2–dc21   [B]   99-046603

ISBN 0 19 850614 7 (Hbk)

J&L Composition Ltd, Filey, North Yorkshire

Printed in Great Britain by Biddles Ltd,
Guildford & King's Lynn

Contents

TO IDA, JOSHUA, LISA, AND ZANE
and in grateful memory to those portrayed here, who are no
longer with us

On biographers

Nemo igitur Vir Magnus sine aliquo adflatu divino umquam fuit.
(No one was ever a Great Man without a certain divine touch.)

Marcus Tullius Cicero, *De Deorum Natura*, Book II, p. 167.

Plutarch, a first-century Greek, has often been called the father of biography. In his forty-six *Parallel Lives*, pairs of biographies, one Greek and one Roman, he masterfully matched narrative with anecdote, and analysis with high drama. Another early biographer to be remembered is Tacitus, Plutarch's Roman contemporary, for his *Life of Agricola*, his father-in-law. Among other works of long, but not that long, ago, Benvenuto Cellini's sixteenth-century (auto)biography stands out as one of the most singular and fascinating books in existence.

In our days, biographies range from lengthy tomes that go on and on forever to gossipy stories detailing someone or other's intimate life. That last category also has its predecessors. Examples: the sixteenth-century Abbé Pierre de Brantôme's *Dames Galantes*, unblushing accounts of scandalous anecdotes of the French court, or the seventeenth-century Gédéon Tallemant, Sieur de Réaux, who chronicled the many amorous adventures of such ladies as Ninon de l'Enclos in his *Historiettes*. Unlike modern vulgar output, however, these two volumes show a speed of wit, a lightness of touch, and an aptness of language which make for quite pleasant reading.

Among early English biographers, the best remembered are James Boswell, whose eighteenth-century *Life of Samuel* ('Dictionary') *Johnson* is veritably sacred wherever English is spoken; and John Lockhart, whose nineteenth-century *Life of Walter Scott* may well be the most admirable biography in the English language after Boswell.

And then there was John Aubrey, who in the seventeenth century perfected the short biography with his *Brief lives*, records of gossip with friends, which never moralized and only rarely turned to scandal. Aubrey, one of the 98 original Fellows of the Royal Society, knew Newton and men who had known Shakespeare ('His Playes tooke well.') The sharpness of his every phrase is striking; for example, this is what he wrote about Descartes: 'He was too wise a man to encomber himselfe with a Wife; but as he was a man, he had the desires and appetities of a man; he therefore kept a good hansome woman that he liked.'

No such delectations are found in early dictionaries of biography. The earliest one I know is Pierre Bayle's *Dictionnaire Historique et Critique*, the first volume of which appeared in 1697. The first one in English, the *Dictionary of National Biography*, was the creation of Leslie Stephen, best known today as the father of Virginia Woolf. The style of its first volume, which came out in 1885, is one of Victorian high seriousness and lacks all human insight. Less formal tributes are found in those *Dictionary* supplements that have appeared since 1950, when things were printed that earlier could be expressed only in conversation.

Browsing through the works of these past masters has led me to adopt the style for the present book.

———•———

In 1970 there appeared the first of the 14 volumes, followed by four supplements, of the *Dictionary of Scientific Biography*, a project ably directed by its Editor-in-Chief Charles Coulston Gillispie. Since every entry has its own specialized author, one will find differences in style and quality among the various contributions, but on the whole it provides a splendid and indispensable wealth of information on scientists from ancient to recent times, with added references to each person's main writings and obituaries (all those included are deceased).

Whenever I began collecting my thoughts on a person who appears in what follows, I would invariably turn to this *Dictionary* for a first orientation. The information so obtained is necessary but not at all sufficient for my own purpose, since it only tells what people did but not who they were.

As is in fact stated in the *Dictionary's* preface (Volume 1), that work was designed 'to make available reliable information on the history of science through the medium of articles on the *professional* lives of scientists... Authors were asked to place emphasis on the *scientific* accomplishments... *personal* biography has intentionally been kept to the minimum ...' (all italics are mine).

I, on the other hand, endeavor in what follows to present a blend of personality and work of those described, in other words I shall attempt to bring these people back to life, helped by the fact that I have known all of them personally, some better, some less well. This variance in level of acquaintance largely explains the variance in length of the entries that follow. They do not, repeat not, reflect on the relative importance of those portrayed. Regarding personal aspects, I have never been interested in entering others' bedrooms.

The present portraits are not full-fledged biographies like the ones I have published earlier, two on Albert Einstein[1,2] and one on Niels Bohr.[3] More recently I was invited, and accepted the offer, to write a contribution on Einstein for a major new Danish encyclopedia. I of course made use of my earlier books but had the challenging task to compress into 2000 words what earlier had taken me over 800 printed pages. It seemed fitting to include here this microbiography, translated into English from the original Danish, which I consider the essence of Einstein. A similarly highly compressed sketch of Bohr is another portrait included here, this one my opening address at a UNESCO conference in 1998.

The other portraits in this volume nearly all refer to people who have already appeared in my just-mentioned books as well as in my autobiography.[4] There they acted as supporting cast. Here they are presented in their own right, one might say. Most of what I write about them I have not told before, but minor repetition of earlier writing is of course inevitable. Some entries are much extended versions of earlier publications that have appeared in widely scattered places; about half are entirely new. I have of course made grateful use of various biographies by others on a number of my subjects but have not attempted to emulate these. My strategy differs, in fact, from most of them. Rather than going into painstaking detail, I have aimed at a more compact style in which only the central themes of the life and work are emphasized.

It is a pleasure to acknowledge with gratitude the help and advice I have enjoyed in gathering material.

On Feigenbaum: from Mitchell himself, the result of many late evening discussions.

On Jost: from Hilde, his widow; Walter Hunziker.

On Kramers: from Jan, his son; Jaap Goedkoop.

On Pauli: from Charles Enz, Hilde Jost, Karl von Meyenn.

On Rabi: from Chauncey G. Olinger, Jr.

On Wigner: from Martha Wigner Upton, his daughter; Frederick Seitz; Arthur Wightman.

On Uhlenbeck: from Else, his widow; Ockie, his son; Eugenius Marius, his brother.

I am very grateful to the A. P. Sloan Foundation for financial support that helped me in preparing this book.

Thank you, Jan Maier, for your ever fine help in typing the manuscript.

I am much beholden, as always, to my dear wife Ida for critical comments and steady encouragement.

References

1. A. Pais, *Subtle is the Lord*, Oxford University Press, Oxford and New York,1982. Translated so far into ten languages; detailed references to these are found in A. Pais, *A Tale of Two Continents*, chapter 31, refs. 15-24, Princeton University Press and Oxford University Press, 1997.

2. A. Pais, *Einstein Lived Here*, Oxford University Press, 1994. Translations: *Einstein woonde hier*, Bert Bakker, Amsterdam, 1995; *Einstein boede her*, Rhodos, Copenhagen, 1995; *Einstein è vissuto qui*, Boringhieri, Turin, 1995; *Ich vertraue auf Intuition*, Spektrum, Heidelberg, 1995; *Einstein viveu aqui*, Gradiva, Lisbon, 1996.

3. A. Pais, *Niels Bohr's Times*, Oxford University Press, 1991. Translations: *Il Danese tranquillo*, Boringhieri, Torino, 1993; *Niels Bohr og hans tid*, Spektrum, Copenhagen, 1994.

4. A. Pais, *A Tale of Two Continents* (ref. 1).

Niels Bohr at his country house in Tisvilde, Denmark, early 1960s. (Courtesy of Niels Bohr Archive, Copenhagen.)

Niels Bohr, the man and his science*

Introduction

Winston Churchill has written in Volume 1 of his *History of the English Speaking Peoples*:

> No one can understand history without continually relating the long periods which are constantly mentioned to the experience of our brief lives. Five years is a lot. Twenty years is the horizon . . . Fifty years is antiquity.

These words fittingly describe the times of Niels Bohr's life, which has spanned revolutionary changes in science itself as well as making a dramatic impact on society. As a first example, consider what Federico Mayor, Director General of UNESCO, wrote only a few years ago:

> In October 1988 an immense power of destruction was, perhaps for the first time in human history, being dismantled precisely because of the enormity of the risk it entailed for our species.[1]

Now compare this with the state of affairs at the time of Bohr's birth, when practical applications of atomic energy, for good or evil, were not even visible on the far horizon. In fact, as the curtain rises, the reality of atoms is still under debate, the atomic nucleus is not yet discovered. All that changed during Bohr's life, much of it under his own influence. He was the first to understand how atoms are put together, he played a leading role in the development of the theory of the atomic nucleus, and he was influential in creating nuclear medicine at his Institute. He was also the first to bring to the attention of leading statesmen the need for openness between West and East, a need resulting from the advent of formidable new weapons developed during and after the Second World War. Time and again he would stress that openness was essential for political world stability.

....
* Opening address, given on May 27, 1998, at the conference on 'Niels Bohr and the evolution of physics in the 20th century,' held at the UNESCO building in Paris.

Even more profound than new discoveries and perceptions regarding the structure of matter are new physical laws discovered in the same period. Here the key concepts are relativity theory and quantum theory. Bohr was the principal figure in elucidating the revisions of the philosophical foundations of physics for a comprehension of quantum phenomena.

After this bird's eye view of Bohr's scientific legacy, I turn to an account of Bohr the man and the scientist.

On the morning of October 24, 1957, Robert Oppenheimer and I took an early train from Princeton to Washington. We were on our way to the Great Hall of the National Academy of Sciences, where, that afternoon, the first Atoms for Peace Award was to be presented to Niels Bohr. It was a festive event. James Killian read the award citation, from which I quote:

> Niels Henrik David Bohr, in your chosen field of physics you have explored the structure of the atom and unlocked many of Nature's other secrets. You have given men the basis for greater understanding of matter and energy. You have made contributions to the practical uses of this knowledge. At your Institute for Theoretical Physics at Copenhagen, which has served as an intellectual and spiritual center for scientists, you have given scholars from all parts of the world an opportunity to extend man's knowledge of nuclear phenomena. These scholars have taken from your Institute not only enlarged scientific understanding but also a humane spirit of active concern for the proper utilization of scientific knowledge.
>
> In your public pronouncements and through your world contacts, you have exerted great moral force in behalf of the utilization of atomic energy for peaceful purposes.
>
> In your profession, in your teaching, in your public life, you have shown that the domain of science and the domain of the humanities are in reality of single realm. In all your career you have exemplified the humility, the wisdom, the humaneness, the intellectual splendor which the Atoms for Peace Award would recognize.

Killian then presented the award (a gold medal and a check for $75 000) to Bohr, while a smiling President Eisenhower looked on.[2] In his brief response Bohr stressed the need for international understanding: 'The rapid advance of science and technology in our age . . . presents civilization with a most serious challenge. To meet this challenge . . . the road is indicated by worldwide cooperation.'

Next, the President addressed Bohr, calling him 'a great man whose mind has explored the mysteries of the inner structure of atoms, and whose spirit has reached into the very heart of man.'[3]

Killian's citation eloquently describes that combination of qualities we find in Bohr and only in Bohr: creator of science, teacher of science, and spokesman not only for science *per se* but also for science as a potential source for the common good.

As a creator he is one of the three men without whom the birth of that uniquely twentieth-century mode of thought, quantum physics, is unthinkable. The three, in order of appearance, are: Max Planck, the reluctant revolutionary, discoverer of the quantum theory, who did not at once understand that his quantum law meant the end of an era in physics now called classical; Albert Einstein, discoverer of the quantum of light, the photon, founder of the quantum theory of solids, who at once realized that classical physics had reached its limits, a situation with which he never could make peace; and Bohr, founder of the quantum theory of the structure of matter, also immediately aware that his theory violated sacred classical concepts, but who at once embarked on the search for links between the old and the new, achieved with a considerable measure of success in his correspondence principle.

How different their personalities were. Planck, in many ways the conventional university professor, teaching his courses, delivering his PhDs. Einstein, rarely lonely, mostly alone, who did not really care for teaching classes and never delivered a PhD, easily accessible yet so apart, ever so friendly yet so distant. And Bohr, always in need of other physicists, especially young ones, to help him clarify his own thoughts, always generous in helping them clarify theirs, not so much a teacher of courses nor a supervisor of PhDs but forever giving inspiration and guidance to so many engaged in post-doctoral and senior research, father figure extraordinary to physicists belonging to several generations, including this speaker.

Bohr's researches, his teachings, his endeavors in the political sphere, and his relations with other major figures of his time—these are among the themes to be developed in this paper. But there are more. There is also Bohr the philosopher, the administrator, the fund raiser, the catalyst in promoting physical applications to biology, the helper of political refugees, the co-founder of international physics institutes as well as the nuclear power projects in Denmark, and, last but not least, the devoted family man. A composite picture will emerge of a life so full and dedicated that one wonders how a single individual could have managed so much.

Bohr's spectrum of activities was broad; the intensity with which he attacked whatever task lay before him was high. All who knew him well were aware of his immense powers of concentration which one could often note simply by looking at him. A story will illustrate this.

Bohr's aunt, Hanna Adler, once told me of an experience she had long ago when she sat in a Copenhagen streetcar together with Bohr's mother and the two young sons, Harald and Niels. The boys were hanging on their mother's lips as she was telling them a story. Apparently there was something peculiar about these two young faces in concentration, for Miss Adler overheard one lady in the streetcar remark to her neighbour, 'Stakkels mor' (that poor mother).

As I have been told time and again, those who have read recollections and biographies of Bohr often tend to come away with the overall reaction that his life story is too good to be true. I, too, believe that his was a wonderful life and that he was a good man, capable of both bringing and receiving happiness. I do not consider him, however, as an angelic figure to whom struggle, ambition, disappointment, and personal tragedy were alien.

Which brings me to some personal recollections.

In January 1946 I arrived in Copenhagen for the first time from my native Holland, the first of the post-Second World War generation to come to Bohr's Institute from abroad for a longer period of study. The morning after my arrival I went to the secretary, Mrs Betty Schultz, who told me to wait in the library where she would call me as soon as Professor Bohr was free to see me. I had sat there reading for a while, when someone knocked at the door. I said come in. The door opened. It was Bohr. My first thought was, what a gloomy face.

Then he began to speak.

Later I have often been puzzled about this first impression. It vanished the very moment Bohr started to talk to me that morning, never to return. True, one might correctly describe Bohr's physiognomy as unusually heavy or rugged. Yet his face is remembered by all who knew him for its intense animation and its warm and sunny smile.

Soon thereafter I had my first opportunity to talk physics with Bohr. I told him of problems in quantum electrodynamics I had worked out during my years in hiding in Holland. While I was telling him what I had done, he smoked his pipe; he looked mainly at the floor and would only rarely look up at the blackboard on which I was enthusiastically writing down various formulae. After I finished, Bohr did not say much, and I felt a bit disheartened with the impression that he could not care less about the whole subject. I did not know him well enough at the time to realize that this was not entirely true. At a later stage I would have known right away that his curiosity was aroused, as he had neither remarked that this was very interesting nor said that we agreed much more than I thought—his favorite ways of expressing that he did not believe what he was told.

Bohr had in fact become quite interested in what I had told him. One day in May he asked me whether I would be interested in working with him on a daily basis during the coming months. I was thrilled and accepted. The next morning I went to Carlsberg. The first thing Bohr said to me was that it would only be profitable to work with him if I understood that he was a dilettante. The only way I could react to this unexpected statement was with a polite smile of disbelief. But evidently Bohr was serious. He explained how he had to approach every new question from a starting point of total ignorance. It is perhaps better to say that Bohr's strength lay in his formidable intuition and insight rather than in erudition. I thought of his remarks of that morning some years later, when I sat at his side during a colloquium in Princeton. The subject was nuclear isomers. As the speaker went on, Bohr got more and more restless and kept whispering to me that it was all wrong. Finally, he could contain himself no longer and wanted to raise an objection. But after having half-raised himself, he sat down again, looked at me with unhappy bewilderment, and asked 'What is an isomer?'

The first subject of work was the preparation of Bohr's opening address to the International Conference on Fundamental Particles to be held in July 1946 in Cambridge, England. I must admit that in the early stages of our collaboration I did not follow Bohr's line of thinking a good deal of the time and was in fact often quite bewildered. I failed to see the relevance of remarks such as, for example, that Erwin Schrödinger was completely shocked in 1926 when he was told of the probability interpretation of quantum mechanics, or references to some objection by Einstein in 1927 which apparently had no bearing whatever on the subject at hand. It did not take very long before the fog started to lift, however. I began to grasp not only the thread of Bohr's arguments but also their purpose. Just as many sports players go through warming-up exercises before entering the arena, so Bohr would relive the struggles which had taken place before the content of quantum mechanics was understood and accepted. I can say that in Bohr's mind this struggle started afresh every single day. Einstein appeared forever as his leading spiritual sparring partner; even after Einstein's death Bohr would argue with him as if he were still alive.

Sometime later the Bohr family went to their summer house in Tisvilde. I was invited to stay with them, so that the work could continue. It was a wonderful experience. A good deal of the day was spent working in a separate little pavilion on the grounds. All during this period, his son Aage Bohr joined in as well. We would go for a swim in the afternoon and often work more at night. In fact after Aage and I had retired, Bohr would still come in sometimes, in a shoe and a sock, to impart to us just one further thought that had occurred to him that very minute, and would keep talking for an hour or so.

Other evenings were spent in the family circle, and sometimes Bohr would read one or more of his favorite poems. He liked especially to quote the following lines by Schiller:

> . . . Wer etwas Treffliches leisten will,
> Hätt' gern etwas Grosses geboren,
> Der sammle still und unerschlafft
> Im kleinsten Punkte die höchste Kraft.

These lines have been translated[4] as

> Ah! he would achieve the fair,
> Or sow the embryo of the great,
> Must hoard—to wait the ripening hour—
> In the least point the loftiest power.

Like everything Bohr did, large or small, he was able to put his whole being into it and he could convey beautifully how small the point was and how lofty the power.

Bohr was an indefatigable worker. When he was in need of a break in the discussions, he would go outside and apply himself to the pulling of weeds with what can only be called ferocity. At this point I can contribute a little item to the lore about Bohr the pipe smoker. It is well known that to him the operations of filling a pipe and lighting it were interchangeable but the following situation was even more extreme. One day Bohr was weeding again, his pipe between his teeth. At one point, unnoticed by Bohr, the bowl fell off the stem. Aage and I were lounging in the grass, expectantly awaiting further developments. It is hard to forget Bohr's look of stupefaction when he found himself holding a thoughtfully lit match against a pipe without bowl.

Bohr devoted tremendous effort and care to the composition of his articles. However, to perform the physical act of writing, pen or chalk in hand, was almost alien to him. He preferred to dictate. On one of the few occasions that I actually did see him write, Bohr performed the most remarkable act of calligraphy I shall ever witness.

It happened during that summer in the pavilion in Tisvilde, as we were discussing the address Bohr was to give on the occasion of the tercentenary celebration of Newton's birth. Bohr stood in front of the blackboard (wherever he dwelt, a blackboard was never far) and wrote down some general themes to be discussed. One of them had to do with the harmony of something or other. So Bohr wrote down the word *harmony*. It looked about as follows:

However, as the discussion progressed, Bohr became dissatisfied with the use of harmony. He walked around restlessly. Then he stopped and his face lit up. 'Now I've got it. We must change *harmony* to *uniformity*.' So he picked up the chalk again, stood there looking for a moment at what he had written before, and then made the single change:

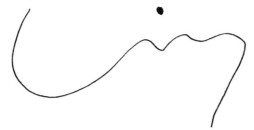

with one triumphant bang of the chalk on the blackboard.

In the fall of 1946 Bohr and I were in Princeton, where I helped him prepare a lecture. Bohr was not a good public speaker, yet he was a man of the greatest lucidity of thought. Nor was that entirely due to the fact that Bohr's voice did not carry far, which made it impossible to hear him at the back of a large audience. The main reason was that he was in deep thought as he spoke. I remember how that day he had finished part of the argument, then said, 'And . . . and . . .,' then was silent for at most a second, then said, 'But . . .,' and continued. Between the 'and' and the 'but' the next point had gone through his mind. However, he simply forgot to say it out loud and went on somewhere further down his road. To me, the story was continuous as I knew precisely how to fill in the gaps Bohr had left open. And so it has come to pass more than once that I have seen an audience leave a talk by Bohr in a mild state of bewilderment, even though he had toiled hard in preparing himself in great detail. Still, when he would come up to me afterwards with the characteristic question: '*Jeg håber det var nogenlunde*' (I hope it was tolerable), I could assure him that it was much more than that. In spite of linguistic shortcomings, this unrelenting struggle for truth was a powerful source of inspiration.

My own first direct experience of the impact of Einstein on Bohr happened in 1948, at the Institute for Advanced Study in Princeton. At that time Bohr was a temporary visitor there, I a permanent member. One day Bohr came to my office. He was in a state of angry despair and kept saying 'I am sick of myself,' several times. I was concerned and asked what had happened. He told me he had just been downstairs to see Einstein. As always they had got into an argument about the meaning of quantum mechanics. And, as remained true to the end, Bohr had been unable to convince Einstein of his views. There can be no doubt that Einstein's lack of assent was a very deep frustration to Bohr. It is our good fortune that this led Bohr to keep striving at clarification and better formulation. And not only that: it was Bohr's own good fortune, too.

Another day Bohr came into my office and started as follows: '*Du er så klog . . .*' (you are so wise). I started to laugh (no formality was called for with him) and said: 'All right, I understand.' Bohr wanted me to come down to his office and talk. We went there, and it should be explained that Bohr at that time used

Einstein's own office in Fuld Hall. At the same time, Einstein himself used the adjoining small assistant's office: he had a dislike of the big one, which he did not use anyway. After we had entered, Bohr asked me to sit down ('I always need an origin for the coordinate system') and soon started to pace furiously around the oblong table in the center of the room. He then asked me if I could note down a few sentences as they emerged during his pacing. At such sessions, Bohr never had a full sentence ready. He would often dwell on one word, coax it, implore it, to find the continuation. This could go on for several minutes. At the moment the word was 'Einstein.' There was Bohr, almost running around the table and repeating 'Einstein . . . Einstein . . .' It would have been curious sight for someone not familiar with him. After a little while he walked to the window, gazed out, repeating every now and then: 'Einstein . . . Einstein . . .'

At that moment the door opened very softly and Einstein tiptoed in. He indicated to me with a finger on his lips to be very quiet, an urchin smile on his face. He was to explain a few minutes later the reason for his behavior. Einstein was not allowed by his doctor to buy tobacco. However, the doctor had not forbidden him to steal tobacco, and this was precisely what he set out to do now. Always on tiptoe, he made a beeline for Bohr's tobacco pot, which stood on the table at which I was sitting. Meanwhile Bohr, unaware, was standing at the window, muttering 'Einstein . . . Einstein . . .' I was at a loss what to do, especially because I had at that moment not the faintest idea what Einstein was up to.

Then Bohr, with a firm 'Einstein', turned around. There they were, face to face, as if Bohr had summoned him forth. It is an understatement to say that for a moment Bohr was speechless. I myself, who had seen it coming, had felt distinctly uncanny for a moment, so I could well understand Bohr's own reaction. A moment later the spell was broken when Einstein explained his mission and soon we were all bursting with laughter.

The periods of closest contact which I had with Bohr are those mentioned so far. In subsequent years I saw him often, either in Denmark or in the US, but no longer for protracted periods of time.

In the fall of 1961 we were both present at the Solvay Congress in Brussels. It was the 50th anniversary of the first one, and Bohr gave an account, both charming and fascinating, of the developments during that period.[5] He was present at the report I gave at that meeting, after which we talked in the corridor and spoke of the future of particle physics. It was the last time I spoke to him.

Descent and early years

Niels Bohr descended from an upper class background. His father was professor of physiology at the University of Copenhagen, its rector during 1905–6, and was twice proposed for the Nobel Prize in physiology or medicine. His mother hailed from a Jewish banking family. Her father was co-founder of two major

Danish banks and a member of parliament. Niels was born on October 7, 1885, at Ved Stranden 14, one of Copenhagen's handsomest mansions, then the home of his maternal grandmother. He had an older sister, Jenny, and a younger brother, Harald, who became a renowned mathematician. All who knew Niels in his early years have recalled[6] a close-knit, harmonious, and stimulating family. When I saw the brothers together, it struck me that one could see in Harald's face—but not in Niels'—some traits of his Jewish ancestry. Soon after Niels' birth the family moved to the professorial apartment at Bredgade 62, where he would live until he received his doctorate.

In his school years Niels was tall and strong like a bear. During his adolescence he would occasionally beat-up classmates. He did well in school but was not ambitious. From early on he showed special gifts for mathematics and physics, was not good at foreign languages, but very good at Danish. In physical exercises he was one of the best, especially at soccer. His brother was even better at that, becoming a member of the Danish soccer team that won the silver medal at the 1908 Olympics.

There is a charming story about Bohr and soccer. After he had been appointed professor in Copenhagen, he presented himself at a public audience to the King, as is the Danish custom. Dress: morning coat and white gloves, the latter not to be removed when shaking hands with the monarch. Accordingly Bohr called on Christian X, a rather stiff military type. I have it on good authority that this event went about as follows. After the introduction the King said he was pleased to meet the famous soccer player Bohr, whereupon Niels replied something like, I am sorry but Your Majesty must be thinking of my brother. The King was taken aback since according to the rules of the game one does not contradict the monarch during a public audience. So Christian started all over again, saying how pleased he was, etc. Bohr now became very uncomfortable and replied that indeed he was a soccer player, but that he had a brother who was the *famous* soccer player. Whereupon the King said, '*Audiensen er forbi*' (the audience is over), and Bohr took his leave, walking backwards, as custom demands.

In 1903 Bohr entered Copenhagen University. He had chosen physics as his major, astronomy, chemistry, and mathematics as minor subjects. His chemistry teacher has recalled that Bohr was second to none in breaking glassware. Oh, that must be Bohr, he is said to have remarked when one day the laboratory was rocked by explosions.[7]

However that may be, Bohr's first scientific publication describes some lovely physics experiments he had performed. In order to execute these he had to cope with a complication. The University had no physics laboratory. So he did this work in his father's physiology laboratory. He dictated the resulting paper[8] to

Harald, the first example of his life-long routine to do the work himself but let others do the writing.

In 1910 Niels obtained his master's degree, and in May 1911 he publicly defended his doctor's thesis wearing the customary white tie and tails. A newspaper noted that the majority of those attending were soccer players.

The thesis is entitled: 'Studies on the electron theory of metals.'[9] It is an extension of the classical theory initiated by Lorentz. Of particular interest is his inevitable failure to explain *classically* some paradoxes related to the Hall effect. About these he stated:

> It does not seem possible at the present stage of the development of the electron theory to explain the magnetic properties of bodies from this theory.

It could just be that these experiences encouraged him to push into areas beyond, into the mysteries of quantum physics, as he was soon to do.

The year 1911 can be said to mark the end of the first phase of Bohr's life. Meanwhile the second phase had begun. In 1909 he first met his future wife, Margrethe Norlund. They were married on August 1, 1912. The finest comment on the meeting of Niels and Margrethe was made shortly after Niels' death by Richard Courant, friend of the Bohrs for many decades:

> Some people have speculated about the lucky circumstances which combined to make Niels so successful. I think the ingredients of his life were by no means matters of chance but deeply ingrained in the structure of his personality . . . It was not luck, rather deep insight, which led him to find in young years his wife, who, as we all know, had such a decisive role in making his whole scientific and personal activity possible and harmonious.[10]

I have been privileged to know Margrethe well. She was a most charming yet formidable lady.

Bohr, father of the atom

In 1911, Bohr sent the following letter to the Carlsberg Foundation:

In English: 'The undersigned takes the liberty of requesting a travel stipend of 2500 kroner for one year's study at Universities abroad.' The amount requested—and received—may seem puny, but remember that since that time the Danish kroner has suffered deflation by a factor of about forty. More striking is the fact that neither a vita nor a research proposal was appended, showing that Bohr was already sufficiently known by the powers that be.

The following September Bohr arrived at the Cavendish Laboratory in Cambridge, hoping to work under the guidance of J. J. Thomson. I have been told that their first meeting went roughly as follows. He entered the office, opened J. J.'s book *Conduction of Electricity Through Gases*, pointed at a certain formula and politely said: 'This is wrong.' About that encounter Bohr said, later in life:

Kjøbenhavn d. 20 Juni 1911.

Undertegnede tillader sig at ansøge om et Rejsestipendium paa 2500 Kr til et etaarigt Studieophold ved udenlandske Universiteter

ærbødigst

Niels Bohr
Dr. phil.

Til Carlsbergfondets Direktion

Facsimile of Bohr's application to the Carlsberg Foundation.

It was a disappointment that Thomson was not interested to learn that his calculations were not correct. That was also my fault. I had no great knowledge of English and therefore I did not know how to express myself. And I could say only that this is incorrect. And he was not interested in the accusation that it was not correct . . . Thomson was a genius who actually showed the way to everybody. *Then* some young man could make things a little better . . . The whole thing was very interesting in Cambridge but it was absolutely useless.[11]

Then, while still attached to Cambridge, Bohr met Rutherford and his whole life changed.

———————

Times were not yet ripe for tackling the theory of atomic structure when the twentieth century began. As one physicist has written: 'It is perhaps not unfair to say that, for the average physicist of that time, speculations about atomic structure were something like speculations about life on Mars—very interesting for those who like that kind of thing, but without much hope of support from convincing scientific evidence and without much bearing on scientific thought and development.'[12] The first major step toward clarifying this issue was Rutherford's discovery that the bulk of the atomic mass resides in a tiny central body, the nucleus. That work was published in May 1911—half a year before Bohr met Rutherford for the first time. Which goes to show once again that it is not enough to be smart, one also has to be at the right place, Rutherford's laboratory in Manchester, and at the right time, March 1912, when Bohr moved there.

Rutherford was the most important scientific figure in Bohr's life, not just because his discovery of the nucleus led to Bohr's most important work, his discovery of the structure of the atom as a whole, but also because Rutherford's personal and scientific style profoundly influenced Bohr. Later he said of him: 'To me he had almost been like a second father.'[13]

Rutherford had stated that an atom consists of a nucleus plus electrons orbiting around it, either unaware or unconcerned of the paradoxes this picture posed. Bohr's early thoughts on that problem are contained in a memorandum[14] sent to Rutherford on July 6, 1912. The most important line in this document concerns his realization that its understanding demands a new 'hypothesis for which there will be given no attempt at a mechanical foundation (*as it seems hopeless*),' (my italics). He had realized that atomic stability cannot be understood on the basis of classical physics but that one somehow needed the young quantum theory.

Later in July Bohr returned to Denmark to get married, and to take up a junior position at the University. Friends have characterized him at that time as: 'Somewhat introvert, saintly, extremely friendly, yet shy[15] . . . an incessant worker, always in a hurry, serenity and pipe smoking came later.'[16]

It was only in February 1913 that Bohr realized the need for spectroscopic data to reach his goal. This resulted in a paper,[17] published in July, that marks the birth of quantum *dynamics*. His main piece of information was the divine guess made by Johann Balmer, a Swiss schoolmaster, who in 1885 had proposed his formula

$$ v_{mn} = R \left[\frac{1}{n^2} - \frac{1}{m^2} \right], $$

($n = 1, 2, 3, \ldots m > n$ and integer) for the hydrogen spectrum. Already in 1885 the 'Rydberg constant' R was known to one part in ten thousand, correct to one part in a thousand:

$$ R = 3{,}2916 \times 10^{15} \text{ inverse secs.} $$

Now to Bohr's paper on hydrogen.[17] He begins by noting that, according to the classical theory, 'the electron will no longer describe stationary orbits,' but will fall inward to the nucleus due to energy loss by radiation. Then he plunges into the quantum theory. His first postulate: an atom has a state of lowest energy, the ground state, which *by assumption* does not radiate, one of the most audacious hypotheses ever introduced in physics. His second postulate: higher 'stationary states' of an atom will turn into lower ones such that the energy difference E is emitted in the form of a light quantum with frequency v given by $E = hv$ (h is Planck's constant).

I shall not discuss in detail Bohr's quantum constraint on the hydrogen orbits. Suffice it to say that it is equivalent to the one we learned in school: the orbital angular momentum L is restricted to the values

$$L = n(h/2\pi), \qquad\qquad n = 0, 1, 2, \ldots$$

Not only does the Balmer formula follow at once, but R now appears in terms of fundamental constants

$$R = (2\pi^2 e^4 m / h^3) \text{ inverse secs.}$$

This prediction of R, 'inside the experimental errors in the constants entering in the expression for the theoretical value,' is the first triumph of quantum dynamics and the most important equation that Bohr derived in his life. It represented a triumph over logic. Never mind that discrete orbits violated the laws of physics then known. Nature had told Bohr that he was right anyway and had advised him that a new logic was called for which should also explain the serious conflict of the Bohr theory with classical causality: how does an electron choose beforehand to which stationary state it shall pass when emitting a light quantum? All these issues were clarified after 1925 when quantum mechanics arrived. Bohr was of course well aware of all these problems. As was written of him at the time of his death: 'The tentative character of all scientific advance was always on his mind, from the day he first proposed his hydrogen atom, stressing that it was merely a model beyond his grasp. He was sure that every advance must be bought by sacrificing some previous certainty and he was forever prepared for the next sacrifice.'[18]

Bohr's work of 1913 caused a veritable explosion of activity in quantum physics, in Europe as well as in the United States. As he wrote to Rutherford, 'The whole field has from a very lonely state suddenly got into a desperately crowded one.'[19] I must restrict myself to Bohr's own contributions during the next few years. These are: his formulation of the correspondence principle which states, roughly speaking, that for large wave lengths the theory should be in formal accord with classical mechanics and electrodynamics; his prediction of the ratio of Rydberg constants for singly ionized helium and hydrogen, agreeing with experiment to five significant figures; his formulation of selection rules for electric dipole transitions; and his proof that the chemical properties of the elements are largely determined by the configuration of the outermost shell of electrons, which may be said to make him the founder of quantum chemistry. He also struggled with one of the several problems which his theory could not cope with: the spectrum of helium, not understood until 1926.

The best characterization of Bohr's activities during those years was given in 1949 by the 70-year-old Einstein: 'That this insecure and contradictory foundation was sufficient to enable a man of Bohr's unique instinct and tact to discover the major laws of the spectral lines appeared to me as a miracle—and appears to me as a miracle even today. This is the highest sphere of musicality in the sphere of thought.'[20]

Those years of struggle in the *clair-obscur* left an indelible mark on Bohr's style, once again best expressed by Einstein: 'He utters his opinions like one perpetually groping and never like one who believes to be in the possession of definite truth.'[21] As Bohr himself often used to say, never express yourself more clearly than you think.

Bohr as administrator and fundraiser

In April 1916 Bohr was appointed to the newly created chair of theoretical physics in Copenhagen. On March 3, 1921 his own Institute for Theoretical Physics (the later Niels Bohr Institute) was formally opened. Soon physicists from far and wide came to work there, the world's leading center in theoretical physics during the 1920s and 1930s. The international character of the enterprise was manifest from the start. By 1930 some 60 physicists, hailing from Austria, Belgium, Canada, China, Germany, Holland, Hungary, India, Japan, Norway, Poland, Romania, Switzerland, the United Kingdom, the United States, and the USSR had spent time in Copenhagen.[22] By the time of Bohr's death the number of visitors who spent at least a month in Copenhagen had risen to over 400. At the opening ceremonies of the Institute Bohr had stated its main theme to be: 'To introduce a constantly renewed number of young people into the results and methods of science,'[23] covering not only theory but also a lively experimental program, all directed and supervised by Bohr himself, who also personally oversaw several extensions of his Institute's buildings. Among the mighty contributions produced in Copenhagen by those young people I note: Heisenberg's uncertainty relations; Dirac's transformation theory, the Dirac statistics, and his first paper on quantum electrodynamics; Frisch and Meitner's theory of nuclear fission; and the experimental discovery of a new element, hafnium, named after Copenhagen. Moreover, beginning in 1929, Bohr organized a series of international conferences at his Institute, remembered as the most outstanding gatherings of their kind during these years. No wonder that in those days he was called 'director of atomic theory.'[24]

So did Bohr fulfill his tasks as teacher and administrator. But that was still not all. Bohr also became his own raiser of funds, from Denmark and abroad. When in 1923 he came to the United States to negotiate funding by the Rockefeller Foundation, *The New York Times* called him 'A modern Viking who comes on a great errand . . . [25] Working with Dr. Bohr is regarded by scientists as working with the foremost of the exponents of the new atomic physics, which is revolutionizing science.'[26] Bohr is unique, I believe, in being able to combine all these activities with an intense and most important research program of his own at the frontiers of physics. He worked under strains which stretched his formidable physical strength to the limit—and beyond. A few times, overexertion would force him to take some weeks' rest.

In 1922 Bohr received the Nobel Prize. These days, such awards make front page news in the world press. It was not always like that. To find the first word of Bohr's prize in *The New York Times*, turn to page 4, the middle of column 2, of its November 10 edition to find, in its entirety, the following item:

> Nobel prize for Einstein
> The Nobel Committee has awarded the physics prize for 1921 to Albert Einstein, identified with the theory of relativity, and that for 1922 to Professor Neils [*sic*] Bohr of Copenhagen.

At the traditional Nobel banquet, Bohr proposed 'A toast to the vigorous growth of the international work on the advancement of science which is one of the high points of existence in these, in many respects, sorrowful times",[27] words spoken shortly after the end of the First World War.

Complementarity

In 1925 quantum mechanics arrived. In March 1927 Heisenberg stated his uncertainty principle. On September 16, 1927, at the Volta Meeting in Como, Bohr enunciated for the first time the principle of complementarity, which embodies the physical interpretation of the uncertainty relations.[28]

From then on and for the rest of his life Bohr focussed on the language of science, the way in which we communicate. In 1927 he stated straight away his main theme:

> Our interpretation of the experimental material rests essentially upon the classical concepts.

It sounds simple enough but is also most profound. Let me enlarge. In the classical era one verified the validity of theories by comparing them with experimental observations made with balances, thermometers, voltmeters, etc. The theories have been modified in the quantum era but—and this was Bohr's point—their validity continues to be verified by the same readings of a balance's equilibrium position, a thermometer's mercury column, a voltmeter's needle, etc. The phenomena may be novel, their modes of detection may have been modernized, but detectors should be treated as classical objects; their readings continue to be described in classical terms.

'The situation thus created is of a peculiar nature,' Bohr remarked.[27] Consider for example the question: can I not ask for the quantum mechanical properties of a detector, say a voltmeter? The answer is yes, I can. Next question: but should I then not abandon the limited description of the voltmeter as a classical object, and rather treat it quantum mechanically? The answer is yes, I must. But in order to register the voltmeter's quantum properties I need *another* piece of apparatus with which I again make classical readings. In Bohr's own rather cryptic words: 'The concept of observation is in so far arbitrary as it depends upon which objects are included in the system to be observed.'[28]

These considerations led Bohr to introduce his refinement of language demanded by quantum mechanics. Thus he said (I paraphrase): the question of whether an electron is a particle or a wave is a sensible question in the classical context, where the relation between the object of study and detector either needs no specification or else is a controllable relation. In quantum mechanics that question is meaningless, however. There one should rather ask: does the electron (or any other object) *behave* like a particle or like a wave? That question is answerable, but only if one specifies the experimental arrangement by means of which 'one looks' at the electron. That is what Bohr meant in Como, where he introduced the concept of complementarity:

> An independent reality in the ordinary [that is, classical] physical sense can ... neither be ascribed to the phenomena nor to the agencies of observation ... The very nature of the quantum theory ... forces us to regard the space-time coordination and the claim of causality, the union of which characterizes the classical theories, as complementary but exclusive features of the description, symbolizing the idealization of observation and definition, respectively.[28]

Let me say what Bohr meant in my own words. Wave and particle behavior mutually exclude each other. The classical physicist would say: if two descriptions are mutually exclusive, then at least one of them must be wrong. The quantum physicist will say: whether an object behaves as a particle or as a wave depends on your choice of experimental arrangement for looking at it. He will not deny that particle and wave behavior are mutually exclusive but will assert that both are necessary for the full understanding of the object's properties.

It can be said that with Bohr's paper of 1927 the logic of quantum mechanics as we know it today reached it closure. It was Heisenberg[29] who coined the term *der Kopenhagener Geist*, the spirit of Copenhagen, for this fundamentally new interpretation of the foundation of quantum physics.

Bohr's Como lecture did not bring down the house, however. He himself would later frown on expressions he used there, such as 'disturbing the phenomena by observation.' Such language may have contributed to the considerable confusion that for so long has reigned around this subject. It has been said of his philosophical writings:[30] 'Against the sometimes maddening frustration brought about by these essays is the fact that nobody has succeeded in saying anything better in the 60 years since Bohr started talking about the problem.'[31] To me these writings are not at all frustrating, however, since I have had the privilege of many discussions with Bohr about these problems.

A month after Como the great masters gathered at the fifth Solvay Congress in Brussels. It was there that Einstein expressed for the first time his critical attitude toward quantum mechanics, which he maintained until his death. This forced Bohr to improve his language. His finest expose is found in the volume[32] for Einstein's 70th birthday. I know that article so well because in Princeton I helped him prepare it. In this paper he recalled his position[33] regarding the so-called EPR paradox,[34] a misnomer since that paper is logically flawless. They simply concluded that Bohr's view is incompatible with the assumption that quantum mechanics is complete. Einstein's statement[32] that quantum mechanics is 'not reasonable' is *his* problem.

Also in that Einstein book Bohr repeated[35] the correct language which it had taken him 20 years to formulate that clearly: *to define the term 'phenomenon' to include both the object of study and the mode of observation*:

> Phrases often found in the physical literature, as 'disturbance of phenomena by observation' or 'creation of physical attributes of objects by measurements', represent a use of words like 'phenomena' and 'observation' as well as 'attribute' and 'measurement' which is hardly compatible with common usage and practical definition and, therefore, is apt to cause confusion. As a more appropriate way of expression, one may strongly advocate limitation of the use of the word phenomenon to refer exclusively to observations obtained under specified circumstances, including an account of the whole experiment.[35]

I am now ready to state why I consider Bohr to be not only a major figure in physics but also one of the most important twentieth-century philosophers. As such he must be considered the successor to Kant, who had considered causality as a 'synthetic judgement a priori,' not derivable from experience. Causality is, in Kant's own words, 'a rule according to which phenomena are sequentially determined. Only by assuming that rule is it possible to speak of experience of something that happens.' This view must now be considered *passé*. Since Bohr the very definition of what constitutes a phenomenon has undergone changes that, unfortunately, have not yet sunk in sufficiently among professional philosophers.

Again according to Kant, constructive concepts are intrinsic attributes of the 'Ding an sich,' a viewpoint desperately maintained by Einstein, but abandoned by quantum physicists. In Bohr's words: 'Our task is not to penetrate in the essence of things, the meaning of which we don't know anyway, but rather to develop concepts which allow us to talk in a productive way about phenomena in nature.'[36] After Bohr's death Heisenberg wrote that Bohr was 'primarily a philosopher, not a physicist,'[37] a judgement that is arguable yet particularly significant if one recalls how greatly Heisenberg admired Bohr's physics.

From many discussions with Bohr I know that complementarity was his contribution most precious to him. There lay his inexhaustible source of identity in later life. He would not consider himself a philosopher, however, as witness his favorite definition of an expert and a philosopher. An expert is someone who starts out knowing something about some things, goes on to know more and more about less and less, and ends up knowing everything about nothing. Whereas a philosopher is someone who starts out knowing something about some things, goes on to know less and less about more and more, and ends up knowing nothing about everything. I like to think that Pascal's words, 'To ridicule philosophy is truly philosophical,' might have appealed to him.[38]

Much has been written on how Bohr was influenced by his reading of various philosophers. I consider such speculations as far-fetched, to say the least. I do know, however, that he admired William James, and spoke with respect of Buddha and Lao Tse.

Bohr gave much thought to extending complementarity to fields outside physics, being well aware that those ideas were mostly preliminary. The fields he probed were biology, where his ideas are now obsolete; human cultures where on the issue of nature versus nurture he emphatically sided with the latter; and psychology, where I consider his ideas of lasting value. Samples: 'Words like thoughts and sentiments . . . have since the origins of language been used in a typically complementary manner.'[39] And: 'It must be recognized that in any situation which calls for the strict application of justice there is no room for display of love and that, conversely, the ultimate exigencies of a feeling of love may conflict with all ideas of justice.'[40] Such complementary modes of thinking have had a lasting and liberating influence on my own life.

The principal and all-pervasive theme in these thoughts was the use of language. He was fond of telling the following story which he liked to apply to himself. Once upon a time a young rabbinical student went to hear three lectures by a famous rabbi. Afterwards he told his friends: 'The first talk was brilliant, clear and simple. I understood every word. The second was even better, deep and subtle. I didn't understand much, but the rabbi understood all of it. The third was by far the finest, a great and unforgettable experience. I understood nothing and the rabbi didn't understand much either.'[41] He also would often use some of his self-created aphorisms such as: It is not enough to be wrong, one must also be polite; or: Some subjects are so serious that one can only joke about them.

Finally I mention Bohr's own succinct summary of his philosophy, where the emphasis is once again on the use of language.

> There is no quantum world. There is only an abstract quantum physical description. It is wrong to think that the task of physics is to find out how nature is. Physics concerns what we can say about nature . . . What is it that we humans depend on? We depend on our words. Our task is to communicate experience and ideas to others. We are suspended in language.[41]

Bohr's role in nuclear physics and biology

On December 11, 1931, the Danish Academy of Sciences and Letters chose Bohr to be the next occupant of the *Aeresbolig*, the residence of Honor in the Carlsberg breweries. At about that time Bohr commenced the new task of redirecting his Institute toward the young field of nuclear physics, moving the experimental thrust from atomic spectroscopy to nuclear processes. That demanded a lot of money for construction, equipment, and operating expenses. This time Bohr the fundraiser pulled out all the stops. On April 25, 1938, the 25th anniversary of Bohr's completion of the hydrogen atom paper, the new laboratory space was inaugurated in the presence of King Christian X. Whereupon, a newspaper wrote: 'The institute locks its doors again for publicity. One prefers to work unnoticed until results are available.'[42] Those began coming in late 1938, when the Copenhagen cyclotron, which ranks among the first of its kind in Europe, began producing an intense source of neutrons generated by a 4 MeV deuteron beam. In 1939 another accelerator, this one of Cockcroft–Walton type, began producing 1 MeV neutrons. Also in that year plans took shape for building a 2 MeV van de Graaff, not used for scientific work until 1946.

Meanwhile the miserable Nazi time in Germany had begun, leading Niels and his brother Harald to join the board of the Danish committee for support to refugee intellectuals. Niels found financial support for offering temporary hospitality to a number of physicists who, with few exceptions, were to rise to prominence elsewhere.

As if all that was not enough, Bohr also managed, in the 1930s, to make an important contribution to the theory of nuclear reactions. These, he proposed, should be treated as a two-step process.[43] In the first, the incoming projectile merges with the bombarded nucleus into a single unit, the compound nucleus, which is well separated in time from the second stage, the break-up of this compound. Hans Bethe has written: 'The compound nucleus dominated the theory of nuclear reactions at least from 1936 to 1954 . . . At Los Alamos when we tried to get [probabilities] the compound nucleus model could explain many phenomena.'[44]

Bohr's final contribution to nuclear physics (and his last major one to physics), made in 1939 at age 53, was his discovery that only the rare isotope U235 undergoes fission when uranium is bombarded with *slow* neutrons.[45] This led to his well-known papers with Wheeler on fission theory.[46]

There is still more in the 1930s, to wit, Bohr's own role in promoting applications of nuclear physics to biology. In the 1920s he had attracted Georg von Hevesy to Copenhagen, where he (H.) made the first applications of isotopic tracers to the life sciences. Hevesy came back again in 1935–43 to continue his tracer studies, which led to applications to nuclear medicine, a discipline unquestionably founded by Hevesy, with Bohr acting as godfather.

Finally, as if he did not have enough to do, Bohr was president of the Kongelige Danske Videnskabernes Selskab (Royal Danish Academy of Sciences and Letters) from 1939 until his death in 1962.

The Second World War changed Bohr's life profoundly. In 1943, warned of his impending arrest by the Germans, he escaped to England. To the end of the War he served as consultant for atomic bomb projects. For the rest of his life his main concern was the political implications of the new weapons, as you will hear from my friend Ove Nathan.

The final years

I turn to Bohr's final years, beginning with him at age 60, still in full vigor, still running up steps two at a time.

Bohr has now reached the zenith of his influence. He has become a public figure of the first rank, he and Margrethe often being called Denmark's second royal family. High dignitaries visit his home. On his 70th birthday (1955) the King and Queen come to congratulate him, and the Prime Minister addresses the Danish people by radio to honor him.[47] Foreign notables visit Carlsberg, among them Queen Elizabeth II and Prince Philip of England, the Queen of Siam, the Crown Prince (now the Emperor) of Japan, Jawaharlal Nehru (Prime Minister of India), David Ben Gurion (Prime Minister of Israel), Adlai Stevenson. When the newspaper *Politiken* asks its readers to vote on which men and women have put the greatest stamp on developments in Denmark during that era, Bohr tops the list.

Along with these consuming activities, the Bohrs still found time for, and took pleasure in, receiving junior and senior physicists in their home.

For some of the post-war years Bohr remained active in research but more and more he assumed the roles of elder statesman and senior philosopher. He continued writing on complementarity, gave many occasional addresses and traveled widely, to the United States, where in 1950 I helped him put finishing touches to his open letter to the UN, to Iceland, Israel, Yugoslavia, Greenland, India, the USSR. He was active in the founding of CERN, of NORDITA, and of laboratories at Risø, vibrant parts of the Bohr legacy.

On Sunday, November 18, 1962, Bohr died of heart failure in his Carlsberg home. Physicists and other friends, young and old, sent expressions of sorrow and sympathy to Margrethe Bohr and her family. So did dignitaries from various parts of the world.

President Kennedy wrote to Mrs Bohr: 'I am deeply saddened by Professor Bohr's death. American scientists, indeed all American citizens who knew doctor Bohr's name and his great contributions, have respected and venerated him for more than two generations . . . We are forever indebted to him for the scientific inspiration he brought along on his many visits to the United States, and especially for his great contribution to the atomic center at Los Alamos. Please accept my condolences and deep sympathy.'[47] Other messages included those from the Prime Minister of Israel, the King of Sweden, and the Chancellor of West Germany.[48] At CERN the flags of all member nations flew at half mast. Bohr was eulogized at the United Nations in New York.[49] At a UNESCO meeting in Paris a minute of silence was observed.[48]

Bohr's ashes were interred in the family grave in Assistens Kirkegaard in Copenhagen, where they now rest next to those he loved most: his wife (who died 22 years later), his parents, his brother Harald, and his son Christian.

After the death of Rutherford in 1937, Bohr's speech in his memory included these words.

> His untiring enthusiasm and unerring zeal led him on from discovery to discovery and among these the great landmarks of his work, which will forever bear his name, appear as naturally connected as the links in a chain.
>
> Those of us who had the good fortune to come in contact with him will always treasure the memory of his noble and generous character. In his life all honours imaginable for a man of science came to him, but yet he remained quite simple in all his ways. When I first had the privilege of working under his personal inspiration he was already a physicist of the greatest renown, but nonetheless he was then, and always remained, open to listen to what a young man had on his mind. This, together with the kind interest he took in the welfare of his pupils, was indeed the reason for the spirit of affection he created around him wherever he worked . . . The thought of him will always be to us an invaluable source of encouragement and fortitude.[50]

I know of no better way of concluding than by applying these words to Niels Bohr himself.

References

In what follows CW stands for *Niels Bohr, Collected Works*, North Holland, Amsterdam, volumes published starting in 1972. NBA stands for Niels Bohr Archive, Copenhagen.

1. F. Mayor, *The New Page*, Dartmouth Publishing, Aldershot, England, 1995.

2. Picture in J. R. Killian, *Sputnik, Scientists and Eisenhower*, p. 24, MIT Press, Cambridge, MA ,1977.

3. *The New York Times*, October 25, 1957.

4. Translation by P. E. Pinkerton of Heinrich Düntzer's *Poetical Works, Life of Schiller*,

Dana Estes, Boston, 1902.

5. N. Bohr, in *La théorie Quantique des Champs* (R. Stoops, Ed.), Interscience, New York, 1962.

6. E. g. A. V. Jørgensen, *Naturens verden*, 1963, p. 225.

7. N. Bjerrum, unpublished MS, NBA.

8. N. Bohr, *Trans. Roy. Soc.* **209**, 281, 1909; reprinted. in CW, Vol. 1, p. 29.

9. CW, Vol. 1, p. 294.

10. R. Courant, in *Niels Bohr* (S. Rozental, Ed.), p. 304, North-Holland, Amsterdam, 1967.

11. N. Bohr, interviews with T. S. Kuhn, L. Rosenfeld, A. Petersen, and E. Rüdinger, November 1 and 7, 1962, NBA.

12. E. N. da Costa Andrade, *Proc. Roy. Soc.* **A244**, 437, 1958.

13. CW, Vol. 1, p. 106.

14. CW, Vol. 2, p. 577.

15. R. Courant, ref. 10, p. 159.

16. J. R. Nielsen, *Phys. Today*, October 1963, p. 22.

17. N. Bohr, *Phil. Mag.* **26**, 1, 1913; CW, Vol. 2, p. 159.

18. *The New York Times*, November 19, 1962.

19. N. Bohr, letter to E. Rutherford, September 6, 1916, NBA.

20. A. Einstein, in *Albert Einstein: Philosopher–Scientist* (P. A. Schilpp, Ed.), Tudor, New York, 1949.

21. A. Einstein, letter to B. Becker, March 20, 1954.

22. P. Robinson, *The Early Years*, p. 51, Akademisk Forlag, Copenhagen, 1979.

23. CW, Vol. 3, p. 293.

24. A. Sommerfeld, letter to N. Bohr, April 15, 1921, NBA.

25. *The New York Times*, November 5, 1923.

26. *Ibid.*, January 7, 1924.

27. CW, Vol. 4, p. 26.

28. N. Bohr, *Nature* **121** (supplement.) 580, 1928; CW, Vol. 6, p. 24.

29. W. Heisenberg, preface to *Die physikalische Prinzipien der Quantentheorie*, Hirzl, Leipzig, 1930.

30. *The Philosophical Writings of Niels Bohr*, 3 vols., Ox Bow Press, Woodbridge, Connecticut, 1987.

31. D. Mermin, *Phys. Today* **42**, February 1989, p. 105.

32. N. Bohr, in ref. 20, p. 199.

33. N. Bohr, *Nature* **136**, 65, 1935; *Phys. Rev.* **48**, 696, 1935; CW, Vol. 7.

34. A. Einstein, B. Podolsky, and N. Rosen, *Phys. Rev.* **47**, 777, 1935.

35. N. Bohr, *Dialectica* **2**, 312, 1948.

36. N. Bohr, letter to H. P. E. Hansen, July 20, 1935, NBA.

37. W. Heisenberg, ref. 10, p. 95.

38. B. Pascal, *Pensées*, Part VII, No. 35.

39. N. Bohr, *Naturw.* **50**, 725, 1963; CW, Vol. 10.

40. N. Bohr, *Studia Orientalia Ioanni Pedersen*, p. 385, Munksgaard, Copenhagen, 1953; CW, Vol. 10.

41. A. Petersen, *Bull. Atom. Sci.*, September 1963, p. 8.

42. *Politiken*, April 6, 1938.

43. N. Bohr, *Nature* **137**, 344, 1936; CW, Vol. 9, p. 152.

44. H. Bethe, in *Nuclear Physics in Retrospect* (R. Stuewer, Ed.) p. 11, University of Illinois Press, 1979.

45. N. Bohr, *Phys. Rev.* **55**, 418, 1939; CW, Vol. 9, p. 343.

46. N. Bohr and J. Wheeler, *Phys. Rev.* **56**, 426, 1056, 1939; CW, Vol. 9, pp. 363, 403.

47. Repr. in *Berlingske Tidende*, November 21, 1962.

48. *Politiken*, November 21, 1962.

49. *The New York Times*, December 2, 1962.

50. N. Bohr, *Nature* **140**, 752, 1937.

Max Born, about 1959. (Courtesy of AIP Emilio Segrè Visual Archives.)

Max Born*

It is the main purpose of this essay to discuss Born's two papers written in 1926, where, for the first time, a statistical element was introduced in the fundamental laws of physics. After a brief account of Born's life, followed by a summary of his earlier involvements with quantum physics, including his bringing the new quantum mechanics to the United States, I turn to the motivation for, and contents of, the 1926 papers and the reactions to them by his colleagues.

The life

Born was born in Breslau, Germany (now Wrocław, Poland), the son of Gustav Born, a professor of anatomy and Margarethe née Kauffmann. He received his early education in his native city, including three semesters at the University. In 1904 he entered the University of Göttingen, where in 1907 he took his doctorate. In 1913 he married Hedwig Ehrenberg. They had three children, Irene (later Mrs Newton-John, a famous singer), Margaret, and Gustav, who became a prominent biologist.

In 1915 Born was appointed extraordinary professor in Berlin, in 1919 followed a professorship in Frankfurt, in 1921 one in Göttingen, where he stayed until 1933, when a law against Jewish civil servants forced him to resign. In 1936 he was appointed professor in Edinburgh, where he stayed until 1954, when he and his wife returned to Germany, where he spent the rest of his life in Bad Pyrmont.

Born's oeuvre includes more than 300 articles in physics journals and more than 20 books. He became renowned and will long be remembered for his contributions to relativity theory (he and Einstein were close friends), the dynamics of crystal lattices, optics—and quantum physics.

In his later years Born was active in drawing attention to the dangers confronting man in the atomic age. It was during that period (in 1955) that I once spent a long afternoon with him in Geneva, discussing physics rather than politics.

* This is an extended version of an address given on October 21, 1982 at a meeting of the Optical Society of America held in Tucson, Arizona, on the occasion of the centenary of Born's birth.

The end of a revolution

The introduction of probability in the sense of quantum mechanics—that is, probability as an inherent feature of fundamental physical law—may well be the most drastic scientific change yet effected in the twentieth century. At the same time, this advent marks the end rather than the beginning of a scientific revolution, a term often used but rarely defined.

In the political sphere, revolution is a rather clear concept. One system is swept away, to be replaced by another with a distinct new design. It is otherwise in science, where revolution, like love, means different things to different people. Newspapermen and physicists have perceptions of scientific revolution which need not coincide. Nor would individual members of these or other professions necessarily agree on what a scientific revolution consists of. In London, for example, *The Times* of November 7, 1919 headed its first article on the recently discovered bending of light by: 'Revolution in science . . . Newtonian ideas overthrown.' Einstein, on the other hand, in a lecture given in 1921, deprecated the idea that relativity is revolutionary and stressed that his theory was the natural completion of the work of Faraday, Maxwell, and Lorentz. I happen to share Einstein's judgment, while other physicists will quite reasonably object that the abandonment of absolute simultaneity and of absolute space are revolutionary steps.

However, all of us would agree, I think, that *The Times* statement 'Newtonian ideas overthrown,' being unqualified, tends to create the incorrect impression of a past being entirely swept away. That is not how science progresses. The scientist knows that it is in his enlightened self-interest to protect the past as much as is feasible, whether he be a Lavoisier breaking with phlogiston, an Einstein breaking with the aether, or a Max Born breaking with classical causality.

These tensions between the progressive and the conservative are never more in evidence than during a revolutionary period in science, by which I mean a period during which (i) it becomes clear that some parts of past science have to go and (ii) it is not yet clear which parts of the older edifice are to be reintegrated in a wider new frame. Such periods are initiated either by experimental observations that do not fit into accepted pictures or by theoretical contributions that make successful contact with the real world at the price of one or more assumptions which are in violation of the established corpus of theoretical physics.

The era of the so-called old quantum theory, the years from 1900 to 1926, constitutes the most protracted revolutionary period in modern science. Six theoretical papers appeared during that time which are revolutionary in the above sense: Planck's on the discovery of the quantum theory (1900); Einstein's on the light quantum (1905); Bohr's on the hydrogen atom (1913); Bose's on what came to be called quantum statistics (1924); Heisenberg's on what came to be known as matrix mechanics (1925); and Schrödinger's on wave mechanics (1926). If these papers have one thing in common it is that they contain at least one theoretical step which (whether the respective authors knew it then or not) could not be justified at the time of writing.

The end of this revolutionary period (I consider only nonrelativistic quantum mechanics) is not marked by a single date, nor was it brought about by a single person, but rather by three: Heisenberg, Born, and Bohr. The end phase begins in 1925 with the abstract of Heisenberg's extraordinary first paper on quantum mechanics, which reads: 'In this paper it will be attempted to secure foundations for a quantum theoretical mechanics which is exclusively based on relations between quantities which in principle are observable.' With these words Heisenberg states specific desiderata for a new axiomatics. His paper is the correct first step in the new direction. The end phase continues in 1926 with Born's remarks on probability and causality, and comes to a conclusion in 1927 with Heisenberg's derivation of the uncertainty relations and Bohr's formulation of complementarity. At that stage the basic ingredients had been provided which, in the course of time, were to allow for a consistent theoretical foundation of quantum mechanics, including a judgment of the way the new theory contains the old, the classical, theory as a limiting case.

Let us now turn to Max Born, illustrious descendant of the tribe of Abarbanel.[1] 'My father was a scientist . . . My mother's family was Silesian, a very old Jewish family there . . . [Her] parents were great industrialists—textiles.'[2]

Born and the quantum: 1912 to 1926

Born's active preoccupation with the quantum theory dates back to 1912, when he and Theodore von Kármán became the first to apply quantization conditions to collective modes of a many-body system: the normal modes of vibration of a crystal lattice. Ionic crystals were again at issue when, six years later, Born and Alfred Landé computed some of their properties in terms of Bohr's model for an ion: a set of electrons moving in planar orbits around the nucleus. They found that this picture did not work well: crystals were predicted to be too soft, their compressibility came out too high. The calculations indicated 'that the electrons in a single atom are uniformly distributed in [all] spatial directions rather than in plane disks . . . The planar orbits do not suffice, the atoms are evidently [three-dimensional] spatial structures . . . in this sense we must demand a generalization of the theory',[3] a statement memorable for its prescience. Born's third confrontation with the limitations of the old quantum theory occurred another five years later, in 1923. This time he addressed that mystery, celebrated in its time, the spectrum of the helium atom.[4] As others had before them, he and his young assistant Heisenberg concluded that the quantum rules of the old theory could not even qualitatively account for the helium spectrum.[5]

Thus Born belongs to that select group of physicists who knew early that there was some truth to the old quantum theory, yet that this theory (if indeed one may call it that) was in deep ways totally inadequate. He had arrived at this knowledge not as a cynic on the sidelines, but as a participant in the struggles with quantum problems. He knew that a new mechanics was called for, and he was the one to name it, in 1924, even before its discovery: quantum mechanics.[6]

Heisenberg said later that 'It was the peculiar spirit of Göttingen, Born's faith that nothing short of a new self-consistent quantum mechanics was acceptable as the goal in fundamental research that enabled [my] ideas to come to full fruition.'[7] Indeed, during the 1920s, the final decade in which physics at the frontiers was quintessentially European, a new generation was preparing at four main schools for what was to come: Bohr's in Copenhagen, Born's in Göttingen, Rutherford's in Cambridge, and Sommerfeld's in Munich. The list of Born's early assistants is impressive: Pauli, Heisenberg, Jordan, Hund, Hückel, Nordheim, Heitler, and Rosenfeld. At least 24 students received their PhD with Born in Göttingen, among them Delbrück, Elsasser, Flügge, Hund, Jordan, Goeppert-Mayer, Nordheim, Oppenheimer, and Weisskopf. Visitors drawn to Göttingen in the 1920s (not only to Born, of course, but also to James Franck and to David Hilbert) include Blackett, Bohr, K. Compton, Condon, Davisson, Dirac, Ehrenfest, Fermi, Ph. Frank, Herzberg, Houtermans, Hylleraas, Joffe, Kapitza, Kramers, von Neumann, Pauling, Reichenbach, H. P. Robertson, Teller, Uhlenbeck, V. Fock, Wentzel, N. Wiener, and Wigner. 'In the winter of 1926,' Compton recalled, 'I found more than twenty Americans in Göttingen at this fount of quantum wisdom.'[8] Born has remembered: 'There came a lot of people from America and from Russia and from Italy and it was a terrible strain for me at that time. It was very quickly going like that—that the younger people took it over and made it so complicated that I couldn't follow it any more . . . There was Oppenheimer, to whom I gave a paper as a thesis for his doctor's degree. It was a complicated paper and he did it very well.'[9]

It must be remembered that Born was in his middle forties when he did his work on the statistical interpretation of quantum mechanics. By that time he was already a renowned physicist and teacher, had published more than a hundred research papers, and had written six books. Likewise, Bohr was already a stellar figure in his forties when he gave the complementarity interpretation of quantum mechanics. However, the creators of quantum mechanics— Heisenberg, Dirac, Jordan, and Pauli—were in their twenties in 1925, the years when it began. Thus the period 1925 to 1927 would become known in Göttingen as the years of 'Knabenphysik': boy physics. Schrödinger does not easily fit into this simplistic scheme; he was 38 at that time. It does not seem out of place, however, to note here the remark, once made to me by Hermann Weyl, that Schrödinger did his great work during a late erotic outburst in his life. Nor should it be forgotten that Schrödinger was the only one among the creators of the new mechanics who never found peace with what he had wrought.

Let us recall a few dates, all in 1925, all referring to the times of receipt by journals: July 29, Heisenberg's first paper on quantum mechanics;[10] September 27, recognition by Born and Jordan that Heisenberg's mechanics is a matrix mechanics[11] and first proof of the relation $pq - qp = h/2\pi i$, where p is a momentum, q is the corresponding coordinate, and h is Planck's constant; November 7, independent proof of the same relation by Dirac[12]; and November 16, first comprehensive treatment of the foundations of matrix mechanics, by Born, Heisenberg, and Jordan.[13]

It was Born who first brought the new dynamics to America. On November 2, 1925, he left Göttingen for a visit to the Massachusetts Institute of Technology (MIT).

> The day before I left there appeared a parcel of papers by Dirac, whose name I had never heard. And this contained exactly the same as was to be in our paper [with Jordan]. In turning it in we were about four weeks earlier than him, but not in publication. And I was absolutely astonished. Never have I been so astonished in my life; that a completely unknown and apparently young man could write such a perfect paper. But I didn't know who he was. Only a half year later, when I came to England, I met him.[9]

Born's 1925 journey actually was his second visit to America. Already in 1911 he had gone to Chicago, invited by Albert Michelson. On that occasion 'I traveled around a lot, gave no lectures, only a few small seminars . . . [But on my visit to MIT] I had of course a huge audience.'[14]

Part of Born's series of lectures at MIT, from November 14, 1925 to January 22, 1926, was devoted to quantum theory. Their published version[15] is the first book to appear which deals with quantum mechanics. Before returning to Göttingen, Born also lectured at the Universities of Chicago, Wisconsin, and California (Berkeley), at Caltech, and at Columbia University.

At the same time Born left for the United States, interest in quantum mechanics was spreading. Others had begun thinking, but few had as yet much of a grasp of what was happening. The mathematics was unfamiliar, the physics intransparent. In September, Einstein wrote to Ehrenfest about Heisenberg's paper: 'In Göttingen they believe in it (I don't).'[16] At about that same time Bohr considered the work of Heisenberg to be 'a step probably of fundamental importance' but noted that 'it has not yet been possible to apply [the] theory to questions of atomic structure.'[17] Whatever reservations Bohr initially may have had, these were dispelled by early November (ref. 17, footnote 17), when word reached him[18] that Pauli had done for matrix mechanics what he himself had done for the old quantum theory: derive the Balmer formula for the discrete spectrum of hydrogen.

Let us return to MIT. Born was one of the authors of the first paper on quantum mechanics to be written in the United States. Heisenberg's mechanics, as it stood then, was specifically designed for dealing with discrete energy spectra. At MIT, Born and Norbert Wiener developed a general operator calculus that could be applied to the discrete as well as to the continuous case. They were proud to be the first to solve a continuum problem: the motion of a free particle in one dimension.[19] (Their methods have since been superseded.) As we will see, Born's early involvement with continuum problems was crucial for his discovery of the quantum mechanical probability concept.

Max Born and Norbert Wiener at MIT in November or December 1925, during which time they completed the first paper on quantum mechanics written in the United States. (Courtesy of the MIT Museum and Historical Collection Cambridge, MA.)

Summer of 1926

By the time Born returned to Göttingen from his American journey, Schrödinger had discovered wave mechanics and had derived the complete spectrum of the hydrogen atom.[20] Uhlenbeck told me: 'The Schrödinger theory came as a great relief, now we did not any longer have to learn the strange mathematics of matrices.' Rabi told me how he looked through Born's book *Atommechanik* for a nice problem to solve by Schrödinger's method, found the symmetric top, went to Kronig, and said: 'Let's do it.' They did.[21] Wigner told me: 'People began making calculations but it was rather foggy.'

Indeed, until the spring of 1926 quantum mechanics, whether in its matrix or its wave formulation, was high mathematical technology of a new kind, manifestly important because of the answers it produced, but without clearly stated underlying physical principles. Schrödinger was the first, I believe, to propose such principles in the context of quantum mechanics, in a note completed not later than May, which came out on July 9.[22] He suggested that waves are the only reality; particles are only derivative things. In support of this monistic view he considered a suitable superposition of linear harmonic oscillator wave functions and showed (his italics): 'Our wave group holds *permanently together*, does *not* expand over an ever greater domain in the course of time,' adding that 'it can be anticipated with certainty' that the same will be true for the electron as it moves in high orbits in the hydrogen atom. Thus he hoped that wave mechanics would turn out to be a branch of classical physics—a new branch, to be sure, yet as classical as the theory of vibrating strings or drums or balls.

Schrödinger's calculation was right; his anticipation was not. The case of the oscillator is very special: wave packets do almost always disperse. Being a captive of the classical dream, Schrödinger missed a second chance at interpreting his theory correctly. On June 21, 1926 his paper[23] on the nonrelativistic time-dependent wave equation was received. It contains in particular the one-particle equation (I slightly modify his notations)

$$i\hbar \frac{\partial \psi}{\partial t} = \left(- \frac{\hbar^2}{2m} \Delta + V \right) \psi$$

(where ψ is the wave function, t is time, $\hbar$ is Planck's constant divided by 2π. Δ is the Laplace operator, and V is a potential), and its conjugate, and the corresponding continuity equation,

$$\frac{\partial \rho}{\partial t} + \operatorname{div} j = 0 \qquad (1)$$

$$\rho = \psi^\star \psi$$

$$j = \frac{i\hbar}{2m} (\psi^\star \nabla \psi - \nabla \psi^\star \psi)$$

Equation (1), Schrödinger believed, had to be related to the conservation of electric charge.

Born had no truck with Schrödinger's interpretation. 'We were in a rather acrimonious debate about this . . . He was very offensive—as he always was when somebody objected to him. It never disturbed our friendship, but there was a violent discussion between us.'[9]

The break with the past came in a paper by Born received four days later, on June 25, 1926. In order to make his decisive new step, 'It is necessary [Born wrote half a year thereafter[24]] to drop completely the physical pictures of Schrödinger which aim at a revitalization of the classical continuum theory, to retain only the formalism and to fill that with new physical content.'

In his June paper,[25] entitled 'Quantum mechanics of collision phenomena,' Born considers (among other things) the elastic scattering of a steady beam of particles with mass m and velocity v in the z-direction by a static potential which falls off faster than $1/r$ at large distances. In modern language, the stationary wave function describing the scattering behaves asymptotically as $\exp(ikz) + f(\theta,\varphi)\exp(ikr) / r$, $k = m v / \hbar$. The number of particles scattered into the element of solid angle $d\omega = \sin\theta \, d\theta \, d\varphi$ is given by $N \, |f(\theta,\varphi)|^2 \, d\omega$, where N is the number of particles in the incident beam crossing a unit area per unit time. In order to revert to Born's notation, replace $f(\theta,\varphi)$ by Φ_{mn}, where 'n' denotes the initial-state plane wave in the z-direction and 'm' the asymptotic final state in which the wave moves in the (θ,φ) direction. Then, Born declares, 'Φ_{mn} determines the probability for the scattering of the electron from the z-direction into the direction $[\theta,\varphi]$.'

At best, this statement is vague. Born added a footnote in proof to his evidently hastily written paper: 'A more precise consideration shows that the probability is proportional to the square of Φ_{mn}.' He should have said 'absolute square,' but he clearly had got the point, and so the correct expression for the transition probability concept entered physics by way of a footnote.

Born has recalled Schrödinger's reaction to his new ideas: 'I wrote about it to Schrödinger, and it made him furious, because he didn't want that.'[9]

I will return shortly to the significant fact that Born originally associated probability with Φ_{mn} rather than with $|\Phi_{mn}|^2$. As I learned from recent private discussions, Dirac had the same idea at that time. So did Wigner, who told me that some sort of probability interpretation was then on the minds of several people and that he, too, had thought of identifying Φ_{mn} or $|\Phi_{mn}|$ with a probability. When Born's paper came out and $|\Phi_{mn}|^2$ turned out to be the relevant quantity, 'I was at first taken aback but soon realized that Born was right,' Wigner said.

If Born's paper lacked formal precision, causality was brought sharply into focus as the central issue:

One obtains the answer to the question, *not* 'what is the state after the collision' but 'how probable is a given effect of the collision.' . . . Here the whole problem of determinism arises. From the point of view of our quantum mechanics there exists no quantity which in an individual case causally determines the effect of a collision . . . I myself tend to give up determinism in the atomic world.

However, he was not yet quite clear about the distinction between the new probability in the quantum mechanical sense and the old probability as it appears in classical statistical mechanics: 'It does not seem out of the question that the intimate connection which here appears between mechanics and statistics may demand a revision of the thermodynamic-statistical principles.'

One month after the June paper, Born completed a sequel with the same title.[26] His formalism is firm now and he makes a major new point. He considers a normalized stationary wave function ψ referring to a system with discrete, non-degenerate eigenstates ψ_n and notes that in the expansion

$$\psi = \Sigma c_n \psi_n,$$

$|c_n|^2$ is the statistical probability for the system to be in the state n. In June he had discussed probabilities of transition, a concept that, at least phenomenologically, had been part of physics since 1916, when Einstein had introduced his A and B coefficients in the theory of radiative transitions—and at once had begun to worry about causality as an ingredient in fundamental physical laws, the first physicist to do so. Already in 1920 he had written to Born: 'That business about causality causes me a lot of trouble. Can the quantum absorption and emission of light ever be understood in the sense of the complete causality requirement, or would a statistical residue remain? I must admit that there I lack the courage of my convictions. But I would be very unhappy to renounce *complete* causality.'[27]

Where Einstein's courage failed, Born's did not: in his second 1926 paper[26] he introduced *the probability of a state*. That had never been done before. He also expressed beautifully the essence of wave mechanics: 'The motion of particles follows probability laws but the probability itself propagates according to the law of causality.'

During the summer of 1926 Born's insights into the physical principles of quantum mechanics developed rapidly. On August 10 he read a paper before the meeting of the British Association at Oxford[28] in which he clearly distinguished between the 'new' and the 'old' probabilities in physics:

The classical theory introduces the microscopic coordinates which determine the individual processes only to eliminate them because of ignorance by averaging over their values; whereas the new theory gets the same results without introducing them at all . . . We free forces of their classical duty of determining directly the motion of particles and allow them instead to determine the probability of states.

> Whereas before it was our purpose to make these two definitions of force equivalent, this problem has now no longer, strictly speaking, any sense.

The history of science is full of gentle irony. In teaching quantum mechanics, most of us arrive at Eq. (1), note that something is conserved, and identify that something with probability. But Schrödinger, who discovered that equation, did not make that connection and never liked quantum probability, while Born introduced probability without using Eq. (1).

In this article I do not at all attempt to describe all aspects of the history of probability in quantum physics. However, I cannot refrain from mentioning a remark found in a paper, completed in December 1926, in which for the first time in print the probability for a many-particle system with coordinates $q_1, \ldots, q_f$ is introduced: '$| \psi(q_1, \ldots, q_f) |^2 \, dq_1, \ldots, dq_f$ is the probability that, in the relevant quantum state of the system, the coordinates simultaneously lie in the relevant volume element of configuration space.' The paper is by Pauli and deals with gas degeneracy and paramagnetism. The remark, inspired by Born's work, is found—once again—in a footnote.[29]

What made Born take this step?

In 1954 Born was awarded the Nobel Prize 'for his fundamental research, especially for his statistical interpretation of the wave function.' In his acceptance speech Born, then in his seventies, ascribed his inspiration for the statistical interpretation to 'an idea of Einstein's [who] had tried to make the duality of particles—light-quanta or photons—and waves comprehensible by interpreting the square of the optical wave amplitudes as probability density for the occurrence of photons. This concept could at once be carried over to the ψ-function: $| \psi |^2$ ought to represent the probability density for electrons.'[30] Similar statements are frequently found in Born's writings in his late years. On the face of it, this appears to be a perfectly natural explanation. Had Einstein not stated that light of low intensity behaves as if it consisted of energy packets $h\nu$? And is the intensity of light not a function quadratic in the electromagnetic fields? In spite of this plausibility, and in spite of the fact that I must here dissent from the originator's own words, I do not believe that these contributions by Einstein were Born's guide in 1926.[31]

My own attempts at reconstructing Born's thinking (necessarily a dubious enterprise) are exclusively based on his two papers on collision phenomena and on a letter he wrote to Einstein, also in 1926. Recall that Born initially thought, however briefly, that ψ rather than $| \psi |^2$ was a measure of the probability. I find this impossible to understand if it was true that, at that time, he had been stimulated by Einstein's brilliant discussions of the fluctuations of quadratic quantities (in terms of fields) referring to radiation. Nevertheless, it is true that Born's inspiration came from Einstein: not Einstein's statistical papers bearing on light, but his never published speculations during the early 1920s on the dynamics of light quanta and wave fields. Born states so explicitly in his second paper[26]: 'I start from a remark by Einstein on the relation between [a] wave field and light-quanta; he said approximately that the waves are only there to show the way to the corpuscular light-quanta, and talked in this sense of a 'ghost field' [*Gespensterfeld*] [which] determines the *probability* [my italics] for a light-quantum . . . to take a definite path.'

It is hardly surprising that Einstein was concerned that early with these issues. In 1909 he had been the first to write about particle–wave duality. In 1916 he had been the first to relate the existence of transition probabilities (for sponta-neous emission of light) to quantum theoretical origins—though how this rela-tion was to be formally established he did, of course, not yet know. Little con-crete is known about his ideas of a ghost field or guiding field (*Führungsfeld*). The best description we have is from Wigner,[32] who knew Einstein personally in the 1920s:

> [Einstein's] picture has a great similarity with the present picture of quantum mechanics. Yet Einstein, though in a way he was fond of it, never published it. He realized that it is in conflict with the conservation principles . . . This Einstein never could accept and hence never took his idea of the guiding field quite seri-ously . . . The problem was solved, as we know, by Schrödinger's theory.[33]

Born was even more explicit about his source of inspiration in a letter to Einstein written in November 1926 (for reasons not clear to me this letter is not found in the published Born–Einstein correspondence):

> About me it can be told that physicswise I am entirely satisfied since my idea to look upon Schrödinger's wave field as a '*Gespensterfeld*' in your sense proves better all the time. Pauli and Jordan have made beautiful advances in this direction. The probability field does of course not move in ordinary space but in phase- (or rather, in configuration-) space . . . Schrödinger's achievement reduces itself to something purely mathematical; his physics is quite wretched [*recht kümmerlich*].[34]

Thus it seems to me that Born's thinking was conditioned by the following circumstances. He knew and accepted the fertility of Schrödinger's formalism but not Schrödinger's attempt at interpretation:

> He [Schrödinger] believed . . . that he had accomplished a return to classical think-ing; he regarded the electron not as a particle but as a density distribution given by the square of his wave function $|\psi|^2$. He argued that the idea of particles and of quantum jumps be given up altogether; he never faltered in this conviction . . . I, however, was witnessing the fertility of the particle concept every day in [James] Franck's brilliant experiments on atomic and molecular collisions and was

convinced that particles could not simply be abolished. A way had to be found for reconciling particles and waves.[35]

His quest for this way led him to reflect on Einstein's idea of a ghost field. It now seems less surprising that his first surmise was to relate probability to the ghost field, not to the '(ghost field)^2.' His next step, from ψ to $|\psi|^2$, was entirely his own. We owe to Born the beginning insight that ψ itself, unlike the electromagnetic field, has no direct physical reality.

Born's work on the statistical interpretation occupies a singular position in his oeuvre. It is his most innovative contribution. At first glance this choice of scientific problem seems somewhat unlike Born. As Heisenberg once said, 'Born was more of a mathematician,'[36] more the man for the '*problème bien posé*.' It seems not entirely far-fetched, however, to consider Born's problem of June and July 1926 to be just of that kind: 'A way had to be found for reconciling particles and waves.' It should also be noted that Born may not have realized at once the profundity of his contribution, which helped bring to an end the quantum revolution. In a later interview he reminisced as follows about 1926: 'We were so accustomed to making statistical considerations, and to shift it one layer deeper seemed to us not very important.'[9]

Changing of the guard

In March 1926, Einstein wrote to Born: 'The Heisenberg–Born concepts leave us all breathless, and have made a deep impression on all theoretically oriented people.'[37] Those lines had been written before Schrödinger had come out with his wave mechanics. When Einstein wrote again to Born, in December 1926, replying to Born's of November,[34] Schrödinger's work had appeared, as had Born's probability interpretation, for which Einstein did not care at all, as is seen from that oft-quoted December letter: 'Quantum mechanics is certainly imposing. But an inner voice tells me that it is not yet the real thing. The theory says a lot but does not really bring us any closer to the secret of the "old one." I, at any rate, am convinced that *He* is not playing dice.'[38] That remained Einstein's opinion for the rest of his life. Sample—Einstein to Born in the mid-1930s: 'I still do not believe that the statistical method of the quantum theory is the last word, but for the time being I am alone in my opinion.'[39]

Also, the attitude of the other leaders of the once dominant Berlin school—Planck, von Laue, and Schrödinger—continued to range from skepticism to opposition. In the first week of October 1926 Schrödinger went to Copenhagen, at Bohr's invitation, to discuss the state of the quantum theory. Heisenberg also went. Later, Bohr often told others (including me) that Schrödinger reacted on that occasion by saying that he would rather not have published his papers on wave mechanics, had he been able to foresee the consequences. Schrödinger continued to believe that one should dispense with particles. Born continued to refute him. After Schrödinger's death, Born, mourning the loss of his old friend, wrote of their arguments through the years: 'Extremely coarse [*saugrob*] and tender; sharpest exchange of opinion, never a feeling of being offended.'[40]

After Born's work, Lorentz could no longer grasp the changes wrought by the quantum theory. In the summer of 1927 he wrote to Ehrenfest:

> I care little for the conception of $\psi\psi^*$ as a probability . . . In the case of the H-atom, the difficulty in making precise what is meant if one interprets $\psi\psi^*$ as a probability manifests itself in that for a given value of E (one of the eigenvalues) there is also a [nonvanishing] probability outside the sphere which electrons with energy E cannot leave.[41]

The quantum revolution was over by October 1927, the time of the fifth Solvay conference. In March of that year, Heisenberg had derived the uncertainty relations; in September, Bohr had lectured for the first time on complementarity. The printed proceedings of this Solvay meeting[42] appeared in 1928. They open with a tribute by Marie Curie to Lorentz, who had presided over the conference in October, and who had died shortly thereafter. Next follows a list of the participants, which includes Planck, Einstein, Bohr, de Broglie, Born, Schrödinger, and the youngsters, Dirac, Heisenberg, Kramers, and Pauli. Then come the texts of the papers presented. Taken as a whole, this record reads as an account of a changing of the guard.

What was created in those stirring years is still with us. To this day there are physicists, some of them quite thoughtful, who are uncomfortable with the probability interpretation. However, there are neither experimental nor theoretical arguments that force us to believe in the necessity for a revision of the rules of the nonrelativistic quantum theory. I do not care to speculate about the future, but I would like to conclude by repeating a comment, made more than a quarter of a century ago, which is still timely: 'It has been well said that the modern physicist is a quantum theorist on Monday, Wednesday, and Friday, and a student of gravitational relativity theory on Tuesday, Thursday, and Saturday. On Sunday the physicist is neither, but is praying to his God that someone, preferably himself, will find the reconciliation between these two views.'[43]

More on the reception of Born's probability concept

It is a bit odd—and caused Born some chagrin—that his papers on the probability concept were not always adequately acknowledged in the early days. '[It] made me very angry [that] they missed the main point.'[9] Heisenberg's own version[44] of the probability interpretation, written in Copenhagen in November 1926, does not mention Born. One finds no reference to Born's work in the two editions of Mott and Massey's book on atomic collisions, nor in Kramers' book on quantum mechanics. In his authoritative *Handbuch der Physik* article of 1933, Pauli refers to this contribution by Born only in passing, in a footnote. Jörgen Kalckar from Copenhagen wrote to me about his recollections of discussions with Bohr on this issue. 'Bohr said that as soon as Schrödinger had demonstrated the equivalence between his wave mechanics and Heisenberg's matrix mechanics, the "interpretation" of the wave function was obvious ... For this reason, Born's paper was received without surprise in Copenhagen. "We had never dreamt that it could be otherwise," Bohr said.' A similar comment was made by Mott:

> Perhaps the probability interpretation was the most important of all [of Born's contributions to quantum mechanics], but given Schrödinger, de Broglie, and the experimental results, this must have been very quickly apparent to everyone, and in fact when I worked in Copenhagen in 1928 it was already called the 'Copenhagen interpretation'—I do not think I ever realized that Born was the first to put it forward.[45]

In response to a query, Casimir, who started his university studies in 1926, wrote to me: 'I learned the Schrödinger equation simultaneously with the interpretation. It is curious that I do not recall that Born was especially referred to. He was of course mentioned as co-creator of matrix mechanics.' The same comments apply to my own university education, which started a decade later.

Postscript: the Born approximation

It is otherwise with another contribution found in the second of Born's 1926 papers on collisions: the Born approximation, taught in every sensible course on quantum mechanics and still in steady use wherever quantum physics is practiced. Of course, later generations of students rarely had grounds for consulting Born's original paper. Long before preparing this article I had occasion to do so, however: once in the course of refining the Born approximation,[46] and another time when Res Jost and I became interested in the convergence of the Born expansion for the scattering by a static, spherically symmetric potential which, with suitable normalization, can be written as $\lambda V(r)$, where λ is the potential strength. Write the scattering wave function ψ as a power series in λ. The question was whether, under certain conditions imposed on $V(r)$, this power series, the Born expansion, converges. We found general conditions on V for which ψ can be written as the quotient of two convergent power series in λ, and from this result obtained a way of determining the radius of convergence for the Born expansion.[47]

Having finished our work, we wondered what had been done earlier about this convergence question. We searched the literature, found nothing more concrete than assertions that the expansion will be the more trustworthy the higher the energy or the smaller the quantity $|\lambda|$, until we finally discovered that Born had considered our question in his second paper of 1926 on collision theory.[26] He first discussed the one-dimensional case for potentials such that $|V(x)| <$ constant $\cdot$ x^{-2}, and correctly showed that under these circumstances his expansion converges uniformly for any finite interval. This result may have led him to conclude, for the three-dimensional case: 'The convergence of the procedure can easily be shown on the assumption that V tends to zero as r^{-2}; but we will not go into detail.' That statement, alas, was incorrect.

Returning to our own work, we were encouraged to inquire whether we could also do something for relativistic field theories. We failed. The kernels encountered in that case were too singular for our methods to apply. To this day, proofs or disproofs of the convergence of the Born expansion in field theory remain an important challenge, yet to be met.[48]

References

1. Some time after Born's Sephardic ancestors came to Germany, the family name was changed to Born. (Mrs Irene Newton John-Born, private communication.)

2. M. Born, interview by T. S. Kuhn, October 18, 1962; transcript in Niels Bohr Archive (NBA), Copenhagen.

3. M. Born and A. Landé, *Verh. Deutsch. Phys. Ges.* **20**, 210, 1918; reprinted. in ref. 4.

4. *Max Born, Ausgewählte Abhandlungen*, Vol. 1, p. 356, Vandenhoeck and Ruprecht, Göttingen, 1963.

5. M. Born and W. Heisenberg, *Zeitschr. f. Physik* **16**, 229, 1923.

6. M. Born, *Zeitschr. f. Physik* **26**, 379, 1924; reprinted in ref. 4, Vol. 2, p. 61.

7. N. Kemmer and R. Schlapp, *Biogr. Mem. Fellows R. Soc.* **17**, 17, 1971.

8. K. T. Compton, *Nature (London)* **139**, 238, 1937.

9. Ref. 2, interview October 17, 1962.

10. W. Heisenberg, *Z. Phys.* **33**, 879, 1925.

11. M. Born and P. Jordan, *ibid.*, **34**, 858, 1925; reprinted in ref. 4, Vol. 2, p. 124.

12. P. A. M. Dirac, *Proc. R. Soc. London Ser. A* **109**, 642, 1925.

13. M. Born, W. Heisenberg, P. Jordan, *Zeitschr. f. Physik* **35**, 557, 1926; reprinted in ref. 4, Vol. 2, p. 155.

14. M. Born, interview by P. P. Ewald, June 1960; transcript in NBA.

15. M. Born, *Probleme der Atomdynamik*, Springer, Berlin, 1926; in English: *Problems of Atomic Dynamics* MIT Press, Cambridge, MA, 1926; reprinted by Ungar, New York, 1960.

16. A. Einstein, letter to P. Ehrenfest, September 20, 1925.

17. N. Bohr, *Nature (London)* **116**, 845, 1925.

18. *Wolfgang Pauli Scientific Correspondence*, Springer Verlag, New York, 1979, Vol. 1, pp. 252–4.

19. M. Born and N. Wiener, *J. Math. Phys. (Cambridge, Mass.)* **5**, 84, February 1926; *Zeitschr. f. Physik* **36**, 174, 1926; reprinted in ref. 4, Vol. 2, p. 214.

20. E. Schrödinger, *Ann. d. Phys. (Leipzig)* **79**, 361, 1926.

21. R. de L. Kronig and I. I. Rabi, *Phys. Rev.* **29**, 262, 1927.

22. E. Schrödinger, *Naturwissenschaften* **14**, 644, 1926.

23. E. Schrödinger, *Ann. d. Phys. (Leipzig)* **81**, 109, 1926.

24. M. Born, *Gött. Nachr.* 1926, p. 146; reprinted in ref. 4, Vol. 2, p. 284.

25. M. Born, *Zeitschr. f. Physik* **37**, 863, 1926; reprinted in ref. 4, Vol. 2, p. 228.

26. M. Born, *Zeitschr. f. Physik* **38**, 803, 1926; reprinted in ref. 4, Vol. 2, p. 233.

27. A. Einstein, letter to M. Born, January 27, 1920, in *The Born–Einstein Letters* (I. Born, Ed.), p. 23, Walker, New York, 1971.

28. M. Born, *Nature* **119**, 354, 1927.

29. W. Pauli, *Zeitschr. f. Physik* **41**, 81, 1927, footnote on p. 83.

30. M. Born, in *Nobel Lectures in Physics 1942–1962*, p. 256, Elsevier, New York 1964.

31. Nor do I believe that Born was guided by the Bohr–Kramers–Slater theory, proposed in 1924, abandoned in 1925 [W. Heisenberg, in *Theoretical Physics in the Twentieth Century*, Interscience, New York, 1960, p. 44] or that his ideas were 'formed in the trend of Einstein–de Broglie's dualistic approach' [H. Konno, *Jpn. Stud. Hist. Sci.*, **17**, 129, 1978].

32. E. Wigner, in *Some Strangeness in the Proportion*, Addison-Wesley, Reading, MA, 1980, p. 463.

33. The conflict with the conservation laws arose because Einstein had in mind one guide field per particle. By contrast, the Schrödinger waves are 'guiding fields' in the configuration space of all particles at once.

34. M. Born, letter to A. Einstein, November 30, 1926.

35. M. Born, *My Life and My Views*, Scribner's, New York, 1968, p. 55.

36. Oral history interview of Heisenberg by T. Kuhn, 1963, Archives of the History of Quantum Physics, Niels Bohr Library, American Institute of Physics, New York.

37. A. Einstein, letter to M. Born, March 7, 1926, in ref. 27, p. 88.

38. A. Einstein, letter to M. Born, December 4, 1926, in ref. 27, p. 90.

39. A. Einstein, letter to M. Born, undated, probably 1936, ref. 27, p. 124.

40. M. Born, *Phys. Bl.* **17**, 85, 1961; reprinted in ref. 4, Vol. 2, p. 691.

41. H. A. Lorentz, letter to P. Ehrenfest, August 29, 1927.

42. *Électrons et Photons*, Gauthier-Villars, Paris, 1928.

43. N. Wiener, *I am a Mathematician*, MIT Press, Cambridge, MA, 1956, p. 109.

44. W. Heisenberg, *Z. Phys.* **40**, 50, 1926.

45. N. F. Mott, Introduction to ref. 35, pp. x–xi.

46. A. Pais, *Proc. Cambridge Philos. Soc.* **42**, 45, 1946.

47. R. Jost and A. Pais, *Phys. Rev.* **82**, 840, 1951.

48. I am grateful to Professor K. P. Lieb from Göttingen for a helpful correspondence.

Left to right: Oppenheimer, Dirac, Pais, in the common room of the Institute for Advanced Study, Princeton, 1948. (Courtesy of Archives Institute for Advanced Study.)

Paul Dirac: aspects of his life and work[1]

'Of all physicists, Dirac has the purest soul.'

Niels Bohr

In the year 1902, the literary world witnessed the death of Zola, the birth of John Steinbeck, and the first publications of *The Hound of the Baskervilles, The Immoralist, Three Sisters*, and *The Varieties of Religious Experience*. Monet painted *Waterloo Bridge*, Elgar composed *Pomp and Circumstance*, Caruso made his first phonograph recording, and the Irish Channel was crossed for the first time by balloon. In the world of science, Heaviside postulated the Heaviside layer, Rutherford and Soddy published their transformation theory of radioactive elements, Einstein started working as a clerk in the patent office in Bern, and, on August 8, Paul Adrien Maurice Dirac was born in Bristol, one of the children of Charles Dirac, a native of Monthey in the Swiss canton of Valais, and Florence Holten, daughter of a British sea captain. There was also a brother two years older, Reginald, whose life ended in suicide in 1924, and Beatrice, a sister four years younger. About his father Dirac has recalled:

> My father made the rule that I should only talk to him in French. He thought it would be good for me to learn French in that way. Since I found that I couldn't express myself in French, it was better for me to stay silent than to talk in English. So I became very silent at that time—that started very early.[2]

About his brother's suicide, Dirac has said:

> It was a great shock to my family, of course . . . I suppose he was just very depressed and that kind of life, where we were brought up without any social contact at all must have been very depressing to him as well as to me and having a younger brother who was brighter than he was, must have depressed him also, quite a lot . . . For instance, I got a first class in my engineering and he got a third class . . . He got an engineering job and he used to, in the Midlands, Coventry for

---

[1] Address to the Royal Society, London, given on November 13, 1995, on the occasion of the unveiling that day of a memorial plaque to Dirac in Westminster Abbey.

some time Wolver Hampton and he used to, well I think that he would have liked to come home even though there wasn't much social life at home because the small amount of vacation that he would get, he would immediately spend the time by traveling to Bristol and back again at the end of it spending as much time at home as he could . . . He did have a girlfriend . . . [After Reginald's death] my father did suggest that this girl should come and visit us and then my mother said oh no, she mustn't, she might go after me . . . I was twenty-two years old at the time but my mother still thought that I needed to be protected from girls. I rather resented it but the result was I never met her . . .

There was some mystery connected with my brother's death because he left his job three months before he died and what he did during those last three months, no one was able to find out. He didn't tell his landlady that he left his job. He continued to leave regularly in the morning and come home in the evening. The landlady did not know that he left his job. He continued to pay his rent regularly. He just went through his savings. When they were gone, he killed himself. The police made extensive inquiries but they were unable to find out what he did during those last three months . . .

We didn't correspond with each other, in fact we never talked to each other for a good many years . . . For one thing, we had to talk in French or we'd get into a row and that was one reason for not talking.'[2]

Some family life.

The first edition of Dirac's book, *The Principles of Quantum Mechanics*, has stood on my shelves since my graduate days in Holland. Learning from it the beauty and power of that compact little Dirac equation was a thrill I shall never forget. Years later, in January 1946, I first met Dirac and his wife on a brief visit to their home at 7 Cavendish Avenue in Cambridge. I saw much more of him in the autumn of that year when we met at the Institute for Advanced Study in Princeton. He had spent academic 1934–35 there, and also, during my own time at the Institute, the fall term of 1946, and academic 1947–48, 1958–59, and 1962–63. In the course of all these visits to Princeton I came to know Dirac quite well. A friendship developed. In the course of joint talks and walks and wood chopping expeditions, I developed a good grasp of his views on physics. I also met him elsewhere, especially in Tallahassee where, in 1972, at age 70, he had started a new career: professor of physics at the Florida State University.

I shall presently tell of those encounters with Dirac, and of my impressions of his personality. First, however, I should like to speak of his career prior to the time of my personal contacts with him.

Young Paul first attended the Bishop Road primary school, then, at age 12, the secondary school at the Merchant Venturer's Technical College, both in Bristol, where his father taught French. Much later he has recalled that '[This] was an excellent school for science and modern languages. There was no Latin or Greek, something of which I was rather glad, because I did not appreciate the value of old cultures . . . I played soccer and cricket . . . and never had much success. But all through my schooldays, my interest in science was encouraged and stimulated.'[3]

At the suggestion of his father, Dirac started in 1918 to study at the electrical engineering department of the University of Bristol, from which he graduated with first-class honors in 1921. Forty years later he wrote:

> I would like to try to explain the effect of this engineering training on me. I did not make any further use of the detailed applications of this work, but it did change my whole outlook to a very large extent. Previously, I was interested only in exact equations. Well, the engineering training which I received did teach me to tolerate approximations, and I was able to see that even theories based on approximations could sometimes have a considerable amount of beauty in them . . . I think that if I had not had this engineering training, I should not have had any success with the kind of work that I did later on . . . I continued in my later work to use mostly the nonrigorous mathematics of the engineers, and I think that you will find that most of my later writings do involve nonrigorous mathematics . . . The pure mathematician who wants to set up all of his work with absolute accuracy is not likely to get very far in physics.[4,5]

During those years as an engineering student,

> A wonderful thing happened. Relativity burst on the world . . . It is easy to see the reason for this tremendous impact. We had just been living through a terrible and very serious war . . . Everyone wanted to forget it. And then relativity came along . . . It was an escape from the war.
>
> Previously, as a schoolboy I had been much interested in the relations of space and time. I had thought about them a great deal, and it had become apparent to me that time was very much like another dimension, and the possibility had occurred to me that perhaps there was some connection between space and time, and that we ought to consider them from a general four-dimensional point of view. However, at that time the only geometry that I knew was Euclidean geometry.[4]

In 1921, Dirac looked without success for an engineering job. Then, to his luck, he was offered free tuition for two years to study mathematics at the University of Bristol.

Those years conclude what one may call the prelude to Dirac's scientific career.

———————

In the autumn of 1923, Dirac enrolled at Cambridge with a maintenance grant from the Department of Scientific and Industrial Research. Nine years later he would succeed Joseph Larmor to the Lucasian Chair of Mathematics, once held by Newton.[6] It was Ralph Fowler who, in Cambridge, introduced Dirac to the old quantum theory, and it was from him that he first learned of the atom of Rutherford, Bohr, and Sommerfeld.

Dirac first met Bohr in May 1925 when the latter gave a talk in Cambridge on the fundamental problems and difficulties of the quantum theory. Of that occasion Dirac said later:

> People were pretty well spellbound by what Bohr said . . . While I was very much impressed by [him], his arguments were mainly of a qualitative nature, and I was not able to really pinpoint the facts behind them. What I wanted was statements which could be expressed in terms of equations, and Bohr's work very seldom provided such statements. I am really not sure how much my later work was influenced by these lectures of Bohr's . . . He certainly did not have a direct influence, because he did not stimulate one to think of new equations.[4]

In July 1925 Dirac first met Heisenberg, also in Cambridge. In that month, Heisenberg's first paper on quantum mechanics had come out. 'I learned about this theory of Heisenberg in September, and it was very difficult for me to appreciate it at first. It took two weeks; then I suddenly realized that the non-commutation was actually the most important idea that was introduced by Heisenberg.'[7] The result was Dirac's first paper on quantum mechanics.[8] Prior to that time he had already published seven respectable papers which had not caused any particular response. Number eight caused a stir, however. It contained the relation $pq - qp = h/2\pi i$, independently derived shortly before by Born and Jordan. The respective authors were unaware of one another's results. Born has described his reaction upon receiving Dirac's paper: 'This was—I remember well—one of the greatest surprises of my scientific life. For the name Dirac was completely unknown to me, the author appeared to be a youngster, yet everything was perfect in its way and admirable.'[9]

In those days, Dirac invented several notations which are now part of our language: q-numbers, where 'q stands for quantum or maybe queer'; c-numbers, where 'c stands for classical or maybe commuting.'[4] He has described his work habits in those years: 'Intense thinking about those problems during the week and relaxing on Sunday, going for a walk in the country alone.'[4] Dirac was forever much attracted by the beauty of nature, particularly of mountain areas. He liked to climb mountains, for which he practiced by climbing trees on the Gog-Magog hills outside Cambridge, even then wearing his perennial dark suit. He avoided technical climbs but nevertheless ascended impressive peaks, in the Rockies, the Alps, and the Caucasus. In 1936, accompanied by Igor Tamm, he managed to reach the 5640-metre-high top of the Elbruz, Europe's highest mountain, but collapsed at a high altitude, where he had to rest for 24 hours before completing the descent.[10]

In May 1926, Dirac received his PhD on a thesis entitled 'Quantum Mechanics.'[11] Meanwhile Schrödinger's papers on wave mechanics had appeared, to which Dirac reacted with initial hostility, then with enthusiasm. He quickly applied the theory to systems of identical particles.[12] At almost the same time, that problem also attracted Heisenberg,[13] whose main focus, on a few particle systems, resulted in his theory of the helium atom.[14] Dirac's paper[12] (August 1926), on the other hand, will be remembered as the first in which quantum mechanics is brought to bear on statistical mechanics. Recall that the earliest work on quantum statistics, by Bose and by Einstein, predates quantum mechanics. Also, Fermi's introduction of the exclusion principle in statistical problems, though published[15] after the arrival of quantum mechanics, is still executed in the context of the 'old' quantum theory.[16] All these contributions were given their quantum mechanical underpinnings by Dirac, who was, in fact, the first to give the correct justification of Planck's law, which started it all: 'Symmetrical eigenfunctions . . . give just the Einstein–Bose statistical mechanics . . . (which) leads to Planck's law of black-body radiation.'[12]

It is edifying to remember that it took some time before it was sorted out when Bose–Einstein and Fermi–Dirac statistics, respectively, apply. Dirac in August 1926: 'The solution with anti-symmetric eigenfunctions (F. D. statistics) . . . is probably the correct one for gas molecules, since it is known to be the correct one for electrons in an atom, and one would expect molecules to resemble electrons more closely than light-quanta.'[12] Other great men were not at once clear either about this issue, Einstein, Fermi, Heisenberg, and Pauli among them.[16]

Having obtained his doctorate, Dirac was free to travel and, in September 1926, he went to Copenhagen. 'I admired Bohr very much. We had long talks together, long talks in which Bohr did practically all the talking.'[4] It was there that he worked out the theory of canonical transformations in quantum mechanics since known as the transformation theory.[17] 'I think that is the piece of work which has most pleased me of all the works that I've done in my life . . . The transformation theory (became) my darling.'[7] In this paper, Dirac introduced an important tool of modern physics, the δ-function, about which he remarked right away: 'Strictly, of course, $\delta(x)$ is not a proper function of x, but can be regarded as the limit of a certain sequence of functions. All the same, one can use $\delta(x)$ as though it were a proper function for practically all the purposes of quantum mechanics without getting incorrect results.'[18]

Dirac's stay in Copenhagen—lasting till February 1927—is also highly memorable, because it was there that he completed the first[19] of two papers in which he laid the foundations of quantum electrodynamics. The sequel[20] was written in Göttingen, the next important stop on his journey.

Preceding these two papers, Dirac had already given[12] a theory of induced

radiative transitions by treating atoms quantum mechanically but still considering the Maxwell field as a classical system.[21] However, 'one cannot take spontaneous emission into account without a more elaborate theory.'[12] Here, Dirac
echoed Einstein who, already in 1917, still the days of the old quantum theory,
had stressed that spontaneous emission 'make[s] it almost inevitable to formulate a truly quantized theory of radiation.'[22] In his Copenhagen paper,[19] Dirac
did just that. He proceeded to quantize the electromagnetic field, thereby giving
the first rational description of light quanta, and then derived from first principles Einstein's phenomenological coefficient of spontaneous emission.[23]

The theory was not yet complete, however: 'Radiative processes . . . in which
more than one light quantum take(s) part simultaneously are not allowed on
the present theory.'[19] How young quantum mechanics still was. Early in 1927,
Dirac did not yet know that these processes are perfectly well included in his
theory. All one had to do was extend perturbation theory from first order (used
by him in the treatment of spontaneous emission) to second order. So, in his
Göttingen paper,[20] he developed[24] second order perturbation theory, which
enabled him to give the quantum theory of dispersion.[25] He further noted[26] that
the theory could now also be applied to the Compton effect, a subject that had
interested him earlier.[27]

In Göttingen Dirac met Robert Oppenheimer, who lived in the same pension
and with whom he became close friends. Dirac found the catholic interests of
Oppenheimer, who spent much time reading Dante in the original, very difficult to understand. It is said that Dirac once asked him: 'How can you do both
physics and poetry? In physics we try to explain in simple terms something that
nobody knew before. In poetry it is the exact opposite.'

In the year 1927, of which I speak, Dirac was elected Fellow of St John's College
in Cambridge and began lecturing on quantum mechanics. In 1929 he was
nominated Praelector in mathematics and physics, a post with only nominal
duties. In 1930 he was elected Fellow of the Royal Society. As of September 30,
1932, he became the Lucasian professor, a post he was to hold until 1969. Out of
his lectures to students grew his book on quantum mechanics, the first edition
of which appeared in 1930. I may note here that in all he published about 200
papers.

Dirac devoted only a small part of his duties to teaching and almost none to
administration. He preferred to work by himself and created no school. It has
been written of him that he was one of the few scientists who could work even
on a deserted island.[28] While it lay therefore not in his nature to seek out
research students, he nevertheless delivered a fair number of PhDs.[29]

When Dirac wrote an article or gave a lecture he considered it unnecessary to
change his carefully chosen phrases. When somebody in the audience asked him

to explain a point he had not understood, Dirac would repeat exactly what he had said before, using the very same words.[30] Be that as it may, his style of lecturing was admirable, as I have been privileged to notice frequently. Some of his students have put it well: 'The delivery was always exceptionally clear and one was carried along in the unfolding of an argument which seemed as majestic and inevitable as the development of a Bach fugue.'[31] Nevertheless I tend to agree with Sir Nevill Mott, who has said: 'I think I have to say his influence was not very great as a teacher . . . He never would advise a student to examine the experimental evidence and see what it means . . . He would never, between his great discoveries, do any sort of bread-and-butter problem. He would not be interested at all.'[32]

I return to the year 1927, when I left Dirac in Göttingen. From there he went to Leiden and concluded his travels of that year by attending the Solvay conference in Brussels (in October), where he met Einstein for the first time. From discussions with Dirac, I know that he admired Einstein. The respect was mutual ('. . . Dirac, to whom, in my opinion, we owe the most logically perfect presentation of (quantum mechanics)'[33]). Yet, the contact between the two men remained minimal, largely, I would think, because it was not in Dirac's personality to seek for father figures.

That 1927 Solvay conference marks the beginning of the well-known debate between Bohr and Einstein on the interpretation of quantum mechanics. Fifty years later Dirac said: 'This problem of getting the interpretation proved to be rather more difficult than just working out the equations.'[7] As time went by he expressed reservations not only regarding quantum field theory but also, though less strongly, in relation to ordinary quantum mechanics,[34,35] but never more clearly than in 1979 when he and I were both in Jerusalem to attend the Einstein centennial celebrations:

> In this discussion at the Solvay Conference [of 1927] between Einstein and Bohr, I did not take much part. I listened to their arguments, but I did not join in them, essentially because I was not very much interested. I was more interested in getting the correct equations. It seemed to me that the foundation of the work of a mathematical physicist is to get the correct equations, that the interpretation of those equations was only of secondary importance . . . It seems clear that the present quantum mechanics is not in its final form . . . I think it is very likely, or at any rate quite possible, that in the long run Einstein will turn out to be correct, even though for the time being physicists have to accept the Bohr probability interpretation, especially if they have examinations in front of them.[36]

Later I shall comment further on Dirac's position.

Dirac has recalled a conversation with Bohr during the 1927 Solvay conference.

Bohr: 'What are you working on?' Dirac: 'I'm trying to get a relativistic theory of the electron.' Bohr: 'But Klein has already solved that problem.'[4]

Dirac disagreed.

By the time of the 1927 Solvay conference, a relativistic wave equation was already known: the scalar wave equation, stated independently by at least six authors,[37] Klein and Schrödinger among them. One could not, it seemed, associate a positive definite probability density with that equation, however. That Dirac did not like at all, since the existence of such a density was (and is) central to his transformation theory. 'The transformation theory had become my darling. I was not interested in considering any theory which would not fit in with my darling . . . I just couldn't face giving up the transformation theory.'[7] That is why, as said, Dirac disagreed with Bohr. Accordingly, he began his own search for a relativistic wave equation that does have an associated positive probability density. Not only did he find it but, in the course of doing so, he also discovered the relativistic quantum mechanical treatment of spin.

That was a major novelty. In May 1927, Pauli had proposed[38] that the electron satisfy a two-component wave equation which does contain the electron spin, explicitly coupled to the electron's orbital angular momentum. Nothing determined the strength of that coupling, the 'Thomas factor,' which had to be inserted by hand 'without further justification.' This flaw, Pauli noted, was due to the fact that his equation did not satisfy the requirements of relativity. The theory was, in his words, provisional and approximate.

In his equation, Pauli described the spin by 2×2 matrices, since known as the Pauli matrices. It appears that Dirac had discovered these independently: 'I believe I got these (matrices) independently of Pauli, and possibly Pauli also got them independently from me.'[4] Always in quest of a relativistic wave equation with positive probability density, Dirac continued playing[39] with the spin matrices.

> It took me quite a while . . . before I suddenly realized that there was no need to stick to quantities . . . with just two rows and columns. Why not go to four rows and columns.'[4]

Quite a while, actually, was only a few weeks. Toward the end of his life, Dirac reminisced: 'In retrospect, it seems strange that one can be so much held up over such an elementary point (!)'[40]

Thus, early in 1928, was born the Dirac equation[41, 42] with the positive density its author had so fervently desired. To his great surprise, he had stumbled on much more, however.

> It was found that this equation gave the particle a spin of half a quantum. And also gave it a magnetic moment. It gave just the properties that one needed for an electron. That was really an unexpected bonus for me, completely unexpected.[7]

Spin was a necessary consequence, the magnetic moment and the Sommerfeld fine structure formula came out right, the Thomas factor appeared automatically; and for kinetic energies small compared to mc^2 (m = electron mass) all the results of the nonrelativistic Schrödinger theory were recovered. Dirac had played hard and played well. His discovery ('once you got the right road it jumps at you without any effort'[43]), ranking as it does among the highest achievements of twentieth-century science, is all the more remarkable since it was made in pursuit of what eventually turned out to be a side issue, positive probabilities.[44]

Along with its spectacular successes, the Dirac equation was, for a few years, also a source of great trouble, however.

Pauli's wave functions have two components, corresponding to the options spin up and spin down. But Dirac's wave functions had four. The question: why four? led to monumental confusion about which, in the 1960s, Heisenberg recalled: 'Up till that time [1928], I had the impression that, in quantum theory, we had come back into the harbor, into the port. Dirac's paper threw us out into the sea again.'[45]

From the outset,[41] Dirac had correctly diagnosed the cause for this doubling of the number of components. There are two with positive, two with negative energies, each pair with spin up/down. What to do with the negative energy solutions? 'One gets over the difficulty on the classical theory by arbitrarily excluding those solutions that have a negative energy. One cannot do this in the quantum theory, since, in general, a perturbation will cause transitions from states with E positive to states with E negative.'[41] He went on to speculate that negative energy solutions may be associated with particles whose charge is opposite to that of the electron. In that regard, Dirac did not yet know as clearly what he was talking about as he would one and a half years later. This undeveloped idea led him to take the problem lightly, initially: 'Half of the solutions must be rejected as referring to the charge $+e$ of the electron.'[41] In a talk given in Leipzig, in June 1928, he no longer spoke of rejection, however. Transitions to negative energy states simply could not be ignored. 'Consequently, the present theory is an approximation.'[46]

While in Leipzig, Dirac, of course, visited Heisenberg (recently appointed there), who must have been well aware of these difficulties. In May, he had written to Pauli: 'In order not to be forever irritated with Dirac, I have done something else for a change,'[47] the something else being his quantum theory of ferromagnetism. Dirac and Heisenberg discussed several aspects of the new theory.[48] Shortly thereafter, Heisenberg wrote again to Pauli: 'The saddest chapter of modern physics is and remains the Dirac theory,'[49] mentioned some of his own work, which demonstrated the difficulties, and added that the magnetic electron had made Jordan *trübsinnig* (melancholic). At about the same time, Dirac, not feeling so good either, wrote to Oskar Klein: 'I have not met with any success in my attempts to solve the $\pm e$ difficulty. Heisenberg (whom I met in Leipzig) thinks the problem will not be solved until one has a theory of the proton and electron together.'[50]

Early in 1929, both Dirac and Heisenberg made their first trip to the United States, Dirac lecturing at the University of Wisconsin, Heisenberg at the University of Chicago. In August of that year, the two men boarded the steamer *Shinyo Maru* together in San Francisco, stopped over in Hawaii,[51] then went on to Japan, where they both lectured in Tokyo and Kyoto. I was curious whether they had discussed the problematics of the Dirac equation during their trip, so I asked Dirac. He replied:

> In 1929, Heisenberg and I crossed the Pacific and spent some time in Japan together. But we did not have any technical discussions together. We both just wanted a holiday and to get away from physics. We had no discussions of physics, except when we gave lectures in Japan and each of us attended the lectures of the other. I do not remember what was said on these occasions, but I believe there was essential agreement between us.[52]

Heisenberg has told a story of that trip which gives a rare glimpse of Dirac's attitudes towards the opposite sex:

> We were on the steamer from America to Japan, and I liked to take part in the social life on the steamer and, so, for instance, I took part in the dances in the evening. Paul, somehow, didn't like that too much but he would sit in a chair and look at the dances. Once I came back from a dance and took the chair beside him and he asked me, 'Heisenberg, why do you dance?' I said, 'Well, when there are nice girls it is a pleasure to dance.' He thought for a long time about it, and after about five minutes he said, 'Heisenberg, how do you know *beforehand* that the girls are nice?'[53]

In the meantime, Weyl had made[54] a new suggestion regarding the extra two components: 'It is plausible to anticipate that, of the two pairs of components of the Dirac quantity, one belongs to the electron, one to the proton.' In December 1929, Dirac (back in Cambridge) dissented:[55] 'One cannot simply assert that a negative energy electron *is* a proton, since this would violate charge conservation if an electron jumps from a positive to a negative energy state.'[56] Rather, 'Let us assume . . . that all the states of negative energy are occupied, except, perhaps for a few of very small velocity,' this occupation being one electron per state, as the exclusion principle demands. Imagine that one such negative energy electron is removed, leaving a hole in the initial distribution. The result is a rise in energy and in charge by one unit. This hole, Dirac noted, acts like a particle with positive energy and positive charge. 'We are . . . led to the assumption that the holes in the distribution of negative energy electrons are the protons.'[56]

The identification of holes with particles is fine, but why protons? Dirac later remarked: 'At that time . . . everyone felt pretty sure that the electrons and the protons were the only elementary particles in Nature.'[57] (Recall that, in 1929, the atomic nucleus was still believed to be built up of protons and electrons![58])

Just prior to submitting his paper, Dirac wrote a letter[59] to Bohr which shows that he knew quite well that, at least in the absence of interactions, his holes should have the same mass as the electrons themselves. It was his hope (an idle one) that this equality would be violated by electromagnetic interactions:

> So long as one neglects interaction, one has complete symmetry between electrons and protons; one could regard the protons as the real particles and the electrons as the holes in the distribution of protons of negative energy. However, when the interaction between the electrons is taken into account, this symmetry is spoilt. I have not yet worked out mathematically the consequences of the interaction . . . One can hope, however, that a proper theory of this will enable one to calculate the ratio of the masses of protons and electron.

Actually the 'complete symmetry' of which Dirac wrote, charge conjugation invariance, extends to the electromagnetic interactions as well. For want of a better procedure, Dirac briefly considered the mass m in his equation to be the average of the proton and the electron mass.[60]

The hole theory was in this fumbled state when Dirac reported on its status at a meeting of the British Association for the Advancement of Science in Bristol. According to *The New York Times*[61] he bewildered his audience—no wonder. 'Later Doctor Dirac was asked to discuss this theory but he shook his head, saying he could not express his meaning in simpler language without becoming inaccurate.'

The confusion lasted all through 1930 when first Oppenheimer,[62] then, independently, Tamm[63] noted that the proton proposal would make all atoms unstable because of the process: proton + electron → photons. In November 1930, Weyl took a new stand[64] in regard to the protons:

> However attractive this idea may seem at first, it is certainly impossible to hold without introducing other profound modifications . . . indeed, according to (the hole theory), the mass of the proton should be the same as the mass of the electron; furthermore . . . this hypothesis leads to the essential equivalence of positive and negative electricity under all circumstances . . . the dissimilarity of the two kinds of electricity thus seems to hide a secret of Nature which lies yet deeper than the dissimilarity between the past and future . . . I fear that the clouds hanging over this part of the subject will roll together to form a new crisis in quantum physics.

Then, in May 1931, Dirac bit the bullet[65] (or, in his words, he made 'a small step forward'[43]): 'A hole, if there were one, would be a new kind of particle, unknown to experimental physics, having the same mass and opposite charge of the electron.' Dirac eventually called the new particle anti-electron. Just before the year's end, Carl Anderson made the first announcement[66] of experimental evidence for the anti-electron. The name positron first appeared in print in one of his later papers.[67] The prediction and subsequent discovery of the positron rank among the great triumphs of modern physics.

That, however, was not at once obvious.

The detection of the positron was considered by nearly everyone as a vindication of Dirac's theory. Yet its basic idea, a positron as a hole in an infinite sea of negative electrons, remained unpalatable to some, and not without reason. Even the simplest state, the vacuum, was a complex consisting of infinitely many particles, the totally filled sea. Interactions between these particles left aside, the vacuum had a negative infinite 'zero point energy' and an infinite 'zero point charge.' Pauli did not like that. Even after the positron had been discovered, he wrote to Dirac: 'I do not believe in your perception of 'holes' even if the 'anti-electron' is proved.'[68] That was not all, however. Pauli to Heisenberg one month later: 'I do not believe in the hole theory, since I would like to have asymmetries between positive and negative electricity in the laws of nature (it does not satisfy me to shift the empirically established asymmetry to one of the initial state).'[69]

The zero point energy and charge are actually innocuous and can be eliminated by a simple reformulation of the theory.[70] Even thereafter, the theory is still riddled with infinities caused by interactions, however. To this day, the influence of interactions cannot be treated rigorously. Rather, one uses the fact that the fundamental charge e is small, more precisely that the dimensionless number $a = e^2/\hbar c \cong 1/137$ is small, and expands in a. To leading power in a, theoretical predictions were excellent for processes like photo-electron scattering, the creation and annihilation of electron–positron pairs, and many others. Contributions to these same processes stemming from higher powers in a are invariably infinitely large, however. One was faced with a crisis: how to cope with a theory which works very well approximately but which makes no sense rigorously. As Pauli put it in 1936 during a seminar given in Princeton: 'Success seems to have been on the side of Dirac rather than of logic.'[71] Or, as Heisenberg put it,[72] in a letter to Pauli (1935): 'In regard to quantum electrodynamics, we are still at the stage in which we were in 1922 with regard to quantum mechanics. We know that everything is wrong. But, in order to find the direction in which we should depart from what prevails, we must know the consequences of the prevailing formalism much better than we do.' Heisenberg was, in fact, one of that quite small band of theoretical physicists who had the courage to explore those aspects of quantum electrodynamics which remained in an uncertain state until the late 1940s, when renormalization would provide more systematic and more successful ways of handling the problem.

The first steps toward renormalization go back once again to Dirac. In August 1933, he had written[73] to Bohr:

Peierls and I have been looking into the question of the change in the distribution of negative energy electrons produced by a static electric field. We find that this changed distribution causes a partial neutralization of the charge producing the field . . . If we neglect the disturbance that the field produces in negative energy electrons with energies less than $-137mc^2$, then the neutralization of charge produced by the other negative energy electrons is small and of the order 136/137 . . . The effective charges are what one measures in all low-energy experiments, and the experimentally determined value of e must be the effective charge on an electron, the real value being slightly bigger . . . One would expect some small alterations in the Rutherford scattering formula, the Klein–Nishina formula, the Sommerfeld fine structure formula, etc., when energies of the order mc^2 come into play.

Transcribed in the modern vernacular, Dirac's effective charge is our physical charge; his real charge our bare charge; his neutralization of charge our charge renormalization; and his disturbance that the field produces in negative energy electrons our vacuum polarization.[74]

In quantitative form, the results Dirac had mentioned to Bohr are found in his report[75] to the seventh Solvay conference (October 1933), the paper that marks the beginning of positron theory as a serious discipline. There, Dirac also gives the finite contribution to the vacuum polarization[76] which, in 1935, was to be evaluated by Uehling[77] for an electron moving in a hydrogen-like atom—a result which, in turn, was to provide the direct stimulus for the celebrated Lamb shift experiments of 1946.

With Dirac's Solvay report, his exquisite burst of creativity at the outer frontiers of physics, spanning eight years, comes to an end.

The years 1925–33 are the heroic period in Dirac's life, during which he emerged as one of the principal figures in twentieth-century science and changed the face of physics. He himself has called those years in his scientific career 'the exciting era.'[78] My foregoing sketch of that period is not, by any means, complete. For example, in 1931, Dirac produced[65] the first application of global topology to physics, his proof that the existence of magnetic monopoles implies, quantum mechanically, that electric charge is quantized. He returned to this subject some 20 years later[79] (he lectured upon it[80] at the Pocono conference, March 31 – April 1, 1948) and, once again, nearly 30 years thereafter.[81] As these intervals illustrate, Dirac remained scientifically active for the 50 years following the developments that came to a close in 1933.

I shall turn shortly to a summary of those later undertakings by Dirac but will first make some comments on his personal life in the 1930s.

In 1933, Dirac received the Nobel Prize 'for his discovery of new fertile forms of the theory of atoms and for its applications,' sharing the award with

Schrödinger. 'At first he was inclined to refuse the prize because he did not like publicity, but when Rutherford told him: 'A refusal will get you much more publicity,' he accepted.'[82] At that time he had ceased all contact with his father, so he only took his mother along to Stockholm, where he delivered his Nobel lecture.[83]

Much to his dismay, the Nobel Prize did make Dirac a public person. A London paper characterized him 'as shy as a gazelle and modest as a Victorian maid,' and called him 'The genius who fears all women.'[84]

Well, not quite all.

As mentioned before, Dirac was in Princeton during academic 1934–35. That autumn, Eugene Wigner, professor of physics at Princeton University, received a visit from his sister, Margit Wigner Balasz (Manci to her friends), who lived in her native Budapest. Manci and Paul met. 'He spoke to me about his difficult, I should say very difficult, childhood, I told him about mine, which also left some sad memories about my unhappy marriage.'[85] In the summer of 1935 Paul visited Manci in Budapest. Manci has written a loving, tender account of their courtship.[85] They married on January 2, 1937. 'So started a very old-fashioned Victorian marriage.'[85] Paul gave up his bachelor quarters in St John's College. The couple moved into the house on Cavendish Avenue, where I first met them. They were joined by Manci's two children from her previous marriage, Monica and Gabriel—who became a mathematician of distinction—who both adopted the name Dirac. Paul and Manci had two daughters, Mary and Florence. 'Paul, although not a domineering father, kept himself aloof from his children.'[85]

After Paul's father's death in 1936, Paul wrote to Manci: 'I feel much freer now.'[85] His mother became a frequent visitor to Cavendish Avenue. It was there that she died, in 1941.

As promised, I now continue with an account of Dirac's later work, and begin with some lesser known of his researches. First, in 1933 he collaborated with his good friend Pyotr Kapitza on a theoretical study of the reflection of electrons from standing light waves.[86] This 'Kapitza–Dirac effect' was not experimentally observed until 1986.[87]

Secondly, also in 1933, Dirac invented a centrifugal method for separating gaseous isotope mixtures. Kapitza encouraged him to carry out the experiments himself, which Dirac did but did not complete. Dalitz has given a detailed account[88] of how, after 1940, construction projects of atomic bombs revived interest in that work, and how Dirac became an informal consultant for that project. He also contributed in a quite different way to the war effort, being a member of the small fire fighter team of St John's College, Cambridge, during the period when fire raids were expected (according to a letter dated April 28, 1993 from H. Peisir to R. Hovis, now in the archives of St John's).

Interesting though these two topics are, they must be considered as digressions from Dirac's main later pursuits of fundamental issues, in which he continued to show his high mathematical inventiveness and craftsmanship but no longer that almost startling combination of novelty and simplicity that mark his heroic period.

Without pretence to completeness, and in fairly random order, here are some main themes which, as I see it, convey the flavor of his thinking in his later years.

Elaborations of Hamiltonian dynamics. These include studies of the special relativistic dynamical evolution of systems on various types of hypersurfaces, in classical theory[89] and in quantum mechanics.[90] Also, investigations of constrained Hamiltonian systems,[91,92] leading to his Hamiltonian formulation of general relativity.[93] That work, in turn, aroused his interest in gravitational waves.[94] Did Dirac coin the name graviton? According to *The New York Times* of January 31, 1959, 'Professor Dirac proposed that the gravitational wave units be called gravitons.'

Related to Dirac's lifelong interest in general relativity are his papers on wave equations in conformal,[95] de Sitter,[96] and Riemannian spaces.[97] He lectured on general relativity until in his seventies.[98]

Cosmological issues, in which he had already become interested in his Göttingen days.[99] He did not publish on this subject until 1937.[100] From then on, until the end of his life, he was much intrigued by the possibility that the fundamental constants in nature actually are not constant but depend on time in a scale set by the cosmological epoch, the time interval between the big bang and the present.[101] It was his hope that simple relations should emerge between such extremely large but roughly comparable numbers as the ratio of epoch to atomic time intervals and the ratio of electric to gravitational forces between an electron and a proton.[102] No definitive advance was ever achieved. Others followed these exploits with more interest than enthusiasm.

The aether. A brief period (1951–53) of speculations to the effect that quantum mechanics allows for the existence of an aether.[103]

Quantum electrodynamics. One further contribution still belongs to the heroic period. In March 1932, Dirac proposed a 'many-time formalism' in which an individual time is assigned to each electron.[104] This new version of the theory, equivalent to earlier formulations,[105] marks an important first step toward the manifestly covariant procedures that were to play such a key role from the late 1940s on.

A few years later, Dirac turned highly critical of quantum electrodynamics. On the one hand, the work he produced as a result of this negative attitude has not in any way enhanced our understanding of fundamental issues. On the other hand, these later struggles are of prime importance for an understanding of Dirac himself. His radically modified position resulted from his work[75] on vacuum polarization in which he had encountered the infinities that, as said, constituted a crisis in the quantum field theory of the 1930s.

Dirac's drastic change in attitude is starkly expressed in a brief paper he wrote in 1936, his first publication following his involvement[75] with the implications of positron theory. I regard it as significant that this article followed a period during which he had not published at all for more than a year. The *a propos* was a fleeting experimental doubt about the validity of the theory of photon–electron scattering. Dirac reacted[106] as follows: 'The only important part (of theoretical physics) that we have to give up is quantum electrodynamics . . . we may give it up without regrets . . . in fact, on account of its extreme complexity, most physicists will be very glad to see the end of it.'

At this point, it should be recalled that the germs of the difficulties with the infinities date back to the classical era. A classical electron considered as a point particle has an infinite energy due to the coupling to its own electrostatic field. With this in mind, Dirac adopted the strategy of attempting to modify the classical theory first, so as to rid it of *its* infinities, and thereupon to revisit the quantum theory in the hope that also there all would be well. At that time, that approach was followed also by others, Born, Kramers, and Wentzel among them. Even today, there remains a much needed understanding of what lies beyond the infinities. There are overwhelming reasons, however, why a return to the classical theory is the wrong way to go.[107]

Be that as it may, Dirac tried several times to reformulate the classical theory of the electron. His first attempt[108] dates from 1938. 'A new physical theory is needed which should be intelligible both in the classical and in the quantum theory and our easiest path of approach is to keep within the confines of the classical theory.' He started from the observations that Lorentz's classical theory of the electron's motion is not rigorously valid for high accelerations, since Lorentz's electron has a finite radius. Dirac, instead, started from a zero radius electron and was able to find a rigorous classical equation of motion for it which is free of the classical infinities but which exhibits new pathologies; it has solutions corresponding to accelerations even in the absence of external fields. He did find a not very palatable constraint that eliminates these unwanted solutions—but there was more trouble. New infinities arose upon quantizing the theory.[109] In order to eliminate these, Dirac introduced[110] what amounts to photons of negative energy. He attempted to eliminate the physical paradoxes resulting from this new postulate by introducing an indefinite metric in Hilbert space.[111] That, however, leads to still further difficulties, critically analyzed by Pauli.[112] These new postulates were never discussed in the context of positron theory.

Unable to find a satisfactory quantum version of his point electron, Dirac never mentioned this theory again in later years. By 1946, he tended to the view that the infinities are a mathematical artifact resulting from expansions in a that are actually invalid.[113]

Shortly thereafter, in the years 1947–78, quantum electrodynamics took a new turn when the renormalization program was systematically developed. That technique does not fully resolve the problem of the infinities. The electron's mass and charge unalterably remain infinite. To a very large extent, these two infinities can be rendered harmless, however, in the sense that predictions to arbitrarily high orders in a can now be made for the scattering, creation, and annihilation processes mentioned earlier, where, before, the leading order in a had worked so well, but the higher orders had been intractable. As a result, quantum electrodynamics could now be confronted with experiment to vastly improved orders of magnitude. The results were spectacular. With good reason, Feynman has called[114] the new version of quantum electrodynamics 'the jewel of physics—our proudest possession.'

Dirac would have none of it.

In 1951, he wrote: 'Recent work by Lamb, Schwinger and Feynman and others has been very successful . . . but the resulting theory is an ugly and incomplete one.'[115] He had a deep aversion to the way infinite masses and charges are manipulated in the renormalization program. In that year, he started all over again for a second time in his search for a new, classical, point of departure. 'The troubles . . . should be ascribed . . . to our working from the wrong classical theory.'[115] His new suggestion may be considered as the extreme opposite of what he had proposed in 1938. This time, he began with a classical theory that does not contain discrete particles at all. 'The notion of electrons should be built up from a classical theory of the motion of a continuous stream of electricity[116] rather than the motion of point charges. One then looks upon the discrete electrons as a quantum phenomenon.'[117] After 1954, this model, too, vanished from his writings without leaving a trace.

Thus, from the early 1950s on, Dirac went his own lonely way. He accepted the successes of the renormalization method. In fact, in the mid-1960s, he lectured on the anomalous magnetic moment and Lamb shift calculations.[118] He never wavered in his belief, however, that quantum electrodynamics needed a new starting point. In later years, he would occasionally seek new remedies in a reformulation not so much of classical as of quantum theory.[119] In 1970, he invented the last of the Dirac equations, a relativistic wave equation with positive energies only.[120]

———————

From September 1970 to January 1971, Dirac was visiting professor at the Florida State University in Tallahassee. During that time he was offered a permanent position there, which he accepted. In 1972 he started a new life as professor in Florida. One of his colleagues there has told me:

> At that time he was also courted by the New York State University at Stony Brook and by Miami. He declined those offers, principally because he could not go for walks there . . . In Tallahassee he walked about a mile to work . . . He was fond of swimming in nearby Silver Lake and Lost Lake, also sometimes at the seashore.
>
> Dirac was most happy in Tallahassee, he really changed. In Cambridge he only went to the University for classes and seminars but otherwise worked at home. In Tallahassee he came diligently all day, ate lunch with the boys, took a nap after lunch. His wife would pick him up in the late afternoon . . . We treated him like one of the boys . . . did not indulge in much red carpet treatment. He liked that.'[121]

Dirac's writings in the Florida period are simply prolific. He published over 60 papers in those last 12 years of his life, most of them reviews of past events, including a short book on general relativity.[122] I cherish a 'Dear Bram' letter he wrote to me[52] in those days, thanking me for a copy of my scientific biography of Einstein. On the back flap of that volume one finds words of praise by Dirac for that book.

Dirac's last paper (1984), entitled 'The inadequacies of quantum field theory,'[123] contains his last judgment on quantum electrodynamics: 'These rules of renormalization give surprisingly, excessively good agreement with experiments. Most physicists say that these working rules are, therefore, correct. I feel that is not an adequate reason. Just because the results happen to be in agreement with observation does not prove that one's theory is correct.' The paper concludes with Dirac's final published scientific words:

> I have spent many years searching for a Hamiltonian to bring into the theory and have not yet found it. I shall continue to work on it as long as I can, and other people, I hope, will follow along such lines.

Dirac died on October 20, 1984, aged 82. He was buried in the Roselawn Cemetery in Tallahassee. It was his family's wish that he should rest where he left the world.

———————

It has been correctly said of Dirac that his life was mostly science and his science was physics. That is reflected in what I have discussed so far: mostly his science with only brief digressions about other features of his life. I would be remiss, however, if I did not flesh out these latter aspects some more.

Dirac's ascetic lifestyle, his indifference to discomfort or food has been likened to Gandhi.[124] He neither touched alcohol nor smoked. He shunned publicity and honors, of which he nevertheless received many.[125] Regarding religion, he tended towards atheism, as he has publicly expressed only once.[126] As Pauli once said: 'There is no God and Dirac is his prophet.'[127] Manci Dirac has written to me, however: 'Paul was no atheist. Many times did we kneel side by side in chapel, praying. We all know he was no hypocrite.'[128]

Throughout his life, Dirac maintained a minimal, sparse (not terse), precise, and apoetically elegant style of speech and writing. Sample: his comment on the novel *Crime and Punishment*: 'It is nice, but in one of the chapters the author made a mistake. He describes the sun as rising twice on the same day.'[129] Once, when Oppenheimer offered Dirac some books to read, he politely refused, saying that reading books interfered with thought.[130]

After his marriage Dirac became a keen gardener, and tried to deal with horticultural problems from first principles, which did not always lead to good results.[131]

I turn to my personal contacts with Dirac, mainly those at the Institute in Princeton, which began in the fall of 1946. At that time we would often have lunch together. It was on one of those occasions that I had my first exposure to the Dirac style of exhaustive inquiry. Because of a large appetite and a Dutch background, I would regularly eat three sandwiches at that time. One day, Dirac queried me. (Between each answer and the next question there was a half minute's pause.) 'Do you always eat three sandwiches for lunch?' 'Yes.' 'Do you always eat the same three sandwiches for lunch?' 'No, it depends on my taste of the day.' 'Do you eat your sandwiches in some fixed order?' 'No.' Some months later, when a young man named Salam visited me at the Institute, he said: 'I have regards for you from Professor Dirac in Cambridge. He wants to know if you still eat three sandwiches for lunch.' Dirac and I again often lunched together when he came back to the Institute for academic 1947–48. On an early occasion, Dirac looked at my plate and noted, triumphantly: 'Now you only eat two sandwiches for lunch.' Another recollection: a corridor conversation at the Institute. D.: 'My wife wants to know if you can come for dinner tonight.' P.: 'I regret. I have another engagement.' D.: 'Goodbye.' Nothing unfriendly implied. Nothing else said like 'Some other time perhaps.' The question had been posed and answered, the conversation was finished.

Everything had been arranged at the Institute for Dirac's next visit in academic 1954–55. It was not to be. The events of the troubled spring of 1954 were summarized in the 'News and Views' column of *Physics Today*, July 1954, under two headings: The Oppenheimer Case; Dirac denied Visa. Dirac had been informed by the American Consulate in London that he was ineligible for a visa under Section 212A of the Immigration and Naturalization Act, the infamous McCarran Act which (to quote *Physics Today*) 'Covers categories of undesirables ranging from vagrants to stowaways.' The reasons for this decision have never become quite clear, but it was believed that Dirac's seven pre-War visits to Russia, three in the course of his three trips around the world, and all for scientific purposes, had something to do with it.[132] The event, widely reported in the world press,[133] caused some American physicists to write to *The New York Times*: 'If this is what the McCarran Act means in practice, it seems to us a form of cultural suicide.'[134] It was a quite bad, yet by no means the worst, case of harm done during that period. It passed.

In 1988 I requested and received Dirac's FBI files, which contain only one line which I find moderately pertinent: 'The reason for Dirac's [1954] visit here was to discuss with Oppenheimer an invitation from Cambridge University to accept an offer as a professor. Dr. Oppenheimer, bitter over the [security clearance] vote against him, will accept that British offer.' For the rest these documents are monumentally uninteresting.

Later Dirac was to spend two more academic years in Princeton. During all those visits I would draw him out, time and again, about his discontent with quantum electrodynamics. He would concede the successes of renormalization but forever was of the opinion that the remaining mass and charge infinities 'ought not to be there. They remove them artificially.'[123] This diagnosis may well be much better than the cures he proposed.

Other recollections: his evident pride at having invented the bra and ket notations, announced in a paper[135] specially written for this purpose. His reply to my question, posed in the early 1960s, why space reflexion and time reversal invariance do not appear in his book on quantum mechanics: 'Because I did not believe in them.' Indeed, in 1949, he had written: 'I do not believe there is any need for physical laws to be invariant under these reflections, although all the exact laws of nature so far known do have this invariance.'[136]

By far the most revealing insight I gained from those discussions concerned the Dirac way of playing with equations, which can be summed up like this: first play with pretty mathematics for its own sake, then see whether this leads to new physics.

Throughout most of his life, that attitude is manifest in his writings. At age 28:

> There are, at present, fundamental problems in theoretical physics . . . the solution of which . . . will presumably require a more drastic revision of our fundamental concepts than any that have gone before. Quite likely, these changes will be so great that it will be beyond the power of human intelligence to get the necessary new ideas by direct attempts to formulate the experimental data in

mathematical terms. The theoretical worker in the future will, therefore, have to proceed in a more direct way. The most powerful method of advance that can be suggested at present is to employ all the resources of pure mathematics in attempts to perfect and generalize the mathematical formalism that forms the existing basis of theoretical physics, and after each success in this direction, to try to interpret the new mathematical features in terms of physical entities,[65]

just what is happening these days. At age 36: 'As time goes on, it becomes increasingly evident that the rules which the mathematician finds interesting are the same as those which Nature has chosen.'[34] At age 60: 'I think it's a peculiarity of myself that I like to play about with equations, just looking for beautiful mathematical relations which maybe don't have any physical meaning at all. Sometimes they do.'[2] At age 78:

> A good deal of my research work in physics has consisted in not setting out to solve some particular problem, but simply examining mathematical quantities of a kind that physicists use and trying to fit them together in an interesting way, regardless of any application that the work may have. It is simply a search for pretty mathematics. It may turn out later that the work does have an application. Then one has good luck.[40]

In that last paper he gave three examples of the way he played: the Dirac equation, monopoles, and the last Dirac equation. His own judgment, at age 69: 'My own contributions since [the] early days have been of minor importance.'[137]

What kinds of mathematics did Dirac consider pretty? 'The research worker, in his efforts to express the fundamental laws of Nature in mathematical form, should strive mainly for mathematical beauty. He should take simplicity into consideration in a subordinate way to beauty . . . It often happens that the requirements of simplicity and beauty are the same, but where they clash the latter must take precedence.'[34] It is, of course, idle to argue about such subjective issues as the distinction between beauty and simplicity.

Dirac was a very private man, not much given to reminiscing about other personalities or past events. He would only rarely talk about himself. On a few occasions, he would reveal some of his emotions in his writings, however. I find it striking that, as mentioned, he would refer to the transformation theory as 'my darling.'[7] Equally notable are his rare utterances about anxiety. When, at age 60, he was asked about his feelings on discovering the Dirac equation, he replied: 'Well, in the first place, it leads to great anxiety as to whether it's going to be correct or not . . . I expect that's the dominating feeling. It gets to be rather a fever . . .'[2] At age 67: 'Hopes are always accompanied by fears, and, in scientific research, the fears are liable to become dominant.'[138] At age 69: 'I think it is a general rule that the originator of a new idea is not the most suitable person to develop it, because his fears of something going wrong are really too strong . . .'[137]

As my last example of Dirac talking about himself I quote from a letter[139] to me by a colleague: 'I had a conversation with him about a year and a half before his death . . . I asked him to come and talk at the University of Florida, and he said: 'No! I have nothing to talk about. My life has been a failure . . .' and then went on to talk about the infinities [in quantum electrodynamics]!!' It is typical for many great men that in their own minds failure outweighs success.

———— • ————

I should next like to add two Dirac stories to the immense lore about him.

One day Niels Bohr came into my office in Princeton, shaking his head while telling me of a discussion he had just with Dirac. It was in the early 1950s, during the time of the Cold War. Bohr had expressed his dislike of the abusive language the American press was using in reference to the Russians. Dirac had replied that all this would come to an end in a few weeks' time. Bohr had asked why. Well, Dirac had remarked, by then the reporters will have used up all the invective in the English language, so therefore they will have to stop.

The other story is not about Dirac, but one that I have heard Dirac tell more than once, with relish. In a small village, a newly appointed priest went to call on his parishioners. On a visit to a quite modest home, he was received by the lady of the house. He could not fail to notice that her place was teeming with children and asked her how many the couple had. Ten, she replied, five pairs of twins. Astonished, the priest asked: You mean you always had twins? To which the woman replied: No, Father, sometimes we had nothing. Precision at that level had an immense appeal to Dirac.

———— • ————

My final story about Dirac concerns a letter to me by a friend of his and mine.[140] It concerns my very first encounter with the Diracs, in January 1946, during which Paul had queried me about my war experience. The letter says in part:

> It was about two weeks before his death . . . Margit and I were sitting at his bedside. He was pale, thin, and unusually talkative . . . He said that very near the end of the War you had been captured by the Germans and that you were about to be executed . . . The unusual thing about the situation was that he repeated the story in its entirety at least four times . . . Margit finally got through to him and made him stop . . . Some day perhaps you can tell me about it.

———— • ————

As I look back on the almost 40 years I knew Dirac, all memories are fond ones. I share Niels Bohr's opinion of him: 'Of all physicists, Dirac has the purest soul.'[141] In some, but only some, ways he reminds me of Einstein: one of the century's great contributors, always going his own way, not making a school, compelled by the need for beauty and simplicity in physical theory, in his later years more addicted to mathematics than was good for his physics, continuing his activities in pure research until close to his death. In other respects, I never knew anyone quite like him.

References

(In these notes D. stands for P.A.M. Dirac.)

1. Address to the Royal Society, London, given on November 13, 1995, on the occasion of the unveiling that day of a memorial plaque to Dirac in Westminster Abbey. Parts of this paper were taken from my earlier writings about D., found in: *Aspects of Quantum Theory* (A. Salam and E. P. Wigner, Eds), p. 79, Cambridge University Press, 1972; in *Inward Bound*, Oxford University Press, 1986; and in *Reminiscences about a Great Physicist* (B. Kursunoglu and E. P. Wigner, Eds), p. 93, Cambridge University Press, 1987. My principal secondary sources have been the fine writings by R. H. Dalitz and R. Peierls, *Biogr. Mem. Fell. Roy. Soc.* **32**, 139, 1986; and by H. S. Kragh, *Dirac*, Cambridge University Press, 1990.

2. T. Kuhn, interview with D., May 7, 1963, Niels Bohr Archive, Copenhagen.

3. D., 'A little "prehistory,"' *The Old Cathamian*, p. 9, 1980.

4. D., in *History of Twentieth Century Physics* (C. Weiner, Ed.), p. 109, Academic Press, New York, 1977.

5. D., interview in *Florida State University Bulletin*, Vol. 3, February 1978.

6. For an account of D.'s Cambridge days, see R. J. Eden and J. C. Polkinghorne, in *Aspects of Quantum Theory*, ref. 1, p. 1.

7. D., Report KFKI-1977-62, *Hung. Ac. of Sc.*

8. D., *Proc. Roy. Soc.* **A109**, 642, 1925.

9. M. Born, *My Life*, p. 226, Scribner, New York, 1978.

10. *Reminiscences about I. E. Tamm* (E. Feinberg, Ed.), Nauka, Moscow, 1987.

11. Cf. D., *Proc. Camb. Phil. Soc.* **23**, 412, 1926.

12. D., *Proc. Roy. Soc.* **A112**, 661, 1926. For many more details about Dirac's early years and his contributions to quantum mechanics during 1925–26, see J. Mehra and H. Rechenberg, *The Historical Development of Quantum Theory*, Vol. 4, part 1, Springer, New York, 1982.

13. W. Heisenberg, *Zeitschr. f. Physik* **38**, 411, 1926.

14. W. Heisenberg, *Zeitschr. f. Physik* **39**, 499, 1926.

15. E. Fermi, *Rend. Lincei* **3**, 145, 1926; *Zeitschr. f. Physik* **36**, 902, 1926; reprinted in *Enrico Fermi, Collected Works*, Vol. 1, pp. 181, 186, University of Chicago Press, 1962. In ref. 4, pp. 133, 134, Dirac has given a charming account of the time sequence of his and Fermi's contributions.

16. For the history of quantum statistics in the days of the old quantum theory, see *Inward Bound*, ref. 1, chapter 13, section (d).

17. D., *Proc. Roy. Soc.* **A113**, 621, 1927.

18. Rigorous treatments lead to the theory of distributions; cf. I. Halperin and L. Schwartz, *Introduction to the Theory of Distributions*, Toronto University Press, 1952.

19. D., *Proc. Roy. Soc.* **A114**, 243, 1927.

20. D., *Proc. Roy. Soc.* **A114**, 710, 1927.

21. This so-called semi-classical procedure (discussed in detail by W. Pauli, *Handbuch der Physik*, Vol. 24/1, sections 15, 16, Springer, Berlin, 1933) allows for a good approximate but not rigorous treatment of induced processes; radiative corrections are not properly accounted for.

22. A. Einstein, *Phys. Zeitschr.* **18**, 121, 1917. See further A. Pais *Subtle is the Lord*, chapter 21, section (d), Oxford University Press, New York, 1982.

23. D. was aware[19] that he missed a factor two in this coefficient because he had not yet treated polarization properly.

24. Independently of Schrödinger, *Ann. der Phys.* **81**, 109, 1926.

25. A far more detailed analysis of D.'s two founding papers on quantum electrodynamics has been given by R. Jost, in *Aspects of Quantum Theory*, ref. 1, p. 61.

26. Ref. 20, p. 719.

27. D., *Proc. Roy. Soc.* **A111**, 405, 1926; *Proc. Camb. Phil. Soc.* **23**, 500, 1926.

28. L. Infeld, *Quest*, p. 203, 2nd edn, Chelsea, New York, 1980.

29. See especially the account of D.'s research students by Dalitz and Peierls, ref. 1, pp. 155–7.

30. H. B. G. Casimir, *Haphazard Reality*, p. 72, Harper and Row, New York, 1983.

31. R. Eden and J. Polkinghorne, in *Tributes to Paul Dirac* (J. C. Taylor, Ed), p. 5, Hilger, Bristol, 1987.

32. N. F. Mott, interviewed by T. S. Kuhn, March 1962, Niels Bohr Archive, Copenhagen.

33. A. Einstein, in *James Clerk Maxwell*, p. 66, New York , 1931.

34. D., *Proc. Roy. Soc. Edinburgh* **59**, 122, 1939.

35. D., *Sci. Am.* **208**, 45, May 1963.

36. D. in *Albert Einstein, Historical and Cultural Perspectives* (G. Holton and Y. Elkana, Eds), p. 79, Princeton University Press, 1982.

37. O. Klein, *Zeitschr. f. Physik* **37**, 895, 1926; E. Schrödinger, *Ann. der Phys.* **81**, 109, 1926; V. Fock, *Zeitschr. f. Physik* **38**, 242, 1926; Th. de Donder and H. van den Dungen, *Comptes Rendues* **183**, 22, 1926; J. Kudar, *Ann. der Phys.* **81**, 632, 1926; W. Gordon, *Zeitschr. f. Physik* **40**, 117, 1926.

38. W. Pauli, *Zeitschr. f. Physik* **43**, 601, 1927.

39. He was looking for a four-dimensional generalization of $\sigma \cdot \mathbf{p}$. Later he was to play briefly with wave equations for higher spin; D., *Proc. Roy. Soc.* **A155**, 447, 1936.

40. D., *Int. J. Theor. Phys.* **21**, 603, 1982.

41. D., *Proc. Roy. Soc.* **A117**, 610, 1928.

42. D., *Proc. Roy. Soc.* **A118**, 351, 1928.

43. Ref. 2, interview May 14, 1963.

44. It was later shown by Pauli and Weisskopf (*Helv. Phys. Acta* **7**, 709, 1934) that the scalar wave equation is amenable to a treatment compatible with the transformation theory.

45. W. Heisenberg, interviewed by T. Kuhn, July 12, 1963, Niels Bohr Library, American Institute of Physics, New York.

46. D. *Phys. Zeitschr.* **29**, 561, 712, 1928.

47. W. Heisenberg, letter to W. Pauli, May 3, 1928; reprinted in *Wolfgang Pauli, Scientific Correspondence*, Vol. 1, p. 443, Springer, New York, 1979; referred to as PC below.

48. Ref. 46, p. 562, footnote 2.

49. W. Heisenberg, letter to W. Pauli, July 31, 1928; PC, Vol. 1, p. 466.

50. D., letter to O. Klein, July 24, 1928, copy in Niels Bohr Library.

51. S. F. Tuan, *Dirac and Heisenberg in Hawaii*, unpublished manuscript.

52. D., letter to A. Pais, October 21, 1982.

53. W. Heisenberg, in *The Physicist's Conception of Nature* (J. Mehra, Ed.), p. 816, Reidel, Dordrecht, 1973.

54. H. Weyl, *Zeitschr. f. Physik* **56**, 330, 1929.

55. Other pertinent developments which had meanwhile taken place include the derivations of the Klein–Nishina formula for Compton scattering; and of the Klein paradox. See further *Inward Bound*, ref. 1, chapter 15, section (f).

56. D., *Proc. Roy Soc.* **A126**, 360, 1929; also *Nature* **126**, 605, 1930.

57. D., ref. 4, p. 144.

58. See *Inward Bound*, ref. 1, chapter 14.

59. D., letter to N. Bohr, November 26, 1929, copy in Niels Bohr Library.

60. D., *Proc. Camb. Phil. Soc.* **26**, 361, 1930.

61. *The New York Times*, September 9, 1930.

62. J. R. Oppenheimer, *Phys. Rev.* **35**, 562, 1930.

63. I. Tamm, *Zeitschr. f. Physik* **62**, 545, 1930.

64. H. Weyl, *The Theory of Groups and Quantum Mechanics*, pp. 263–4 and preface, Dover, New York.

65. D., *Proc. Roy. Soc.* **A133**, 60, 1931.

66. C. D. Anderson, *Science* **76**, 238, 1932.

67. C. D. Anderson, *Phys. Rev.* **43**, 491, 1933.

68. W. Pauli, letter to D., May 1, 1933; PC, Vol. 2, p. 159.

69. W. Pauli, letter to W. Heisenberg, June 16, 1933; PC, Vol. 2, p. 169.

70. Cf. *Inward Bound*, ref. 1, chapter 16, section (d).

71. *The Theory of the Positron and Related Topics*, report of a seminar conducted by W. Pauli, notes by B. Hoffmann, Institute for Advanced Study, Princeton, 1935–36, mimeographed notes.

72. W. Heisenberg, letter to W. Pauli; PC, Vol. 2, p. 386.

73. D., letter to N. Bohr, August 10, 1933, copy in Niels Bohr Library.

74. The existence of vacuum polarization was also independently diagnosed by W. H. Furry and J. R. Oppenheimer, *Phys. Rev.* **45**, 245, 343, 1934.

75. D., in *Rapports du Septième Conseil de Physique*, p. 203, Gauthier-Villars, Paris, 1934; cf. also D., *Proc. Camb. Phil. Soc.* **30**, 150, 1934.

76. A numerical error in the coefficient of that finite term was corrected by W. Heisenberg, *Zeitschr. f. Physik* **90**, 209, 1934.

77. E. Uehling, *Phys. Rev.* **48**, 55, 1935.

78. Ref. 4, p. 140.

79. D., *Phys. Rev.* **74**, 817, 1948.

80. D., in dittoed notes of the Pocono conference, p. 72, unpublished.

81. D., in *New Pathways in Science* (A. Perlmutter, Ed.), Vol. 1, Plenum Press, New York, 1976; see further E. Amaldi and N. Cabibbo, in *Aspects of Quantum Theory*, ref. 1, p. 183.

82. Dalitz and Peierls, ref. 1, p. 150.

83. D., 'Theory of electrons and positrons,' in *Nobel Lectures in Physics, 1922–1941*, p. 320, Elsevier, Amsterdam, 1965.

84. *Sunday Dispatch*, November 19, 1933.

85. Margit Dirac, in Kursunoglu and Wigner, ref. 1, p. 3.

86. D., and P. Kapitza, *Proc. Cambr. Phil. Soc.* **29**, 297, 1933.

87. P. Gould *et al.*, *Phys. Rev. Lett.* **56**, 827, 1986.

88. R. H. Dalitz, in *Reminiscences about a Great Physicist*, ref. 1, p. 69; also Dalitz and Peierls, ref. 1, p. 152.

89. D., *Rev. Mod. Phys.* **21**, 392, 1949.

90. D., *Phys. Rev.* **73**, 1092, 1948; *Proceedings of the Second Canadian Mathematical Congress 1949*, p. 10, University of Toronto Press, 1951.

91. D., *Can. J. Math.* **2**, 129, 1950; **3**, 1, 1951; *Proc. Roy. Soc.* **A246**, 326, 1958; *Proc. Roy. Irish Acad.* **A63**, 49, 1964.

92. See also F. Rohrlich, in *High Energy Physics* (B. Kursunoglu and A. Perlmutter, Eds), p. 17, Plenum Press, New York, 1985.

93. D., *Proc. Roy. Soc.* **A246**, 333, 1958; *Phys. Rev.* **114**, 924, 1959; also in *Recent Developments in General Relativity*, p. 191, Pergamon Press, London, 1962. See further D., *Proc. Roy. Soc.* **A270**, 354, 1962; *Gen. Rel. and Grav.* **5**, 741, 1974.

94. D., *Phys. Rev. Lett.* **2**, 368, 1959; *Proceedings of the Royaumont Conference 1959*, p. 385, Editions du CNRS, Paris, 1962; *Phys. Bl.* **16**, 364, 1960.

95. D., *Ann. of Math.* **37**, 429, 1935.

96. D., *Ann. of Math.* **36**, 657, 1935.

97. D., in *Max Planck Festschrift 1958*, p. 339, Deutscher Verlag der Wissenschaften, Berlin, 1958.

98. D., *General Theory of Relativity*, Wiley, New York, 1975.

99. Ref. 4, p. 149.

100. D., *Nature* **139**, 323, 1001, 1937; also *ibid.*, **192**, 441, 1961.

101. D., Report CTS-T. Phys. 69-1, Center for Theoretical Studies, Coral Gables, Florida, 1969; *Comm. Pontif. Acad. of Sci* **2**, No. 46, 1973; **3**, No. 6, 1975); *Proc. Roy. Soc.* **A338**, 446, 1974; *Nature* **254**, 273, 1975; in *Theories and Experiments in High Energy Physics* (B. Kursunoglu *et al.*, Eds), p. 443, Plenum Press, New York, 1975); *New Frontiers in High Energy Physics* (A. Perlmutter and L. Scott, Eds), p. 1, Plenum Press, New York, 1978; *Proc. Roy Soc.* **A365**, 19, 1979.

102. See further F. J. Dyson, in *Aspects of Quantum Theory*, ref. 1, p. 213.

103. D., *Nature* **168**, 906, 1951; **169**, 146, 1952; *Physica* **19**, 888, 1953; *Sci. Monthly* **78**, 142, 1954.

104. D., *Proc. Roy. Soc.* **A136**, 453, 1932.

105. Cf. e.g. D., V. Fock and B. Podolsky, *Phys. Zeitschr. der Sowjetunion* **2**, 468, 1932.

106. D., *Nature* **137**, 298, 1936.

107. *Inward Bound*, ref. 1, chapter 16, section (c); chapter 18, section (a).

108. D., *Proc. Roy. Soc.* **A167**, 148, 1938; see also ref. 92.

109. D., *Ann Inst. H. Poincaré* **9**, 13, 1939.

110. D., *Comm. Dublin Inst. Adv. Studies* **A1**, 1943.

111. D., *Proc. Roy. Soc.* **A180**, 1, 1942.

112. D., *Rev. Mod. Phys.* **15**, 175, 1943.

113. D., *Comm. Dublin Inst. Adv. Studies*, **A3**, 1946; *Proceedings of the International Conference on Fundamental Particles and Low Temperatures, Cambridge, June 1946*, p. 10, Taylor and Francis, London, 1946; *Proceedings of the 8th Solvay Conference 1948* (R. Stoops, Ed.), p. 282, Coudenberg, Brussels, 1950.

114. R. P. Feynman, *Quantum Electrodynamics, the Strange Story of Light and Matter*, Princeton University Press, 1985.

115. D., *Proc. Roy. Soc.* **A209**, 251, 1951.

116. See also D., in *Deeper Pathways in High Energy Physics* (B. Kursunoglu *et al.*, Eds), Plenum Press, New York, 1977.

117. See further D., *Proc. Roy. Soc.* **A212**, 330, 1952; **223**, 438, 1954; also D., *Proc. Roy. Soc* **A257**, 32, 1960; **268**, 57, 1962.

118. D., *Lectures on Quantum Field Theory*, Belfer School of Science, Yeshiva University, New York, 1966.

119. Cf. D., *Nuov. Cim. Suppl.* **6**, 322, 1957; *Nature* **203**, 115, 1964; **204**, 771, 1964; *Phys. Rev.* **139B**, 684, 1965.

120. D., *Proc. Roy. Soc.* **A322**, 435, 1971; **328**, 1, 1972; and in *Fundamental Interactions in Physics and Astrophysics* (G. Iverson, Ed.), p. 354, Plenum Press, New York, 1973.

121. Interview with Professor Joe Lannutti, January 30, 1986.

122. D., *General Theory of Relativity*, ref. 98.

123. D., in *Proceedings of Loyola University Symposium, New Orleans, 1984*; reprinted in *Reminiscences about a Great Physicist*, ref. 1, p. 194.

124. N. F. Mott, *A life in Science*, p. 42, Taylor and Francis, London, 1986.

125. For a list see *Dirac*, ref. 1, p. 356, note 20.

126. D., *Chem. Zeitung* **95**, 880, 1971.

127. Quoted by Heisenberg in *Schritte und Grenzen*, Piper, Munich, 1971.

128. Manci Dirac, letter to A. Pais, November 25, 1995.

129. G. Gamow, *Thirty Years that Shook Physics*, p. 121, Doubleday, New York, 1966.

130. L. Alvarez, *Adventures of a Physicist*, p. 87, Basic Books, New York, 1987.

131. R. Peierls, in ref. 31, p. 36.

132. *Washington Post* and *Times Herald*, September 24, 1954.

133. E.g. *The New York Times*, May 27, June 11, 1954; *New York Herald Tribune*, May 28, 1954; *The Times* (London), June 18, 1955; *The Financial Times* (London), August 6, 1954.

134. *The New York Times*, June 3, 1954.

135. D., *Proc. Camb. Phil. Soc.* **35**, 416, 1939.

136. Ref. 89, p. 393.

137. D., *The Development of Quantum Theory*, Gordon and Breach, New York, 1971.

138. D., *Eureka* No. 32, 2–4, October 1969.

139. P. Ramon, letter to A. Pais, February 22, 1996.

140. J. Lannutti, letter to A. Pais, May 19, 1986.

141. Quoted by R. Peierls in ref. 130.

Albert Einstein in Pasadena 1931. Distinguished colleagues: (front left) A. A. Michelson, first American Nobel Prize winner in physics; (right) Caltechs's Nobel laureate Robert Millikan; (back row) Walter Adams of Mount Wilson; Walther Meyer, assistant to Einstein; Max Farrand of the Huntington Library. (A. Pais, Private Collection.)

Albert Einstein*

Einstein, Albert, this century's most renowned scientist, was born in Ulm, in the kingdom of Württembery, now part of Germany, the son of Hermann Einstein, a small businessman, never very successful, and Pauline née Koch. In 1881 Maria, his only sibling, was born. In 1880 the family moved to Munich, where Einstein attended public school and high school, always doing well. (The story that he was a poor pupil is a myth, probably caused by his dislike of formal education.) In those years he also received violin lessons privately and, in order to comply with legal requirements, instruction in the elements of Judaism. As a result of this inculcation, Einstein went through an intense religious phase at age about eleven, following religious precepts in detail and (he later told a friend) composing songs in honor of God. A year later, this phase ended abruptly and forever as a result of his exposure to popular books on science, to 'the holy geometry book' (as he called it) on Euclidean geometry, to writings of Kant, and more.

In 1895 Einstein took the entrance examination at the Federal Institute of Technology (ETH) in Zurich but failed because of poor grades in literary and political history. In 1896, after a year of study at a high school in Aarau (Switzerland), he did gain admission, however. In that year he gave up his German citizenship and became stateless, in 1901, Swiss.

During his next four years as an ETH student, Einstein did not excel in regular course attendance, relying far more on self-study. In 1900 he passed his final examinations with good grades, which qualified him as high school teacher in mathematics and physics. For the next two years he had to be satisfied with temporary teaching positions until, in June 1902, he was appointed technical expert third class at the Patent Office in Berne.

In January 1903 Einstein married Mileva Marić, of Greek–Catholic Serbian descent, a fellow student at the ETH. In 1902 the couple had a daughter out of wedlock, Lieserl, whose fate remains unknown, and after marriage two sons, Hans Albert, who became a distinguished professor of hydraulic engineering in Berkeley, California, and Eduard, a gifted child, who became a student of

* English translation of a contribution to the *Store Danske Encyclopaedi*.

medicine in Zurich, but then turned severely schizophrenic and died in a psychiatric hospital.

In 1914 the Einsteins separated, in 1919 they divorced. Thereafter Einstein remarried with his cousin Elsa Einstein, who brought him two stepdaughters. He had several extramarital affairs during this second marriage.

None of Einstein's first four papers, published between 1901 and 1904, foreshadowed his explosive creativity of 1905, his *annus mirabilis*, in which he produced: in March, his proposal of the existence of lightquanta and the photoelectric effect, work for which in 1922 he received the Nobel Prize; in April, a paper on the determination of molecular dimensions which earned him his PhD in Zurich; in May, his theory of special relativity; in September, a sequel to the preceding paper containing the relation $E = mc^2$. Any one of these papers would have made him greatly renowned; their totality made him immortal.

Only after all these publications did Einstein's academic career begin: privatdozent in Berne, 1908; associate professor, University of Zurich, 1909, the year of his first honorary degree (Geneva); full professor at the Karl Ferdinand University, Prague, 1911; professor at the ETH, 1912; professor and member of the Prussian Academy of Sciences, Berlin, 1914–32, where he arrived four months before the outbreak of the First World War.

In 1915 Einstein cosigned his first political document, a 'Manifesto to Europeans,' in which all those who cherish European culture were urged to join in a League of Europeans (never realized). Far more important, in that year Einstein completed his masterpiece, perhaps the most profound contribution to physics of the twentieth century: his general relativity theory, on which he had been brooding for the previous eight years. In the special theory all laws of physics have the same form for any two observers moving relatively to each other in a straight line and with constant, time-independent, velocity. In the general theory the same is true for *all* kinds of relative motion. This demands a revision of Newton's thory of gravitation. Space is curved, Einstein now asserted, the amount of curvature depending on how dense matter is at that place— matter determines by its gravitational action 'what shape space is in.'

The superiority of Einstein's over Newton's theory became manifest in 1915, when Einstein could for the first time explain an anomaly in the motion of the planet Mercury (advance of the perihelion). known observationally since 1859. He also predicted that light grazing the sun bends by a factor two larger than predicted by Newton's theory.

In 1916 Einstein completed his most widely known book *On the Special and the General Theory of Relativity, Popularly Explained*, wrote the first paper on gravitational waves and became president of the *Deutsche Physikalische Gesellschaft*. In 1917 he became ill, suffering successively from a liver ailment, a stomach ulcer, jaundice, and general weakness, but nevertheless managed to complete his first paper on relativistic cosmology. He did not fully recover until 1920.

In November 1919 Einstein became the mythical figure he is to this day. In May of that year two solar eclipse expeditions had (in the words of the astronomer Eddington) 'confirm[ed] Einstein's weird theory of non-Euclidean space.' On November 6, the President of the Royal Society declared in London that this was 'the most remarkable scientific event since the discovery [in 1846] of the predicted existence of the planet Neptune.'

The next day *The Times* in London carried an article headlined 'Revolution in Science/New theory of the Universe/Newtonian ideas overthrown.' Einstein had triumphed over Newton (who of course is and remains a stellar figure in science). The drama of that moment was enhanced by the contrast with the recently concluded World War, which had caused millions to die, empires to fall, the future to be uncertain. At that time Einstein emerges, bringing new law and order. From that time on the world press made him into an icon, the θεῖος ανήρ, the divine man, of the twentieth century.

At about that time one begins to perceive changes in the activities of Einstein, now in mid-life. He began writing non-scientific articles. In 1920 he was exposed to anti-semitic demonstrations during a lecture he gave in Berlin. At the same time, Jews fleeing from the East came literally knocking at his door for help. All that awakened in Einstein a deepened awareness of the Jewish predicament, and caused him to speak up and write in favor of Jewish self-expression by means of settling in Palestine, creating there a peaceful center where Jews could live in dignity and without persecution. Thus, he became an advocate of what one may call moral Zionism, though he never was a member of any Zionist organization.

The 1920s was also the period of Einstein's most extensive travels. In 1921 he paid his first visit to the United States for the purpose of raising funds for the planned Hebrew University, being honored on the way, including being received by President Harding. In 1922 his visit to Paris contributed to the normalization of Franco-German relations. Also in that year he accepted membership in the League of Nation's Committee on Intellectual Cooperation. In June, Walter Rathenau, Foreign Minister of Germany, a Jew and an acquaintance of Einstein, was assassinated. After being warned that he, too, might be in danger, Einstein left with his wife for a five months' trip abroad. After short visits to Colombo, Singapore, Hong Kong, and Shanghai, they arrived in Japan for a five-week stay. The press reported that, at a reception, the center of attention was not the Empress, everything turned on Einstein.

On the way back they visited Palestine. In introducing Einstein at a lecture, the president of the Zionist Executive said: 'Mount the platform which has been awaiting you for two thousand years.' Thereafter Einstein spent three weeks in

Spain. In 1925 he journeyed to South America, lecturing in Buenos Aires, Montevideo, and Rio de Janeiro. Apart from three later trips to the United States, this was the last major voyage in Einstein's life.

All these multifarious activities took a lot of Einstein's energies but did not keep him from his physics research. In 1922 he published his first paper on unified field theory, an attempt at incorporating not only gravitation but also electromagnetism into a new world geometry, a subject that was his main concern until the end of his life. He tried many approaches; none of them have worked out. In 1924 he published three papers on quantum statistical mechanics which include his discovery of so-called Bose–Einstein condensation. This was his last contribution to physics which may be called seminal. He did continue to publish all through his later years, however.

In 1925 quantum mechanics arrived, a new theory with which Einstein never found peace. His celebrated dialogue with Bohr on this topic started at the 1927 Solvay conference. They were to argue almost until Einstein's death without ever coming to an agreement.

In 1928 Einstein suffered a temporary physical collapse due to an enlargement of the heart. He had to stay in bed for four months and keep to a salt-free diet. He fully recuperated but stayed weak for a year. 1929 witnessed his first visit with the Belgian royal family, leading to a life-long correspondence with Queen Elizabeth.

Einstein had been a pacifist since his young years but in the 1920s his position became more radical in this respect. For example, in 1925 he, Gandhi, and others signed a manifesto against obligatory military service, in 1930 another supporting world government. In that year and again in 1931 he visited the United States. In 1932 he accepted appointment as professor at the Institute for Advanced Study in Princeton, originally intending to divide his time between Princeton and Berlin. When, however, he and his wife left Germany on December 10 of that year, they would never set foot in Germany again—in January 1933 the Nazis came to power. Though remaining pacifist at heart, Einstein was deeply convinced that they could only be defeated by the force of arms.

Because of the new political situation, Einstein changed his plans, arriving on October 17, 1933 in the US to settle permanently in Princeton, whereafter he left that country only once, in 1935, to travel to Bermuda in order to make from there application for permanent residency. In 1940 he became a US citizen.

Einstein also remained a prominent figure in his new country. In 1934 he and his wife were invited by the Roosevelts and spent a night at the White House. He remained scientifically active, wrote in fact some good papers, but nothing as memorable as in his European days.

In 1939 Einstein wrote to Roosevelt to draw his attention to possible military uses of atomic energy. His influence on these later developments was marginal, however. In 1943 he became consultant to the US Navy Bureau of Ordnance but was never involved in atomic bomb work. In 1944 a copy of his 1905 paper on relativity, handwritten by him for this purpose, was auctioned for six million dollars as a contribution to the war effort. (It is now in the Library of Congress.)

After the war he continued to speak out on political issues, such as his open letter to the United Nations urging the formation of a world government, and his frequent condemnations in the press of McCarthy's activities. After the death of Chaim Weizmann, first president of Israel, Einstein was invited, but declined, to be his successor.

In 1948 Einstein was found to have a large intact aneurysm of the abdominal aorta. In 1950 he wrote his testament, willing his papers and manuscripts to the Hebrew University (where they are now). On April 11, 1955, Einstein wrote his last letter (to Bertrand Russell), in which he agreed to sign a manifesto urging all nations to renounce nuclear weapons. On April 13 Einstein wrote a draft (incomplete) for a radio address which ends: 'Political passions, aroused everywhere, demand their victims.' On the afternoon of that day his aneurysm ruptured. On the 15th he entered Princeton Hospital, where he died on April 18 at 1.15 a.m. His body was cremated that same day. The ashes were scattered at an undisclosed place. The following November his first great-grandson was born.

Mitchell Feigenbaum, 1997. (Courtesy of Gunilla Feigenbaum.)

Mitchell Jay Feigenbaum

One morning, not long ago, it was about eight o'clock, I left my New York apartment on York Avenue for my daily walk, which that day led me along 63rd Street to Central Park, where I walked around for a while, then returned. I had reached the corner of First Avenue when I saw a familiar face, his hair a ragged mane. 'What are you doing here so late?' I inquired. He explained that he had run out of cigarettes, and also wanted to pick up the day's edition of *The New York Times* which he likes to read before going to bed. I wished him good night and walked on.

That was my good friend Mitch Feigenbaum. We live in the same apartment complex and have offices next to each other at the Rockefeller University. With luck we meet there in the late afternoon. The sketch of his life and work to date which is to follow is largely the result of numerous late evening talks with him.

Family

Mitch was born in Philadelphia on December 19, 1944, the son of Abraham Joseph and Mildred, née Sugar, both native New Yorkers. His father is the third of four children. His family hails from Loshitz, near Warsaw, from where Mitch's grandfather emigrated to the United States. Mitch thinks the family name was then Fajgenboim. His mother's father came to the US from Kiev. The name Sugar was made up by Ellis Island officials. She is the second of three children, she also has two half sisters.

Mitch's older brother Edward was decidedly a child prodigy who could read at a very early age. He is now a systems engineer and lives with his wife and two children outside Washington, DC. (He is not to be confused with a famous computer scientist who has the same first and last name.) Glenda, Mitch's younger sister, is an actuary at the Metropolitan Life Insurance Company and lives in New Jersey with her husband and two children.

After receiving a Master's degree in biology from New York University, Abraham Joseph was offered a university job in Rochester, New York, with a salary of $2000 a year. His wife thought that was not enough. Instead he became an analytical chemist at the Naval Shipyard in Philadelphia (we are now into the Second World War), where he had to study insecticides that could kill cockroaches on ships and took catering jobs on weekends to make some extra money.

In 1947—Mitch was two and a half—the family moved back to New York City, where they bought a two-story house in Brooklyn, renting out one floor. The father now obtained a position as analytical chemist with the New York Port Authority. Among his assignments was to test land where Idlewild (now J. F. Kennedy) Airport was to be built.

Mitchell calls his mother 'a physically and mentally powerful woman.' At age 14 she went to study at Hunter College but had to leave two years later in order to bring in money for her family. In her late teens she earned money by playing handball, at which she could beat men; and also by teaching remedial reading. Next she applied for and obtained a job in the knitting department of Lamston's department store in Spanish Harlem. At that point she knew neither Spanish nor how to knit, but quickly picked up both. Mitch characterizes her especially as an educator who served as his first role model. Later that switched to the father. 'I found his ways of thinking more substantial . . . I found him infinitely honest. He underexpressed himself, however, finding speaking in some ways superfluous.'

Early memories

Mitch was 'clean' when half a year old. He started talking 'reasonably late. Before that I just pointed at things, having my brother say what name they had.' His mother tried to teach him reading but he did not like that, in fact he did not read until he went to school. From early on he liked to know 'how things worked,' in the mechanical sense, liked to take things apart and to know 'what things looked like.' From age three he began to listen to music. 'This was very important to me.' He would be up by seven in the morning to listen to music. They had a radio. How does that one work? 'It struck me that a radio is remarkable because it has no phonograph records, and because 'radio waves' go through walls.'

From very early on he liked to sit and muse about things and observe, sitting on the porch. He remembers, at age four or five, calling out to his mother to come to the porch. 'Look at that woman. Why doesn't she fall?' It was a large-breasted lady; Mitch was wondering about her mechanical equilibrium.

From early on Mitch very much liked to draw, especially portraits. He discovered that drawing smooth, perfectly crafted curves could replace the rendering of minutiae. His drawings became more and more abstract, Miro-like. He stopped drawing at about age 21. 'In the end I had nothing new to express; it became cartoons. I did not know what to draw any more.'

School years

Mitch started school at age five, attending the public school PS208 for gifted children. The school had advanced programs. Spanish was taught in first grade, as was shop and typing (the latter being unusual for that time). Until the middle of the first grade he read English very poorly. After his mother had gone to his school to talk that over with the teachers, she taught him at home. As a result he became, one month later, the best reader in his class.

Also in that first grade—Mitch told me—the teacher once asked who wanted to be absent on the Jewish high holidays. He was puzzled. A friend nudged him to raise his hand. 'There were no Jewish traditions in the house. One Passover my mother cooked a ham. Yet there were rabbis among my mother's ancestry.'

By order of the authorities, Mitch had to move to PS251 after some time, which he found completely boring. 'I just sat there looking out of the window.' He was taken out of the class and put in charge of the school's audio-visual system. When in second grade he helped sixth graders with arithmetic and reading. His teachers were not indifferent to him. 'Some loved me, some hated me.' As to his schoolmates, he never fought with them but rather made them his friends. At age eight he began to lose interest in them. 'I liked parents more than children.' From that time on he had for many years virtually no friends of his age.

In fifth grade his mother taught Mitchell some algebra. He continued to dislike reading. 'I hated libraries and still do.' He did like to read articles on science in the *Encyclopedia Britannica*, however. Understandably he found these largely incomprehensible, and later, when he knew their content, realized that they were probably of no utility to a person of whatever level of understanding. During those years he of course had to take tests, which he passed easily.

When Mitch was about 12 years old he began to develop strong obsessional compulsions about cleanliness—washing his hands all the time. Also, things had to be orderly. When he set his alarm clock he would continue to check whether the lever you had to pull out had not sprung back. This compulsive period came to an end at age 19, for reasons I shall come back to.

At age 12, Mitchell moved to junior high school PS258 in Brooklyn. He was in an SP, a special program, which allowed skipping one year out of three. After one month his algebra teacher sent him away 'because I was always correcting her.' Again he did everything he could not to attend classes. He was once more put in charge of the audio-visual system, a more fancy one this time, and also ran projectors. Furthermore he became secretary of the gym class—which allowed him not to do gym himself—and was on the chess team, 'at which I did medium.' He was also taught French, which he found useless, though later he became more fluent at it as the result of visits to France.

At the end of each year one had to 'take the Regents,' a statewide written examination. Mitch scored 100 out of a 100 in math and science; also high in other subjects.

Also at age 12, Mitch taught himself to play the piano on the instrument at a friend's home. Half a year later his parents bought a piano for his sister. Thereafter Mitchell took some piano lessons, but only six months. He took another half year's lessons when 15 but continued mainly to teach himself and kept playing till at age 19 he left home and no longer had easy access to an instrument. He bought a grand piano after he moved to New York City in 1987. Again he took some exceptionally fine instruction but now only plays infrequently.

The next schooling Mitchell received was at Tilden High School, a good Brooklyn school. He did the three-year curriculum in two and a half. He found the education mostly crummy and the students uninteresting. He was on the math team, which freed him from one school day a week, again worked the audio-visual school systems, and again was gym secretary. His Regents scores were as high as before.

Undergraduate years

Mitch had turned 16 when, in February 1961, he entered the City College of New York, at Convent Avenue and 137th Street in the Bronx. At that time entrance demands were a high-school average higher than 88. Tuition was free except for a $15 admission fee. It was a very good college then, less so later when it was ruled that a high-school diploma sufficed. Mitch traveled between home and CCNY by bus and subway—then costing 15 cents each—which took him one hour 45 minutes each way.

Mitch chose electrical engineering because at about age ten he had found out that these people knew how a radio works—that, as said, had puzzled him greatly as a growing child. Also he had learned that such a degree allowed him to land a job making something like $10 000 a year. It was a five-year program which, however, he completed in three and a half years, taking all the physics and mathematics graduate courses as well. He rapidly realized that it was physics that held the secret of radio waves. He took lots of laboratory courses and went to CCNY summer school to speed things up. His grades were As in subjects in which he was, Cs in those in which he was not, interested. In 1964, at age 19, he obtained the BEE (Bachelor of Electrical Engineering) *magna cum laude*. He missed *summa cum laude* by one thousandth of a point because his lab course grades were only moderate.

Mitch had already taught himself calculus during his last high-school year. That changed his life style of education. Self-instruction became the most important. He had already begun his research as an undergraduate, together with Professor Mansour Javid. His first work dealt with neural networks (then called Adeline) in relation to voice recognition. At that time he also became interested in applications of feedback control to economic problems. In that connection he figured out in 1963 the theory of linear response behavior, a subject that came into general vogue only in 1968.

Graduate education

Mitchell had applied to graduate schools at CalTech, Columbia University, Harvard, MIT, and Princeton, and had been accepted by all. Influenced by experiences of a friend of his brother, he chose MIT, where he started in the summer of 1964. Shortly afterward he became a member of the American Physical Society, of which he is now a Fellow.

As to his living quarters, 'I kept moving,' living in graduate dormitories, then in rooms in Cambridge, Brookline, Belmont. For his six years' stay at MIT—up to and including his PhD—he had financial support from an NSF graduate fellowship for the first three years, then became research assistant to Francis Low. Initially Mitch enrolled in the electrical engineering program, but he knew by now that you need physics to understand how a radio *really* works. Since each student was free to choose his own course schedule, he began concentrating on physics and mathematics. In his first graduate term he applied for a switch to the physics department which was granted the next term.

Since his first term, Mitch had taken courses in quantum and classical mechanics, also in complex functions, in the math department. Of quantum mechanics he recalls not liking the theory of two-body scattering, feeling rather drawn to the idea of studying complex systems. He began to get bored as early as his first term and started, on his own, the study of general relativity theory, reading from cover to cover Landau and Lifshitz's book on that subject, on which he wanted to do his PhD thesis. That turned out to be impossible, however, 'there was no one at MIT during those years to guide that sort of work,' nor anywhere else at that time for that matter. It bothered him that the MIT faculty showed little interest in problems of principle.

During his graduate year Mitch got 100 in all exams, yet received only an overall B mark in his EE course because he would not solve the problems assigned in class. Even before he had finished his graduate studies he was offered an assistant professorship in electrical engineering, which he declined.

As to extracurricular interests: already in his first term he began reading extensively, including philosophy, for example Kant's critique of pure reason, also all of Dostoevski. He also spent several hours a day in the music library, listening to records and reading scores.

One day, in his twentieth year, Mitch drove with some friends to the nearby Lincoln reservoir. While they went for a walk, he strolled by himself to the De Cordova Museum of modern art, which lies on a nearby hill. On the way up he had a revelation. The question came to him: What do people's perceptions, visual, aural, etc. have to do with *the reality* of what they perceive? It came to him that he should know much more than he did about psychology and philosophy. This led him to study the works of Freud, 'the whole stuff.' He also started reading Ernst Mach, Newton's *Principia*, and Galileo's writings. 'I educated myself.' At age 22 he became seriously interested in visual physiology.

I mentioned earlier that, from age eight on, Mitchell had no friends among his contemporaries. So it remained until his last year at CCNY, when he decided he had to do something about that, that he had to make efforts to meet his peers. So he forced himself to go to the cafeteria and strike up conversations, from which he did not derive much inspiration. He did meet several people at this point who were to remain life-long friends, however. His reading of Freud had impressed him very much, but he does not know whether that was of actual help to him in eliminating his obsessional acts. As a result of these readings, self-analysis did become important to him, however.

Another aspect of Mitchell's early years, also mentioned before, was his strongly obsessive behavior. All that vanished when at age 19 he started kissing women. In graduate school he had his first love affair—which in fact was a disaster. At age 23 he started living with a woman. Virtually all his girlfriends—and his two wives—were non-American born.

In 1970 Mitchell received his PhD (the Master's degree is dispensed with at MIT). His thesis advisor was Francis Low, his topic: dispersion relations. This work led to his first publication, jointly with Low.[1] The time had now come for some years of postdoctoral research.

Postdoc positions

Mitchell went first to Cornell for two years, supported half by an instructorship, half by an NSF postdoctoral grant, totalling $10 000 per annum. At that time only 50 such grants were available nationwide. His title was: instructor/research associate. He took teaching seriously, giving courses in variational techniques and advanced nonrelativistic quantum mechanics. He was also partly responsible for a physics course for 500–700 sophomore medical students, in which he managed to include special relativity theory, which, expanded upon, resulted in a paper years later.[2]

During his two years at Cornell, Mitch became completely conversant with everything in theoretical particle physics. He did not find it a domain which illuminated his understanding of the world. Nevertheless he published three more papers on that subject.[3,4,5] Their contents indicate his growing interest in complex systems.

Of the physicists at Cornell, Mitch liked Ed Salpeter and Pete Carruthers. He was impressed with Ken Wilson's skills, liked very much his work on the renormalization group, and was inspired by Ken's lectures on that subject. Mitch respected Bethe's technical abilities but was less impressed with his views on world problems. During his Cornell years, Mitchell met David Finkelstein, from Yeshiva University, whose 'real thinking' about fundamental issues had a strong impact on him.

As Mitch and I were talking about these Cornell experiences the subject naturally turned to his encounters with other physicists. He thinks highly of Steve Weinberg's abilities, mentioning in particular his work on current algebra. He had met Feynman several times but did not have substantial conversations with him until 1981, when he was invited to CalTech and offered a position there. He thinks Feynman and Landau are the last great figures in physics.

After Cornell Mitchell went to the Virginia Polytechnic Institute where Paul Zweifel had obtained funding for one postdoc. He stayed there during 1972–74, his support being again $10 000/year. 'At VPI, Zweifel finished my education on good wines, which had interested me for years and on which I already then knew a lot.' His first job offer, as a graduate student, was as a wine salesman. He has remained an expert on the subject.

Once again Mitchell taught, Banach spaces and C*-algebra among other topics. During his second year he got deeply interested in the nature of time in a discrete universe, inspired by conversations with Finkelstein. He did a lot of work on that subject which, however, has remained unpublished. Also in that year he became professionally interested in the renormalization group.

'These two-year positions made serious work almost impossible. After one year you had to start worrying about where you could go next.'

After Blacksburg, Mitch obtained his first long-term appointment. Carruthers had gone to Los Alamos, where he had become head of the theory department. He offered Mitchell a position there as staff member, with a yearly salary of $22 500 plus funds for travel. Mitch accepted gladly for the science but after considerable soul-searching about the venue, and made his move in 1974.

In 1976, just after recuperating from the ordeal of finishing the most important work of his life—to which I shall turn anon—Mitch met Cornelia Drobowolski at Los Alamos, a German woman who was studying for a Master's degree in German literature. They married in 1978. She brought two young sons, then four and eight, to the marriage. The marriage ended in divorce in 1981, though Mitch has continued to consider both boys as 'his' sons. They remain close and still visit with Mitch in New York.

After the divorce, Mitchell was in dire straits and withdrew from human contacts, most especially in Los Alamos. On the recommendation of friends, he went to consult a Jungian psychiatrist in Santa Fe, whom he saw once a week for eight visits. He found him to be a wise and really humane person who counseled him as well on how to handle practical aspects of his divorce. Mitchell spoke to me with glowing admiration about this man.

In 1986 he married again, with Gunilla Öhman, Swedish born. She is a quite talented artist, both as writer and as painter. My wife and I are happy to count the two of them as dear friends.

Toward chaos[6]

'When I arrived at Los Alamos, Carruthers felt that the time was right, and I was the appropriate person, to see if Ken Wilson's renormalization group ideas could solve the century-old problem of turbulence [a question raised by Wilson himself[7]]. In a nutshell, it couldn't—or so far hasn't—but led me off in wonderful directions.'[8] The wonderful direction was chaos theory, the study of systems that aren't random but appear random. Here and in what follows I shall mean by chaos what is more precisely called dynamical chaos, the apparently random motion of a dynamical system, that is, a system with no random forcing.

Mitchell's work on this subject started in the 1970s. It is a profound extension of *classical* physics, where by then it had a long history. I sketch a few highlights.

First, turbulence, a term coined by Lord Kelvin[9] derived from the French *tourbillon*, which means whirlpool or eddy. That was a few years following the seminal discoveries of the British physicist Osborne Reynolds,[10] after whom the number is named that marks the transition from regular, laminar, flow to chaotic, turbulent, flow as the flow velocity increases.

It was Henri Poincaré who, also in the late nineteenth century, was the first to realize that the physical laws of motion for a system as simple (pardon the expression) as that consisting of sun, earth, moon cannot be rigorously solved because there are not enough constants of the motion,[11,12] one of the characteristic properties of chaos. Another: in the course of time two orbits of a given system that had started out close together will depart exponentially from each other. Their relative distance grows as $e^{\lambda t}$; the positive number λ is called the Liapunov exponent (also dating from the 1890s[13], named after Aleksandr Liapunov). That was very clear to Poincaré:

> If we knew exactly the laws of nature and the situation of the universe at the initial moment, we could predict exactly the situation of that same universe at a succeeding moment. But even if it were the case that the natural laws had no longer any secret for us, we could still know the situation approximately. If that enabled us to predict the succeeding situation with the same approximation, that is all we require, and we should say that the phenomenon had been predicted, that it is governed by the laws. But it is not always so; it may happen that small differences in the initial conditions produce very great ones in the final phenomena. A small error in the former will produce an enormous error in the latter. Prediction becomes impossible.[14]

Incidentally, in this context use of the *term* chaos to describe this situation dates only from 1975, where it first appears in the title of a paper: 'Period three implies chaos.'[15]

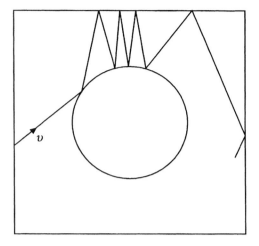

Sinai's billiard.

An elementary example[16] of a chaotic system is Yasha Sinai's billiard: a little sphere moves within a square billiard in which a round obstacle with reflective walls is placed. The motion of the little sphere is deterministic but successive collisions with the obstacle cause neighboring orbits to diverge exponentially. A rough estimate shows that the corresponding Liapunov exponent is given by $\lambda = v/L$, where v is the sphere's velocity and L a representative length.

One last remark on Poincaré's three-body problems. He had discovered that rigorous solutions are impossible but, of course, its orbits can be calculated numerically with high precision—at least for a while. Long-term questions about three-body problems cannot be answered, however. To this day we don't even know whether the solar system is stable; the best present informed numerics indicate that it is *not*. It certainly appears to be so in the short term, but we cannot (yet) give a rigorous answer to the question: can planets escape from the solar system?

Poincaré had no computers. Had those been available to him, he could have tracked three-body orbits for much extended periods of time—while still being unable to answer the escape question till kingdom come.

However that may be, since the 1960s computers have played an absolutely crucial role in advancing the understanding of chaotic phenomena.

One day in the winter of 1961 the research meteorologist Edward Norton Lorenz was in his office at MIT, busy as usual mapping weather on his Royal McBee LGP-30 computer—a quite clumsy one by modern standards. He would print out one parameter or another, the direction of an air stream, air pressure, temperature, and so on. It was 'toy weather,' that is, he used simple, simplified, purely deterministic equations (now known as the Lorenz equations) which mimic the earth's real weather. On that day he wanted to check an earlier result, so he once again typed in the initial conditions, then went out for a cup of coffee. When he returned he saw something quite unexpected. In his own words:

> During our computations we decided to examine one of the solutions in greater detail, and we chose some intermediate conditions which had been typed out by the computer and typed them in as new initial conditions. Upon returning to the computer an hour later, after it had simulated about two months of 'weather,' we found that it completely disagreed with the earlier solution. At first we expected machine trouble, which was not unusual, but we soon realized that the two solutions did not originate from identical conditions. The computations had been carried internally to about six decimal places, but the typed output contained only three, so that the new initial conditions consisted of old conditions plus small perturbations. These perturbations were amplifying quasi-exponentially, doubling in about four simulated days, so that after two months the solutions were going their separate ways.[17]

Here Lorenz had made quantitative[18] the sensitive dependence on initial conditions, which the ever-prescient Poincaré had noted in the paragraph immediately following my previous quotation:

> Why have meteorologists such difficulty in predicting the weather with any certainty? . . . We see that great disturbances are generally produced in regions where the atmosphere is in unstable equilibrium. The meteorologists see very well that the equilibrium is unstable, that a cyclone will be formed somewhere, but exactly where they are not in a position to say; a tenth of a degree more or less at any given point, and the cyclone will burst here and not there, and extend its ravages over districts it would otherwise have spared . . . Here, again, we find the same contrast between a very trifling cause that is inappreciable to the observer, and considerable effects, that are sometimes terrible disasters.[14]

This situation is now popularly known as the butterfly effect: the trifling event of a butterfly fluttering in the air over Kyoto can lead to a disastrous storm over Chicago. Hence, in Lorenz's words: '*Precise very-long-range [weather] forecasting would seem to be non-existent*'[18] (my italics).

'Years later, physicists would give wistful looks when they talked about Lorenz's paper[18]—that beautiful marvel of a paper . . . All the richness of chaos was there . . . By then it was talked about as if it were an ancient scroll, preserving secrets of eternity.'[19] I respect most of all Lorenz's realization that what he had seen was not machine trouble but something profoundly new. There is more novelty in that paper; for example it contains the first picture[20] of an infinitely tangled abstraction now called a strange attractor.[21]

Lorenz's paper[19] marks the beginning of a new era in science, the quantitative study of chaos, resented by some, evangelically embraced by many. It has been written that 'chaos presages the future as none will gainsay.'[22] Intuition in chaos continues to be developed with the help of computers, mathematics has become its experimental tool par excellence. 'The heart of chaos is mathematically accessible.'[23]

By now chaos is ubiquitous. After its start in meteorology one employs chaos theory in studies of turbulence, astronomy and cosmology, laser optics, acoustics, plasma physics, accelerator physics, chemical reactions. Also in animal populations, epidemiology (chaos was found in records of New York's measles epidemics,[24] generally the fraction of a population infected at a given time), the theory of learning (the bits of information that can be remembered after a given period of time), the propagation of rumors (the number of people who have heard a certain rumor after some period of time), the flow of car traffic, the relationship between commodity quantity and price on the stock market.[25] All of which has led to partnerships between physics and other disciplines. Literature on chaos has exploded. A list of publications on that subject published between 1963 and 1983 contains about 1000 items; in the later 1980s more than 2000 further background papers appeared.[26] In 1977 the first conference on chaos was held. Such meetings as well as journals dealing exclusively with chaos now abound.

One last item needs to be mentioned before I turn to Feigenbaum's contributions to the theory of chaos: bifurcations, once again first mentioned by the great Poincaré[27] in lectures given at the Sorbonne in 1900, in the course of describing motions of cylindrical columns of liquids. At that time he used the expression *échange des stabilités* for what now is called bifurcations. It is astonishing to me that, to my knowledge, Poincaré is never mentioned in literature on bifurcation.

The modern era of popular awareness of physical and biological studies in bifurcation began in the 1970s, with the paper 'Simple mathematical models with very complicated dynamics'[28] by Sir Robert McCredie May, then a professor of biology in Princeton, later that university's dean of research, now the chief scientific advisor to the British government. The paper contains 'An evangelical plea . . . not only in research, but also in the everyday world of politics and economics, we would be better off if more people realized . . . the wild things that simple non-linear equations can do.' (As we shall see, that problem was already solved when May wrote his article.)

May's specialty was population biology, particularly the ecological problem of how populations behave over time. That question goes back at least to Thomas Malthus, who had posited a scenario in which populations show unrestrained growth, so that, he feared, they would outrun the food supply. In mathematical terms: let x_t denote a population at time t, and x_{t+1} the same one year later. Then, Malthus assumed, $x_{t+1} = rx_t$, where r represents the rate of growth.

The equation May analyzed was

$$x_{t+1} = f(x_t) \tag{1}$$
$$f(x_t) = rx_t\,(1-x_t),$$

known as the non-linear logistic difference equation. In the jargon of non-linear dynamics $f(x_t)$ is called a map. Here 'population' is treated as a fraction between zero and one. Zero represents extinction, one the maximum population. That equation had been studied well before, but May was the first to appreciate how very rich in information that innocent-looking equation is.

The reader may like to have a simple pocket calculator at hand in order to follow what happens as the growth parameter rises:

For $r < 1$, populations are attracted to zero. Example: $x_1 = 0.4$, $r = 0.5$: $x_2 = 0.12$, $x_3 = 0.053$, . . .

For $r > 4$, all populations tend to minus infinity. Example: $x_1 = .4$, $r = 5$: $x_2 = 1.2$, $x_3 = -1.2$, $x_4 = -13.2$, . . .

Populations behave in a less trivial way when r lies between 1 and 3. Example: $x_1 = 0.02$, $r = 2.7$. The population wobbles up and down, settling finally at the value 0.6296.

The real excitement starts when r lies between 3 and 4. Example: $x_1 = 0.4$, $r = 3.1$. The population sequence in the first eight years is:

0.4	0.744
0.590	0.770
0.549	0.777
0.539	0.770,

to be read as follows: across the first row, then the second, etc. Thus the population is 0.4 in the first year, 0.744 in the second, 0.590 in the third. Bifurcation has set in! The population oscillates between the two values in alternating years. Different values for x_1 converge to the same two-year cycle.

Now start again with $x_1 = 0.4$ but raise r to 3.5 You will find the sequence:

0.4000,	0.8400,	0.4704,	0.8719,
0.3908,	0.8332,	0.4862,	0.8743,
0.3846,	0.8284,	0.4976,	0.8750,
0.3829,	0.8270,	0.4976,	0.8750,
0.3829,	0.8270,	0.5008,	0.8750,
0.3828,	0.8269,	0.5009,	0.8750,
0.3828,	0.8269,	0.5009,	0.8750, etc.,

again to be read in the order first row, second row, etc. We see bifurcation of bifurcation! The two-year cycle has become a four-year cycle. Raising r further yields 8, 16, 32, . . . bifurcations. The range of r values wherein any number of bifurcations occurs diminishes progressively as that number increases until one reaches the accumulation value $r = 3.5699$ . . ., where (as was theoretically proved later) the period has doubled *ad infinitum*. For higher r, the behavior becomes erratic, aperiodic. We have reached the chaos regime.

In 1973 it was conjectured[29] that the behavior described for the logistic dif-ference-equation holds *qualitatively* for all $f(x_t)$ which have a maximum (at $x_t = 0.5$ in the logistic case) and fall off monotonically on both sides.

Within the region of chaos one finds an infinite number of ever smaller r-ranges for which the system becomes again periodic.[30] The behavior of this logistic equation, so elementary looking at first sight, is utterly remarkable. Go figure.

The Feigenbaum numbers

At Los Alamos it soon became clear to his fellow scientists that Mitchell was a very smart man worth talking to—he himself always talked rapidly—when they got stuck on their own work. They knew that he was in deep thought nearly all the time but did not produce any scientific papers. The main problems he was brooding about concerned big, complex, systems, how physics sufficed (if it did) to describe their reality.

By August 1975—Mitch has told me—he had his first new result, obtained by using his first programmable calculator, an original HP65, given him in December 1974 as a perk for having been promoted to staff member at Los Alamos. This is what he found that August, after a round-about path of analyt-ical thought. Let r_i be the parameter value where the i-th bifurcation sets in, and let $\Delta_i = r_{i+1} - r_i$. Then the Δ_i sequence *asymptotically* converges *geometrically*[31] with increasing i.

> By $r_i = 4$ it was already clear that Δ_i was converging geometrically. One sees this by noticing that the difference of successive values decreases by a constant ratio, which quickly appeared to be about 5. By $i = 7$ the next term in the series already solved the equation to machine precision, which was exceeded beyond $i = 8$. But the ratio of differences itself was converging, down to 4.669 before precision dete-riorated . . . Now this was curious and extraordinary . . . What in this florid calcu-lation was providing geometrical convergence? . . . I was so struck by this that I spent part of the day trying to see if 4.669 was close to various simple combina-tions of numbers and so forth. Nothing at all clear turned up . . .
>
> I spent the first week of October visiting CalTech . . . [when] I suddenly was taken aback by a memory. Stein had told me that the doubling was the same for anything that looked like a bump. In the MSS paper[29] I had looked over almost a year earlier, I suddenly recalled that $x_{t+1} = r \sin \pi x_t$ showed identical behavior to Eq. (1). The day I returned home I decided immediately to check if sin x actually

doubled. Indeed it did, but at 1 second per trigonometry the wait was painful. I recalled there was an easy way to guess the next value, and by $n = 4$ again realized there was geometric convergence. By my efforts to fit the ratio, the new result settling down to 4.662 smelled familiar. A quick rummage through my drawer resurrected the sheet with 4.669 for the [logistic difference equation].

Without an instant's hesitation I experienced an overwhelming excitement that I had stumbled upon a piece of the godhead.

I immediately called Stein. No, he didn't know that the doublings converged geometrically and was deeply skeptical that a universal *quantitative* entity could exist. I went over to his office to show him the numbers which had him respond with a repressed anger that I had no right to such suppositions based on just three identical figures. But *twelve* figures would convince him.

Nevertheless, I called my parents that evening [on October 22] and told them that I had discovered something truly remarkable, that, when I had understood it, would make me a famous man.

A colleague, one of the most knowledgeable computer users, gave me a FOR-TRAN instruction list book to look at, and told me next morning he'd help me onto a serious Los Alamos computer. His few hours of instruction on the system, editor and the easiest way to get output were extraordinary. I had, under my own steam, 4.6692 by the end of the day. This wasn't my limitation. Rather, for naive iteration, 1/3 of the precision of the machine is all one can do. So the next day . . . another computation expert gave me crucial pointers on how to use 29 digit CDC double precision arithmetic. Finally, the next day, some four days after the last encounter, I marched into Stein's office with 4.66920160 . . . agreed to 11 figures for four different problems. This time he concurred, and took out his 'dictionary' of numbers—an ordered list of several hundred pages of decimals and what they represent. By the '9' nothing was close.

So far I have told about how a number I called δ was born. With this as really the sole clue, I knew it foreshadowed an entire world.[32]

Up to twelve decimals, his result was

$$\frac{\Delta_i}{\Delta_{i+1}} \to \delta = 4.669201660910 \text{ as } i \to \infty.$$

Mitchell made his next step into this new world in early 1976 when he conceived the crucial idea that the theory was to be expressed in terms of functional equations, and that not just δ but *all* the chaos dynamics must be quantitatively universal. 'This was the great jewel.'[33] The first outcome of this line of thought dealt with the magnitudes ε_i of the separation between the two arms of the i-th bifurcation about the maximum. He found that, asymptotically, this separation is reduced by a constant value a when going from one doubling to the next:

$$\frac{\varepsilon_i}{\varepsilon_{i+1}} \to a \text{ as } i \to \infty.$$

a is 'another universal constant and this one for the actual dynamics!'[34]

'After an extraordinary amount of analytical computer effort, some two and a half months, every day, 22 hours a day, until I required medical attention in mid-March'[34]—he had lived practically on coffee and cigarettes only—he had his functional equation, which 'justified the big dream that dynamics . . . when appropriately complex in behavior, knew how to perform independently of details.'[34] He had completed the search for his 'universal function,' an achievement he has called 'the most extraordinary discovery I have made in my life.'[34]

The analytic part of the work consisted in finding the functional equation for the universal function; the numerical portion in evaluating a which resulted in (again up to 12 decimals)

$$a = 2.502907875095$$

The numerics to find the first three decimals had been performed with his HP65. Thereafter he had to turn to 'wholesale powerful computation.'[34]

When done, the doctor prescribed a modest amount of valium and an enforced vacation.

δ, the period doubling parameter, and a, the separation parameter, are now known as the Feigenbaum numbers. To the best of my knowledge these are the only dimensionless universal numbers named after a person in the twentieth century. Mitchell has calculated their first 100 decimals, others may have gone further. It is not known whether these numbers are transcendental. It would be highly surprising if they were not.

Mitchell's universal function is not known in closed analytic form. (It is analytic over some domain.) All its consequences are obtained by a combination of analytics and significant amounts of numerical calculation. In a paper[35] published in 1992(!), we read: 'Some of us have been wondering for a long time what the *domain of validity of these discoveries* is and what *techniques from dynamics* need to be employed or invented to make a proof' (author's italics). These questions are answered in that paper[35] with the help of newly invented methods.

I shall not try to sketch the contents of that derivation and proof of the universal function because, frankly, I could not follow the arguments myself! Even Mitchell calls that paper 'exceptionally heavy-duty mathematics.' Instead I refer to papers by Feigenbaum; the first,[36] heuristic one, completed in April 1976, was published in 1978, updated in an appended afterword which acknowledged a seminal contribution made by Predrag Cvitanović in May 1976, crucial to the technical paper[37] published in 1979. A letter written in 1979,[38] followed by a full version in 1980,[39] enlarged this work to an arbitrary number of dimensions, thus making the first contact with the real world. He has also published[40] a semi-popular version of this work.

It has been Mitch's good fortune that he had begun this work with the help of a pocket calculator. That had given him time to reflect and to guess ahead.

> I know no one had discovered δ prior to myself . . . So far as I can tell, had I not had a training that made me eschew computers, had I not so thoroughly enjoyed the computation and 'meaning' of numbers . . . and had the HP65 not been so excruciatingly slow, I wouldn't have discovered δ either. It is a *sine qua non* of emergent behavior. But how do you see it if you don't know what it looks like? After all, fate and luck play all too significant a role.[41]

End notes

1. Feigenbaum's two papers[36,37] were both rejected by journals, the first after a half-year delay. Mitchell still keeps the rejection letters in a desk drawer. 'Every novel paper of mine, without exception, has been rejected by the refereeing process. The reader can easily garner that I regard this entire process as a false guardian and wastefully dishonest.'[42] By 1977 over a thousand preprints of the first paper had been shipped, however.

    Mitch lectured far and wide on his work, starting in May 1976, in Princeton, in August at a Gordon conference, in September before his first international audience, at Los Alamos. In 1981 he spoke at CalTech.

    > That colloquium proved to be the most enjoyable and electric one in my career: it rapidly developed into a dialogue between Feynman in the front row and myself. After the talk I went up to his office. 'You know, I'm envious of you,' he said. 'Come on, you of all people can't be envious of *me*.' 'Well, maybe you're right,' he rejoined.[42]

2. During and after 1979, Mitchell continued to publish on chaos theory.[43] Among his other work I note in particular that on the construction of geographical maps. This has led to new improved editions of the *Hammond Atlas*. In the introductory notes[44] to this volume we read:

    > Using fractal geometry to describe natural forms such as coastlines, mathematical physicist Mitchell Feigenbaum developed software capable of reconfiguring coastlines, borders, and mountain ranges to fit a multitude of map scales and projections . . . Dr. Feigenbaum also created a new computerized type placement program which places thousands of map labels in minutes, a task which previously required days of tedious labor.

    Mitchell has written two papers[45] on the mathematics of map making.

3. The previous sketches about chaos refer exclusively to one-dimensional problems. Much important work on chaos in more dimensions and on rigorous mathematics

has meanwhile been performed by him[39] and by others. I refer to refs 26 and 49 for reviews and collections of major reprinted papers on these various topics, and take this opportunity to express my respects and apologies for not going into detail on the work of their authors.

4. In 1982 Feigenbaum left Los Alamos to assume a professorship at Cornell, until 1986. Thereafter he became professor in the Rockefeller University, where he was named the first Toyota professor, a chair endowed by the Toyota Motor Corporation. In 1984 he received a MacArthur Foundation award.

5. In 1979 Albert Joseph Libchaber (born in Paris, still a French citizen), then working at the École Normale Supérieure, and assisted by Jean Maurer, an engineer, published[47] his first preliminary results of observations on bifurcation cascades. The experimental arrangement is astoundingly small, elegant, and simple. A five cubic millimeter rectangular convective cell is filled with liquid helium. The temperature is made to vary from 2.5 to 4.5 degrees Kelvin, the pressure from 1 to 5 atmospheres. When the fluid is heated from below, at low heating rates, no flow occurs. At higher rates, time-independent convection is set up. At yet higher rates, a periodic time-dependence occurs. At still higher rates they first observed a series of successive period doublings, followed by a very chaotic regime with a broad band spectrum.

In this paper[47] there is no mention of Feigenbaum's work. In a more elaborate paper[48] with the appropriate title 'Helium in a small box,' published in 1982, one finds a section, however, entitled 'The period doubling bifurcation to chaos, Feigenbaum scheme,' in which it is noted 'The qualitative picture proposed by Feigenbaum seems to be correct. Quantitatively there are discrepancies which may be associated to the fact that we observe only the very first bifurcations.' Later with more extensive experiments, this discrepancy disappeared. The questions arise: when did the two men know of each other's work and how did they know it? To find out, I went to consult both Albert, also a friend of mine, and Mitchell. This is what I found out.

Albert has told me that, when he began this work, he did not know of Mitchell's theoretical considerations. Then why did he choose this problem? 'It was in the air,' is all he said to me. Mitchell already knew of Albert's data in 1979, as is seen from his Letter[38] which came out in December of that year, where he quoted the first paper of ref. 47 and stated 'We find excellent agreement with the recent experimental data of Libchaber and Maurer.' The two met for the first time soon afterward, in Paris. Feigenbaum has written, '1979 was a banner year . . . Dynamical systems only became "science" after Libchaber's measurements in the summer of 1979 showed that a fluid can make a transition to turbulence via period doubling with the generic values of a and δ.'[42]

Since 1983, Libchaber has held professorships in Chicago, Princeton, and currently in the Rockefeller University. He has received wide recognition, including the French Legion of Honor. He is married and has three talented sons.

6. In 1986 Feigenbaum and Libchaber were in Jerusalem to share the Wolf Prize in physics ($100 000). Mitchell was cited 'for his pioneering theoretical studies

demonstrating the universal character of non-linear systems, which has made possible the systematic study of chaos,' Albert 'for his brilliant experimental demonstration of the transition to turbulence and chaos in dynamical systems.'

In the accompanying press release it is further noted: 'The impact of Feigenbaum's discoveries has been phenomenal. It has spanned new fields of theoretical and 'experimental' mathematics . . . It is hard to think of any other development in recent theoretical science that has had so broad an impact over so wide a range of fields, spanning both the very pure and the very applied.'

7. I regard chaos theory as one of the great revolutions in twentieth-century physics, along with relativity and quantum mechanics. No two of these are alike, of course. In particular chaos has not produced a paradigm shift (if I understand correctly what that peculiar concept means). One physicist has put it well: 'Relativity eliminated the Newtonian illusion of absolute space and time; quantum theory eliminated the Newtonian dream of a controllable measurement process; and chaos eliminates the Laplacian fantasy of deterministic predictability.'[49]

There are some physicists, famous, yes, wise, no, who have stated in print that the end, the completion, of physical theory is in sight. I am not of that persuasion. 'Twenty years ago, no physicist knew of chaos and, what is more important, of its prevalence.'[50] For centuries most of theoretical studies in physics had been focussed on linear systems or on the linear approximations to more realistic situations. It is only in the last 20 years or so that methods have been found to handle some of the mathematical intricacies which non-linearity brings to a realistic description of natural phenomena.

Mitchell and I believe that we know much, yet little indeed. We are both convinced that the truly astonishing developments described in this essay are but early beginnings, that more surprises are to come. When? From where? In other areas too? Who can tell . . .

References

1. M. Feigenbaum and F. E. Low, *Phys. Rev.* **D4**, 3738, 1971.

2. M. Feigenbaum and D. Mermin, *Am. J. Phys.* **56** (1), 1988.

3. M. Feigenbaum, *J. Math. Phys.* **17**, 614, 1976.

4. F. Cooper and M. Feigenbaum, *Phys. Rev.* **D14**, 583, 1976.

5. M. Feigenbaum and L. Sertorio, *Il Nuov. Cim.* **43A**, 31, 1978.

6. On this subject I have much benefited from the fine book *Chaos*, by J. Gleick, Viking Press, New York, 1987.

7. K. Wilson and J. Kogut, *Phys. Reports* **12C**, 76, 1974.

8. M. Feigenbaum, in *Twentieth Century Physics* (L. Brown, A. Pais, and Sir Brian Pippard, Eds), Vol. 3, p. 1829, American Institute of Physics Press, New York, 1995.

9. H. Rouse and S. Ince, *History of Hydraulics*, p. 212, Dover, New York, 1957.

10. O. Reynolds, *Phil. Trans. Roy. Soc.* **174**, 935, 1886; also **186**, 123, 1895.

11. H. Poincaré, *Acta Math.* **13**, 1, 1890.

12. E. T. Whittaker, *A Treatise on Analytical Dynamics*, chapter 14, Cambridge University Press, 1927.

13. Ref. 12, p. 397.

14. H. Poincaré, *La science et la méthode*, Paris, 1908; in English in *The Foundations of Science* (G. Halsted, transl.), Science Press, Lancaster, 1946; see p. 397.

15. J. Yorke and T. Y. Li, *Am. Math. Monthly* **82**, 985, 1975.

16. Copied from N. G. van Kampen, *Nederl. Tÿdschrift Natuurk.* **20**, 321, 1982.

17. *Exploring Chaos* (N. Hall, Ed.), p. 96, Norton, New York, 1993.

18. E. Lorenz, in *Global Analysis* (J. Marsden, Ed.), p. 55, Springer, New York, 1979.

19. First publication: E. Lorenz, *J. Atmospherical Sci.* **20**, 130, 1963.

20. Ref. 6, p. 30.

21. Ref. 18, Fig. 2.

22. Name proposed by D. Ruelle and F. Takens, *Comm. Math. Phys.* **20**, 167, 1971.

23. Quoted in ref. 6, p. 39.

24. Ref. 6, p. 79.

25. Ref. 17, p. 174.

26. See the lists in Hao Bai-Lin, *Chaos*, and in *Chaos II*, World Scientific, Singapore, 1984 and 1990.

27. H. Poincaré, *Figures d'équilibre d'une masse fluide*, p. 162ff., Gauthier-Villars, Paris, 1902.

28. R. M. May, *Nature* **261**, 459, 1976.

29. See e.g. N. Metropolis, M. Stein, and P. Stein, *J. Combinatorial Theory* **A15**, 25, 1973.

30. Ref. 6, pp. 1–4.

31. He gave the details of the argument in ref. 8, pp. 1840–2.

32. Ref. 8, pp. 1842–4.

33. Ref. 8, p. 1845.

34. Ref. 8, p. 1846.

35. D. Sullivan, 'Bounds, quadratic differentials, and renormalization conjectures,' *Proc. Am. Math. Soc. Symposium*, Vol. 2, p. 417, American Mathematical Society, 1992.

36. M. Feigenbaum, *J. Stat. Phys.* **19**, 25, 1978.

37. M. Feigenbaum, *J. Stat. Phys.* **21**, 669, 1979.

38. M. Feigenbaum, *Phys. Lett.* 74A, 375, 1980.

39. M. Feigenbaum, *Comm. Math. Phys.* **77**, 65, 1980.

40. M. Feigenbaum, *Los Alamos Sci.* **1**, 14, 1980; *Physica* **7D**, 16, 1983.

41. Ref. 8, p. 1844.

42. Ref. 8, p. 1850.

43. M. Feigenbaum, *et al.*, *Physica* **D3**, 468, 1981; *et al.*, *Physica* **D5**, 370, 1982; *J. Stat. Phys.* **46**, 5, 1987; **52**, 527, 1988; *Nonlinearity* **1**, 577, 1988.

44. *Hammond Atlas of the World*, p. 9, Hammond Inc., Maplewood, NJ, 1992.

45. M. Feigenbaum, in *Towards the Harnessing of Chaos* (M. Yamaguti, Ed.), p. 1, Elsevier, New York, 1994; and in *Trends and Perspectives in Applied Mathematics* (L. Sirovich, Ed.), p. 55, Springer, New York, 1994.

46. P. Cvitanović, *Universality in Chaos*, Hilger, Bristol, 1984.

47. A. Libchaber and J. Maurer, *J. de Physique* **40**, L419, 1979; also *J. de Physique* **C3**, 51, 1980.

48. A. Libchaber and J. Maurer, in *Nonlinear Phenomena at Phase Transitions and Instabilities* (T. Riste, Ed.), p. 259, Plenum, New York, 1982.

49. Quoted in ref. 6, p. 6.

50. Ref. 8, p. 1823.

Res Jost lecturing in Zurich, 1960s. (Courtesy of Hilde Jost.)

Res Jost

On January 2, 1946 I arrived in Copenhagen to start postdoctoral research. I was the first of the post-War crop of youngsters from abroad to start work at Niels Bohr's Institut for Teoretisk Fysik (in 1965 renamed Niels Bohr Institute). There, shortly afterwards, on the 15th, I made the acquaintance of another young arrival from abroad.[1] He was Res Jost. We were of the same age, both born in 1918. He was the best friend I ever had. I also knew his father well, and continue to have affectionate relations with his wife and three children.

What follows is mainly the story of our almost half a century's friendship rather than a systematic detailed analysis of Jost's oeuvre.

Res Wilhelm Jost was born on January 10, 1918 in Berne, the son of Wilhelm Jost and Hermine née Spycher. He had a one-year younger sister, Katherine. His father, who grew up in the hills of Wynigen, Canton Berne, worked himself through the hierarchy of the school system: elementary school teacher, secondary school teacher, finally teacher at a Gymnasium. For 38 years he taught physics at the Städtische Gymnasium of Berne. It was he who first introduced his son to the fundamentals of physics.

Res received his elementary and secondary education in Berne. After having obtained his *Maturität* (high school diploma) he entered the University of Berne where, until winter 1943, he studied mathematics, theoretical physics, and chemistry. During those years he was called up a number of times for military service in the Swiss army. In November 1943 he received the *Diploma für das hohere Lehramt*, which entitled him to teach at the Gymnasium level, which he did, part-time, in Berne.

From the summer of 1944 until the beginning of 1946 Res studied at the University of Zurich. There he became deeply impressed by the courses given by the mathematician Heinz Hopf and the physicist Gregor Wentzel, under whose guidance he attained the degree of 'Dr Phil. II,' on a PhD thesis dealing with meson theory.[2] In January 1946 he went on his first journey outside Switzerland, to become a postdoctoral student in Copenhagen.

Res and I got along well from the day we met. We would often eat and talk together, especially about our work, which had gone in different directions. I had become interested in the possible existence of elementary particle spectra, work of which only a new word, the term lepton,[3] has survived, had made some calculations on neutron–proton scattering,[4] and had soon become involved in daily work with Bohr. Res was deeply impressed by Bohr, even though he spent rather little time with him. He had become immersed in the theory of the scattering matrix (S-matrix), formulated in 1943 by Heisenberg, and of great interest in Copenhagen, where Christian Møller had elaborated Heisenberg's ideas.

Heisenberg had conjectured that the zeros of the S-matrix on the imaginary axis in the k-plane (k is the asymptotic momentum) would give the bound states. Meanwhile it had been found out, however, that for potential scattering, 'false zeros' can arise that do not correspond to bound states. Whereupon Jost gave a general criterion for bound states: for given angular momentum the S-matrix can always be written, he showed, as[5] $S(k) = f(k)/f(-k)$. Bound states are given by the zeros of $f(k)$, any false zeros by the poles of $f(-k)$. $f(k)$ is now known as the Jost function. It appears for the first time in his paper completed in Copenhagen,[6] and was treated by him in much more detail a year later.[7] Ever since, the Jost function has played an important role in scattering theory.

One remnant of our Danish days has remained in our later conversations, whether face to face or by phone. At the end, one of us would invariably say: *mange tak*, many thanks, the other would reply: *selv tak*, thanks yourself.

On the following September 26, I left Copenhagen, Res departed four days later. I was bound for Princeton, where I had received a Fellowship from the Institute for Advanced Study (hereinafter called the Institute), which one year later was converted to a five-year appointment. In 1951 I became a full professor at the Institute. Res had left Copenhagen for Zurich with an appointment as assistant to Wolfgang Pauli at the ETH (*Eidgenössische Technische Hochschule*, Swiss Federal Institute of Technology), a post he was to hold until October 1949. In an unpublished autobiographical sketch he has written: 'The influence of this singular teacher has formed me most decidedly.'

In 1947, Pauli wrote to a colleague: 'I am very satisfied with my assistant Jost.'[8] Res had indeed quickly become productive in his new position. In that year he first published work done some years earlier on the mathematical theory of counters,[9] then came the paper[7] on false zeros mentioned earlier, next he solved a problem set him by Pauli,[10] concerning soft photons emitted in Compton scattering.[11] Finally, he published a theorem on entropy in wave mechanics.[12]

One will note the strong mathematical bent in all these papers. So it remained throughout Jost's career. He was in fact to become one of the leading mathematical physicists of his time.

The year 1947 saw major advances in quantum electrodynamics, stimulated by discoveries of a small displacement (Lamb shift) of certain lines in the hydrogen spectrum, and of a small anomaly of the magnetic moment of the electron, both as compared with Dirac's predictions of 1928. New mathematical techniques, known as the renormalization program for radiative corrections, were developed almost at once to cope with these effects. It was just the kind of novelty that was up Jost's alley.

Several of his next papers (together with coworkers) are devoted to applications of this new program: radiative corrections to Compton scattering for spinless particles[13] and a treatment of vacuum polarization.[14] In the next paper, a more refined treatment of vacuum polarization,[15] we find Jost's first use of the graph techniques meanwhile perfected by Richard Feynman. This paper is of particular interest because of questions of principle addressed therein. First: why are all charges renormalized to the same amount, that is, for example, why do the proton and the positron have the same renormalized electric charge? It was shown how this comes about to order e^2. Secondly, Pauli had conjectured that the fine structure constant might be fixed by requiring a correlation of divergences to order e^2 and e^4. This conjecture was proven incorrect.

We, in Princeton, had followed this work with great interest. I urged Oppenheimer to invite some of the young Zurich theorists to the Institute. That fit quite well with another long-standing invitation, to Pauli, to spend academic 1949–50 with us. So it came about that in the autumn of 1949 he appeared in Princeton, soon followed by his 'children,' as he put it,[16] Jost, Luttinger, and Villars.

Jost came accompanied by his bride. Earlier in 1949 he was married in Berne to Hilde Fleischer, a native of Vienna, herself a PhD in physics, who found a job at the Princeton University Library. Theirs was a splendid union. In particular, Hilde's cheery outlook on life, always aiming towards the positive side, was a great support to Res, who tended to be less sanguine by nature. Later a colleague said about Res:

> Surpassing everything else was the care for your family . . . Your Hilde [was a] loving, never wavering support who with incredible emotional strength never left your side. I recall that once, when we were still young, you said to me that there are many important things in life—science, art, nature, politics, and others—but only one thing was really decisive, a good marriage and a harmonious family life.[17]

I became fond of Hilde right away. (Later she told me that she had heard about me from Res and had imagined me to be a grey-haired older man.) Since I would often be invited for dinner to their apartment, I soon found out that she was a fine cook. Her Wiener schnitzels were excellent, her Sacher torte was superb. After-dinner discussions would range far and wide. For the first time I realized Res' broad and deep extrascientific interests in history, literature, music, the visual arts. Through the years it has always enriched me to talk with him about all those subjects.

Res' first Princeton paper[18] deals with a calculation, using S-matrix methods, of the angular and momentum distribution of a nucleus as it recoils after pair production by an incident photon. It is his only work in which comparisons with current experiments were used. He made such a strong impression at the Institute that in the spring of 1950 he was offered and accepted a five-year membership, thus extending his first stay to 1955. In later years he would return several more times, to spend the fall term of 1957, academic 1962–63, and the fall term of 1968.

The next great event in Res' life was the birth of his first son, in 1951. In that year Hilde had gone to Berne for the delivery. On her return Res went to fetch her. I can still remember seeing them walk to their apartment, Res holding little baby Resli in a carrying bag. I was most honored and pleased to become his *Götti*, godfather, and felt likewise when Res agreed to become godfather to my son Joshua. Resli has grown up to be a tall, vigorous fellow, for years a fine handball player, and is currently the head of the gastroenterology department of the Kantonsspital Winterthur. The Josts were to have two more children, who likewise have done well in mature life: Beat (b. 1957), experimental physicist, currently staff member at CERN; and Inge (b. 1960), who became a student of law, and is now personnel manager at the firm Allopro, in Baar, Switzerland (both were also born in Berne). After Resli's birth, Hilde gave up her career forever. She was, and is, a splendid mother.

During 1951–52, Res and I collaborated on two projects, our only joint papers.

The first of these deals with the quantum theory of potential scattering and is an elaboration of an approximation method first proposed by Max Born in 1926.[19] Brooding about integration methods devised by Feynman, it struck me one day that it would be possible to use them for a calculation in closed form of the second Born approximation for scattering by a Yukawa potential. The gist of Born's method is to expand the scattering amplitude in terms of powers of the potential coupling strength. Up till then very little was known beyond the first power, that is, the first approximation. The prospect of going one step further was exciting.

That evening I had to buy something in Thorne's drugstore on Nassau Street. There I met the Josts and told Res of my idea. He too got excited and suggested we go to a blackboard to have a closer look, which we did. So began a period of several months' intense joint labor; evenings we would often work until three in the morning.

It did not take us long to solve the Yukawa problem. It was only natural that next we were led to a much tougher question: what is the radius of convergence of the Born series? We could give an exact answer for one particular potential[20] but for S-states only. Could we do something for general potentials, independent of angular momentum restrictions? The answer was yes, using a new method based on the Fredholm theory of integral equations. Jost's profound mathematical knowledge was indispensable to get that far. Emboldened by this success we dared to ask whether our methods could be extended to quantum field theory. A few days of rumination showed us that this ambition could not be fulfilled. Later, our Fredholm method was successfully applied to nonrelativistic dispersion relations.[21]

As we began preparing our paper[22] on the subject, the question arose of whether others had studied the convergence question before us. We went back and back in the literature, found nothing, until we came to Born's paper[19] of 1926, where we saw a correct proof of general convergence for one-dimensional scattering, followed by the incorrect statement, without proof, that this result can directly be extended to three dimensions.[23]

When we received proofs, the pedantic editor of the *Physical Review* demanded that in our references we supply the initials of authors of books which everyone knows by last names only. That went too far, we felt, so you will find in our printed paper references to A. B. Whittaker and C. D. Watson, A. B. Frank and C. D. Mises . . .

Our second joint paper[24] deals with problems in particle physics. It is the first paper that introduces a rigorous selection rule which has come to be known as G-parity. This work has played a crucial role in my later work, since it was the first occasion on which I learned to apply invariance principles.

In the summer of 1952 I saw Res in action in a quite different capacity: as a mountaineer. In June of that year the Josts and I were in Copenhagen to attend an international physics conference. While there we planned to take some vacation together in the Swiss mountains. Some weeks later I joined them in Zurich, from where, together with Res' father, we went by car to Pontresina in Canton Graubünden, where we settled in Pension Remi. We made an excursion to nearby St Moritz. Another day we went up the Schafsberg, more of a hike, but a good long one. Res' father, then in his early eighties, went along. I admired the old man's ways, going slowly but steadily, rarely pausing for a moment's rest. From him, a seasoned mountaineer in his younger days, I learned the climber's rule: below 4000 meters walk slowly, higher up go as fast as you can.

Guided by Res I found some edelweiss that day. (I had no idea what they looked like.) I plucked a few of those delicate white flowers, and for years they have hung behind glass in my office.

Meanwhile Res and I had made a plan to do something more serious, climb the nearby Piz Albris. We estimated that the ascent would take about five hours;

we planned to leave early, so we could be back by dinner time. That, however, did not come to pass.

All went as planned on the way up. The climb was not very technical, yet did require that now and then Res, an expert in the mountains, had to belay me, the novice. After we reached the top we had a piece of bread and sausage and some water. Looking over the beautiful landscape, we noticed another possible way back to the valley, steeper but considerably shorter. We decided to try that one and began our slow descent. There came a point where I, in front, belayed by Res, saw trouble ahead. If we continue this way, I told him, we will hit a good-sized waterfall. We retraced our steps part of the way until we found a narrow lateral ledge along which we proceeded sideways, stepping very carefully. The going was slow, the sun went down, we were still on the slope. Whereupon Res decided that safety demanded that we spend the night there to wait for sunrise before going further. We sat for quite a while until I felt like moving a little bit. That was lucky, since I discovered a safe way to get down. Slowly, slowly, we went on, reaching the road by eleven in the evening. We still had to walk another hour to reach our Pension. On we went, when a car stopped next to us. Are you the two men from the Pension Remi who were on the Albris? Indeed we were. Shouts of joy from the car.

What had happened meanwhile was that Hilde, seriously alarmed, had called a local three-man mountain rescue squad who were on their way to save us when we met them. Together we drove to the Pension where we were embraced by a tearful Hilde. All of us were given food and hot tea, then sat for hours as the locals told stories of other rescues which did not end as happily as ours.

Also in later years I have spent happy times with the Josts in Switzerland. We would vacation together, in Saas Fee, and in Lauenen, from where, in 1961, Res and I made another climb, the ascent of the Wildhorn—this time with a guide. I was always welcome as their houseguest wherever they lived. In October 1964 they moved into their final residence in Unterengstringen, a house they themselves had largely designed. Not only was it a beautiful comfortable home, but also it had its own heatable swimming pool, realizing Hilde's dream of taking a swim every day. I have never seen Res in their pool, water was not his element. On hikes in the neighborhood I noticed another quality of Res. He was an expert in finding edible mushrooms.

———— • ————

I return to Princeton in 1952. Res had begun a series of investigations on the 'inverse problem'; given the scattering phase shifts and the values of the bound state energies, to what extent is the scattering potential determined? And on the related issue of equivalent potentials: can different potentials lead to the same phase shifts and bound states? That work, begun with his good friend Walter Kohn, kept him busy on and off for the next three years.[25] Then his time in

Princeton was up. In the spring of 1955 he and his family went back to Zurich, where an appointment as *extraordinarius* at the ETH was awaiting him.

During the first few years after his return, Res had unexpectedly and undeservedly to endure grave personal attacks from the side of Pauli, who in those last few years of his life had turned quite hostile to him. It caused an irreparable rift between the two men.

Pauli's attitude was, I am sure, due to his mental instability at that time, which I noticed from personal observations (in New York, in April 1957). Similar observations (with which I concur) about that sad state of affairs are found in Heisenberg's autobiography.[26] Only once did Res comment publicly on this nasty situation: 'I was under the spell of this unique personality until he ousted me [from his inner circle].'[27] In 1989 he sent me a lengthy memorandum on this matter, entitled 'The rift with Pauli,' from which I quote the following.

> Summer 1955. Return to Zurich. Harmonious relations with Wolfgang and Franca [his wife]. Walks with Pauli. On one of these he asks me whether it makes sense to commit his dreams to paper. I fervently say yes, telling him that later times will turn to his person and will gain essential insights from his written dreams. Shortly afterward Pauli gave me two dreams in writing. I read them. They shocked me. I had the impression of a man who is threatened by dark powers. At our next encounter I told him that I could not discuss his dreams: that was too dangerous for me. Pauli appeared to understand this. Now I believe that at that point something broke between us.
>
> Autumn 1956. Trips to the U.S.—Seattle, Pittsburgh, finally a week in Princeton. Return to Zurich, where I at once call Pauli, to whom I mention my invitation to the Princeton Institute. I mention that I would only go to Princeton if he had not the same plan—he had precedence of course. Shortly afterward I receive a typed letter from Pauli in which he deplores my invitation from the Institute and is afraid that the administration may consider this as competing requests for leave of absence. I am astonished by this bureaucratic communication, since we see each other daily. With my ticket in hand I look up Pauli and tell him I would rather have this orally. It makes no sense to involve the secretary in such things. Pauli replies: 'The text was not written by the secretary' (so probably by Franca) . . . My relation with Pauli cooled noticeably . . . In 1957 my relations with him were ruined . . . [In 1958] it becomes clear to me that I must leave Zurich.

In 1958, Res wrote a letter[28] to the president of the ETH board from which I quote.

> The good relations [with P.] lasted until the autumn of 1956, when Herr Pauli suddenly and completely broke off the personal relations with me and my wife, which until then had been very animated. I shall not go into his motivation that I had surreptitiously obtained an invitation to Princeton. Shortly afterward he began his attacks on my scientific work . . . Unfortunately I must admit that Herr

Pauli had chosen his victim with great skill, since I am somewhat helpless in the face of these smaller and larger taunts. It does not seem correct to me, however, that Herr Pauli wrote to his assistant about these matters, ordering him that he show the relevant parts of his letter to me. It is no pleasure to be exposed to the negative traits of a very prominent scholar.

What was behind this most regrettable episode? I agree with the opinion of Fierz, who has written:

Pauli considered Res Jost as 'junior partner' but RJ believed that he considered him as a kind of 'higher assistant' and that did not suit him at all. A conflict flared up as a result of this misunderstanding which I consider to be a father-son conflict . . . I was always aware of the distance between me and Pauli, which I have heeded. It was dangerous to come too close to him, especially because of the very difficult personality of his wife, who always jealously guarded over the status of her husband.[29]

Pauli died in December 1958. The next February Res wrote to Oppenheimer: 'I now direct my plans entirely on remaining in Switzerland. What seemed impossible only a few months ago now becomes very probable . . . I do not yet have official confirmation of my promotion.'[30] In this letter he also asks Oppenheimer's opinion about who should succeed Pauli. Later in 1959 it was Res himself who was officially chosen to be Pauli's successor. Even thereafter he could not shake the harrowing experiences of the late 1950s, as is seen, for example, from what he wrote to Fierz ten years later: 'Above all you have not been exposed to the greatest tyrant of those times, Pauli . . .'[31]

Meanwhile, undaunted, Jost had begun in Zurich his researches on issues of principle in quantum field theory, his most famous and profound contributions to mathematical physics. I mention their highlights only, and those very briefly, since this is not the place in which to go into detail, and, more so, since this work lies beyond my range of expertise, though I have followed it in outline.

These activities began with his paper, jointly with Harry Lehmann, on causal commutators.[32] Next follows his series of papers on the CTP theorem,[33] culminating in its masterful derivation in terms of the complex extension on the Lorentz group.[34] This work forms part of his studies in axiomatic field theory, a new field of endeavor that started in the 1950s, of which he was one of the cofounders, and on which he published a monograph.[35] In those years Res also found time to pursue questions in another area dear to him: classical mechanics.[36]

Beginning in the later 1950s, Jost exerted his important influence as a teacher, in fact creating his own school. His students, several of whom have made their names internationally, have always endeavored to follow the high standards he set for himself.

In those years I continued to see Res fairly frequently, in Switzerland and elsewhere. In particular, I recall us being together in Seattle, in September 1956, for a physics conference; and our joint visit to Otto Stern near Berkeley, California, where he lived part of the time in his years of retirement. Also in that period we maintained steady contact by correspondence.

I had left the Institute when, in the fall of 1968, Res spent his last period of membership there. He came to the Rockefeller University, however, where I had been appointed in 1963, to give a series of lectures on classical mechanics, entitled 'Attempts of an old professor to learn modern methods.'

Here ends my cursory review of Res' original contributions to science—but not of his full oeuvre.

Jost was in many respects unique among the great physicists of his time. Also during his years of greatest creative strength and in the glow of international recognition he came time and again to grips with the past and with the problems of our time.

Thus wrote the editors of *Das Märchen vom Elfenbeinernen Turm* (The Myth of the Ivory Tower),[37] a collection of seventeen essays by Res, many of them never published before, addressed to a scientifically interested general public. Some deal with the history of physics, some with the relations between mathematics and physics, a few with ethical issues raised by modern science. They were written between 1966 and 1986, all in the strong, beautiful style which shows Res' mastery of language, especially of German.

The title of this collection is also the title of one of the essays.[38] Here we meet Res the scholar, delving into the origins of the concept, 'ivory tower,' which led him via the Song of Songs of Solomon to an essay by Charles Augustin Sainte-Beuve. At issue here is how to justify the life of the modern scholar who, supported by public funds, can lead the contemplative life. Jost takes the discovery of DNA as an example for showing that this life is not always as contemplative as those who use the term 'ivory tower' as a term of abuse may imagine.

Res' historical essays tell of some of the greatest physicists of the nineteenth and twentieth centuries. Several deal with Max Planck, beginning[39] with the complex prehistory[40] of his famous law which marks the beginning of quantum physics. I recall a statement by one of Planck's contemporaries, told to me by Jost. Planck made so many mistakes that he *had* to end up finding his law. Then follow discussions of the relations of Planck with Boltzmann,[41] and with Ernst Mach.[42] Yet another gives a well-deserved critique of the critique of Planck's work by Thomas Kuhn.[43]

Two other essays deal with Einstein. The first is an account of his Zurich period[44] about which, late in life, he once said to a friend: '[Switzerland] is the most beautiful part of the world I know. I like that land to the same extent that it did not care for me,' on which Jost commented: 'He was more correct than we care.' This essay also includes the story of Einstein's *annus mirabilis*, the year 1905, which he spent in Berne. The second Einstein essay concerns the centennial celebration of Einstein's birth, in Princeton, which both Res and I attended. It is a reprint[45] of Res' lengthy learned commentary on my paper at that conference, dealing with 'Particles, fields, and the quantum theory.'[46]

Next follows the text of a lecture Jost gave on Michael Faraday, on the occasion of the 150th anniversary of his discovery of electromagnetic induction. With his customary elegance, Res gives a succinct account of Faraday's life and work, adding the little-known story of Faraday's irritation upon hearing of the claim by two gentlemen from Florence that they had anticipated his discovery of induction. Next we find an essay on Émile du Bois-Raymond's concepts of the physical world.

Res' last historical contribution, dealing with quantum field theory, is a paper[48] in honor of Dirac, '[whose] scientific production in the years 1925–28 . . . is hardly equalled in the history of physics . . . Three physicists above all are prominent by their contributions to quantum electrodynamics in the first third of our century: Max Planck, Albert Einstein, and P. A. M. Dirac.'

Five essays on 'Mathematics and physics' follow. The volume ends with three more, carrying the collective title '*Wissen und Gewissen*,' that is, 'Knowledge and conscience,' a translation which inevitably spoils Res' elegant choice of words. One of these three deals with the concept of 'ivory tower,' already mentioned, another with 'Physics, yesterday and tomorrow.'[49] Where is science going? Res answers this question in the most sensible way I can imagine: 'I don't know an answer that satisfies even the slightest standard of credibility.'

The final essay of this wonderful collection, which I recommend to everyone, scientist or not, deals with 'Science between yearning and sin.'[50] Res, once again at his best, illuminates his points with comments that start with Newton and end with Oppenheimer. Its concluding sentence expresses opinions shared by many of us: 'It is cold comfort that those in power insisted on taking away once and for all the carefully considered judgment, the knowledge and conscience from him who personified these qualities, Robert Oppenheimer.'

This superb book begins with Res' personal recollections,[51] originally delivered in 1984 in response to his being awarded the Planck medal. It is largely a eulogy on Planck, whom Res heard lecture in his [R.'s] young years.

I conclude the review of Res' writings by noting that he published twenty book reviews, all in the *Zeitschrift für Angewandte Mathematik und Physik* (ZAMP),[52] in the years from 1957 to 1973. Of particular interest are Jost's words of praise for the book by Pauli: 'The strikingly beautiful use of language, which links balance with perfect clarity, should be particularly emphasized . . . We [should be] grateful for these essays.'[52]

Res also wrote a few obituaries,[53] notably one for Robert Oppenheimer. 'No one who has enjoyed the Oppenheimer's hospitality in Olden Manor [their Princeton home] will ever forget that.'[53] He also wrote in a Zurich paper on the occasion of the centenary of Bohr's birth, characterizing him well: 'A spirit of dialectic ability and enormous perseverance, who was able to endure and make fertile the contradictions between phenomena forced upon us by observation.'[53]

In September 1972 I received a letter from Res[54] which gave me a shock. In the preceding June he had been hospitalized with a serious heart attack. One day in August, having recuperated somewhat, he fell, unconscious, and damaged a vertebra. 'I could not work. That, however, I don't take seriously since, at my age, one hardly can produce anything of lasting value.'[54] From that time on he turned to his historical essays as his main interest.

To help cheer him up, I initiated proceedings for his nomination to Foreign Member of the US National Academy of Sciences; he was elected in 1974.

In his later years, Res was quite active with help in the preparation of the publication of Einstein's collected works, both in scientific matters and in obtaining financial support from Swiss sources. In volume 5 of these papers, published[55] in 1993, one will find the dedication 'To the memory of Res Jost, *Fortiter in re, suaviter in modo*': forceful in affairs, mild in execution.

In 1987 it was diagnosed that Res suffered from a melanoma. He was operated on, successfully it appeared, but was much weakened afterward.

In 1988 friends of mine had organized a one-day physics symposium followed by a festive dinner, at the Rockefeller University, in honor of my seventieth birthday. I wanted very much for Res and Hilde to attend; we would take care of expenses. After some discussion by telephone, they accepted, to my great contentment, and spent a few days in New York. On arrival Res told me that he did not have the strength, however, to speak at the occasion. I told him not to worry, I was just happy that he and Hilde were present.

In 1989, a second operation turned out to be necessary. Res appeared to respond well to after-treatment, but then, one night, became lame on the left side and was hospitalized.

I was in Denmark at that time and decided to visit him, which I did. On return I kept in close touch with Hilde, who told me that his state was deteriorating. Whereupon, in September 1990, I went back to Zurich again, staying several days, spending part of each with him in his hospital room. He could no longer speak but I could see that he responded to me when I talked to him. It was heartbreaking to see this good man, who always had been so strong physically and was so helpless now. In all those months, until the end, Hilde was constantly at his bedside.

On October 3, 1990, Res Jost died in the hospital. In the family's announcement, sent out the next day, it was said that he took his final suffering 'with courage and humor.'

In the obituary for Res, found in the *Neue Zürcher Zeitung*, we find these words:

> On October 3, 1990, Professor Res Jost died after a long, serious illness, borne with courage and understanding . . . Res Jost was known for his modesty and reserve regarding his own work, for his extraordinary personal integrity, his generosity and benevolence toward colleagues and pupils, his great courage and striking scientific criticism, his comprehensive erudition and deep understanding of the connection between science and history . . . Many of us lose a fatherly friend . . . We are grateful for all he has given us.[56]

Another obituary spoke of 'His wonderful sense of language, his pithy sense of humor, his laughter, and his deep humanity.'[57]

On October 8, 1990, colleagues spoke at a memorial service held in Weiningen's reformed church. One, Walter Kohn, recalled his collaboration with Res, 'which usually lasted from about eleven in the morning until three or four at night . . . I recall how toward midnight Hilde would come down to cheer us up and bring us a tasty bite to eat,' spoke of 'his sparse humor and exuberant laughter,' and remembered that 'long walks was one of his greatest passions.'[58]

J. B. Blaser, another colleague, said: 'Now you have to leave us, dear Res . . . but you have given us so much . . . with greatest gratitude we shall retain in lively memory all we were allowed and share with you. Adieu Res . . .'[17]

Of all the people I have known and who have passed before me, I miss no one more than Res. He was my best friend.

References

In what follows RJ stands for Res Jost.

1. I found the dates of our arrival and departure among documents at the Niels Bohr Archive in Copenhagen.

2. RJ, *Helv. Phys. Acta* **19**, 113, 1946.

3. C. Møller and A. Pais, *Cambridge Conference on fundamental particles and low temperatures*, p. 181, Taylor and Francis, London, 1947.

4. Ref. 3, p. 177.

5. $f(k)$ is the value of the function $f(k,r)$ at $r = 0$, where $f(k,r)$ is that solution of the Schrödinger equation which for large r behaves as an incoming spherical wave with amplitude normalized to unity: $f(k,r) \rightarrow e^{-ikr}$, $r \rightarrow \infty$.

6. RJ, *Physica* **12**, 509, 1946.

7. RJ, *Helv. Phys. Acta* **20**, 256, 1947.

8. W. Pauli, letter to H. B. G. Casimir, January 2, 1947, reprinted in W. Pauli, *Wissenschaftliche Briefwechsel* (K. von Meyenn, Ed.), Vol. III, p. 411, Springer, New York, 1993.

9. RJ, *Helv. Phys. Acta* **20**, 173, 1947.

10. W. Pauli, letter to A. Bohr, March 30, 1947, ref. 8, p. 432.

11. RJ, *Phys. Rev.* **72**, 815, 1947.

12. RJ, *Helv. Phys. Acta* **20**, 491, 1947.

13. RJ and E. Corinaldesi, *Helv. Phys. Acta* **21**, 183, 1948.

14. RJ and J. Rayski, *Helv. Phys. Acta* **22**, 457, 1949.

15. RJ and J. Luttinger, *Helv. Phys. Acta* **23**, 201, 1950.

16. W. Pauli, letter to I. Rabi, December 19, 1949, ref. 8, p. 722.

17. J. P. Blaser, in his address at the memorial service for RJ, October 8, 1990.

18. RJ, J. Luttinger, and M. Slotnick, *Phys. Rev.* **86**, 189, 1950.

19. M. Born, *Zeitschr. f. Phys.* **38**, 803, 1926.

20. The Hulthén potential, $V(r) = e^{-r}/(1 - e^{-r})$.

21. N. N. Khuri, *Phys. Rev.* **107**, 1148, 1957.

22. RJ and A. Pais, *Phys. Rev.* **82**, 840, 1951.

23. Ref. 19, p. 816.

24. A. Pais and RJ, *Phys. Rev.* **87**, 871, 1952.

25. RJ and W. Kohn, *Phys. Rev.* **87**, 977, 1952; **88**, 382, 1952; RJ and R. Newton, *Helv. Phys. Acta* **29**, 410, 1955; RJ, *ibid.* **29**, 410, 1956.

26. W. Heisenberg, *Der Teil und das Ganze*, pp. 316–20, Piper Verlag, Munich, 1969. For more on this episode see my essay on Pauli in this book.

27. RJ, *Phys. Blätter* **40**, 178, 1984.

28. RJ, letter to the President of the ETH Board, *Schulratsakten* 1958, Nr. 8191/624, copy in the ETH Hauptbibliothek, Zurich.

29. M. Fierz, letter to the President of the ETH Board, July 26, 1994, quoted in the *Schulratsakten*.

30. RJ, letter to J. R. Oppenheimer, February 13, 1959.

31. RJ, letter to M. Fierz, October 28, 1967.

32. RJ and H. Lehmann, *Nuovo Cim.* **5**, 1598, 1957.

33. RJ, *Helv. Phys. Acta* **30**, 409, 1957; **33**, 773, 1960; **36**, 77, 1963; also with M. Fierz, *ibid.* **38**, 137, 1965.

34. See Jost's contribution to *Theoretical Physics in the Twentieth Century*, p. 107, Interscience, New York, 1960.

35. RJ, *The General Theory of Quantized Fields*, American Mathematical Society, Providence, RI, 1965.

36. See e.g. RJ, *Helv. Phys. Acta* **41**, 965, 1968.

37. RJ, *Das Märchen vom Elfenbeinernen Turm* (K. Hepp, W. Hunziker, and W. Kohn, Eds), Springer, New York, 1995.

38. Ref. 37, p. 261.

39. Ref. 37, p. 23.

40. For which see also A. Pais, *Subtle is the Lord*, chapter 19, section(a), Oxford University Press, 1982.

41. Ref. 37, p. 35.

42. Ref. 37, p. 53.

43. Ref. 37, p. 67.

44. Ref. 37, p. 99.

45. RJ, *Some Strangeness in the Proportion* (H. Woolf, Ed.), p. 252, Addison-Wesley, Reading, MA, 1980.

46. Ref. 45, p. 197.

47. Ref. 37, p. 117.

48. Ref. 37, p. 153.

49. Ref. 37, p. 249.

50. Ref. 37, p. 271.

51. Ref. 37, p. 11.

52. Books by D. Hartree, ZAMP **9a**, 215, 1958; R. Leighton, **10**, 528, 1959; D. ter Haar, **10**, 330, 1959; E. Kemble, **10**, 325, 1959; J. Schwinger, **10**, 325, 1959; *Handbuch der Physik*, Vol. 34, **10**, 216, 1959, M. Planck, **10**, 111, 1959; *Handbuch der Physik*, Vol. 5, part 1, **10**, 110, 1959; anniversary volume for L. Meitner, O. Hahn, and M. von Laue, **11**, 336, 1960; U. and L. Fano, **11**, 248, 1960; Max Planck Festschrift 1958, **11**, 85, 1960; W. Pauli, **12**, 578, 1961; Landau and Lifshitz, **13**, 528, 1962; M. von Laue, **13**, 620, 1962; J. von Neumann, **14**, 391, 1963; Landau and Lifshitz **15**, 216, 1964; V. Arnold and A. Avez, **21**, 681, 1970; E. Prugovecki, **24**, 146, 1973; J. Bradley **25**, 258, 1973; H. Lipkin, **25**, 699, 1974.

53. Of Max Schafroth, *Neue Zürcher Zeitung* (NZZ), June 8, 1959; J. R. Oppenheimer, NZZ, February 21, 1967; W. Heitler, *Vierteljahresschr. Naturf. Ges. Zurich* **128**, 139, 1983; F. Bloch, NZZ, October 14, 1983; E. Stückelberg, NZZ, September 9, 1984; N. Bohr, NZZ, November 9, 1985.

54. RJ, letter to A. Pais, September 19, 1972.

55. *The Collected Papers of Albert Einstein* (M. Klein *et al.*, Eds), Vol. 5, Princeton University Press, 1993.

56. J. Fröhlich, K. Hepp, and W. Kohn, NZZ, October 6/7, 1990.

57. W. Kohn, D. Ruelle, and A. Wightman, *Phys. Today* **45**, February 1992, p. 120.

58. W. Kohn, address at the memorial service for RJ, October 8, 1990.

Oskar Klein in 1920. (Courtesy of Niels Bohr Archive, Copenhagen.)

Oskar Klein*

Oskar Benjamin Klein was born on September 15, 1894 in Stockholm, the third child of Gottlieb Klein and Antonie (Toni) née Levy. Learning and culture belonged to the family tradition. His father hailed from Homonna, a town in the Southern Carpathians, where the family ran a small shop. He left home early. In 1873 he received a Dr Phil. degree from the University of Heidelberg. In 1877 he finished his rabbinical studies, begun with Abraham Geiger, the founder of a liberal movement in Judaism. In 1883 he moved to Stockholm as Sweden's first chief rabbi. Oskar's mother was the daughter of an orientalist.

Klein himself has recalled[1] how his interest in science arose.

'I started school at an age which was not at all early, just when I was seven . . . My science interest began very early. It came mostly from being glad to hear and see things about animals. For a time I thought I would be a biologist. That state lasted rather long.'[1] His father, who always tried to find books that interested him, had given him Darwin's *Origin of Species*.

> So when I was something like 14, 15 I read about Darwin . . . I have always kept my interest [in biology] and have recently [in 1940, collaborated with] one of our good cytologists[2] . . . When I was about 14 I used to go around with my mother's opera glasses and look at stars. When we came home from some party I saw Sirius, that was a very great event. Then the next year I started to do some chemistry by trying to do fireworks. Some young friend lent me a book by Ostwald [*Schule der Chemie*] translated into Swedish. That was really an interesting book . . . I tried to make as many experiments as I could in connection with it . . . Then I began to read a little more advanced books and had very great trouble. Then I knew very little mathematics, but afterward I found mathematics rather easy. But that took me quite a time.[1]

Klein's father, who knew Svante Arrhenius, was invited one day to come for lunch at his home.

> That was in the summer of 1910, just before I was sixteen. And then my father asked if his two boys could come after lunch, and we came, my younger brother

* Extended version of the opening address at the Oskar Klein Centenary Symposium held in Stockholm, September 19–21, 1994. Earlier version published in *Proceedings of the Oskar Klein Symposium* (U. Lindström, Ed.), p. 1, World Scientific, Singapore, 1995.

and I, and I met Arrhenius and Ostwald. That was of course a great event. And then Arrhenius asked me if I wouldn't come in the fall and work a little bit in his laboratory. By that time he had started to work on radiochemistry.

Then, it must have been in the spring of 1911, I met [Arrhenius's deputy] and he asked if I didn't want to make some little work. I did that in my free time from school.[1]

It led to Klein's first paper, published when he was 18, dealing with the solubility of zinc hydroxide in alkalis.[3]

When still in high school, Klein began reading books on physics, Lorentz's *Lectures on Theoretical Physics* ('I hardly knew the word at that time'), Helmholtz on mechanics. Arrhenius lent him Rutherford's book (in English) on radioactive transformations. 'Physics and chemistry, these things I learned mostly by myself, [also] later at the University. I learned a good bit of mathematics studying by myself in the same way . . . I got used to doing things my own way.'[1]

In 1912 Klein finished high school and started his University studies. In the spring of 1914 he finished his examination for *fil. cand.* Whereupon Arrhenius wrote a letter to Jean Perrin, asking whether Klein could work a year with him in Paris. Klein actually went to France to improve his French but soon had to return to Sweden when the First World War broke out. From June 1915– September 1916 he did his military service, then went back to Arrhenius as *amanuens* (scientific assistant). In April 1917 he completed a 48-page paper on his measurements of dielectric constants of alcohols in various solvents.[4]

In the autumn of that year the young Dutch physicist Hendrik Kramers (Hans to his friends, which were to include Klein and myself) came to Stockholm from Copenhagen. He had come to Denmark in 1916, as the first of more than 400 foreign visitors who would spend at least one month under the tutelage of Niels Bohr in his lifetime. (Kramers actually stayed ten years.)

Kramers came to Arrhenius's institute and we had some private talks together . . . about quantization, the adiabatic principle, that kind of thing . . . I don't remember when I first heard of Bohr's papers. I think it was in my second University year, in the fall of 1913 . . . When one first heard about the quantum it was very mysterious . . . Then after I began to read a little. I understood a little on the formal side, but my insight into the physics was very vague. I read a bit of those quantization papers of Sommerfeld and Schwarzschild.[1]

Those readings occurred during Klein's last year (1917–18) at Arrhenius's laboratory. 'I was amazed by Bohr's explanation of the Rydberg constant. But I was far from understanding the deep background of this result, being more impressed by the explicitly mathematical papers of Sommerfeld, Einstein, and Debye.'[5]

Then Arrhenius's son, a friend of Klein, had him apply for a fellowship for studies abroad, which was granted. 'I chose primarily Einstein and Debye . . . but since Bohr was so near I wrote to him first.'[5] Meanwhile he had published an article on the freezing points of binary solutions of electrolytes.[6]

In Klein's first letter ever to Bohr, dated March 27, 1918, he tells of his interest in quantum physics and of his desire to work under Bohr's guidance, asking if Bohr receives pupils from abroad. A week later Bohr replied that he would be very happy to see him in Copenhagen, adding that 'It will be a great pleasure to give you whatever counsel I can give regarding your studies.'[7] Klein thanked Bohr,[8] noting that he had to do military service in the autumn and telling him of his recent publication.[6] It may be noted that Klein's first few letters to Bohr were in Swedish, thereafter he would forever write him in good Danish. Just before Klein left for Denmark he completed a minor paper[9] which is of interest, however, since it deals with X-ray scattering, a subject on which he would make such important contributions a decade later.

When Klein arrived in Copenhagen in May 1918, as the second foreigner to come work with Bohr, he did not proceed to Bohr's institute on Blegdamsvej for the simple reason that it did not yet exist. Copenhagen University had in fact no physics institute of any kind whatever at that time. Shortly after May 5, 1916, when Bohr's appointment as Denmark's first professor in theoretical physics came through, he was housed, for the next four years, in a small office of less than 150 square feet in the Polytekniske Læreanstalt at Sølvtorvet (now called the Technical University of Denmark). Initially he had to share this small space with Kramers. When Klein arrived, he had to work in the library adjoining Bohr's office, as did Adalbert Rubinowicz, the Pole, and Svein Rosseland , the Norwegian astrophysicist, who both came in 1920. The grounds for the Bohr institute which we know and love were in fact bought from the Copenhagen *Kommune* (Municipality) in August 1918, during Klein's first visit.

In reflecting on Bohr's contributions to physics, one must never forget that he took the initiative, supervised the building, raised the funds for, and by himself administered an institute which in the 1920s and 30s was *the* Mecca of theoretical physics.

During Klein's first stay, 'I learned a great deal from Kramers—which he had gotten in turn from Bohr. I heard from Bohr largely generalities and I had not much occasion to see him at that time.'[1] (Bohr had then of course his hands full with the installation of his new institute.) Klein has remembered the great hospitality with which Bohr and his wife received him in their home in Hellerup.

Upon his return to Stockholm in September, Klein wrote to Bohr,[10] thanking him for his stay, and mentioning that he was about ready with his paper on the 'virial work' dealing with osmotic pressure in electrolytes[11], work showing how well versed he was in statistical mechanics. Bohr's reply,[12] a 14-page letter, makes clear how seriously he took Klein's work, as is also seen from Klein's acknowledgment of gratitude to Bohr for 'valuable counsel.'

In December Klein reports to Bohr that Kramers will come for a visit and will teach him quantum theory. He hopes he has not bothered Bohr too much with all his stupidities. After Kramers came, in January 1919, the two men took off for a skiing trip in Dalarna, a region in middle Sweden. And, of course, they discussed physics, notably the idea that the separation of the Hamilton–Jacobi equation (an important tool for quantization techniques) was only possible in elliptic coordinates. 'We managed to get something done on this problem but nothing was published.'[1] (Klein worked on this question from 1919–21. An unpublished fragment of this research is in the NBA.) By that time he had also begun to think about a topic for his PhD thesis.[13]

From June until late November 1919 Klein was in Copenhagen again.

> Bohr put me first on some problems about ring molecules. The results were negative. But, of course, it was a good experience. I had occasion to talk to Bohr during those times. And I got a very much stronger impression of Bohr himself, and his way of reasoning which made an enormous impression on me . . .
>
> I also remember that Bohr took me on a rather long walk in the north of Sjælland, and then he told me a bit of his general ideas, both on physics and on general philosophy, including his father's ideas on teleology . . . He mentioned that the use of [classical] mechanics was provisional and that it was very strange that one should be able to quantize by means of mechanical orbits . . . The rest of us also very soon got it, i.e., that the whole thing is not satisfying as it is. One should see how far one could go with [classical] mechanics, but there were obvious limits.[1]

Bohr's scientific work in those years was mainly concerned with what, some years later, he called the correspondence principle.

In the summer of 1919 Klein became for the first time Bohr's closest collaborator. In the spring Kramers had gone to Leiden to take his doctor's degree, and then had remained in Holland, first for a holiday, and then because of illness. Bohr had joined Kramers in Leiden and had given a lecture (in English) on his recent work, which he wanted to rework upon his return. Klein had to help him do that. He has described how they worked together.

> The place where we worked was a hired room not far from the country house where Bohr and his family stayed during this and some of the following summers before they moved into their own house at Tisvilde Hegn. With some writing paper and a pencil in front of me I was placed at a table around which Bohr wandered, alternately dictating in English and explaining in Danish, while I tried to get the English text onto paper. Sometimes there were long interruptions either

for pondering over what was to follow, or because Bohr had thought about something outside the theme which he had to tell me about . . . Often, also, work was
interrupted by short running trips or cycling to the shore together with the family
for bathing.

The aim of the dictation was a presentation of the essence of the quantum theory of atoms and molecules. The Leiden lecture was never published, however. Its
contents were included in a later paper written in connection with a lecture in
Berlin the following spring.

In the fall of 1919 Klein went to Lund to attend a small conference where Bohr
and Arnold Sommerfeld lectured. 'Then we thought that Bohr saw so much
deeper than Sommerfeld but I [now] think, like young people often do, we
underestimated Sommerfeld.'[1] After Klein's return to Stockholm, he received a
letter from Bohr, who was pleased that he (K.) had enjoyed his stay. So did he.[15]

'Around New Year 1920 Bohr went with me and some of my Swedish friends
on a skiing tour to Dalarna, where he impressed everybody by his practical ability. This occasioned the following amusing compliment (in Swedish) by one of
the company: "The only criterion that the professor is a professor is that the
professor always forgets his gloves."'[14] Afterward Bohr wrote to Klein, thanking
him for his stay in their family home, and telling him how happy he was to have
met Klein's mother.[16]

Also in 1920 Klein spent some time in Copenhagen.[17] During that visit he collaborated with Rosseland on a paper dealing with the statistical equilibrium of
a mixture of atoms and free electrons. At issue was the theoretical interpretation
of the famous experiments by James Franck and Gustav Heitz on electron–atom
collisions,[18] which, these authors had shown, lead to processes

larger electron energy $\rightarrow$ atomic excitation energy + lower electron energy

Klein has recalled:

> One morning when we were sitting in the library of the Læreanstalt, Rosseland
> began to talk about it. He wondered how there could be temperature equilibrium.
> Then it occurred to me how one could formulate it . . . in analogy with Einstein's
> paper [of 1917 on a mixture of atoms and electromagnetic radiation]. Then in the
> evening Bohr had taken me to the theatre . . . and I told him about this . . . And he
> advised that Rosseland and I should publish together.[19]

Which they did.[20] It is Klein's first contribution of substance, purely theoretical
and of lasting importance. Their point is this. It was believed until then that
electrons colliding with atoms always lose energy. But, they note, that cannot be
since it would violate the second law of thermodynamics. Their saving remark
is to introduce 'collisions of the second kind,' according to which an electron
gains rather than loses energy in colliding with an atom, the latter making a
transition to a lower stationary state, that is, the same process displayed above

but with the direction of the arrow reversed. The successful application of this concept to atomic, molecular, and celestial physics considerably enhanced Klein's reputation.

I may mention the application which I consider the most spectacular. In the 1860s lines were discovered in the spectra of nebulae which indicated the presence of an unknown substance, assumed to be a new element, named nebulium. References to this otherwise elusive element are found in the literature for more than 60 years—until in 1927 it became clear that the mysterious lines were actually due to transitions from metastable states of nitrogen and oxygen.[21] Why had these lines never been seen on earth? Because under terrestrial conditions pressures are higher and these states lose energy more readily through collisions of the second kind!

The Klein–Rosseland paper has the honor to be the first ever to be published under the byline *Institut f. teoretisk Fysik*, even though that Institute did not yet formally exist. The byline is dated November 17, 1920, but the Institute was only formally inaugurated on March 3, 1921.

Klein's next work was his doctor's thesis.

> I was then toiling with the forces between ions in strong electrolytes, trying to apply Gibbsian statistical mechanics to these problems; and Bohr showed me his deeper view of this subject, telling me how Gibbs' general canonical distribution gave the very definition of temperature. All this meant a new epoch for me, and an essentially happy one, although I had more troubles than results from my own work, which, however, led to my thesis on generalized Brownian motion, meant as a foundation for a theory of solutions of interacting particles.[19]

In this work Klein built further on earlier work by Einstein and Marian von Smoluchowski. He acknowledged Arrhenius and Bohr 'for the benevolent interest with which they have guided my studies during several years.'[22]

On May 25, 1921, at ten in the morning, Klein began the defense of this thesis. His opponents included Ivar Fredholm, the distinguished Swedish mathematician, and Kramers.

> I never liked such official things, but mine was very easy. First of all, Kramers was an old friend of mine, so we had a quite lively discussion. Professor Fredholm was very kind and nice, so there was not much opposition . . . Often at these times one had a very official dinner [but we had mine] at home. We were living outside of Stockholm in a villa, and that was very nice.[23]

In September 1921 Klein came to Copenhagen again, for a year this time. Bohr asked him to make some calculations on van der Waals forces. 'That was a very difficult mathematical problem, . . . that went very very slowly.'[23] This work was not published.

At that time Bohr himself was immersed (as he had been since 1920) in attempts at understanding the periodic table of elements. By then it had become obvious, not least through efforts by Bohr and Kramers, that the successes in understanding the spectrum of hydrogen could not be extended to heavier atoms. Already helium was a mess—not surprising since neither Pauli's exclusion principle nor spin were yet known. Whereupon Bohr decided to concentrate on atomic *ground states* only, that is, on the interpretation of the periodic table. In June 1922 he went to Göttingen to give seven lectures on these matters, an event later called the Bohr *Festspiele* (festival). It was a great event in Klein's life to be present. He has written:

> I must abstain from mentioning all the distinguished physicists, old and young, who were present at Bohr's lectures, where I had accompanied him as his assistant; to do so would make an almost homeric ship's catalogue. Bohr, who had earlier met with considerable criticism and lack of understanding, had at this time become one to whom all listened with reverence, so that the discussions about the lectures were rather concerned with whether Bohr had meant this or that, than the matter itself.[14]

After their return, Bohr wrote to Klein thanking him for his help on their joint journey, adding that he was happy to hear that Klein had enjoyed it too.[24]

Among the physicists Klein met for the first time in Göttingen were Pauli and Ehrenfest. We owe to Klein one of the best Pauli stories:

> During those Göttingen days Ehrenfest and Pauli also met for the first time. From that time dates the first story of their [P. and E.'s] 'war of jokes' which concerned a very original, profound, but also very controversial article on statistical mechanics which Ehrenfest and his wife had written for the *Enzyklopädie der Mathematischen Wissenschaften*. On that occasion, Ehrenfest stood a little away from Pauli, looked at him mockingly and said: 'Herr Pauli, I like your article better than I like you! [Pauli had written the article on relativity for that same *Enzyklopädie*]. To which Pauli very calmly replied: 'That is funny, with me it is just the opposite!'[25]

In December 1922 Bohr was in Stockholm to receive the Nobel Prize. Klein was there and has remembered: 'At the obligatory lecture, for which he had chosen to talk about the constitution of atoms, he discovered that he had forgotten his notes and slides at the hotel, so he had to begin without them, while they were fetched. This, however, was rather an advantage, because it forced him to improvise, such as he did in private conversations.'[14]

We have now reached a turning point in Klein's activities.

Firstly, 1922 marks the beginning of Klein's semi-popular writings on physics, the first of its kind being essays on Bohr's theory of the atom,[26] the second on the discovery of hafnium.[27] Shortly afterward he published his first paper on philosophical issues, a refutation of objections to relativity theory by Swedish philosophers.[28]

Secondly, Klein began looking for a job. He first tried Stockholm.

> I gave one series of two lectures a week on atomic theory where I tried to give a review of Bohr's theory, and one series on statistical thermodynamics. So it was rather hard work; I had to do, practically, the reading and writing at the same time. I hoped that I should get a position as lecturer, dozent, in Stockholm, but they had no money.[23]

In November Klein wrote to Bohr[29] that he had applied for a docentship in Lund. He did go there but

> in Lund I had no real position. I was promised five thousand kronor a year, but also for a rather uncertain period . . . [Then I asked Bohr] if he thought there might be a possibility for some position at an English university. Bohr said that he didn't believe that there would be because now they had many people in England. But he said that he had just been asked by an American theoretical physicist if he could think of someone willing to have a position in Ann Arbor. He hadn't thought of me because he thought I had my things arranged and wanted to stay in Sweden. He didn't know that conditions were very uncertain. Then he said that he would propose me.[23]

Which Bohr did. In a statement[30] in support of Klein's application for a scholarship to go to America, he wrote that he knew Klein's work intimately, and that Klein was 'an uncommonly talented young physicist. One is justified in having great expectations of his future scientific activities.'

Thirdly, there is an approximate rule which says that a male physicist who has spent more than one year in Denmark will marry a Danish girl. (I myself am a case in point.) The first to do so was Kramers, the second Klein. On August 15, 1923, he was in Aarhus to marry Gerda Agnete Koch, daughter of a medical doctor, who had studied Danish literature at the University of Copenhagen. The young couple derived great delight from the groom's descent from a rabbi, whereas the bride could count bishops and priests among her ancestry. They were to have six children.

When, in September 1923, the newlyweds took off for Ann Arbor, Michigan, where Klein was to teach, the quantum theory was in deep crisis. One major difficulty was that no one understood the behavior of atoms in a magnetic field. Klein has recalled a wonderful story. 'Pauli told me of that time when he was walking in Copenhagen and dejected and thinking of [this so-called] anomalous Zeeman effect, and suddenly he heard a deep, earnest voice behind him say 'Think of the Lord.' It was one of those street corner preachers.'[19]

It is not sufficiently known that Klein himself made an important contribution toward deepening the crisis. That work dealt with the action of crossed electric and magnetic forces on a hydrogen atom. He found that in this case the theory allowed for transitions between 'allowed' and 'forbidden' quantum orbits, which was bad. 'When Bohr came to Ann Arbor in early December 1923, I told him about it and he got very interested.'[23] In early January Klein sent his manuscript to Bohr, who informed him[31] that, 'after having made some minor corrections, he had sent it to the *Zeitschrift für Physik*.'[32] The difficulty raised by Klein was resolved soon after the discovery of quantum mechanics.

In his reply to Bohr's last letter,[33] Klein wrote that he had decided to stay for another academic year, when his salary would be increased. The family was about 'to move into a small house where we shall live all by ourselves.' He told Bohr of his current work on the interaction between the rotation of a diatomic molecule and a precessing electronic angular momentum within the molecule.[34]

Klein also mentioned that he was 'extremely anxious to learn about the new work on radiation.' This refers to the ill-fated attempt[35] by Bohr, Kramers, and John Slater (BKS) to avoid the introduction of photons, an issue that had become topical because of the discovery of the Compton effect in 1923. In June 1924 Klein wrote Bohr again,[36] telling him of the birth of his first son, of teaching summer school on atomic theory, and of being engrossed in the BKS paper. In August he wrote to Kramers[37] that his 'book on light'[38] had just been sent off.

<hr />

While in Ann Arbor, Klein conceived the idea for what has become known as the Kaluza–Klein theory. I confine myself here to a few brief historical remarks about its origins.

The mathematician and consummate linguist Theodor Kaluza was the first to suggest that unification of gravitation and electromagnetism might be achieved by extending space-time to a five-dimensional manifold. He must have had that idea already in 1919, for in that year Einstein wrote to him: 'The idea . . . of a five dimensional cylinder world would never have dawned on me . . . At first glance I like your idea enormously[39] . . . the formal unity of your theory is startling.'[40] In 1921 he communicated Kaluza's work to the Prussian *Akademie der Wissenschaften*.[41]

Klein did not start working along these lines until 1924, and did not publish[42,43] until 1926. It was not until that year that he first heard of Kaluza.

> When Pauli came to Copenhagen [in early 1926], I showed him my manuscript
> on five-dimensional theory and after reading it he told me that Kaluza some years
> before had published a similar idea in a paper I had missed. So I looked it up . . .
> and quoted it in the paper I then wrote in a spirit of resignation . . . In the paper I
> tried to rescue what I could from the shipwreck.[5]

It might have cheered him had he known what Einstein wrote to Ehrenfest shortly afterward: 'Klein's paper is beautiful and impressive, but I find Kaluza's principle too unnatural.'[44] I have explained elsewhere the relative merits of the two authors and the technical details of their work.[45] Here I only note briefly that Kaluza completely suppressed any dependence on the fifth coordinate, nor did he ask why we have not seen a fifth dimension if there is one. Klein, on the other hand, took the extra dimension seriously, assuming it to have a circular topology, so that the fifth coordinate is periodic.

In the late 1960s Klein told how his active interest in unified field theory arose:

> [In the autumn of 1924] I gave a lecture course on electromagnetism, towards the end of which I derived the general relativistic Hamilton-Jacobi equation for an electric particle moving in a combined gravitational and electromagnetic field. Thereby, the similarity struck me between the ways the electromagnetic potentials and the Einstein gravitational potentials enter into this equation, the electric charge in appropriate units appearing as the analogue to a [fifth] momentum component, the whole looking like a wave front equation in a space of [five] dimensions. This led me into a whirlpool of speculation, from which I did not detach myself for several years and which still has a certain attraction for me.
>
> I became immediately very eager . . . to find out whether the Maxwell equations for the electromagnetic field together with Einstein's gravitational equations would fit into a formalism of five-dimensional Riemann geometry (correspond-ing to four space dimensions plus time) like the four-dimensional formalism of Einstein. It did not take me a long time to prove this in the linear approximation, assuming a five-equation, according to which an electric particle describes a five-dimensional geodesic.[5]

In the summer of 1925 Klein succeeded in going beyond the linear approxi-mation. He found that the usual energy–momentum four-vector had become a five-vector of energy–momentum–electric charge; and that space in the fifth dimension is a closed circle with a circumference of about 10^{-30} centimeters.

I turn next to the influence of Klein's unification theory on his ideas about quantum physics. This is the most complex scientific thinking of his career. As he has recalled:

> The strong impressions this [unification] made on me came from the attempt to find a wave background to the quantization rules . . . [5] In earlier years Bohr him-self—and that played a role for me—had said that since you cannot get a connect-ed picture of quantum phenomena and four dimensions that maybe you could in a higher number of dimensions . . .[46] [This reference to Bohr explains the other-wise mysterious footnote in ref. 42, p. 906.]
>
> I remember I was thinking of the fifth dimension already in the summer [of 1922] in Goettingen . . . [*In the autumn of 1924] I had the main idea of wave mechanics.* [My italics.] It was only a sketch on a few sheets of paper, but I could not find it later on when I wanted to find it. It may have been left in Ann Arbor . . . Then I was trying to find the stationary states of the harmonic oscillator. But I knew too little about the mathematics there, so I had not found it when Schrödinger's work came about the hydrogen atom.[23]

In his published papers Klein has summarized his quantum ideas like this: 'The new quantum mechanics of Schrödinger can be derived from a wave equation in a five dimensional space . . . the origin of Planck's constant may be sought in the periodicity in the fifth dimension.'[43]

In June 1926 Klein reported to Bohr[42] on his visit to Leiden, telling that Ehrenfest was pleased with his lectures on five dimensions. Uhlenbeck, who was in the audience, later told me: 'I remember that when Klein told us of his ideas which would not only unify the Maxwell with the Einstein equations but also bring in the quantum theory, I felt a kind of ecstasy! Now one understands the world!' Klein's Leiden lectures stimulated Uhlenbeck and Ehrenfest to publish a paper on the 'Graphic visualization of the de Broglie phase waves in the five-dimensional world of O. Klein.'[48]

Klein himself continued brooding about his five-dimensional theory. His fine article, submitted in December 1926,[49] dealing with the application of wave mechanics to electrodynamics with the help of the correspondence principle, ends with comments on wave mechanics in five dimensions. Which led Pauli to write to Bohr: 'I cannot refrain from congratulating you for having brought Klein so far that he has only touched briefly on the fifth dimension in the concluding section.'[50] Four months later, Pauli again to Bohr: 'Many regards to Klein. From the bottom of my heart I wish speedy recovery for his physics.'[51]

Klein kept going, however. In 1927 he submitted a long paper on his five-dimensional theory in which he explained that this formalism unifies five conservation laws: three of the components of momentum, one of energy and one of electric charge.[52] Also in later years one finds Klein returning to these ideas, now here, now there. In his own words: 'After a short attack of 'five-dimensional' in the summer of 1933,[53] I had a more violent one in 1937, when I gave a paper[54] at a conference in Warsaw in 1938,'[5] to which I shall come back later. Klein's next mention of five dimensions that I have found occurs another 20 years later (1957), in a discussion of charge conjugation and parity non-invariance.[55]

It would appear, therefore, that during all of Klein's life the fifth dimension was one of his favorite toys. Yet when in 1969, at age 75, he looked back on his work in an address 'From a life in physics,'[5] he recalled how at Easter time of 1927, when he and Pauli were in Copenhagen, the two of them drank a bottle of wine on the death of the fifth dimension. Add to this his comment, also made in 1969: 'Dirac may well say that my main trouble came from trying to solve too many problems [to wit, the geometrizations of electromagnetism as well as of the quantum theory] at a time,'[5] and one must conclude that, toward the end of his life, Klein repudiated all he had written on this subject since 1927!! Modern string theorists, who believe that many-dimensional theories will lead to the holy grail, may like to reflect on Klein's change of heart.

I return to the summer of 1925, when the Kleins returned from America to Denmark. In June Klein wrote to Bohr of his plans to come to Copenhagen that autumn.[56] In September he wrote again: he had been ill with flu, followed by infectious hepatitis.[57] He was really quite sick. In December, Mrs Klein wrote Bohr[58] that her husband was still in hospital but 'much better now.'

In January Klein himself wrote again, from his home this time, that he was feeling much better and had meanwhile read the papers of Heisenberg, Born, and Jordan.[59] During Klein's forced absence from physics, its frontiers had made major moves. Quantum mechanics had been discovered, in matrix form by Heisenberg (July 1925) in wave language by Schrödinger (January 1926).

The Copenhagen scene had changed too. Kramers, appointed *Lektor* (associate professor) in Copenhagen in 1923, left in March 1926 to become professor in Utrecht. He was succeeded in May 1926 by Heisenberg, who was to hold that position until June 1927. Heisenberg, the most independent personality in the Copenhagen entourage, was not a suitable character to succeed Kramers as Bohr's most intimate collaborator. That task fell to Klein after his arrival in March 1926, for a stay that was to last five years. Thus it came to pass that he became the most important eye witness to the birth of complementarity.

In the fall of 1926 physicists had begun to become accustomed to calculate with matrix mechanics, a particle picture, and with the Schrödinger theory, a wave picture. The mathematical equivalence of these two pictures was known by then, but the deeper physical connection between these two languages was still unclear. That was the situation when, in October of that year, Schrödinger came to Copenhagen to discuss his ideas with Bohr, in the presence of Heisenberg, who wrote later: 'No real understanding could be expected since, at the time, neither was able to offer a complete and coherent picture of quantum mechanics.'[60]

After Schrödinger's departure, Bohr and Heisenberg continued to struggle with the interpretation of quantum mechanics but, however hard they tried, they could not come to a common opinion. Heisenberg has recalled:

> We talked back and forth about these problems and sometimes got a bit impatient with each other about it. I would perhaps try to say, 'Well, this is the answer.' Then Bohr gave the contradictions would say, 'No, it can't be the answer,' and so on . . .
> In the end, shortly after Christmas, we both were in a kind of despair. In some way we couldn't agree and so we were a bit angry about it[61] . . . Both of us became utterly exhausted and rather tense. Hence Bohr decided in February 1927 to go skiing in Norway, and I was quite glad to be left behind in Copenhagen, where I could think undisturbed about these hopelessly complicated problems.[62]

Klein has left us his impressions of Bohr's state of mind as he left for Norway:

He was very tired that time and I believe that the new quantum mechanics caused him both pleasure and very great tension. He had probably not expected that all this would come so suddenly but rather that he himself perhaps might have contributed more at that time. At the same time he praised Heisenberg almost like a kind of Messiah and I think that Heisenberg himself understood that that was a bit exaggerated.[63]

Right after Bohr's departure for Norway, Heisenberg, now in peace and quiet in Copenhagen, made one of his greatest discoveries: the uncertainty relations. When Bohr came back from Norway, Heisenberg showed him the paper he had written on this subject. According to Klein: 'Bohr read the paper and was at first very taken with it but when he began to look more closely he became very disappointed,'[63] because he saw that there was a serious error in the paper, not in its general conclusions but in the way Heisenberg had treated the example of detecting the electron's position with a γ-ray microscope. According to Heisenberg:

Bohr tried to explain that it was not right and I shouldn't publish the paper. I remember that it ended by my breaking out in tears because I just couldn't stand this pressure from Bohr . . .

So actually Bohr went out to the country for reasons I don't know. And I also went to the country to a different place. I remember that Bohr and I once met while we were out walking—the two places are not very far from each other. I don't know whether we agreed to meet or whether we met by coincidence, but there was Bohr and Oskar Klein on the one side and I was on the other side and the three of us had a discussion.

In the last stages [of the discussion], say around February and March, Klein was very much involved. But in some way I would feel that Oskar Klein thought it was his duty, being an old friend of Bohr, that he must defend Bohr against the young man Heisenberg. Perhaps it was also a bit of an issue of who finally clarified the whole thing and so on. So Klein wanted to help Bohr and I was perhaps sometimes a bit too harsh and too quick with saying something, I don't know. So Klein took part quite frequently in these discussions and also helped to clarify. After all, he's a very good physicist . . . I think besides Bohr, Klein and myself there was nobody in these discussions; only Pauli by correspondence.[61]

Klein has remembered: 'Both the results and the failures in Heisenberg's work became a source of inspiration to Bohr, and from then he worked almost day and night on these questions.'[64]

That work had in fact already begun while Bohr was in Norway. During that skiing vacation he had conceived his first ideas on complementarity. The task of assisting Bohr in composing a paper on this new concept fell to Klein.

Bohr began eagerly . . . in April, and then we went to [the Bohr summer house in] Tisvilde . . . and Bohr dictated and the next day all he had dictated was discarded and we began anew. And so it went all summer and after a time Mrs Bohr became unhappy . . . one time when I sat alone in the little room where we worked she came in crying . . . and then Bohr had to go to the Como meeting and then, under strong pressure by his brother Harald, he really tried to get an article written down.[63]

Bohr presented his views on September 16, 1927 at the meeting held in Como on the occasion of the centenary of the death of Alessandro Volta. The manuscript of his lecture appears to be lost but many drafts of his paper have been preserved in the Niels Bohr Archive, nearly all in Klein's handwriting. Let Heisenberg have the last word: 'We concluded, not least thanks to Oskar Klein's participation, that the uncertainty relations were just a special case of the more general complementarity principle.'[65]

This episode brought Bohr and Klein and their families very close. Bohr's oldest son has recalled: 'Memories of our childhood are linked with many 'uncles' of various nationalities, among them . . . Uncle Klein.'[66] When Heisenberg left Copenhagen in June 1927 for a professorship in Leipzig, Klein became his successor as *Lektor*. He also continued to assist Bohr and even wrote letters in his behalf.[67]

Already during the Bohr–Heisenberg episode, Kramers had advised Klein: 'Do not enter this conflict, we are both much too kind and gentle to participate in that kind of struggle.'[68] Both Klein and his wife have insisted that Klein did his most original and daring work when Bohr was away from Copenhagen.[68]

Be that as it may, Klein did his best physics by far in his Copenhagen years from 1926–29. Several of the articles he produced in that period will forever be known by his name.

1. I already mentioned his paper, completed in December 1926,[49] in which he determined atomic transition probabilities before Dirac did so in a more satisfactory way by quantizing the electromagnetic field. *The first section of that paper contains his relativistic scalar wave equation, since known as the Klein–Gordon equation.*

    The physicist Stanley Deser, a son-in-law of Klein, has recalled: 'Not getting credit for discovering the Schrödinger equation was the one injustice I have ever heard him complain of.'[69] I can well understand that feeling even though I do not agree. I accept of course Klein's recollection[23] that he already had the main idea of wave mechanics in 1924. I also understand his reason for not publishing at that time: 'I knew too little about the mathematics.'[23] But if you do not publish you cannot claim credit—that is the rule of the game. I may note incidentally that others besides Klein and, independently, Gordon,[70] should be remembered in connection with the discovery of the scalar wave equation.[71]

2. In 1927 Klein and Pascual Jordan introduced a novel method for dealing with those quantum–mechanical systems that obey Bose–Einstein statistics.[72] The fundamental

importance of their technique, known by the rather unfortunate name second quantization, has been emphasized by Heisenberg:

> Bohr's view of complementarity found a very impressive representation in the mathematical scheme of the quantum theory, when Jordan, Klein, and Wigner[73] were able to show that, starting from a simple (three-dimensional) theory of material waves in Schrödinger's sense, one could quantize this theory and so come back to the Hilbert space of quantum mechanics. The complete equivalence of the particle and the wave pictures in quantum theory was thus demonstrated for the first time.[74]

Technically, Jordan and Klein treated the wave function of a *single* particle as a *field* which in turn should be subject to the laws of quantum mechanics. Their method has not only provided basic tools in elementary particle theories but is also of great importance in solid state physics.

3. In October 1928, Klein and Yoshio Nishina finished their paper[75] on the Compton scattering of a photon by a Dirac electron. Douglas Hartree wrote to Klein[76] of the great interest in this work in Cambridge, mentioning that Rutherford had referred to their paper in his presidential address[77] to the Royal Society.

   This work led to a correspondence with Lise Meitner in Berlin, who had found experimental deviations from the Klein–Nishina results.[78] (This was known for some time as the Meitner–Hupfeld effect.[79]) After those were understood, it became evident that the 'Klein–Nishina formula' was in fact a major success of the Dirac theory. It has been said, fittingly I think, that the derivation of this formula 'was, in its day, as heroic a deed as any of the radiative correction calculations of the late 1940s and—unlike many of those—it was done right the first time.'[69]

4. It was Klein again who, two months later, pointed out serious trouble for the Dirac theory—as it was understood in 1929: electrons moving in steep, strong electric potentials appeared to be reflected such that they accelerate in the direction opposite to the applied force![80]

   It appears that Klein stumbled on this bizarre effect, still known as the 'Klein paradox,' during his work with Nishina on Compton scattering. I deduce this from a letter Pauli wrote to Bohr: 'Klein should absolutely publish immediately his considerations of the autumn [of 1928] about the reflections according to the Dirac theory!'[81] One month later, Pauli to Klein: 'It is simply scandalous and shows lack of consideration for those of your fellow men engaged in physics that you still have not published your considerations about the curious reflections of electrons.'[82] Pauli's pressure on Klein to publish his paradox stemmed of course from his (P.'s) belief at that time that the Dirac theory was wrong.

   The year 1929 marks the beginning of a fairly steady correspondence between Klein and Pauli, no doubt initiated because of the former's growing interest in quantum electrodynamics[49] and in the Dirac theory, subjects of abiding interest to Pauli. Much of what Pauli had to say about Klein had been critical up till that time, as noted. Those comments reflect on Pauli's role as the conscience of physics, and should not be confused with his personal feelings. Thus, in early 1930 Pauli ended a letter to Klein like this: 'Most cordially, your old friend W.P.'[83]

5. The fifth and last of this group of Copenhagen papers, not as well known as the others, impresses me because it shows the width of Klein's interests and his versatility in handling theoretical techniques. It deals with a new method for handling the quantum theory of the asymmetric top, a molecule without rotational symmetry,[84] a problem already complex classically. Klein tackled it with the help of the correspondence principle, demonstrating that, in his words, 'In Copenhagen people would claim that they could "quantize your grandmother."'[69]

In 1929 Klein applied for Fredholm's chair in Stockholm, vacant after his death in 1927. Sommerfeld wrote a letter of recommendation, as did Bohr,[85] who stated that he had known Klein since 1918, and had at once been impressed by his inventiveness, his scientific enthusiasm, and his indefatigable struggles with difficult problems. Bohr went on to note that when Klein went to the US, he had, like few others, a firm grasp of atomic theory, both qua content and limitations, and stressed Klein's selfless help to others, and in the education of students. Klein won the position and in January 1931 went to Stockholm as professor in mechanics and mathematical physics. After 1945 he also taught at the Institute for artillery officers and engineers. In 1951 he became, in addition, director of the Institute of Physics in Oslo. In 1953 he was elected member of the Nobel committee on physics.

Shortly before arriving in Stockholm, Klein had received a letter from his good friend Pauli which read in part:

> You have now arrived at the goal of our social class, are *Oberbonze* [big shot] in Stockholm, and can from now on live as a middle class bourgeois, free of material cares . . . Now you only need to pray to the God of the middle class that he will forever protect your bank account . . . I would hardly congratulate you, however, if these were the only prospects which your Stockholm professorship offer you and your fellow citizens. Actually I can do so in good conscience, however, since I hope that you will now fulfill the words: 'Go and *teach* the people.' Your great pedagogical ability was always one of your strongest suits and for this there will be a broad area of application in Sweden. Until now there was practically almost no theoretical physics in Sweden . . . a mismatch compared with experimental physics which is so brilliantly represented by Manne Siegbahn and Erik Hulthén. Now one needs in Sweden a person familiar with *modern* theoretical physics who should add to the great school of Swedish experimental physicists an equally good one of theoreticians. If you were to succeed in doing that—which I not only hope but even consider probable—then you will be entitled to be quite satisfied and will no longer have to worry about the God of the middle class nor about the fifth dimension (or similar topics).
>
> This last comment leads me to review your activities in pure research up till now . . . I am not of the opinion that finding new laws of nature and indicating new directions is one of your great strengths, although you have always developed

a certain ambition in this direction . . . I find much more beautiful those of your papers which deal with applications of known theories, without such kinds of ambitions, such as for example the one on crossed [electric and magnetic] fields,[32] potential barriers in the Dirac theory,[80] the paper with Nishina about the new scattering formula,[75] etc. . . . May this series of papers continue beautifully for a long time (*in spite* of the professorships which will put other demands on your time).

This wise letter, written with Pauli's customary frankness, has given us an appreciation by a contemporary—though one might perhaps not guess that Pauli was six years younger—of the strengths and weaknesses not only of Klein but also of Swedish physics. Of all the letters the two men exchanged during a quarter century of correspondence, this one is the finest.

———————

In the early years following his arrival in Stockholm, Klein continued his fine work in diverse areas of physics. First, in 1931, came his fundamental paper[87] on the young discipline of quantum statistical mechanics (its beginnings date from the late 1920s). Modifying the expression of entropy to take account of the quantum mechanical uncertainty relations he provided the quantum mechanical version for the second law of thermodynamics. His proof is now called the Klein lemma (Klein's belief that thermodynamic irreversibility is specifically of quantum origin is not correct, however).

In 1932 Klein worked on the derivation of the intramolecular potential of diatomic molecules from spectroscopical information,[88] improving and considerably enlarging on earlier results. The method, still widely used in spectroscopical analysis, is now called the RKR method.[89]

In 1933 he worked out a recursion procedure for one-dimensional quantum–mechanical problems that yields the quasi-mechanical answer in first approximation.[90]

In those years Klein continued to keep in close contact with Bohr. In 1931 he sent him his paper on the second law of thermodynamics,[91] while Bohr asked Klein[92] to join him in being opponent in the thesis defense of Christian Møller. In 1932 Klein thanked Bohr for the recent instructive Copenhagen conference[93] and, in December, spent a few weeks with Bohr in Carlsberg.[94]

In 1933 Klein wrote to Bohr: 'Also in Sweden we are terrified by the conditions in Germany.'[97] Klein even thought of moving his family to the U.S.[69] Recurrent letters tell of his attempts to help refugee physicists.[98] One of these was Walter Gordon, who had been a professor of physics in Hamburg until his dismissal in 1933. Klein helped to provide funds for him so that he could resettle in Stockholm. There Gordon died in 1939 'after a period of serious suffering.'[99] Klein was also good friends with Lise Meitner, another German émigré who had settled in Stockholm.

Klein's researches in the later 1930s produced two memorable results. Firstly, the so-called Klein transformation, which states that one has the freedom of making independent fermion fields either commute or anticommute.[100] Secondly, in a paper[54] presented in Warsaw in 1938, he anticipated some, but not all, aspects of the Yang–Mills theory of 1954. (Unfortunately the presentation is obscured by elements of his five-dimensional ideas.) He wrote to Bohr to ask if his work could also be published in the *Physical Review*. 'As the subject is of current interest, I should not wait long with publication.'[101] I have not seen any reply by Bohr. Alas, this important paper has lain hidden for many years in a conference report. Also from that period date his sensitive obituary of Ehrenfest,[102] and his first paper on a historical topic dealing with seventeenth-century debates between physicists and philosophers.[103]

***

After the outbreak of the Second World War, Bohr managed, in 1940, to visit the Kleins in Stockholm,[104] but efforts failed to get Klein to Copenhagen in those years.[105] I have written elsewhere[106] about Klein's help during Bohr's escape from Denmark to Sweden in 1943.

***

It was in 1946, a year after the War, that I first met Klein, in the home of Niels Bohr, and also Klein's wife, a handsome, cheery woman. My first impressions of him were that he was a very gentle man, perhaps a bit shy. My only other recollection of that occasion is that we engaged in friendly conversation.

I met Klein again in 1949 at the Institute for Advanced Study in Princeton, when he spent the fall term there as visiting professor. (At that time I was professor there.) During those months we had a number of long conversations, as a result of which I came to know him much better. I recall in particular the evident pleasure with which he told me of a meeting he had had with Einstein.

Klein was 50 when the War ended. By then his best work lay behind him, as is only natural. Still, after 1940 he produced some 30 papers. In my opinion, the best of these is a short one he wrote in 1948, dealing with a simple relation between β-decay and the decay of the recently discovered muon.[107]

It is striking how much more varied are the subjects he addressed in this later work of his than those he had published on earlier. Thus, in the most complete published bibliography of his papers, given in ref. 108, we find papers on superconductivity;[109] biochemistry;[110] particle physics;[111] and on interwoven issues in general relativity;[112] stellar evolution;[113] and cosmology, notably his model worked out jointly with Hannes Afvén.[114]

Klein also wrote on other subjects: popular articles on nuclear physics;[115] atomic energy, after the War;[116] in honor of Bohr on his fiftieth, sixtieth, and seventieth birthdays;[117] an affectionate obituary of Pauli, who died in 1958 ('Pauli's unexpected death came as a heavy blow everywhere in the world where theoretical physics is practiced.'[25]). His interests in history are manifest in papers on the thirteenth-century scholar Jordanus Nemerarius,[118] on seventeenth-century science, already mentioned,[103] on Newton,[119] and on Pascal compared to Bohr.[120,121] His life-long interest in biology can be seen, for example, in the article 'Biology and atomic physics' which he contributed to *Svenska Dagbladet* of January 11, 1933. (It deals with Bohr's ideas on complementarity in biology, which are now obsolete.)

In mid-life, Klein wrote on philosophical issues.[122] He became particularly interested in possible analogies between science and religion. 'He wanted to show that the physical concepts of causality, relativity, and complementarity also had a relevance, even a parallel, in the ethical and religious sphere . . . Biblical ethics are highly relativistic, said Klein.'[123] In his own words: 'We have a formal equivalence between the biblical demand of equal rights for all men and the demand of the relativity principle that the role of all observers are equivalent independent of their state of motion, [a parallel] as close as one could wish.'[124] Such ideas caused Bohr to write to Klein[125] that he did not agree with his opinions on the Bible and modern science. (Neither do I.)

A few final comments.

Klein and Pauli corresponded until—as far as I have seen—November 1955, shortly before Pauli's death in 1958. Among his many letters I single out a few which I find particularly interesting.

On December 4, 1930, Pauli wrote his famous letter to a physics meeting in Tübingen, in which he proposed what became known as the neutrino hypothesis.[126] It speaks for his closeness to Klein in those years that the very first subsequent letter dealing with this subject was his one to Klein, sent off less than a week later, in which he communicates for the first time his thoughts on forces acting on this hypothetical particle.[127]

In the 1930s, Pauli himself became actively interested in more-dimensional relativity theory. In 1933 he published an alternative five-dimensional version, known as projective relativity theory.[128] In 1935 he wrote to Klein: 'I cannot decide whether to believe that the whole formalism should be accidental and physically meaningless.'[129]

In 1953 Pauli came back one more time to more dimensions. This time the *à propos* was of my own making. At a conference in Leiden (June 22–26, 1953) I had reported on my recent work which dealt with a *six*-dimensional theory.[130] Details are not relevant for present purposes, but I should note that Pauli, who also was in Leiden, became very interested, as is shown in his comment after my talk.[131] Back in Zurich, Pauli wrote to Klein: 'If there is something to this idea, then your [five-dimensional] is contained as a subspace in this [six-dimensional] space, so that a connection Kaluza–Klein–Pais would be established.'[132] That summer Pauli worked intensely on this six-dimensional proposal.[133] Klein's own last comment to Pauli that I have seen is in a draft letter dated June 8, 1954, available in the Niels Bohr Archive: 'I should like to find a Lagrange function which contains the good parts of the 5-dimensional theory without their shortcomings.'

In Bohr's last letter to Klein, he thanked him for his greetings on his 75th birthday.[134] In Klein's last letter to Bohr, he sent good wishes for the year 1961.[135] Bohr died in 1962. Klein wrote what may be called the official Swedish obituary. 'As the creator of new physics as well as personality he ranked among the greatest of our time.'[136]

In 1962 Klein retired from his professorship but continued to be scientifically active. In 1965 he received an honorary degree from Copenhagen. In the last year of his life his mind began to wander. He was 82 when, on February 5, 1977, he died of old age.[137] He was one of the most prominent Swedish physicists ever.

When, in 1969, Klein looked back on his life in science, he concluded with these words: 'A study of the history of science—not the history of philosophy— shows that the natural attitude of a scientist is to be inspired by the great predecessors, just as they themselves were by their predecessors, but always taking the liberty of doubting when there are reasons for doubt.'[5]

References

In what follows, NBA stands for Niels Bohr Archive in Copenhagen.

1. O. Klein, interview by T. S. Kuhn and J. L. Heibron, September 25, 1962, NBA.

2. O. Klein and J. Runnström, *Ark. f. Kemi, Mineralogi och Geologi* **14A**, No. 4, 1940, under the byline Wenner-Grens Institute for Experimental Biology.

3. O. Klein, Reports from the Nobel Institute 2, No. 18, 1912; see also *Z. Anorg. Chem.* 1917, p. 157.

4. O. Klein, Reports from the Nobel Institute 3, No. 24, 1917.

5. O. Klein, in *From a Life in Physics*, p. 59, Supplement of the IAEA Bulletin, printed by the IAEA in Vienna, 1969. Reprinted in *The Oskar Klein Memorial Lectures* (G. Ekspong, Ed.), p. 103, World Scientific, Singapore 1991.

6. O. Klein and O. Svanberg, Reports from the Nobel Institute 4, No. 1, 1918.

7. N. Bohr, letter to O. Klein, April 5, 1918, NBA.

8. O. Klein, letter to N. Bohr, April 8, 1918, NBA.

9. O. Klein, *Phil. Mag.* **37**, 207, 1919.

10. O. Klein, letter to N. Bohr, September 9, 1918, NBA.

11. O. Klein, Reports from the Nobel Institute 5, No. 6, 1919.

12. N. Bohr, letter to O. Klein, October 23, 1918, NBA.

13. O. Klein, letter to N. Bohr, May 19, 1919, NBA.

14. O. Klein, in *Niels Bohr* (S. Rozental, Ed.), p. 74, North-Holland, Amsterdam, 1967.

15. N. Bohr, letter to O. Klein, December 18, 1919, NBA.

16. N. Bohr, letter to O. Klein, January 12, 1920, NBA.

17. O. Klein, letter to N. Bohr, December 23, 1920, NBA.

18. J. Franck and G. Hertz, *Verh. Deutsch. Phys. Ges.* **15**, 34, 373, 613, 929, 1913; **16**, 12, 457, 512, 1914; **18**, 213, 1916.

19. Ref. 1, interview on February 20, 1963.

20. O. Klein and S. Rosseland, *Zeitschr. f. Physik* **4**, 46, 1920.

21. I. S. Bowen, *Nature* **120**, 473, 1927.

22. O. Klein, *Ark f. Mat. Astr. och Fys.* **16**, 1, 1921.

23. Ref. 1, interview on February 25, 1963.

24. N. Bohr, letter to O. Klein, July 3, 1922, NBA.

25. O. Klein, *Kosmos* **37**, 9, 1959.

26. O. Klein, *Kosmos* **2**, 54, 1922; **3**, 72, 1923.

27. O. Klein, *Svensk kemisk Tidskr.* **35**, 157, 1923.

28. O. Klein, *Nordisk Tidskr.* **46**, 446, 1923.

29. O. Klein, letter to N. Bohr, November 20, 1922, NBA.

30. N. Bohr, May 1, 1923, no addressee, NBA.

31. N. Bohr, letter to O. Klein, January 31, 1924, NBA.

32. O. Klein, *Zeitschr. f. Physik* **22**, 109, 1924.

33. O. Klein, letter to N. Bohr, May 6, 1924, NBA.

34. O. Klein, *Phys. Rev.* **25**, 109, 1925.

35. N. Bohr, H. Kramers, and J. Slater, *Phil. Mag.* **47**, 705, 1924.

36. O. Klein, letter to N. Bohr, June 30, 1924, NBA.

37. O. Klein, letter to H. A. Kramers, August 24, 1924, NBA.

38. O. Klein, *Vad vi veta om ljuset* (What we know about light), *Natur och Kultur* 41–2, 1925.

39. A. Einstein, letter to Th. Kaluza, April 21, 1919.

40. A. Einstein, letter to Th. Kaluza, May 5, 1919.

41. T. Kaluza, *Verh. Preuss. Ak. der Wiss.* 966, 1921.

42. O. Klein, *Zeitschr. f. Physik* **37**, 895, 1926. English translation in *The Oskar Klein Memorial Lectures*, ref. 5, p. 67.

43. O. Klein, *Nature*, **118**, 516, 1926. English translation in *The Oskar Klein Memorial Lectures*, ref. 5, p. 81.

44. A. Einstein, letter to P. Ehrenfest, September 3, 1926.

45. A. Pais, *Subtle is the Lord*, chapter 17, section (b), Oxford University Press, London, 1982.

46. Ref. 1, interview on July 16, 1963.

47. O. Klein, letter to N. Bohr, June 22, 1926, NBA.

48. G. E. Uhlenbeck and P. Ehrenfest, *Zeitschr. f. Physik* **39**, 495, 1926.

49. O. Klein, *Zeitschr. f. Physik* **41**, 407, 1927.

50. W. Pauli, letter to N. Bohr, March 29, 1927. Reprinted in *W. Pauli, Scientific Correspondence*, Vol. 1, p. 389, Springer, New York, 1979.

51. W. Pauli, letter to N. Bohr, August 6, 1927, ref. 50, p. 402.

52. O. Klein, *Zeitschr. f. Physik* **46**, 188, 1927.

53. O. Klein, *Arkiv Mat. Astr. och Fysik* **25A**, No. 15, 1936.

54. O. Klein, in *Les Nouvelles théories de la physique*, p. 77, Nÿhoff, The Hague, 1939. English translation in *The Oskar Klein Memorial Lectures*, ref. 5, p. 85.

55. O. Klein, *Nucl. Phys.* **4**, 677, 1957.

56. O. Klein, letter to N. Bohr, June 17, 1925, NBA.

57. O. Klein, letter to N. Bohr, September 17, 1925, NBA.

58. Mrs G. Klein, letter to N. Bohr, December 20, 1925, NBA.

59. O. Klein, letter to N. Bohr, January 23, 1926, NBA.

60. W. Heisenberg, *Physics and Beyond*, p. 73, Harper and Row, New York, 1971.

61. W. Heisenberg, interview by T. S. Kuhn, February 25, 1963, NBA.

62. Ref. 60, p. 77.

63. O. Klein, interview by L. Rosenfeld and J. Kalckar, November 7, 1968, NBA.

64. O. Klein, ref. 14, p. 88.

65. W. Heisenberg, ref. 14, p. 106.

66. H. Bohr, ref. 14, p. 335.

67. Samples: O. Klein, letter to C. Darwin, November 3, 1927; to E. Schrödinger, December 10, 1930, NBA.

68. M. Dresden, *H. A. Kramers*, p. 481, Springer, New York, 1987.

69. S. Deser, in *Proceedings of The Oskar Klein Centenary Symposium* (U. Lindström, Ed.), p. 49, World Scientific, Singapore, 1995.

70. W. Gordon, *Zeitschr. f. Physik* **40**, 117, 1927.

71. See A. Pais, *Inward Bound*, p. 289, Oxford University Press, 1986.

72. P. Jordan and O. Klein, *Zeitschr. f. Physik* **45**, 751, 1927.

73. Some time later Jordan and Wigner had developed second quantization for systems that obey Fermi–Dirac statistics, P. Jordan and E. P. Wigner, *Zeitschr. f. Physik* **47**, 631, 1928.

74. W. Heisenberg, in *Niels Bohr and the Development of Physics* (W. Pauli, Ed.), p. 15, McGraw-Hill, New York, 1955.

75. O. Klein and Y. Nishina, *Nature* **122**, 398, 1928; *Zeitschr. f. Physik* **52**, 853, 1929.

76. D. Hartree, letter to O. Klein, December 20, 1928, NBA.

77. E. Rutherford, *Proc. Roy. Soc.* **A122**, 1, 1929.

78. L. Meitner, letters to O. Klein, January 29, May 9, June 16, 1930, NBA.

79. See L. Brown and D. Moyer, *Am. J. Phys.* **52**, 130, 1984.

80. O. Klein, *Zeitschr. f. Physik* **53**, 157, 1929. The effect arises when electrons hit a potential barrier that varies by more than mc^2 over a distance of the order h/mc.

81. W. Pauli, letter to N. Bohr, January 16, 1929, ref. 50, Vol. 1, p. 485.

82. W. Pauli, letter to O. Klein, February 18, 1929, ref. 50, Vol. 1, p. 488.

83. W. Pauli, letter to O. Klein, February 10, 1930, ref. 50, Vol. 2, p. 2.

84. O. Klein, *Zeitschr. f. Physik* **58**, 730, 1929. The problem had been solved earlier by H. A. Kramers and G. P.Ittman, *Zeitschr. f. Physik* **53**, 553, 1929.

85. I quote from Bohr's draft, dated February 6, 1929, which was followed by a shorter version, February 12, 1929, both in NBA.

86. W. Pauli, letter to O. Klein, December 12, 1930, ref. 50, Vol. 2, p. 43.

87. O. Klein, *Zeitschr. f. Physik* **52**, 767, 1931.

88. O. Klein, *Zeitschr. f. Physik* **76**, 226, 1932.

89. After R. Rydberg, a young Swede who made the first steps, *Zeitschr. f. Physik* **73**, 376, 1931, Klein, and A. L. G. Rees who introduced further modifications.

90. O. Klein, *Zeitschr. f. Physik* **80**, 792, 1933; also *Proceedings of the Scandinavian Mathematical Congress* 1934, p. 243.

91. O. Klein, letter to N. Bohr, July 21, 1931, NBA.

92. N. Bohr, letter to O. Klein, February 19, 1931, NBA.

93. O. Klein, letter to N. Bohr, May 14, 16, 1932, NBA.

94. O. Klein, letter to N. Bohr, January 3, 1933, NBA.

95. O. Klein, 'Relativitetsteori,' *Natur och Kultur*, No. 118, 1933; letter to N. Bohr, June 17, 1934, NBA.

96. O. Klein, '*Orsak och Verkan*,' *Natur och Kultur*, No. 126, 1935; letter to N. Bohr, January 28, 1935, NBA.

97. O. Klein, letter to N. Bohr, June 20, 1933, NBA.

98. See also F. Aaserud, *Redirecting Science*, p. 117, Cambridge University Press, 1990.

99. O. Klein, letter to W. Pauli, October 1940, ref. 50, Vol. 3, p. 40.

100. O. Klein, *J. de Physique* **9**, 1, 1938.

101. O. Klein, letters to N. Bohr, June 30, 1938; also May 23, 1938, NBA.

102. O. Klein, *Kosmos* **11**, 15, 1935.

103. O. Klein, *Lychnos*, p. 136, Uppsala, 1939.

104. N. Bohr, letter to O. Klein, December 16, 1940, NBA.

105. N. Bohr, letters to O. Klein, June 6, 1941, February 7, 1942; O. Klein, letters to N. Bohr, June 25 and December 21, 1941, NBA.

106. A. Pais, *Niels Bohr's Times*, chapter 21, section (c), Oxford University Press, 1991.

107. O. Klein, *Nature* **161**, 897, 1948.

108. *Proceedings of the Oskar Klein Centenary Symposium*, ref. 69, p. 203.

109. O. Klein, *Ark. Mat. Astr. och Fys.* **33B**, No. 2, 1945; with J. Lindhard, *Rev. Mod. Phys.* **17**, 305, 1945; *Nature* **169**, 578, 1952; *Ark. f. Fys.* **5**, 459, 1952.

110. O. Klein, *Ark. Kemi*, **14A**, 1, 1940.

111. O. Klein, *Teknisk Tidskr.* (Stockholm), **69**, 137, 1939; *Ark. Mat. Astr. och Fys.* **30A**, No. 3, 1943; **34A**, No. 1, 1946; *Nature* **161**, 897, 1948; in *Zur Theorie der*

Elementarteilchen, p. 1, Mosbach, Baden, 1949; *Ark. f. Phys.* **16**, 191, 1959; *Phys. Rev. Lett.* **16**, 63, 1966.

112. O. Klein, *Elementa* **18**, 9, 1935; *Rev. Mod. Phys.* **21**, 531, 1949; *Ark. f. Fys.* **7**, 487, 1954; *Helv. Phys. Acta*, Supplement. **4**, 58, 1956; *Nuov. Cim.* **6**, 344, 1957; *Norsk. Vid. Forh.* **31**, 47, 1958; *Ark. f. Fys.* **17**, 517, 1960; in *Festschrift* Heisenberg, p. 58, Vieweg, Braunschweig; in *Recent Developments in General Relativity*, p. 293, Pergamon, New York, 1962; *Astrophys. Norv.* **9**, 161, 1964; *Nucl. Phys.* **21B**, 253, 1970.

113. O. Klein, *Ark. Mat. Astr. och Fys.* **31A**, No. 14, 1944; **33B**, No. 1, 1945; **34A**, No. 19, 1947.

114. O. Klein and H. Alfvén, *Ark. f. Fys.* **23**, 187, 1962; H. Alfvén, *Sci. Am.* April 1967, p. 106; O. Klein, *Nature* **211**, 1337, 1966; *Ark. f. Fys.* **39**, 157, 1969; *Science* **171**, 339, 1971.

115. O. Klein, *Kosmos* **14**, 7, 1936; in *Vetenskap av i dag*, p. 247, Gebers, Stockholm, 1940; in *Vi och vår värld*, p. 327, Stockholm, 1941.

116. O. Klein, *Industrietidn. Norden* **74**, 23, 35, 45, 1946.

117. O. Klein, *Fys. Tidskr.* **33**, 102, 1935 (50th); *Nordisk Tidskr.* **11**, 408, 1935 (50th); *Fra Fysikkens Verden*, Oslo, 1945, p. 110 (60th); *Festschrift*, p. 18, North-Holland, 1945 (60th); *Niels Bohr and the Development of Physics*, ref. 74, Pergamon, 1955 (70th); 'Et in Arcadia ego' (70th), unpublished manuscript, NBA.

118. O. Klein, *Nucl. Phys.* **54**, 345, 1964.

119. O. Klein, *Kosmos* **20**, 116, 1942.

120. O. Klein, *Lychnos*, Uppsala, 1942, p. 65; *Fys. Tidskr.* **60**, 65, 1962.

121. See also O. Klein, *Nucl. Phys.* **57**, 345, 1964.

122. O. Klein, *Nordisk Tidskr. Vet. Konst och Industri* **10**, 489, 1934; **19**, 465, 1943; *Theoria*, 1938, p. 59. See also ref. 28.

123. K. Jonsson, in *Center on the Periphery*, p. 16, Watson, Canton, MA, 1993.

124. O. Klein, *Ord och Bild*, p. 471, Stockholm, 1941.

125. N. Bohr, letter to O. Klein, March 6, 1940, NBA.

126. Ref. 50, Vol. 2, p. 39.

127. W. Pauli, letter to O. Klein, December 12, 1930, ref. 50, Vol. 2, p. 43.

128. W. Pauli, *Ann. de Phys.* **18**, 305, 337, 1933. Reprinted in *Collected Scientific Papers by Wolfgang Pauli* (R. Kronig and V. Weisskopf, Eds), Vol. 2, p. 630, Wiley, New York, 1964.

129. W. Pauli, letter to O. Klein, July 18, 1935; also August 8, 1935, ref. 50, Vol. 2, pp. 423, 424.

130. A. Pais, *Physica* **19**, 869, 1953.

131. W. Pauli, *Physica* **19**, 887, 1953.

132. W. Pauli, letter to O. Klein, July 14, 1953, ref. 50, Vol. 4.

133. A. Pais, *A Tale of Two Continents*, chapter 23, section 1, Oxford and Princeton University Presses, 1997.

134. N. Bohr, letter to O. Klein, October 27, 1960, NBA.

135. O. Klein, letter to N. Bohr, December 22, 1960, NBA.

136. O. Klein, *Kung. Vetenskaps-Societetens Årsbok 1963*, p. 33, Almquist, Uppsala, 1964.

137. For obituaries see S. Deser, *Phys. Today* June 1977, p. 67; C. Møller, *Fys. Tidskr.* 75, 169, 1977; I. Fischer Hjalmars, and B. Laurent, *Kosmos* 1978, p. 19. English translation in *The Oskar Klein Memorial Lectures*, ref. 5, p. 1.

Hans Kramers in the main auditorium of the Niels Bohr Institute, Copenhagen, 1936.
(Courtesy of the Niels Bohr Archive, Copenhagen.)

Hendrik Anthony Kramers: a personal view of his life and science*

I did my undergraduate work in Amsterdam, graduating in February 1938, whereafter I studied theoretical physics with George Uhlenbeck in Utrecht. All through the spring of 1938 I paid him regular visits from Amsterdam, where I still lived. After a while Uhlenbeck told me that he would soon put me to work on a theory problem. But first, he said, I had to study the textbook on quantum mechanics by Hendrik Anthony Kramers,[1] Hans to his friends, of whom I was to become one, and Holland's most prominent theoretician of the period. I did all right. During one of my visits to Uhlenbeck, the door to his room suddenly opened, no knocking first, and a man stormed in, did not say hello, and planted himself squarely in front of the blackboard. After a few moments' study of what was written there he turned to Uhlenbeck and finally spoke, saying: You need a *schleifenintegral*, a technical mathematical term. It was my first encounter with Kramers, of whom I was to see much in later times.

In the spring of 1939 Uhlenbeck informed me that during the coming fall term he was taking a leave of absence to be visiting professor at Columbia University in New York. That was of course a disappointment for me. Before leaving he told me that he had spoken about me to Kramers in Leiden, who had expressed himself willing to receive me now and then for discussions. So a few days a month I journeyed to Leiden, also attending on occasion the famous so-called Ehrenfest colloquium there. Talks with Kramers showed him to me to be a man of quite unusual depth in his thinking, not only on physics but also in regard to numerous other aspects of human culture. He was very musical and, as I was soon to hear for myself, played the cello very well. I remember a story he once told me about music. One evening he was attending a concert of music he was particularly fond of. Suddenly, in the middle of it all, he got up and left, because, he told me, he had

* Extended version of a lecture delivered on September 14, 1995, at the Eindhoven University of Technology, The Netherlands, to commemorate the centennial of Kramers' birth.

found himself sitting there calculating in his head the energy levels of an oxygen atom, unable to concentrate on the music at the same time. That was too much for him. He never went to a concert again but continued to make his own music because that he could do with undivided attention.

My acquaintance with Kramers grew into a friendship that would last until his death in 1952.

I shall have much to say about my relationship with Kramers, not only how I came to understand that he was one of the great twentieth-century physicists, a fact which is perhaps not sufficiently appreciated in wider circles, but also how he saved my life. First, however, I should like to tell something about his scientific career.[a]

Hans was born in Rotterdam on December 17, 1894, in the family home at Coolsingel 47 in Rotterdam. His father, a medical doctor, was a strong, pragmatic person; his mother, Suzanne née Breukelman, was sensitive and kind, his family life was close-knit. He came from an upper middle class, tolerant Calvinist milieu with Victorian traits, not particularly wealthy but comfortably off. He had four siblings, all boys. All five did well in later life. Two became physicians, one a chemical engineer. Hans and his oldest brother Jan, who was a leading scholar in Arabic, became eminent university professors in Leiden.

Hans showed early interests in reading and in writing stories and poems, in other words in literature rather than in science. His friendship with Jan Romein, a distinguished Dutch historian, began at age five and lasted till Hans' death.

Kramers went through the usual Dutch education, six years of primary school followed by five years of high school. In those years his interest in literature deepened and widened to include literary criticism, philosophy, cultural history, and theology. In high school he handled mathematics and physics with ease and began developing increasing interests in physics and chemistry. When at age 17 he finished high school, he was widely read and also had developed an interest in music. As already mentioned, he became a good cellist. He now resolved to enter university to study physics. That was not an easy decision for him, however. In his diary he writes wistfully about the demands science will make: 'A man of science must sacrifice his individuality for his field.'[3]

Kramers could not enter a Dutch university without further ado, however, because his schooling had not provided training in Latin and Greek, at that time a legal prerequisite for university study in any discipline. That law was abrogated only in 1918.[b] In 1911–12 Kramers had therefore to spend his time learning Latin and Greek. Rapidly, in only one year, he managed to prepare for the necessary examination. He had learned those languages so well, however, that from then on until the end of his life he read them for pleasure, enjoying especially Cicero, Horace, and Homer.

In September 1912 Kramers entered Leiden University. He was a serious student, taking courses in mechanics, electricity, wave theory, statistical mechanics, and thermodynamics. He also studied mathematics beyond the minimal requirements, at which he became superbly expert.

Hans was also active in extracurricular activities. He joined the Leiden Student Corps, an exclusive, snotty fraternity which, however, he soon quit. For some time he was chief editor of the literary student magazine *Minerva*, and participated in organizing international student exchanges.

The most important contacts in Hans' student years were with Hendrik Antoon Lorentz, Holland's most prominent physicist of his generation, and with Paul Ehrenfest, Lorentz' successor. He took Lorentz' celebrated 'Monday morning' classes, a special topics course. Later he has said that he looked at Lorentz 'like a little, little boy who stares at a real Queen for the first time.'[4] He would often refer to his initials, H. A., as predisposing him to physics since Lorentz' initials were the same.

Hans was also deeply impressed by Ehrenfest's true genius as a teacher. The respect was mutual. When Ehrenfest had to be absent, he would sometimes ask Kramers to take over some of his lectures. Nevertheless the relations between the two men did not develop well, mainly because Ehrenfest considered it a fatal flaw that Kramers had intellectual devotions outside physics. When Hans had passed his examination for the *doctorandus* degree (roughly the equivalent of a Master's degree), Ehrenfest intimated in fact that he should become a high school teacher rather than an active research physicist.

And so, in the spring of 1916, we find Kramers teaching mathematics and physics at a school in Arnhem—but only for about two months. Soon he felt the urge to return to the world of research and to go abroad in order to do so. His choice fell on Denmark, first because that country was not involved in the World War, secondly because in the summer of 1916 an international student conference was to be held in Copenhagen which he could attend as officer. He therefore wrote to Niels Bohr. At that time Hans was 21, Bohr 31.

———————— • ————————

In 1913 Bohr had become world famous as the founder of applications of the quantum theory to dynamics, more precisely to the structure of atoms and molecules. It was not until April 1, 1916, however, that he was appointed professor at the University of Copenhagen, the first to hold a chair in theoretical physics there. At that time the University did not yet have a physics institute, so from 1916–20 Bohr was housed in Copenhagen's *Polytekniske Læreanstalt* (now called the Technical University of Denmark), having at his disposal nothing but a small office of less than 150 square feet.

In August 1916 Bohr received a letter written in Copenhagen by a young Dutchman he had never heard of. It reads in part:

Prof. N. Bohr! To begin let me introduce myself by telling that I am a Dutch student in mathematics and physics. I've studied 4 years in Leiden . . . I passed all examinations. I want to get the *doctor's* title . . . As I didn't like to go to a country that is at war now, I decided to go to Copenhagen . . . Of course I should like to come in acquaintance with *you* in the first place, and also with your brother Harald.[c] I should be very glad if you would permit me to visit you one of these days . . . With all kinds of respects, H. A. Kramers.[5]

After the two had met, Bohr decided to give Kramers a chance, a splendid decision as it turned out. Thus Hans became the first of a long row of assistants to Bohr, many of whom reached great fame. In the fall of 1916 the two began a collaboration which, with minor interruptions, was to last until 1926.

Initially Kramers shared Bohr's small office, financially supported from a grant at Bohr's disposal. Already in 1917 Bohr could write: 'I have been very pleased in my collaboration with Dr. [*sic*] Kramers who I think is extremely able and about whom I have the greatest expectations.'[6] Bohr was in attendance when Kramers defended his Doctoral thesis (on quantum physics) in Leiden, in May 1919. Also in that month Kramers was appointed scientific assistant in Copenhagen. In 1923 he became lecturer. 'The Copenhagen years from about 1916 to 1925 witnessed [Kramers'] meteoric rise from an apprentice in atomic physics to heir apparent to Bohr. [In the days of the old quantum theory] he was the dominant figure next to Bohr in Copenhagen.'[7]

In 1919 Bohr began to look for a secretary and was fortunate to find Betty Schultz, who remembered: 'I went out to his home . . . I took shorthand and knew a little English and such things, but when I came there he didn't ask for anything except whether I had been interested in science. And I said, "no, I do not know what it is," and then I was engaged.'[8] She first reported for work on January 2, 1919 and was housed in Bohr's office. 'And there was professor Bohr and Kramers and I sitting in one room . . . When he should work with Kramers I could go home and Kramers went away when we worked.'[8]

Kramers also started a new tradition. He was the first of the many physicists from abroad who would find a Danish spouse. Bohr was one of the official witnesses at their marriage.

***

Soon after having settled in Denmark, Hans met Anna Petersen, generally known by her fitting nickname, Storm, an outgoing, energetic, exuberant young woman, a convert to Catholicism, who was studying voice in Copenhagen. Hans was not only a gifted cellist but also an accomplished pianist. So it came about that he would accompany Storm at recitals. He had great respect for the way Storm took the leadership in these duets. She fell deeply in love with him. They became engaged in 1917, whereafter their relation went through many ups and downs. That may perhaps have been in part because Storm, who was a bright woman with a lot of common sense and a fine sense of humor (she was good at imitating people, Pauli for example), had had little formal education and was no intellectual match for Hans. More importantly, I think, was Hans' quite general fear of irrevocable decisions, his unwillingness or inability to commit himself. When in 1920 Storm turned out to be pregnant, they married on October 25 of that year, in Copenhagen's *Marmor Kirken.*

Their relation did not change much after marriage, however. In the course of time, Kramers' feelings of incompleteness in their union intensified. In the late 1930s he started a relationship with another woman that was important to him, but he never broke his marriage with Storm, who gave him three daughters and a son. Jan Kramers, Hans' son, has told me that Hans' wife knew about this other woman, that his children also met her, and that in this matter Storm showed exemplary tolerance.*d*

Back to the Copenhagen days. Bohr was understandably not content with his working quarters. In April 1917 he approached Danish authorities with the request for an institute for himself and his coworkers. After many hurdles had been cleared, that institute was opened on March 3, 1921. The day before, Kramers, its first junior appointee, gave a tour of the place for newspaper reporters. Bohr gave the main address at the inauguration, in which he thanked Kramers for his contributions to research and to teaching. Meanwhile they themselves had had to move their books and papers to the new location.

On the occasion of the opening of the new institute, Arnold Sommerfeld, another early leader in the quantum enterprise, sent congratulations, calling Bohr 'the director of atomic physics'[10]—in the sense of the man who gave direction not just by his own researches but also by inspiring others. The new institution was called *Institut for Teoretisk Fysik.* In 1965, the year in which Bohr would have been 80, it was renamed *Niels Bohr Institutet.*

The beginnings of Kramers' scientific career were entirely dominated by Bohr's spirit and inspiration. Conversely, Bohr came to rely on Kramers almost from the time he arrived. In 1917 he sent him to Stockholm to present his theories of atomic phenomena. When in 1918 the Swedish physicist Oskar Klein came to work in Copenhagen, the second young man to do so, Bohr left it largely to Kramers to initiate Klein in the mysteries of quantum physics. When others came for short visits, Bohr, very busy not only with his research but also with the organization of his new institute, often sent them on to Kramers to do the honors. As Pauli once said at that time: 'Bohr is Allah and Kramers is his Prophet.'

In some respects one may say that Bohr and Kramers complemented each other. Kramers had a strong bent and great gifts for mathematics. Bohr, on the other hand, had an unparalleled talent for discerning, one might even say divining, how progress could be made by judicious use of experimental data. That is what Heisenberg had in mind when he said: 'Bohr was not a mathematically minded man. He was, I would say, Faraday but not Maxwell.'[11] He could have added that Kramers was more like Maxwell than Faraday.

———— • ————

I now turn to the discussion of Kramers' scientific activities. I should note at the outset that his scientific papers have been collected into a book[12] edited by several of his friends and pupils in order (as they state in the preface) 'to commemorate in a concrete way his exceptionally gifted personality.' A list of Kramers' publications, which includes non-scientific papers, has also been published.[13]

Almost at once after Kramers' arrival Bohr proposed a collaboration on helium. In November Bohr wrote to Rutherford: 'I have used all my spare time in the last months to make a serious attempt to solve the problem of the ordinary [i.e. non-ionized] helium spectrum . . . working together with . . . Kramers . . . I think really that at last I have a clue to the problem.'[14]

Initially Bohr was optimistic. He wrote to colleagues that the theory 'was worked out in the fall of 1916'[15] and of having obtained 'a partial agreement with the measurements.' Some 200 pages of Bohr's calculations, never published, remain in the Niels Bohr Archives.

Bohr's faith waned, however, as time went by; more and more he left the problem to Kramers, who continued to tackle it with his considerable mathematical ingenuity. Bohr himself came back several times to helium, in most detail in part of his Solvay report (1921)[16] and in the fourth of his Göttingen lectures.[17] Eventually Kramers published the helium results in a paper[18] submitted in December 1922. Six years of hard work had gone into these efforts. An interesting feature of his final helium model is that it was no longer plane, the two electrons move in different planes. Perhaps the most important of his negative results concerns Bohr's and Ehrenfest's idea that classical mechanics should apply to electrons while moving in stationary orbits. 'We must draw the conclusion that already in this simple case mechanics is not valid.'[18]

It should be noted at this point, first, that Kramers had an exceptionally deep knowledge of classical mechanics, and, second, that in the years he struggled so valiantly with the helium problem, the main ingredients for its solution were as yet unknown. There was as yet no spin, nor was the exclusion principle known. The helium problem was only resolved in 1926, after the discovery of quantum mechanics.

Kramers was involved in other physics problems as well during the years of his struggles with helium. For example, in 1919 he published on general relativity.[19]

Much more important, in 1917 he began his studies of the intensities of spectral lines. He first worked out the general theory in great detail, then applied it to calculate intensities for the fine structure of the hydrogen spectrum and for the Stark effect, the splitting of spectral lines when atoms are exposed to an electric field. His comparison of the results with experiment turned out to work very well. This work, which ranks among the principal confirmations of Bohr's atomic theory, and which established Kramers as one of the masters of this theory, resulted in his Doctor's thesis,[20] which he defended in Leiden on May 1, 1919, in the presence of three Nobel laureates, Bohr, Heike Kamerlingh Onnes, and Lorentz—and of Storm. This work must have taken its toll on Kramers, for soon after his promotion he became ill and remained in a hospital in Rotterdam for a rather long time.

In 1922, Kramers, together with Helge Holst, a librarian at the *Læreanstalt*, published a book in Danish, entitled *Bohr's Atomteori*. In 1923 an English translation appeared[21] with a foreword by Rutherford in which Kramers received well-deserved praise. 'Dr. Kramers is in an especially fortunate position to give a first hand account of this subject, for he has been a valued assistant to Professor Bohr in developing his theories and has himself made important original contributions to our knowledge in this branch of inquiry.' The book was a great success. It spread the fame of Bohr far and wide and was appreciated by physicists and lay persons alike; it was used by many physicists as a first readable introduction to atomic physics.

No one better than Kramers has conveyed the delicacies of operating with Bohr's so-called correspondence principle, which establishes links between the quantum theory and the predictions of the pre-quantum theory, known as the classical theory. This principle had been a major tool in Kramers' work for his Doctor's thesis. On several occasions he emphasized the subtleties in applying correspondence, for the first time in his book with Holst: 'It is difficult to explain in what (the correspondence principle) consists, because it cannot be expressed in exact quantitative laws, and it is, on this account, also difficult to apply. [However,] in Bohr's hands it has been extraordinarily fruitful in the most varied fields.'[22] Also in 1923, in the issue of *Naturwissenschaften*[23] commemorating the first ten years of the Bohr theory, he wrote: 'In this night of difficulties and uncertainty Bohr['s] . . . principle is a bright spot.' And in 1935, on the occasion of Bohr's fiftieth birthday: 'In the beginning the correspondence principle appeared to the world of physicists as a rather mystic wand that did not work outside Copenhagen,'[24] not unlike Sommerfeld, who earlier had called the principle 'a magic wand . . . which allows us to apply the results of the classical wave theory to the quantum theory.'[25]

The year 1923 was a quite productive one for Kramers, when he published his beautiful paper on X-ray absorption,[26] the first application of quantum theory to *continuous* spectra. That work earned him praise from Eddington.[27] He also wrote on the shell model of atoms,[28] on quantization of rotating molecules,[29] on band spectra,[30] and on velocities of chemical reactions.[31]

A paper Kramers co-authored in 1924 brings me back to a little-known episode in his career, in 1921, when he had a brilliant idea about the quantum theory of light.

Recall that in 1905 Einstein had proposed that under certain circumstances light behaves like a beam of particles, photons. The idea was revolutionary for its time and indeed remained controversial until 1923, when Arthur Compton showed experimentally that light scattered by electrons suffers a decrease in frequency that depends on the angle of scattering and that the amount of that decrease can be predicted theoretically by assuming, firstly, the photon concept, and secondly, that energy and momentum are conserved in the scattering process—minimal assumptions that could have been made much earlier.

And they were. From interviews with Kramers' family, friends, and students, Dresden has produced strong evidence[32]—which I find convincing—that in the summer of 1921, before Compton's experiment, Kramers had obtained the correct theory of the effect. Kramers' wife has recalled that at that time her husband was 'insanely excited . . . Bohr and Kramers immediately started a series of daily no holds barred arguments. After these discussions, which left Kramers exhausted, depressed, and let down, [he] got sick and spent some time in hospital,' the reason being that Bohr strenuously objected to Kramers' ideas. Dresden adds that thereafter 'Kramers did not merely acquiesce to Bohr's views, he made Bohr's views his own . . . [afterwards] Kramers and Bohr were scientifically closer, more in tune with each other, than before.' Kramers' writings of 1923 unequivocally show his conversion: 'The theory of light-quanta may . . . be compared with medicine which will cause the disease to vanish but kill the patient . . . The fact must be emphasized that this theory in no way has sprung from the Bohr theory, to say nothing of its being a necessary consequence of it.'[33]

What, then, were Bohr's own views? He did not at all accept the photon concept.[e] Instead, in 1923, he made the alternative proposal that, in processes like light-electron scattering, energy and momentum are not conserved.[34] Note that in 1923 these laws had not yet been experimentally tested at the level of *individual* microscopic processes such as atomic transitions, collisions of electrons with electrons or atoms, etc. Bohr's ideas led to the poor paper[35] by Bohr, Kramers, and John Slater, a young Harvard PhD who had arrived in Copenhagen in late 1923.

The matter was resolved when in early 1925 experiments showed that energy and momentum are indeed conserved in individual events.[f]

If 1924 had started out poorly, Kramers' later work in that year was among his best, indeed outstanding.

———— ■ ————

From the very beginning of the quantum theory of the atom in 1913 it had been clear, especially to Bohr, that the new quantum rules were in conflict with classical theory. During the following years the classical theory was nevertheless held onto, with quantum rules superimposed, in the hope that this procedure might eventually find its logical justification. It was only in the early 1920s that, mainly as a result of failures, the much more radical insight began to emerge that actually classical models might have to be abandoned in the atomic domain, in particular that the concept of atomic orbits was highly suspect.

To be critical of atomic orbits was one (good) thing, to do atomic physics without them was something else. The first successful effort in that direction is due to Kramers, and dates from 1924. Born has said of that contribution: 'It was the first step from the bright realm of classical mechanics into the still dark and unexplored world of the new quantum mechanics.'[37] Kramers' work deals with the dispersion of light, that is, the emission of secondary light by an atom exposed to and excited by a light beam. Its results were announced in two letters to *Nature*, one[38] submitted in March 1924, one[39] the following July.

According to the classical theory of dispersion, the intensity of the light emitted by an irradiated atom depends on the irradiation frequency and on the classical frequencies of orbital motions of electrons inside the atom. Quantum theory obviously demands that the role of these classical frequencies should somehow be taken over by Bohr's transition frequencies between stationary states. This was the problem that Kramers addressed. As a link with the classical answers he, of course, used the correspondence principle, which in this instance demands that the scattered radiation should continue to depend on the classical frequencies of electron motions in the limit of large quantum numbers. As a quantum theoretical tool he used Einstein's concepts of spontaneous emission; as a *mathematical* trick he replaced the atom by a set of oscillators vibrating with the Bohr frequencies. Combining those ingredients with very clever guesses, he arrived at his so-called *dispersion relation* which expresses the probability for the emission of the secondary light in terms of the irradiation and Bohr frequencies.

The technical details of Kramers' two letters need not concern us here. Most interesting, on the other hand, are his comments on the results:

> [The dispersion relation] contains only such quantities [to wit, transition quantities referring to two stationary states] as allow of a direct physical interpretation on the basis of the quantum theory of spectra and atomic constitution, and exhibits no further reminiscence of the mathematical theory of multiple periodic systems [that is, of orbits].

In later times Kramers' dispersion relations have proved ever more successful. Their first extension was published in 1925, as we shall see in a moment. Next came applications to X-ray data by Kronig[40] and Kramers.[41] I have described elsewhere how these relations, now often called Kramers–Kronig relations, could be derived from progressively more general assumptions, and how they have found important applications in the physics of elementary particles.[42]

Enter Werner Heisenberg, who had arrived in Copenhagen in September 1924 for a half year's stay. Among his first impressions were that 'everybody first talked to Kramers before they talked to Bohr . . . Kramers was, besides Bohr, the man who made the strongest impression on me.'[43]

Heisenberg always got along well with Kramers. He admired his knowledge of physics and languages, especially of German literature, and also his musical talents. 'Well, how can a man know so much?'[43] They used to play music together, Heisenberg at the piano, Kramers on the cello, and also produced a joint paper,[44,45] completed in December 1924, Heisenberg's last contribution in that year. Its redaction was entirely due to Kramers.[46]

In this paper we find for the first time a detailed derivation of Kramers' dispersion relation which the latter had barely sketched in his earlier writing.[38,39] The methodological advances introduced there were absolutely crucial for Heisenberg's first paper on quantum mechanics the next year.

In addition, this famous Kramers–Heisenberg paper also contains new physics. Kramers had dealt only with elastic processes, that is, the frequency of the incident and secondary light are identical but the latter may be emitted in any arbitrary direction. The new paper also contains inelastic processes of the type

$$h\upsilon + E_a = h\upsilon' + E_b$$

where $E_a(E_b)$ is the energy of the initial (final) atomic state and $\upsilon(\upsilon')$ is the frequency of the incident (secondary) light. The states a and b may or may not be the same. The frequency υ' is smaller (larger) than υ if the atom jumps from a lower to a higher (higher to lower) state. These inelastic transitions were not observed until 1928. They are now called Raman scattering, after their discoverer.

Later Heisenberg remarked about this collaboration:

> One felt one had now come a step further in getting into the spirit of the new mechanics. Everybody knew there must be some new kind of mechanics behind it and nobody had a clear idea of it, but still, one felt this was a new step in the right direction . . . Almost one had matrix mechanics at this point without knowing it[47] . . . This new scheme [matrix mechanics] was a continuation of what I had done with Kramers . . . a more systematic continuation of which one could hope, but not know, that it would be a consistent scheme[48] . . . I always regretted that Kramers never got the Nobel Prize.[43]

The Kramers–Heisenberg dispersion formulae are among the few results that have retained to this day their physical and formal validity after quantum mechanics replaced the 'old quantum theory' description, which had begun in 1900 with Max Planck and ended in July 1925 with Heisenberg's matrix mechanics.

Friends and colleagues have often wondered why it was Heisenberg rather than Kramers who discovered quantum mechanics. After all, both men together had come to the very edge of that advance. I cannot answer that question, but would venture the guess that it was Heisenberg's personality, far more aggressive than Kramers', that made the essential difference. Kramers himself has commented on that distinction, writing in 1927 to Klein apropos of a scientific controversy between Heisenberg and Bohr: 'Do not enter this conflict, we are both much too kind and gentle to participate in that kind of struggle. Both Bohr and Heisenberg are tough, hard nosed, uncompromising and indefatigable. We [Kramers and Klein] would just be crushed in that juggernaut.'[49]

In 1925 Kramers published a note on Heisenberg's new theory, but, significantly, only in Dutch, in a little-read Dutch journal.[50]

In 1925 Kramers had been proposed for a professorship in Utrecht. Strong letters by Bohr, Einstein, and Planck, that outstanding threesome of the century's theorists, made it more than obvious that he was the right choice.

It was of course hard for Kramers to leave Bohr after a decade of intense collaboration. He did accept, however. On February 15, 1926, he gave his inaugural address on 'Form and essence'[51] and started his lectures the following May. In that month Heisenberg succeeded Kramers as lecturer in Copenhagen.

In July Kramers wrote to Bohr[52] that he was busy fixing up his new home. He did maintain contacts with Bohr, but these became less frequent as time went by.

On October 30, 1931, Kramers gave another inaugural lecture, on 'Reality and concept formation,'[53] this time as extraordinary professor in the new faculty of Technical Physics at the Institute of Technology in Delft. After Ehrenfest's tragic suicide in September 1933, he wrote two sensitive obituaries[54] about his erstwhile teacher. Soon afterward he moved to Leiden as Ehrenfest's successor, giving an inaugural lecture on 'Physics and physicists.'[55]

I now turn to Kramers' later oeuvre.

In 1926 Kramers wrote a paper[56] on the so-called WKB method that has become a classic. Typical for much of this later work, it is a mathematical elaboration of quantum mechanics. In 1927 he attended the fifth Solvay conference, participating in the lively discussions.[57] He remained silent, however, after

Bohr's address on complementarity, a subject to which Bohr had referred for the first time in a letter to Kramers.[58] Nor would Kramers ever write in later life on the new issues of interpretation raised by quantum mechanics. His style would remain scholarly rather than speculative.

A typical example is his attempt in 1927 at incorporating spin in quantum mechanics, starting from a relativistic generalization of a classical rotating charge distribution. After a highly complex route, he derived a pair of differential equations which are equivalent to an iterated form of the four equations published by Dirac[59] just weeks before Kramers had finished *his* version. This disappointed Kramers so deeply that he gradually withdrew from the frontiers of physics, publishing his own version of spin—which I find rather intransparent—only in his 1938 textbook.[60]

Kramers' collected papers[12] show that after 1927, and until his death in 1952, he published 52 scientific articles which cover a broad range of subjects, of which I have so far mentioned only his work on dispersion relations.[41] Twelve of these[61] deal with concrete quantum mechanical problems, such as multiplet theory, and the quantization of the asymmetric top. A second group[62] deals with properties of paramagnetic substances, notably with their adiabatic demagnetization, an important technique for obtaining ultralow temperatures, a Leiden monopoly at that time.

Kramers made fundamental contributions to the theory of phase transitions. In the second of his papers on ferromagnetism[63] he became the first to realize that *discontinuous* phase transitions can occur only in the 'thermodynamic limit.'[g] He was also the first, together with Gregory Wannier to find the exact position of a phase transition for a particular model of a ferromagnet,[h] showing that *if* there exists a phase transition, then a general argument gives its position. This work is simply a gem of simplicity.[65]

Kramers was also active in studies of diffusion and macromolecular flow, the most important of which is his paper on thermally activated barrier crossing.[66] The chemical world of that time had no direct use for its predictions. Experiments performed in the 1970s and '80s have shown the seminal nature of this work, however, as has been explained in 1990 in a review paper entitled: 'Reaction rate theory: fifty years after Kramers.'[67]

Finally I mention that in 1937 Kramers returned to fundamental issues. In that year he was the first to note a symmetry property of the Dirac equation, which he named charge conjugation.[68] At that time he also began publishing on the interaction of electrons with the electromagnetic field, work to which I will return shortly.

This concludes my incomplete bird's eye view of the oeuvre of one of this century's major physicists.

I now return to recollections of my personal contacts with Kramers—which brings me to the dark days of the Second World War. Recall some dates. On May 10, 1940 German armies invaded Holland. On May 15, Dutch forces laid down arms. Belgium capitulated on May 28, Paris fell on June 14, an armistice with France was signed on June 21.

I spent the day after the fall of Paris with Kramers, in the study of his home on the Poelgeesterweg in Oegstgeest, a suburb of Leiden. The plan had been to discuss some physics issues but neither of us felt like doing that. The loss of Paris had hit us very hard, as it had done to so many other Dutchmen. Nobody had really believed that our country could successfully withstand the German onslaught. But Paris stood as the symbol of Western culture. I do not think that any one of us had reckoned with Paris in German hands—and so quickly. Thus my visit to Kramers turned into hours of gloomy reminiscences about the City of Light. I do not believe I exaggerate when I note that the fate of Paris had hit us harder than even the fall of Holland, than even the black clouds from the fires of burning Rotterdam—which Kramers had seen as they were blowing northward.

As a result of protests by Leiden professors against dismissal of Jewish colleagues, that university was closed in November 1940 (with a brief subsequent reopening) for the duration of the war. On October 22, 1941 the Germans decreed that Jews were to be debarred from participation in non-profit organizations—which included the Royal Dutch Academy of Sciences. As a result five non-Jewish Academy members resigned, among them Kramers.

In June 1942 the use of trains was prohibited to Jews.

These few rather random jottings must suffice to make clear why Kramers and I did not meet further in the early war years—until 1943, the year I went into hiding in a house on the Keizersgracht in Amsterdam.

Soon after I had arrived there, a special place had been constructed where I could hide in case of a German raid on the house. In the attic next to my room, a wooden wall panel had been cut loose, behind which there was a tiny space in which I should crawl in the event. A lock had been attached to the panel's inside so that I myself could close off the wall once I was installed. I regularly trained myself to go rapidly through the necessary motions.

Otherwise, life during the next months was a period of calm and routine. I had one wonderful diversion throughout that period: visits from Kramers, who had been informed of my whereabouts. Ever since his university had been closed down, he had had to find sources of income elsewhere. That is why he had become a consultant for the Bataafsche Petroleum Maatschappij (Shell), one of Holland's major corporations. That brought him once a week to that company's offices in Amsterdam. After consultation with the Koehorst family, my hosts, it was arranged that he would come and visit me on Mondays, after having finished his consultant's duties. He and the Koehorsts took to each other and Hans—as I now called Kramers—was invited to stay for dinner on the days of his visit to me, a treat for Hans in those dark years.

During those visits we had many discussions on Hans' ideas concerning a paradox in the theory of electrons: the fact that they have an infinite energy due to their interaction with the electromagnetic field. His starting point was the classical nonrelativistic electron theory. He had first reported on this work at the Galvani conference of 1937.[69]

I, too, had been working on that problem but had become convinced, correctly as it has turned out, that one should treat it in terms of a relativistic quantum theory, and would therefore argue against Kramers' approach. P: A non-relativistic theory is not a good starting point. K: But we have no reliable relativistic theory. P: I agree but the Dirac theory is still the best we have. I would note that the self-energy problem is inherently a quantum problem and that the electromagnetic field, once quantized, would generate new infinities all over again. He would not deny that, but would keep insisting that one should first remedy the physics of the low-frequency fields and then hope for the best. In his last paper[i] (of 1948[71]) on the subject he put it like this: 'A relativistic treatment would . . . hardly seem possible or promising . . . one should not think too hard of the device: first quantizing the wrong Hamiltonian and trying to make amends later on.' I should have paid closer attention to his wartime ideas, which were nothing less than a mass renormalization program (albeit cast in an outdated framework) instead of searching for a realistic finite theory, as I was doing, an idea neither timely then nor even now.

We talked about other subjects as well, naturally about the war situation. One day the discussion turned to music. Kramers said that my hiding period would be a good time for me to learn to play an instrument, and offered to give me instruction on the cello, his own favorite. I said that sounded great, except that I had no cello. That was not a problem, he replied, he knew a music store in Amsterdam where one could rent one. Shortly thereafter a Koehorst son was delegated to visit that store and rent an instrument. Now I had a wonderful new pastime. The noises I produced caused no problems. My hosts told neighbors in passing that a son had taken up the study of the cello. And so my life went on, by no means unpleasantly, until one Monday in November 1943, when disaster struck.

It was about six o'clock in the evening. We were at dinner, Kramers included, when the bell rang. Whenever that happened, at an unusual hour like this, one of the Koehorst children would go down to open the door in person.

That time it was the Gestapo.

There was a special button near the front door which, on pushing, sounded an alarm upstairs. When it rang, I ran from the table (someone at once took my plate away) to my hiding place. On my way upstairs I heard German spoken below, so I knew enough. I opened the panel in the attic wall and crept inside behind it. Then, dammit, I was so nervous that I could not work the inside lock. I therefore held the panel in position by hand. That way it did not fit perfectly; a narrow open crack remained.

They came upstairs and went into the attic. One man carried a strong torch-light, which at one point he shone straight at my panel. I could see the light through the crack—I can still see that light even as I write these lines. He played the light around for a while. Then they left. For the moment, at least, I had escaped the most dangerous situation in my entire life.

I kept sitting in the tiny space, practically bent double, holding onto the panel, when I heard the door to my room, which lay at the other side of my hiding spot, open softly. Someone entered, I did not at first know who. Then that person sat down on a small bench that stood right at the wall behind which I was folded up. He began to read, not loud but quite softly.

It was Kramers.

Earlier he had lent me a volume of Bradley's *Lectures on Shakespeare*. What this good man was doing now was reading to me from that book, in order to calm my nerves.

Sometime between ten and eleven one of the sons came to the attic to tell me that the coast was clear and I could come out. I vividly remember that I believed I had been cooped up for some 15 minutes. In actual fact it was four hours . . .

It was obvious that I quickly had to leave the Koehorst home and that, wher-ever I went next, visits from Hans should stop. I could not take responsibility for further endangering his life. In fact I did not see him for the rest of the war. Nevertheless the most important event in all my contacts with him occurred before the war was over. That happened at the end of the 'hunger winter' of 1944–45, during which Kramers and his family suffered badly and his health, never too robust, deteriorated sharply.

In March 1945 I was caught by the Gestapo and imprisoned in the house of detention (which they had taken over) on the Weteringsschans in Amsterdam.

Tineke, my non-Jewish girlfriend, at once advised Kramers of my capture. He immediately wrote to Heisenberg, probably stressing that I was a talented apo-litical young physicist, or words to that effect, and sent a copy of the letter to Tineke. As he later told me, he did receive a reply. Heisenberg understood, he wrote, was very sorry, but could not do anything.

It was Tineke who got me out—helped by Kramers' letter.

She had gotten hold of the name and address of a high Nazi official in Amsterdam and decided to call on him. She was indeed received in his office. On his desk stood a photo of Goering, with a dedication *Für meinen Freund . . .*

(to my friend, name forgotten). She showed Kramers' letter to the official and asked for his help. The man did not say a word to Tineke after having read the letter and picked up the phone to call the Weteringsschans. '*Hast du einen Jude Pais dort?*' (*Do you have a Jew P. there?*') Yes, they did. '*Lass ihn gehen.*' (Let him go.)

So it came about that I gained my freedom because of physics, and because of the devotion of Kramers and of Tineke.

———————

The next time I saw Hans was in the winter of 1946, in Copenhagen, when he came to visit Niels Bohr, at whose Institute I was a postdoc at that time. My later encounters with him were all in the United States.

In September 1946 I went by ship to New York, to start a fellowship at the Institute for Advanced Study in Princeton. On board I met an earlier acquaintance, Storm Kramers, who was on her way to join her husband in New York. In January 1946 the General Assembly of the United Nations had adopted a resolution calling for the establishment of the UN Atomic Energy Commission, which in turn had organized a scientific and technical subcommittee. Kramers had been elected its chairman. (As a consequence of the developing cold war, the UNAEC recommended, on May 17, 1948, suspension of its own activities.)

Kramers was a natural choice for this chairmanship, and that not just because of his prominence as a physicist. Indeed, even before the first atomic bomb had been dropped on Japan he had been the first Dutch physicist, and probably one of the first continental Europeans, to have had an inkling of the Anglo-American atomic weapons project. I should explain.

———————

From July 30 until August 4, 1945, a secret meeting took place at the American embassy in London. Present were: the American ambassador; Sir John Anderson, cabinet member in Churchill's government responsible for the supervision of the British atomic bomb efforts; Eelco van Kleffens, the Dutch secretary of state; and a team of scientific advisors which included Kramers. The results of that meeting were recorded in a top-secret document entitled: 'Negotiation of an agreement between the US, the UK, and The Netherlands governments for the control and supply of thorium materials.'

Why thorium? And what did Holland have to do with that?

In 1944 General Leslie Groves, the director of the Manhattan Project, the US atomic bomb effort, had written to the US secretary of state: 'There is every indication that nuclear energy can be produced from thorium. If this is so, it would be practical to use thorium instead of uranium, provided a small amount of uranium was used initially. Thorium compared to uranium is abundant and cheap'[72]—whence the interest in thorium.

Thorium is found in monazite, a mineral mined in the 'tin islands,' Bangka and Billiton, off the coast of Sumatra, in the Dutch East Indies (Indonesia since 1949)—whence the Dutch involvement.

The agreement just mentioned states that the Dutch government gives the UK and the US, exclusive rights to buying Dutch thorium. The document was signed on August 4, 1945.

On that same day van Kleffens composed a memorandum about the negotiations which contains these words: 'It is clear that if one were to succeed in unlocking the nuclear energies of uranium and thorium . . . [then this would imply] tremendous danger for the well-being of nations . . .'[73]

Just before the London meeting broke up, the American Ambassador had privately told van Kleffens that the subject they had been discussing 'would receive considerable publicity within a few days.'[73] In fact, two days later, on August 6, Hiroshima was destroyed by a uranium bomb.

This sequence of events shows that the London negotiations must have made evident to Kramers, even before Hiroshima, why the British and Americans were interested in sources of atomic energy. The bombing of August 6 may well have surprised him slightly less than it did us all. (Being unaware of this story until recently, I could not have asked Kramers about that.)

Two postscripts.

1. Soon after this London meeting it became clear that thorium is of little value as a nuclear fuel. Moreover, from 1955 on, uranium became plentiful after President Eisenhower's Atoms for Peace policy permitted its export to all Allied nations.

2. This is as good a place as any to record a bizarre event.

    One day in 1992 a leading Dutch newspaper came out with a three-page article headed: 'The Kramers Affair.'[74] The piece quotes from an FBI report (date not given) in which it is alleged that Kramers might be an atom spy of a stature similar to the notorious Klaus Fuchs, 'perhaps another Fuchs case.' The newspaper article further recounts that the BVD (Binnenlandse Veiligheidsdienst), the Dutch counterpart of the FBI, also had taken up the investigation of good old Hans' credentials.

    Being familiar with several FBI reports, I am not surprised by this example of their stupidity, I have in fact seen worse. I am saddened, however, to note that Dutch Security as well as an otherwise respectable Dutch newspaper would follow up on such junk.

    I now return to the account of my personal contacts with Kramers.

On 19 September 1946, a meeting of the American Physical Society began in New York which I attended. Kramers was also at the meeting, having broken away from his busy schedule at Lake Success, then the site of the UN. I was sitting next to him at one of the sessions when I saw him scribble something on a slip of paper which he handed to me. It read (verbatim): 'Turn around and pay your respects to Robert Oppenheimer.' I turned and there, right behind me, sat the great man, who up to that moment had been known to me only from newspaper pictures. He grinned pleasantly at me and stretched out his hand, which I shook.

During the fall of 1946 Kramers taught at Columbia. He spent the spring term of 1947 at the Institute in Princeton, where we found many occasions for more discussions and for long walks.

In June 1947 both of us attended the Shelter Island Conference, where just over 20 physicists gathered. Several participants have commented later that this meeting may well have been the most important of its kind in their entire scientific career—also my opinion. Kramers, Oppenheimer, and Victor Weisskopf had been selected as discussion leaders. On the first day Willis Lamb and Isidor Rabi reported on experimental deviations of the Dirac theory—which was soon to lead to the renormalization theory. On the second day Kramers gave his report, dealing with his classical treatment of the electron problem. Conferees may have understood the general drift of his ideas, but not their technical details, which were in fact superseded within weeks after the Conference. Only after Kramers' death was it recognized that the initial renormalization idea was his, though not in the form it has taken since 1948.

Already in those days I noticed how deeply tired Hans was, and no wonder. The war had taken its physical toll on him. In the post-war years he continued his beloved physics but also spent much energy on organizational problems. First there was his work at the UN. Then, from 1946 to 1950, he was Chairman of the International Union of Pure and Applied Physics. Also, he was the driving force behind the founding of the Dutch Foundation for Fundamental Research of Matter (FOM), of the Institute for Nuclear Research in Amsterdam (IKO), and of the Dutch–Norwegian Joint Establishment for Nuclear Energy Research in Kjeller, near Oslo. (Less successful was his initiative to place CERN in Denmark, using Bohr's Institute as a nucleus.[75])

In order to explain the origins of the Kjeller project, I need to go back to 1939.

Early that year, I was then a graduate student in Utrecht, I learned of the discovery of nuclear fission. It was at once clear to all physicists, senior as well as junior, like me, that this opened prospects for new utilizable forms of energy and, worse, of new weapons.

Only very much later did I learn of the response by Wander de Haas, a professor of experimental physics in Leiden, to this event. He had at once called on the Dutch prime minister, proposing that his government buy a sizable quantity of uranium oxide mineral. As a result, this material, containing seven tons of uranium, arrived soon afterward at the Kamerling Onnes Laboratory in Leiden, where it was stored in the basement, and from there transported to Delft—where it was kept hidden through the years of German occupation.[76]

After the war, the Dutch realized that this mineral could be of use in building a Dutch nuclear reactor. Whereupon, in January 1950, Kramers traveled to Oslo, to find out if Norway could provide the heavy water needed for such a reactor. On arrival there, he learned that the Norwegians had already started construction of their own reactor—in Kjeller. Negotiations now began about a collaboration in which Holland would contribute its uranium ore.[77]

First, however, uranium needed to be extracted from the mineral ore, a laborious and costly undertaking. Once again Kramers went on the war path. In November 1950 he could report that the British were willing to exchange the Dutch ore, plus 50 000 guilders per ton, for five tons of pure uranium which, for technical reasons, they could not use themselves.

Kramers was elected the first chairman of the Joint Commission for this cooperation. On November 28, 1951, the Kjeller establishment was officially opened. Kramers gave the final address at this ceremony.

The last time I saw Hans was in the autumn of 1951, when he was again in Princeton as Institute member. Hans was not well in his last years. In August 1947 he suffered a cerebral hemorrhage, from which he recovered. Some years later he was found to have heart trouble. In those times he often complained of fatigue, as he had done off and on earlier as well. In early April 1952 he was hospitalized in Leiden, after a carcinoma in the right lung had been diagnosed. (He had been a heavy cigarette smoker.) The lung had to be removed in its entirety. Thereafter he became lamed on the right side.

I followed these events via letters to Princeton, from where I wrote to him for the last time on April 22.[78] My letter ends like this: 'Life starts all over every single day and one never knows what life will bring until that day is done. Get better soon.' Hans never read that letter. He seemed to recover when, on April 24, 1952, an infection to his left lung brought an end to his rich life. He was buried in Oegstgeest.

A few days after Kramers' death, Bohr wrote a sensitive eulogy of him in a Danish newspaper.[79] In May he[80] and Hendrik Casimir[81] spoke of him at a memorial meeting in Leiden.

I conclude with a few brief comments meant to round off my picture of Hans' life.[j]

Kramers was a man of uncommon intellectual versatility. Playing the cello was only one of his favorite pastimes. He also wrote poetry and translated poems from their original languages into Dutch. He had expert familiarity with the writings of Shakespeare. In the 1930s he was for some years an editor of the Dutch literary journal *Het Kouter*. He has often written about philosophical issues in science. He was a fine and dedicated teacher. Between 1929 and 1952 some 27 aspiring physicists received their doctor's degree under his guidance.

Kramers received many honors, memberships in learned academies, honorary degrees, the Lorentz medal, the Royal Society's Hughes medal. In spite of these many recognitions of his immense scientific contributions, he was forever dissatisfied with his own work. It must have troubled him that he was often so close to seminal discoveries—the Compton effect, quantum mechanics, the Dirac equation—which in the event were made by others. Dissatisfactions in his personal life must have contributed to a self-image that was negative to an unreasonable degree.

It is fitting that I end with what Hans himself has written, late in life, about science:

'Science is for those who study it a source of exultation . . . [It is] as if a force outside ourselves, say an angel, pulled us away from our previous level and brought us, in his mercy, to a higher level in an indescribable, incomprehensible manner.'[83]

Notes

a   Here I make grateful use of Dresden's biography of Kramers.[2]

b   Johannes Diderik van der Waals and Jacobus van't Hoff, in a similar situation in earlier times, had only been able to enter university by special governmental dispensation.

c   Harald Bohr was a mathematician who rose to great prominence.

d   I do not quite agree with the picture of Storm given in ref. 9.

e   I am strongly convinced, but cannot prove, that Bohr rejected the photon because it could not fit into his correspondence principle.

f   For more details of this period, see ref. 36.

g   Defined by $N \rightarrow \infty$, $V \rightarrow \infty$, V/N finite, N = number of particles, V = volume. Uhlenbeck (private communication) has told me that this limit was not yet generally understood at the van der Waals conference in 1937.[64]

h   A two-dimensional Ising model.

i   In 1944 Kramers wrote an excellent review of the status of these issues.[70]

j   A necrology of Kramers by his life-long friend Romein[82] has helped me do so.

References

Abbreviations used in the following:

CW: *Niels Bohr, Collected Works*, North-Holland, Amsterdam, 1972, and later years.

D: M. Dresden, *H. A. Kramers*, Springer, New York, 1987.

K: H. A. Kramers.

NBA: Niels Bohr Archive, Copenhagen.

1. *Die Grundlagen der Quantentheorie*, Akad. Verlagsges., Leipzig, 1938. English translation *The Foundations of Quantum Theory* (D. ter Haar, Transl.), North-Holland, Amsterdam, 1957.

2. D, Chapter 10.

3. Entry in K's diary, 1911, undated.

4. K, address on receiving the Lorentz medal, October 30, 1948.

5. K, letter to N. Bohr, August 25, 1916, reprinted in CW, Vol. 2, p. 537.

6. N. Bohr, letter to C. W. Oseen, February 28, 1917, reprinted in CW, Vol. 2, p. 574.

7. D, p. 463.

8. B. Schultz, interviewed by A. Petersen and P. Forman, May 17, 1963, NBA.

9. D, pp. 114–18, 526–32.

10. A. Sommerfeld, letter to N. Bohr, April 25, 1921, NBA.

11. W. Heisenberg, interview by T. S. Kuhn, February 25, 1963, NBA.

12. 'H.A. Kramers, *Collected Scientific Papers*, North-Holland, Amsterdam, 1956, quoted below as CSP.

13. 'Publications of H. A. Kramers,' *Ned. Tÿdsschr. Natuurk.* **18**, 173, 1952.

14. N. Bohr, letter to E. Rutherford, December 27, 1917, NBA.

15. N. Bohr, letter to A. Sommerfeld, July 27, 1919, CW, Vol. 3, p. 14.

16. CW, Vol. 4, p. 122.

17. CW, Vol. 4, p. 379.

18. K, *Zeitschr. f. Physik* **13**, 312, 1923, CSP, p. 192.

19. K, *Proc. Ac. Amsterdam* **23**, 1052, 1921, CSP, p. 134.

20. K, *Danske Vid. Selsk. Skrifter* **3**, 284, 1919, CSP, p. 3.

21. K and H. Holst, *The Atom and the Bohr Theory of its Structure*, Knopf, New York, 1923.

22. Ref. 21, p. 139.

23. K, *Naturw.* **4**, 550, 1923.

24. K, *Fysisk Tidsskr.* **33**, 82, 1935.

25. A. Sommerfeld, *Atombau und Spektrallinien*, 3rd edn, p. 338, Vieweg, Braunschweig, 1922.

26. K, *Phil. Mag.* **46**, 836, 1923, CSP, p. 156.

27. A. Eddington, letter to K, December 12, 1923, NBA.

28. K, *Naturw.* **11**, 550, 1923.

29. K, *Zeitschr. f. Physik* **13**, 343, 1923, CSP, p. 223.

30. K, *Zeitschr. f. Physik* **13**, 351, 1923, CSP, p. 231.

31. K, *Z. f. Phys. Chem.* **104**, 451, 1923, CSP, p. 249.

32. D, chapter 14.

33. Ref. 21, p. 175.

34. N. Bohr, *Zeitschr. f. Physik* **13**, 117, 1923. English translation in CW, Vol. 3, p. 457, especially chapter 3.

35. N. Bohr, K, and J. Slater, *Phil. Mag.* **47**, 785, 1924, CSP, p. 271.

36. A. Pais, *Niels Bohr's Times*, chapter 11, section (d), Oxford University Press, 1991.

37. M. Born, *My life*, p. 216, Taylor and Francis, London, 1976.

38. K, *Nature* **113**, 673, 1924, CSP, p. 290.

39. K, *Nature* **114**, 310, 1924, CSP, p. 292.

40. R. de L. Kronig, *J. Am. Optical Soc.* **12**, 547, 1926.

41. K, *Atti Congr. Como* **2**, 545, 1927; *Phys. Z.* **30**, 522, 1929; CSP, pp. 333, 347.

42. Cf. A. Pais, *Inward Bound*, p. 499ff., Oxford University Press, 1986.

43. Ref. 11, interview on February 19, 1963.

44. K and W. Heisenberg, *Zeitschr. f. Physik* **31**, 681, 1925, CSP, p. 293.

45. English translation of ref. 44 in B. L. van der Waerden, *Sources of Quantum Mechanics*, p. 223, Dover, New York, 1968.

46. Ref. 45, p. 16.

47. Ref. 11, interview on February 13, 1963.

48. Ref. 11, interview on July 5, 1963.

49. Memorandum of K to O. Klein, undated, NBA.

50. K, *Physica* **5**, 369, 1925.

51. K, *Fys. Tidsskr.* **25**, 128, 1927.

52. K, letter to N. Bohr, July 18, 1926, NBA.

53. K, *Physica* **11**, 321, 1931.

54. K, *Nature* **132**, 667, 1933; *Physica* **13**, 273, 1933.

55. K, *Ned. T. Natuurk.* **1**, 241, 1934.

56. K, *Zeitschr. f. Physik* **39**, 828, 1926, CSP, p. 348.

57. K, in *Électrons et Photons*, pp. 263–70, Gauthier Villars, Paris, 1928.

58. N. Bohr, letter to K, 11 November 1926, NBA.

59. P. A. M. Dirac, *Proc. Roy. Soc. A* **117**, 610; **118**, 35, 1928.

60. Ref. 1, chapter 6.

61. CSP, pp. 375, 382, 388, 395, 405, 411, 423, 437, 453, 629, 654, 669.

62. CSP, pp. 503, 515, 522, 536, 557, 574, 585, 629.

63. CSP, pp. 598, 607, 949.

64. *Physica* **4**, November 23 issue, 1937.

65. K and G. Wannier, *Phys. Rev.* **60**, 252, 263, 1941, CSP, pp. 786, 797.

66. K, *Physica* **7**, 284, 1940, CSP, p. 754.

67. P. Hänggi *et al.*, *Rev. Mod. Phys.* **62**, 251, 1990.

68. K, CSP, p. 697.

69. K, CSP, p. 831.

70. K, CSP, p. 838.

71. K, CSP, p. 845.

72. Quoted in J. van Splunter, *The International History Review* **17**, 485, 1995.

73. Quoted in C. Wiebes and B. Zeeman, *Bÿdragen en Mededelingen over de Geschiedenis der Nederlanden*, **106**, 391, 1991.

74. *NRC Handelsblad*, May 2, 1992.

75. See ref. 36, p. 52.

76. H. Casimir, *Haphazard Reality*, p. 173, Harper and Row, New York, 1983.

77. For the history of the origins of Kjeller see J. A. Goedkoop, *Atoomenergie en haar toepassingen*, **9**, 69, 1967.

78. A. Pais, letter to K, April 22, 1952, now in my private file.

79. N. Bohr, in *Politiken*, April 27, 1952.

80. N. Bohr, *Ned. T. v. Natuurk.* **18**, 161, 1952.

81. H. B. G. Casimir, *ibid* **18**, 167, 1952; also in *Jaarboek Ak. Wetensch. Amsterdam*, 1952–53, p. 1.

82. J. Romein, in *Jaarboek van de maatschappy der Nederlandse letterkunde*, 1951–53, p. 82.

83. K, in *Nederlands' helden in de natuurwelenschappen*, p. 335, Elsevier, Dordrecht, 1946.

Tsung Dao Lee (left) and Chen Ning Yang at the Institute for Advanced Study, Princeton, 1957. (Courtesy of Archives Institute for Advanced Study.)

Tsung Dao Lee and Chen Ning Yang

The decision of the Swedish Academy of Sciences to award the Nobel Prize to the discoverers of the non-conservation of parity in weak interactions so soon after the event most happily expresses the general consensus of opinion concerning the fundamental importance of the discovery. All those who made the personal acquaintance of the young laureates have been impressed by the charm of their personalities no less than by the versatility and profundity of their genius. The following article, racily sketching their brilliant career, will give the reader as apt a picture of their thought as the accompanying photograph of their features— brightened by the perfect Nobel laureate grin. The Editor is grateful to his old pupil and friend A. Pais for his prompt response to a request to write this article [published[1] in 1958]. It is fitting to remember that it was Pais' pioneering endeavor to analyze the invariance properties of elementary particles which gave the initial impetus to the theoretical developments culminating in Lee and Yang's discovery.

(L. Rosenfield, editor of *Nuclear Physics*)

Un physicien éminent me disait un jour á propos de la loi des erreurs: 'Tout le monde y croit fermement parce que les mathématiciens s'imaginent que c'est un fait d'observation, et les observateurs que c'est un théorème de mathématiques.' Il en a été longtemps ainsi pour le principe de la conservation de l'énergie. Il n'en est plus de même aujourd'hui; personne n'ignore que c'est un fait expérimental.

(H. Poincaré)

It seems fair to say that two years ago, to fix a reasonable point in time, nearly all theoretical physicists believed that the general validity of space reflexion invariance had firmly been established by observation.[2] It seems fair to say that at that time few experimentalists thought of devising experiments which might challenge the universal validity of parity conservation.[3] It seems fair to say that the main contribution to physics which Lee and Yang have made so far has been to point out that parity conservation had never been checked in a domain of physics of which much, but not enough, was known two years ago (β-decay, π-decay, μ-decay); and to discuss a series of experimental conditions under which such checks could be made.[4]

The incentive to these investigations came from the puzzling properties of the K-mesons. Various participants of the Sixth Rochester Conference (April 1956) felt and expressed doubts about the universal validity of parity conservation in view of the experimentally found near equality in mass and, above all, in life time of the charged θ- and τ-mesons. Whatever might be the answer to this θ–τ puzzle, it was clear that 'the τ-meson will have either domestic or foreign complications,' as Oppenheimer put it then. Be it recorded here that, on the train back from Rochester to New York, Professor Yang and the present author each bet Professor John Wheeler one dollar that the θ- and τ-mesons were distinct particles; and that Professor Wheeler has since collected two dollars.

Lee and Yang faced the challenge. Immediately after the conference they started a systematic investigation on the then status of experimental knowledge concerning the verification of space reflexion invariance and charge conjugation invariance. Their conclusion was that for one group of interactions neither invariance had so far been established. These reactions are all characterized by their weakness and to these belong the three types of decay processes mentioned above, as well as K-particle and hyperon disintegration. Thus the attention became focused on a whole class of phenomena instead of on an exciting but rather isolated puzzle. Soon a theoretical investigation followed,[5] together with Oehme, on the question of time reversal invariance and on the interrelations between possible violations of 'C-, P- and T-invariance' with the help of the CPT theorem. And then came the great news: neither P- nor C-invariance holds true in β-decay, nor in π-, nor in μ-decay. It will be remembered how the Co^{60}-experiment of Chien Shung Wu (Mrs Yuan) and coworkers[6] provided the first evidence, soon followed by additional evidence from the π–μ–e decay sequence.[7] More recently it has been established that parity is not conserved in Λ^0 decay either, and so, via only a slight theoretical detour, the θ–τ puzzle may be considered to be solved. On January 16, 1957, *The New York Times* carried on its front page an article headlined: 'Basic concept in physics is reported upset in tests/Conservation of parity in nuclear theory challenged by scientists at Columbia and Princeton Institute.'

Thus Lee and Yang's suggestions have led to a great liberation in our thinking on the very structure of physical theory. Once again principle has turned out to be prejudice. The quotation from Poincaré (taken from the preface of his *Thermodynamique*[8]) may be a timely reminder of not too dissimilar struggles of other generations.

———————

Chen Ning Yang (all his friends call him Frank) was born in 1922 in China, in Hofei, in the province of Anhwei. He is the oldest of the five children of Ko-

Chuen Yang, professor of mathematics (PhD, Chicago 1928) at the Southwest Associated University in Kunming, one of the best Chinese universities, later professor at Fudan University in Shanghai. Frank and his family had to endure the devastating war in China (1937–45). 'In 1940 the house that my family rented in Kunming received a direct hit . . . [but] no member of the family was wounded . . . the family survived intact—lean, very lean, but healthy.'[9]

Frank started his university studies at the Southwest Associated University. Later he went to Tsinghua University in the same city, where he received the MSc degree in 1944.[10]

Tsung Dao Lee (T. D. to his friends) was born in 1926 in Shanghai, the third of six children. His father, Tsing Kong Lee, was an agriculturalist. Like Frank, Lee began his studies at the Southwest Associated University. The two men first met in 1945, when Lee was a student and Yang a high school teacher in Kunming. One of Frank's pupils was Miss Chih-Li Tu, now Mrs Yang.

In August 1945 Frank left for the United States. 'There being no commercial passenger traffic between China and the United States at that time, I had to wait several months in Calcutta for a berth in a troop transport. I finally reached New York in late November and went to Chicago around Christmas. January 1946 saw me enrolled as a graduate student at the University of Chicago,'[9] where Fermi's oeuvre and style made a lasting impression on him.[11]

T. D. too went to Chicago. It was there that, in 1946, their friendship started. Yang received his PhD in 1948 under Professor Teller, with a thesis on angular distributions in nuclear reactions.[12] Lee got his in 1950 under Professor Fermi for his work on the hydrogen content of white dwarfs.[13] His first papers[14] deal with astrophysical problems and with the theory of turbulence. Soon after getting his doctorate Yang joined the Institute for Advanced Study in Princeton, at first as a temporary member, eventually (1956) as a full professor. In 1950 Lee went to Berkeley as a lecturer. Here he met Miss Janet Chin, now Mrs Lee.[15] In the Fall of 1951 Lee started a two-year period of membership at the Institute. From that time on the two men have collaborated intimately and steadily. Incidentally, their first joint paper, together with Rosenbluth, deals with weak interactions.[16] In 1953 Lee went to Columbia, where he became a full professor in 1956.

In collaboration with others, Lee has worked on such subjects as π-nucleon scattering[17] and multiple meson production,[18] studied by means of variational methods; and related approaches to the ground state and effective mass of the polaron.[19] Of particular interest is his work on a rigorously solvable renormalizable model of a field theory.[20] It is a model in the sense that one has to do with a problem which is not as rich in physical features as, for example, electrodynamics; at the same time, the model is non-trivial. It enables one to treat renormalizations explicitly without the use of power-series expansions and it leads to new insights on the relation between unrenormalized and renormalized coupling constants. The interesting and spiritual consequences of the model are still under study.

Already in his thesis we find Yang engaged on a program of obtaining physical information which is largely independent of a detailed dynamical description but where extensive use is made of the invariance properties of the problem in hand. In a similar vein are his investigations on the parity[21] of the π^0 meson and on the reflection properties of fermion fields.[22] Further, we mention a not too successful attempt to consider π-mesons as nucleon derivates;[23] and an approach to field theory[24] where one deals directly with the equations of motion for the various fields and sources. In 1952 Yang contracted the celebrated Ising disease, but unlike many of his fellow patients he pulled through by being able to compute the spontaneous magnetization of the two-dimensional lattice.[25] This in turn led to the Yang–Lee theory of phase transitions,[26] a subject to which Yang had been attracted earlier.[27] More recently, and in collaboration with others, new results have been obtained on the many-body problem in quantum theory,[28] some of which will help to put the theory of superfluidity on a more rigorous mathematical basis.

Many of the papers by Lee and Yang on fundamental particles carry a marked element of speculation, such as for example their suggestions on the conservation law of heavy fermions,[29] or on parity conjugation.[30] But invariably they propose experiments to test their conjectures and so, where they have been wrong at times, they have erred in good taste. And they have had the courage to try again.

Their more recent work deals with the two-component formulation of neutrino theory,[31] a topic to which independent contributions had been made by Salam[32] and by Landau[33]; and with the concept of lepton conservation.[34] At the time of writing the experimental situation in β-decay, after having gone through a phase of utter confusion last summer, is still too unclear to enable one to judge the tenability of these appealing ideas. Most recently they have been analyzing the information obtainable from hyperon decay.[35]

The work of T. D. and of Frank is characterized by taste and ingenuity, by physical insight and formal power. Their counsel is sought by theorist and experimentalist alike. In this they have more than a touch of the late Fermi. Their friends wish them many happy and creative years to come.

Addenda

Since it is now 40 years ago that I wrote the preceding lines, it is appropriate that I add some comments on later years. First, I note that both the Lees and the Yangs are blessed with gifted children, Lee with two, Yang with three; and that in 1960 Lee joined the Princeton Institute as a professor.

My brief remarks on their later oeuvre have been greatly helped by having at hand the selected papers by Yang[9] and by Lee,[36] also by editorial comments in both works.

Later joint papers

(a) During the years 1957–60, Lee and Yang wrote a number of very inventive papers on issues in statistical mechanics. These fall in two groups:

    1   Properties of a dilute hard sphere Bose gas by means of the pseudopotential method,[37] using a selective summation of series to eliminate divergences. They obtained information on energy levels, superfluidity, phase transition, and other features.

    2   A series of papers on the many-body problem in quantum statistical mechanics,[38] in which they formulate the grand partition function in terms of average occupation numbers in momentum space, with applications to hard sphere Bose and Fermi gases.

(b) High energy neutrino physics. In 1960, it had been suggested[39] that the interactions of high energy neutrinos and antineutrinos with nucleons and nuclei could provide new information on weak interactions. This suggestion led Lee and Yang to investigate a series of theoretical implications of such experiments—including consequences of the possible existence of weakly coupled charged bosons, $W^\pm$, as transmitters of weak interactions.[40] Sequels to this work are: an analysis of logical and phenomenological aspects of the W-mechanism,[41] and of neutrino reactions without production of W's.[42]

(c) A speculation on larger symmetry groups for strong interactions.[43]

(d) A study of the renormalization question in the quantum field theory of charged W bosons.[44] That paper, submitted in May 1962, is Lee and Yang's last joint effort.

The break

In June 1962, personal and professional relations between Lee and Yang came to an end. This rift has been irreconcilable.

After I was told of this break, I went to see Frank. I told him how deeply saddened I was by what had happened, that I would continue to consider him my friend, and that I would next go to T. D., to tell him the very same. Which I did, adding that I had already told Frank the very same.

My relations with both men have in fact remained affectionate.

In the course of time I have learned a good deal of what had come to pass that June month. I consider that information as privileged and private but should like to observe that in my opinion more knowledge than I possess about Chinese mores would be necessary for greater clarity in this matter. I can refer, however, to comments by Yang[45] and by Lee[46] themselves on these events.

Late in 1962, T. D. returned to Columbia University, as Fermi professor, after 1984 as university professor. In 1966, Frank left the Institute for the State University of New York at Stony Brook with an appointment as Einstein professor, and the directorship of an institute for theoretical physics, created for him.[47]

The two men have remained very productive since having gone their separate ways. I shall briefly indicate highlights of their later work, referring to their selected papers[9,36] for much more detail.

Yang's later work

One item is missing in my synopsis of Yang's earlier publications,[21–35] actually the most important contribution of his career: his papers with Robert Mills on non-Abelian gauge theories.[48] Elsewhere in this book[49] I have explained why that work was initially received with great skepticism by their colleagues, including me: it appeared at that time that the non-Abelian gauge bosons (now called $W^{\pm}$) had to have the absolutely unacceptable mass values zero. When in 1958 I wrote my eulogy[1] to Lee and Yang, I therefore felt no need to mention the Yang–Mills theory. It took until the advent of 'spontaneously broken gauge symmetries,' around 1970, before this vexing issue was resolved. From then on it has been evident that the work by Yang and Mills ranks among the most profound contributions of this century to physical theory.

It had also taken time before Yang himself realized the significance of his work. When asked in the 1990s whether, in 1954, he had understood the tremendous importance of these papers, he replied: 'No. In the 1950s we felt our work was elegant. I realized its importance in the 1960s and its great importance to physics in the 1970s. Its relationship to deep mathematics became clear to me only after 1974.'[50]

Turning now to Yang's later work; he did not publish on gauge fields between 1955 and 1967, when he came back to the subject.[51] Next came a paper in which he broadened the discussion to include remarks on charge quantization and flux quantization.[52] By then he had become interested in the geometric meaning of gauge fields, but wrote in 1972: 'On the mathematical side, the concept of gauge fields apparently is related to fibre bundles. But I do not know really what a fibre bundle is.'[53] Whereupon he sought and received instruction from a mathematician colleague, which led to his excellent, instructive paper,[54] jointly with Tai Tsun Wu, on non-integrable phase factors and global topological connections of gauge theories. This article contains a translation dictionary from gauge field language into bundle terminology, showing that he had mastered the theory of fiber bundles. A series of elaborations followed.[55] From that time on, modern mathematicians have become increasingly interested and have participated in what modern physicists are up to.

In the 1960s, Yang returned to another of his favorite fields of inquiry, statistical physics. He wrote on imperfect Bose gases,[56] flux quantization in super-conductive systems,[57] and long-range order in liquid helium.[58] Together with his brother Chen Ping Yang, now professor emeritus at Ohio State University, he published on critical points in liquid–gas transitions,[59] and solved the problem of one-dimensional chains of spin–spin interactions.[60] Best known in this category is the Yang–Baxter equation, which first appeared in Frank's papers[61] of 1967–68, and which later was published independently by Rodney Baxter[62] in a different context. Today we know that the Yang–Baxter equation is a fundamental mathematical structure with widely varying applications to mathematics and physics.

A third category of papers deals with a variety of topics in high energy phenomenology. Among these I like especially his tests for the single pion exchange model, together with Treiman;[63] and his analysis of CP-violating effects, together with T. T. Wu.[64] There are many more articles from his hand on phenomenological topics.[65]

Lee's later work

Lee, too, published prolifically in subsequent years. Again I restrict myself to some highlights.

Further studies of properties of W bosons.[66] An analysis of divergences related to particles with zero rest mass.[67] A model for CP-violation.[68] Together with Gian Carlo Wick, Lee analyzed the consequences of an indefinite metric in Hilbert space for the purpose of eliminating infinities in quantum field theory.[69] Their collaboration continued with a study of the stability of the vacuum state in a spin zero field theory.[70]

In 1975 Lee began a series of studies of soliton problems[71] and their application to hadron models, for which it was shown that they can reproduce the bag model of hadrons.[72] In the years 1986–92 this work took a new turn with Lee's creation of the field of non-topological solitons applied to stellar objects.[73] This yields new options for cosmological models.

Meanwhile, in the early 1980s, Lee and collaborators had started studies of field theories on a lattice,[74] eventually including effects of gravity.[75] Stimulated by Lee and competently led by Norman Christ, a series of dedicated computers have been constructed, at Columbia's physics department, for the express purpose of performing field theory calculations on lattices within the framework of quantum chromodynamics. This work led Lee to suggest that space and time might *really* be discrete.[76]

Since the discovery of high temperature superconductivity, Lee and coworkers have devoted themselves to trying to understand its mechanism.[77]

Lee has been a strong proponent of using relativistic heavy ion collisions for checking his idea[78] of the existence of phase transitions in the vacuum ('vacuum engineering'). These effects have led to the construction of the RHIC accelerator at Brookhaven National Laboratory. In 1997, Lee assumed the directorship of a theory group at Brookhaven (while retaining his ties with Columbia), supported by funding from Japan.

T. D.'s fine private collection of Chinese art bears witness to one of his important non-scientific interests. He has also lectured on the relations between art and science.[79]

Both Tsung Dao and Frank have, each in their own independent ways, striven to promote a better understanding between the United States and China, and to convince the Chinese government of the importance of basic research and scholarly exchange between the two countries.[80] I should mention in particular a program organized by T. D. which has enabled almost one thousand Chinese students to pursue graduate studies in the United States.

On May 19, 1988 I turned 70. Friends had arranged a symposium in my honor, held at the Rockefeller University on May 13. The speakers, all personal friends, represented a roster of the finest American physicists. I was touched to have both Frank and Tsung Dao among them.

References

1. A. Pais, *Nucl. Phys.* **5**, 297, 1958, enlarged here. Introductory comment by L. Rosenfeld: *ibid.*, **5**, 296, 1958.

2. For a notable case of misgivings see G. C. Wick, A. Wightman, and E. Wigner, *Phys. Rev.* **88**, 101, 1952, footnote 9.

3. For a notable exception see E. Purcell and N. Ramsey, *Phys. Rev.* **78**, 807, 1950.

4. T. D. Lee and C. N. Yang, *Phys. Rev.* **104**, 254, 1956.

5. T. D. Lee, R. Oehme, and C. N. Yang, *Phys. Rev.* **106**, 340, 1957.

6. C. S. Wu *et al.*, *Phys. Rev.* **105**, 1413, 1957.

7. R. L. Garwin, L. Lederman, and M. Weinrich, *Phys. Rev.* **105**, 1415, 1957; J. Friedman and V. Telegdi, *ibid.*, p. 1681.

8. H. Poincaré, *Thermodynamique*, Gauthier Villars, Paris, 1901; also in *La science et l'hypothèse*, p. 155, Flammarion, Paris, 1907.

9. C. N. Yang, *Selected Papers*, pp. 3, 4, Freeman, San Francisco, 1983.

10. C. N. Yang, *J. Chem. Phys.* **13**, 66, 1945.

11. See ref. 9, p. 305.

12. C. N. Yang, *Phys. Rev.* **74**, 764, 1948.

13. T. D. Lee, *Astrophys. J.* **111**, 625, 1950.

14. T. D. Lee, *Phys. Rev.* **77**, 842, 1950; *Astrophys. J.* **112**, 561, 1950; *J. Appl. Phys.* **22**, 524, 1952; *Quart. Appl. Math.* **10**, 69, 1952.

15. Deceased in 1997.

16. T. D. Lee, M. Rosenbluth, and C. N. Yang, *Phys. Rev.* **75**, 905, 1949.

17. T. D. Lee and R. Christian, *Phys. Rev.* **94**, 1760, 1954; the same and R. Friedman, *Phys. Rev.* **100**, 1494, 1955.

18. E. Henley and T. D. Lee, *Phys. Rev.* **101**, 1536, 1956.

19. T. D. Lee, F. Low, and D. Pines, *Phys. Rev.* **90**, 297, 1953; T. D. Lee and D. Pines, *Phys. Rev.* **92**, 883, 1953.

20. T. D. Lee, *Phys. Rev.* **95**, 1329, 1954.

21. C. N. Yang, *Phys. Rev.* **77**, 242, 722, 1950.

22. C. N. Yang and J. Tiomno, *Phys. Rev.* **79**, 495, 1950.

23. C. N. Yang and E. Fermi, *Phys. Rev.* **76**, 1739, 1949.

24. C. N. Yang and D. Feldman, *Phys. Rev.* **79**, 792, 1950.

25. C. N. Yang, *Phys. Rev.* **85**, 808, 1952.

26. C. N. Yang and T. D. Lee, *Phys. Rev.* **87**, 404, 410, 1952.

27. C. N. Yang, *Chinese J. Phys.* **5**, 138, 1944; **6**, 59, 1945; with Y. Y. Li, *ibid.*, **7**, 59, 1947; *J. Chem. Phys.* **13**, 66, 1945.

28. K. Huang and C. N. Yang, *Phys. Rev.* **105**, 767, 1957; the same and J. Luttinger, *Phys. Rev.* **105**, 776, 1957; T. D. Lee and C. N. Yang, *Phys. Rev.* **105**, 1119, 1957; the same and K. Huang, *Phys. Rev.* **106**, 1135, 1957.

29. T. D. Lee and C. N. Yang, *Phys. Rev.* **98**, 1501, 1955.

30. T. D. Lee and C. N. Yang, *Phys. Rev.* **102**, 290, 1956; **104**, 822, 1956.

31. T. D. Lee and C. N. Yang, *Phys. Rev.* **105**, 1671, 1957.

32. A. Salam, *Nuov. Cim.* **5**, 299, 1957.

33. L. D. Landau, *Nucl. Phys.* **3**, 127, 1957.

34. T. D. Lee, *Proceedings of the Seventh Rochester Conference 1957*, section VII, p. 1, Interscience, New York, 1957.

35. T. D. Lee, J. Steinberger, G. Feinberg, P. Kabir, and C. N. Yang, *Phys. Rev.* **106**, 1367, 1957; T. D. Lee and C. N. Yang, *Phys. Rev.* **108**, 1645, 1957.

36. T. D. Lee, *Selected Papers, 1949–1985* (G. Feinberg, Ed.), 3 vols, Birkhäuser, Boston, 1986; *1985–1996* (H. C. Ren and Y. Pang, Eds), Gordon and Breach, New York, 1998.

37. T. D. Lee and C. N. Yang, *Phys. Rev.* **106**, 1135, 1957; **112**, 1419, 1958; **113**, 1406, 1959.

38. T. D. Lee and C. N. Yang, *Phys. Rev.* **113**, 1165, 1959; **116**, 25, 1959; **117**, 12, 22, 897, 1960.

39. M. Schwartz, *Phys. Rev. Lett.* **4**, 306, 1960.

40. T. D. Lee and C. N. Yang, *Phys. Rev. Lett.* **4**, 307, 1960.

41. T. D. Lee and C. N. Yang, *Phys. Rev.* **119**, 1410, 1960; with P. Markstein, *Phys. Rev. Lett.* **7**, 429, 1961.

42. T. D. Lee and C. N. Yang, *Phys. Rev.* **126**, 2239, 1962.

43. T. D. Lee and C. N. Yang, *Phys. Rev.* **122**, 1954, 1961.

44. T. D. Lee and C. N. Yang, *Phys. Rev.* **128**, 885, 1962.

45. C. N. Yang, ref. 9, pp. 30, 53.

46. T. D. Lee, ref. 36, Vol. 3, p. 487; Vol. 1985–1996, p. 163.

47. For the role of Yang at Stony Brook see J. S. Toll, in *Chen Ning Yang* (C. S. Lin and S. T. Yau, Eds), p. 401, International Press, Boston, 1995.

48. C. N. Yang and R. Mills, *Phys. Rev.* **95**, 631; **96**, 191, 1954.

49. See the essay on W. Pauli. See also C. N. Yang, ref. 9, p. 19, and R. Mills, *Am. J. Phys.* **57**, 493, 1989, for their respective recollections of the origins of that work.

50. D. Z. Zhang, interview of Yang, in *C. N. Yang* (C. S. Liu and S. T. Yau, Eds), p. 457, International Press, Boston, 1995.

51. T. T. Wu and C. N. Yang, ref. 9, p. 400.

52. C. N. Yang, *Phys. Rev.* **D1**, 2360, 1970.

53. C. N. Yang, ref. 9, p. 450.

54. T. T. Wu and C. N. Yang, *Phys. Rev.* **D12**, 3845, 1975; See also C. N. Yang, *Phys. Rev. Lett.* **33**, 445, 1974.

55. T. T. Wu and C. N. Yang, *Nucl. Phys.* **B107**, 365, 1976; *Phys. Rev.* **D14**, 437, 1976; **D16**, 1018, 1977; C. N. Yang, *Ann. New York Ac. Sci.* **294**, 86, 1977; *Phys. Rev. Lett.* **38**, 1377, 1977; *J. Math. Phys.* **19**, 320, 2622, 1978.

56. C. N. Yang, *Physica* **26**, 549, 1960.

57. N. Byers and C. N. Yang, *Phys. Rev. Lett.* **7**, 46, 1961.

58. C. N. Yang, *Rev. Mod. Phys.* **34**, 694, 1962.

59. C. N. Yang and C. P. Yang, *Phys. Rev. Lett.* **13**, 303, 1964.

60. C. N. Yang and C. P. Yang, *Phys. Rev.* **150**, 321, 327; **151**, 258, 1966.

61. C. N. Yang, *Phys. Rev. Lett.* **19**, 1312, 1967; *Phys. Rev.* **168**, 1920, 1968.

62. For Baxter's contributions see his article in ref. 50, p. 1.

63. S. B. Treiman and C. N. Yang, *Phys. Rev. Lett.* **8**, 140, 1960.

64. C. N. Yang and T. T. Wu, *Phys. Rev. Lett.* **13**, 380, 1964.

65. Including C. N. Yang and T. T. Wu, *Phys. Rev.* **137**, 708, 1965; C. N. Yang and N. Byers *Phys. Rev.* **142**, 976, 1966; C. N. Yang and J. Benecke, T. Chou, and E. Yen, *Phys. Rev.* **188**, 2159, 1969; C. N. Yang and T. Chou, *Nucl. Phys.* **B107**, 1, 1976; *Phys. Rev.* **170**, 1591, 1968; **D4**, 2005, 1972; **D7**, 2063, 1973; **D17**, 1881, 1978; **D19**, 3268, 1979; **D22**, 610, 1981; *Phys. Rev. Lett.* **20**, 1213, 1968; **25**, 1072, 1970; **46**, 764, 1981.

66. T. D. Lee, Cern Report 61-31, p. 65, 1961; *Phys. Rev.* **128**, 899, 1806, 1968; *Nuov. Cim.* **59A**, 579, 1969; *Phys. Rev. Lett.* **26**, 801, 1971; with J. Bernstein, *Phys. Rev. Lett.* **11**, 512, 1963.

67. T. D. Lee and M. Nauenberg, *Phys. Rev.* **133**, B1549, 1964.

68. T. D. Lee, *Phys. Rev.* **D8**, 1226, 1973; *Phys. Rep.* **9C**, No. 2, 1974; also T. D. Lee and L. Wolfenstein, *Phys. Rev.* **138**, B1490, 1965.

69. T. D. Lee and G. C. Wick, *Nucl. Phys.* **B9**, 209, 1969; **B10**, 1, 1969; *Phys. Rev.* **D2**, 1033, 1970; **D3**, 1046, 1971.

70. T. D. Lee and G. C. Wick, *Phys. Rev.* **D9**, 2291, 1974; **D11**, 1591, 1975; *Rev. Mod. Phys.* **47**, 267, 1975; also T. D. Lee and M. Margulies, *Phys. Rev.* **D11**, 1591, 1975; **D12**, 4008, 1976.

71. N. Christ and T. D. Lee, *Phys. Rev.* **D12**, 1606, 1975; R. Friedberg, T. D. Lee, and A. Sirlin, *Phys. Rev.* **D13**, 2739, 1976; *Nucl. Phys.* **B115**, 1, 32, 1976.

72. R. Friedberg and T. D. Lee, *Phys. Rev.* **D15**, 1694, 1977; **D16**, 1096, 1976; **D18**, 2623, 1978.

73. T. D. Lee, *Phys. Rev.* **D35**, 3637, 1987; R. Friedberg, T. D. Lee, and Y. Pang, *Phys. Rev.* **D35**, 3640, 3658, 1987; T. D. Lee and Y. Pang, *Nucl. Phys.* **B315**, 477, 1989; *Phys. Reports* **22**, 251, 1992.

74. N. Christ, R. Friedberg, and T. D. Lee, *Nucl. Phys.* **B202**, 89, 1982; **210**, 310, 1982.

75. G. Feinberg, R. Friedberg, T. D. Lee, and H. C. Ren, *Nucl. Phys.* **B245**, 343, 1984.

76. T. D. Lee, Phys. Lett. *122B*, 217, 1983; T. D. Lee and R. Friedberg, *Nucl. Phys.* **B225**, 1, 1983.

77. T. D. Lee and R. Friedberg, *Phys. Lett.* **138A**, 423, 1989; *Phys. Rev.* **B40**, 6745, 1989; T. D. Lee, R. Friedberg, and H. C. Ren, *Phys. Rev.* **B42**, 4122, 1990; *Phys. Lett.* **A152**, 417, 423, 1991; *Phys. Rev.* **B45**, 10, 732, 1992; *Ann. of Phys.* **228**, 52, 1993; *Phys. Rev.* **B50**, 10, 190, 1994.

78. T. D. Lee, *Rev. Mod. Phys.* **47**, 267, 1975.

79. See for example T. D. Lee, *Science Spectra* **7**, 26, 1997.

80. For Yang, see ref. 9, p. 518; for Lee, see ref. 36, 1985–1996, pp. XII–XIV.

John and Klari von Neumann in front of their Princeton home, late 1940s. (Courtesy of Marina von Neumann Whitman.)

John von Neumann

Youth

In his native Hungary—he was born in Budapest, on December 28, 1903—he was officially known as Margittai Neumann Janos Lajos. His friends called him Jancsi. In 1913, his father, a lawyer and bank director, had been awarded the Margittai title of nobility by Franz Joseph, in recognition of his contributions to the development of Hungary's economy. (Margitta is the name of a Hungarian town.) He had two younger brothers, Michael and Nicholas. He hailed from a family of non-practicing Jews, though all boys became bar mitzvah, the Jewish rite of initiation to manhood at age 13. Later the family converted to Catholicism. Stanislaw Ulam, a later friend of von Neumann, has written that, however, in his adult years, Jancsi 'never concealed his Jewish origins. In fact, he was very proud of the birth of the State of Israel in 1948.'[1]

In America—he was a US citizen from 1938—he became officially known as John von Neumann. His friends called him Johnny.

Jancsi's education began with years of private tutoring at home, which included training in Hebrew writing and literature by a visiting rabbi. As a child he read all the way through a popular 44-volume set on general history.[2] From a young age on he also developed a special faculty for rapid mental arithmetic, a gift that remained with him throughout his life.

At age ten he was enrolled in the *Agostai Hitvallasu Evangelikus Fogimnázium*, the Lutheran Gimnázium for boys. Its curriculum included eight years of Latin and four years of Greek. The boy thoroughly mastered not only those classical languages—he and his father would often joke with each other in classical Greek[3]—but also excelled in English, and eventually became fluent in German, French, and Italian as well.

Most importantly, soon after having entered the Gimnázium, Johnny's astonishing grasp of mathematics was recognized by one of his teachers, who arranged for Michael Fekete, a young mathematician from the University of Budapest—who himself was to have a distinguished career—to tutor von Neumann regularly at home. That arrangement continued through all of

Johnny's eight Gimnázium years, and resulted in his first mathematics publication, jointly with Fekete.[4]

At school, von Neumann made the first acquaintance with Eugene Wigner, who was one year ahead of him, and who has recalled: 'I never felt I knew von Neumann very well at Gimnázium. Perhaps no one did; he always kept a bit apart. He loved his mother and confided in her, but hardly in others. His brothers greatly admired him, but they were not intimates . . . He joined in class pranks just enough to avoid unpopularity.'[5] In later years, their acquaintance grew into a close friendship, however.

Jancsi's Gimnázium report cards[6] give a synopsis of the boy's strengths and limitations. All his grades were A, except for B's in geometrical drawing, writing, and music, and a C for physical education. Regarding this C,

> As a youth [von N.] had no bent towards physical or sporting activities. And even when later on he drove some very dashing-looking cars with the maximum velocity for which they were designed, he never acquired the mien of a 'sporting type.' He did claim, however, that he had once learned to ride a bicycle . . . In his teens he was somewhat gauche and not quite the type of 'leader.' But there was nothing awkward about his manner in later life, and he gave the impression of considerable collectedness and self-confidence. He was courteous and could be quite jovial . . . He always had the natural air of someone who had been reared from childhood in material comfort.[7]

Jancsi's high school years were interrupted when, a month after the Bela Kun communist uprising in 1919, he and his family fled Budapest to a place they owned in Venice. They returned two months after the Kun regime (which lasted 130 days) was driven out. Von Neumann's outspoken anti-communist attitude dates back to this interlude. In his own words: 'Russia was traditionally an enemy of Hungary . . . I think you will find, generally speaking, among Hungarians an emotional fear and dislike of Russia.'[8] In von Neumann's case, hatred might perhaps be more accurate than dislike.

The next Hungarian régime, led by Admiral Miklos Horthy, distinguished itself by being the first after the First World War to legalize anti-Semitism. Horthy was the first of the modern dictators to introduce the racial principle into anti-Semitism, by declaring Jews to be a separate race rather than a distinct religion. He instituted restrictive anti-Jewish legislation, including the introduction of the *numerus clausus* in universities: not more than five per cent of all students could be Jews. The von Neumann family was not much inconvenienced but the changed atmosphere in Hungary must have hardened Jancsi's aversion to political extremism.

University studies

In 1921, von Neumann finished high school and enrolled in the University of Budapest which, however, he only attended at the end of each semester in order to take the examinations. From 1921 to 1923 he spent most of his time at the University of Berlin where, among others, he heard Einstein lecture on statistical mechanics. There he also met his erstwhile schoolmate Eugene Wigner again.[9]

In 1923 Jancsi enrolled at the *Eidgenössische Technische Hochschule* (Federal Institute of Technology) in Zurich to study chemical engineering, as his father had insisted he do. By that time he was already actively involved in mathematical research, and in contact with Herman Weyl, one of the leading mathematicians of his time, and with George Polya, one of the greatest teachers of mathematics. When Weyl once left for a short while, von Neumann took over his courses for him during that period.[10] In 1925 he obtained a degree in chemical engineering at the Federal Institute. On March 12, 1926 he received, at age 22, his doctorate *summa cum laude* in mathematics, with minors in experimental physics and chemistry, from the University of Budapest. His doctoral dissertation, dealing with the axiomatization of set theory, was not published until 1928.[11]

Von Neumann spent academic 1926–27 as a Rockefeller fellow at the University of Göttingen. In recommending him for this fellowship, the mathematician Richard Courant wrote: 'Mr. von Neumann, in spite of his youth, is a completely exceptional personality . . . who has already done very productive work . . . and whose future development is being watched with great expectation in many places.'[12] In 1927 he was appointed *Privatdozent* at the University of Berlin, the youngest in the university's history. For the next several years he commuted between Göttingen and Berlin. The first half of academic 1929–30 he was *Privatdozent* in Hamburg. In February 1930 he arrived for the first time in Princeton, as visiting lecturer in mathematical physics.

Scientific contributions, the European years

In preparation for reviewing next the papers von Neumann wrote in his European years, from 1923–30, I have his collected works lying on my desk, six volumes, containing over 150 papers, 3631 pages in all.[13] Here and later my surveys of his oeuvre will be quite brief, the principal reason for this being that I, a physicist, master little of his work. One may well ask why, then, I would dare to include in this volume an essay devoted to a renowned mathematician if I am not competent enough to judge his main claim to fame, his mathematical writings. My answer is that Johnny and I were friends—as will be seen later—and that here I endeavor mainly to give a picture of the man.

Von Neumann's work in these years, about 40 papers in all, was greatly influenced by David Hilbert from Göttingen, whose principal aim at that time was to axiomatize everything under the sun.

One group of von Neumann's papers produced in the 1920s, dealing with set theory and the logical foundations of mathematics, includes a rigorous definition for ordinal numbers[14]; a new set of axioms for set theory, now known as the von Neumann–Gödel–Bernays theory;[15] a contribution to Hilbert's proof theory,[16] further elaborated five years later;[17] and a paper on necessary and sufficient conditions for avoiding the logical paradoxes then threatening the foundations of mathematics.[18]

Von Neumann abandoned his researches on the logical foundations of mathematics after 1931, when Kurt Gödel published his undecidability theorem, 'a true theorem such that a formal proof of it leads to a contradiction'[19]—just at the time that von Neumann was busily engaged in trying to develop a proof of just the opposite of Gödel's theorem and was unsuccessful! He (von N.) has remarked that Gödel's stupendous result marks him as the greatest logician since Aristotle. 'His deep admiration for Gödel was mingled with a feeling of disappointment at not having thought himself of undecidability.'[20] For years Gödel was a long-term member of the Institute for Advanced Study without being a professor—which he became only in 1953. That caused Johnny (by then long since a professor there himself) to remark: 'How can any of us be called professor when Gödel is not?'[20]

A second group of von Neumann's articles in the 1920s again shows Hilbert's influence. It begins with a collaboration with Hilbert and the latter's assistant Lothar Nordheim, in which they used (for the first time, I believe) so-called Hilbert spaces (infinite-dimensional vector spaces) in order to achieve an improved version of the mathematical principles underlying Heisenberg's matrix mechanics,[21] work further elaborated in a series of other papers on related matters.[22] These articles are contained and extended in von Neumann's book on the mathematical foundations of quantum mechanics.[23] The book also contains his theory of measurement, in which he argued that indeterminism is an inherent feature of quantum mechanics, rather than a consequence of hidden parameters which, once unveiled, would allow for a deterministic theory. The responses to this work have been judged variously by different people. One has written: 'His formal definition of a physical state as being a point in Hilbert space was as readily accepted by physicists as if it had been the most obvious thing since creation.'[7] But another: 'The mathematically technical character of this account made it much more appealing to the mathematician than to the physicists [including the present author] who have not made substantial use of it.'[24] Von Neumann and Niels Bohr had a spirited discussion on their respective views during a meeting in Warsaw in 1938.[25] I know from personal observation that the two men held each other in great respect.

Physicists will be pleased to know that von Neumann also did straight physics in his European years. This work includes a series of papers jointly with Wigner[26] and, most interestingly, an article in 1928 on Dirac's theory of the electron which then was just a few months old. Every physicist knows that, using bilinear expressions in terms of Dirac's four-component spinor wave functions, one can construct five fundamental covariants (scalar, four-vector, tensor, pseudo four-vector, pseudoscalar), but few will be aware that von Neumann was the first to do so.[27] As he noted in that paper: 'That a quantity with four components [a spinor] is not a four-vector has never yet happened in relativity theory'!

Von Neumann has also contributed to a quite different area of physics, to wit ergodic theory,[28] which has influenced subsequent research on dynamical systems and statistical mechanics. When, shortly before his death, he was asked by the US National Academy of Sciences what he thought were his three greatest achievements, he replied that he considered his most important contributions to have been on the theory of operators in Hilbert space, and on the mathematical foundations of quantum theory and the ergodic theorem.[29] It is significant to note that he began his research in all these subjects during his European years, while in his twenties.

That is still not all he started in this period, however. In 1928 he managed to squeeze his first and basic paper on the theory of games,[30] 'based largely on an analysis of variants of poker,'[31] in between his writings on logic and physics. It has the cozy title: *Zur Theorie der Gesellschaftsspiele* (on the theory of party games) and, in a brief footnote, makes reference to the analogy with some problems in economics. His central result, which has served as a basis for all subsequent work in game theory, is his minimax theorem, which states that for any two-person zero-sum game (a game in which my gains (losses) equal your losses (gains)) there exists an optimal strategy, given in terms of a unique number, the 'minimax' value of the game, which represents the minimum gain and maximum loss each player can expect.

His first effort in economics, presented at a colloquium in Vienna in 1937,[32] has been credited in 1983 by one historian of econometrics as being 'the single most important article in mathematical economics.'[33] Then, together with Oskar Morgenstern, Johnny wrote a book[34] about the theory of games and its application to many economic problems (such as exchange of goods between *n* parties, monopolies, oligopolies, and free trade). This treatise was published in 1944 by the Princeton University Press. 'When deciding to print the book, the Press was cheerfully resigned, for the sake of scholarship, to face the financial deficit they expected. But, in fact, they had to reprint the book in 1947 and again in 1953.' 'A sympathetic front-page article in *The New York Times* in March 1946 [had] made the book a best-seller by academic standards.'[35,36]

> Morgenstern was once asked how a scholar outside the mainstream of economic thinking could make a contribution as original, innovative, and decisive as Johnny's. He replied that Johnny had an extraordinary capacity for picking the brains of a person whom he engaged in casual conversations. Once he saw from these that there was a problem of sufficient mathematical interest to warrant his spending time on it, he homed on to that subject like a guided missile.[37]

After the book had come out, Johnny published a further half dozen papers on games and economic behavior.[38]

The Princeton years

Johnny's first appointment in the United States, as visiting lecturer on quantum theory in Princeton, was for the term of February–June 1930, on a stipend of $3000 plus an allowance of $1000 to cover travel expenses. That position had been arranged by Oswald Veblen, a Princeton professor and a leading American mathematician. 'He liked Johnny very much and considered him almost like a son.'[39]

John traveled to America on the luxury liner *Bremen*, accompanied by Mariette Kovési, his young bride whom he had married in Budapest on January 1, 1930. The two had known each other since childhood. Mariette was a slim, well-dressed, and vivacious young woman, hailing from a wealthy family.

Wigner, who came to Princeton at almost the same time, with a similar appointment, has said: 'Johnny fell in love with America on the first day. He thought: these are sane people who don't talk in those traditional terms which are meaningless. To a certain extent the materialism of the United States, which was greater than that of Europe, appealed to him.'[40] Many years later, von Neumann himself explained his reasons for coming to America:

> I must say that the main reason was partly because conditions in Hungary were rather limited, and I thought the thing I was doing had a better field in America and to a considerable extent because I was much more in sympathy with the institutions of America; and, lastly, because I expected World War II, and I was apprehensive that Hungary would be on the Nazi side, and I didn't want to be caught dead on that side.[42]

Up till 1938 he would visit his native country almost every year, however.

From 1930–33, Johnny spent half the year teaching in Princeton, the other half teaching in Berlin. His lecture courses drew large audiences. In that period he was more involved in the students than through most of his life. Mariette arranged an open house in the evenings, in their rented home. Thus began the von Neumann Princeton parties that were to become famous and grander after they had bought the house on Westcott Road which was to be Johnny's home for the rest of his life.

In 1931 the couple bought their first car. 'Johnny had driven a lot but had never passed a test anywhere. He took the test . . . [and now] was let loose on the roads of America . . . He drove fast down the middle of any road.'[42]

It was Veblen again who arranged for the most important academic appointment in von Neumann's life. He (V.) and Einstein had been named the first professors at the Institute for Advanced Study in Princeton, which had been incorporated in May 1932. In January 1933 Johnny was offered and accepted a professorship there, at an annual salary of $10 000, effective as of April 1, 1933.[43] He started the following September, as its youngest professor at that time, and held that position for the rest of his life.

In 1935 Marina arrived, Johnny's only child. 'Johnny was a besotted father.'[44] Since 1956 she has been Mrs Robert Whitman. She has not only been a good wife and mother, but also a distinguished professor of economics.

John and Mariette divorced amicably in 1937. She later married Horner Kuper, who after the Second World War became director of instrumentation at Brookhaven National Laboratory. It was there that I met Mariette several times, when she was still a vivacious and elegant woman. Johnny had meanwhile become an American citizen and, on December 18, 1938, married again, to Klara ('Klari') Dan, once again a Hungarian woman. I have known Klari for many years, she was a good friend of mine. It was she who taught me the only phrase in Hungarian I know: *Minden kicsi segìt, mondta az egèr, ès belipisilt a tengerbe*, a translation from a saying in my native Dutch: Every little bit helps, said the mouse, and pissed in the sea.

———————

By the time von Neumann arrived in the United States, his contributions to mathematics had already gained him an international reputation. His work in pure mathematics continued during the years up till 1940, 'when he seemed to be advancing at a breathless speed on all fronts of logic and analysis at once, not to speak of mathematical physics.'[45] From 1940 on, events of war began to change the pattern of his activities.

Continuing with my superficial recitation of Johnny's contributions; in the 1930s, in collaboration with F. J. Murray, he produced a series of landmark papers on non-commutative algebras, to which he gave the vague name 'rings of operators,' known also as W^*-algebras and later as 'von Neumann algebras.'[46] An offshoot of these studies was Johnny's 'continuous geometries'[47] (which is a generalization of projective geometry).

Another of von Neumann's important mathematical contributions of this period was a consequence of the discovery in 1933, by his fellow Hungarian Alfred Haar, of the so-called group invariant Haar measure.[48] Johnny showed[49] how Haar's results made possible the partial solution of an unsolved problem posed by Hilbert in 1900. He wrote several more papers[50] on Haar measure; also related papers[51] on almost periodic functions. 'He was upset by Haar's early death.'[52]

In 1936 Alan Turing arrived in Princeton for a two-year stay at the university. His first published paper had been an extension of Johnny's and Gödel's work on logic. Von Neumann may have met him already in 1935 while he was lecturing at Cambridge, England. During his Princeton years, Turing published his seminal paper on what we now call the universal Turing machine,[53] which has profoundly influenced mathematics and mathematical logic, and has laid the theoretical foundation for much of modern computer programming. In 1938 Johnny, deeply interested in Turing's work, offered him the position of his assistant at the Institute which he declined, in order to return instead to his fellowship in Cambridge. He became Britain's master decoder of German wartime ciphers.

Von Neumann and the Second World War

In his testimony before the Special Senate Committee on Atomic Energy, given on January 31, 1946, Johnny summarized his involvement with military matters in the following way:

> I am a mathematician and a mathematical physicist. I am a member of the Institute for Advanced Study in Princeton, New Jersey. I have been connected with Government work on military matters for nearly ten years: As a consultant of Ballistic Research Laboratory of the Army Ordnance Department since 1937, as a member of its scientific advisory committee since 1940; I have been a member of various divisions of the National Defense Research Committee since 1941; I have been a consultant of the Navy Bureau of Ordnance since 1942. I have been connected with the Manhattan District since 1943 as a consultant of the Los Alamos Laboratory, and I spent a considerable part of 1943–45 there.[54]

I may as well add right away Johnny's principal associations in later years related to defense: Naval Ordnance Laboratory (1947–55), Weapons System Evaluation Group (1950–55), Scientific Advisory Board, US Air Force (1951–57), General Advisory Committee US Atomic Energy Committee (AEC) (1952–54), AEC Commissioner (1955–57).[55] It has been said of him that the Pentagon considered him as important as a whole army division.

Clearly, von Neumann's pure research was a casualty of war. 'In 1941, war related work occupied about a quarter of his time . . . by 1943 all of his efforts went that way, and still he could hardly keep pace with his heavy schedule as advisor to several different government organizations.'[56] He himself has written: 'It was through military science that I was introduced to applied science . . . I have certainly succeeded in losing my purity.'[57] Well, not completely. In the years under consideration, he published on the statistics of the gravitational field arising from a random distribution of stars;[58] on other topics in general relativity;[59] and on hydrodynamics.[60]

Why did Johnny become so fascinated with the military in his later years? A comment by a close friend and admirer of his hits the mark, I believe:

> He seemed to admire generals and admirals and got along well with them . . . I believe this was due . . . to his admiration for people who had power. This is not uncommon with those whose life is spent in contemplation. At any rate, it was clear that he admired people who could influence events. In addition, being soft-hearted, I think he had a hidden admiration for people or organizations that could be tough and ruthless. He appreciated or even envied those who at meetings could act or present their views in a way to influence . . . other's thoughts.[60]

War work took von Neumann to Washington for the last few months of 1942 and to England for the first half of 1943, after which he would move almost constantly from one project to the other in the United States. Among the topics he got involved with were mine warfare and countermeasures to it, interaction and reflection of blast waves, shock waves (a number of his papers on this subject have since been published[61]), and, perhaps most important of all, his work on the implosion method for detonating atomic bombs with the help of 'shaped charges,' conventional explosives placed around fissionable material in such a configuration that their detonation would generate a uniform shock wave that compresses the fissionable core to a critical state.

Many if not all of these assignments involved mathematical problems that cannot be solved rigorously. For example, in treating the hydrodynamics of implosions and explosions one needs to have recourse to experimental and/or numerical methods. It was therefore inevitable that Johnny would develop a great interest in the practice and results of what could be done with what were then the fastest and most advanced computers. So it came to pass that in 1944 he came into contact with the ENIAC (Electronic Numerical Integrator and Computer) project at the University of Pennsylvania, a gadget that many people now regard as the first modern computer. He first heard of that project from the mathematician Herman Goldstine, who was then a captain in Army Ordnance (at this writing he is the executive officer of the American Philosophical Society), and who later became his friend and close collaborator. The ENIAC was completed by June 1940.

Johnny became particularly interested in problems for which the ENIAC's storage capacity was inadequate, such as the handling of non-linear partial differential equations. In June 1945 he had completed a hundred-page draft report, issued for limited distribution, crucial parts of which were of his own making, on the logistics of a next generation machine, the EDVAC (Electronic Discrete Variable Computer).

By that time von Neumann already had plans for building his own computer.

Personal recollections. The Johnniac

I arrived in Princeton for the first time in late September 1946, to begin a one-year fellowship at the Institute for Advanced Study. The next month I gave a lecture there on quantum field theory. I had quite some audience: von Neumann, who had brought along a visitor, Alfred North Whitehead, the renowned mathematician from Harvard; also Bohr, Dirac, and Herman Weyl. It may have been my first meeting with von Neumann.

In my life I have met men even greater than Johnny, but none as brilliant. He shone not only in mathematics but was also fluently multilingual and particularly well-versed in history. One of his most remarkable abilities I soon came to note was his power of absolute recall. Goldstine has remembered the same:

> As far as I could tell, von Neumann was able on once reading a book or article to quote it back verbatim; moreover, he could do it years later without hesitation. He could also translate it at no diminution in speed from its original language into English. On one occasion I tested his ability by asking him to tell me how the *Tale of Two Cities* started. Whereupon, without any pause, he immediately began to recite the first chapter and continued until asked to stop after about ten or fifteen minutes. Another time, I watched him lecture on some material written in German about twenty years earlier. In this performance von Neumann even used exactly the same letters and symbols he had in the original. German was his natural language, and it seemed that he conceived his ideas in German and then translated them at lightning speed into English. Frequently I watched him writing and saw him ask occasionally what the English for some German word was.[62]

Johnny could also recite a huge collection of limericks, and taught me the only one in French I have ever heard:

> Il y avait un jeune homme de Dijon,
> Qui ne croyait pas à la religion.
> Il disait: Bien ma foi,
> J'm'en fou d'tous les trois
> Le Père et le Fils et le Pigeon.

The day after he had told me that one I came back to him with an English translation:

> There was a young fellow from Digeon,
> Who did not believe in religion.
> He said: I admit

I don't give a shit
For the Father, the Son, and the Pigeon.

I also had a German translation ready, based on rhyming *Glaube* (faith) with *Taube* (dove).

Johnny also introduced me to a favorite word game of his: find the *nebbish* value of a sentence. The Yiddish word *nebbish* means something like a compassionate 'that's too bad.' The game consisted in finding the ratio of the number of words in a phrase to the number of times one can insert nebbish in a way that enhances the meaning of the sentence. His favorite example, a phrase with maximal ratio one: *cogito nebbish, ergo nebbish, sum nebbish.*

Lighthearted exchanges such as these began shortly after I had settled in Princeton. We were in fact initially drawn to each other by a common fondness for telling jokes, at which he was a master and I not so bad either. It did not last long, however, before we became engaged in more serious conversations. So started a friendship which lasted until Johnny's death. I am pleased to report that it was he who proposed to the faculty, on April 21, 1947, that I be given a five-year membership at the Institute—a suggestion which the faculty accepted.

I would often be invited to the von Neumann's famous parties. From all such experiences I gained my own picture of what kind of man he was.

As a physical specimen, he was plump. Klari has said: 'He liked sweets and rich dishes, preferably with a good nourishing sauce, based on cream. He loves Mexican food . . . When he was stationed at Los Alamos, he would drive 120 miles to dine at a favorite Mexican restaurant . . . He can count anything except calories.'[63] He had a big head with large, vivacious brown eyes, and a waddling walk. He was always dressed in immaculate suits, one of the several expressions of his predilection for a rather sumptuous lifestyle—he would sometimes quote one of his rich uncles: 'It is not enough to be rich, one must also have money in Switzerland.' Generally his physical appearance tended to be on the soft side, behind which great energy and toughness lay barely hidden. He never smoked and drank little. At his parties he would occasionally put up a show of mild inebriation, however, meant to encourage his guests. His manners were polite and cosmopolitan. If, however, 'he is not interested in what is going on around him, he relaxes and falls asleep.'[63] It has been said of him that he was not human but a demigod who 'had made a detailed study of humans and could imitate them perfectly.'[64]

Von Neumann was a very hard worker and could make do with little sleep. 'Each day he would start writing before breakfast. Even at his parties he would leave his guests to go to his study for half an hour or so, to record what was on his mind . . . He could not be a very attentive "normal" husband. This might account in part for his not-too-smooth home life.'[65]

Johnny did have an eye for women, however, in an outward way. He would always look at a woman's legs and figure. 'At Los Alamos the secretaries had desks that were open at the front. Some of them stuck cardboard there because, they said, Johnny had a habit of leaning forward, muttering, and peering up their skirts.'[66]

Von Neumann had an uncanny ability for solving very complex calculations in his head, as is nicely illustrated by an event recalled by Goldstine.

> One time an excellent mathematician stopped into my office to discuss a problem that had been causing him concern. After a rather lengthy and unfruitful discussion, he said he would take home a desk calculator and work out a few special cases that evening. The next day he arrived at the office looking very tired and haggard. On being asked why he triumphantly stated he had worked out five special cases of increasing complexity in the course of a night of work; he had finished at 4.30 in the morning.
>
> Later that morning von Neumann unexpectedly came in on a consulting trip and asked how things were going. Whereupon I brought in my colleague to discuss the problem with von Neumann, who said: 'Let's work out a few special cases.' We agreed, carefully not telling him of the numerical work in the early morning hours. He then put his eyes to the ceiling and in perhaps five minutes worked out in his head four of the previously and laboriously calculated cases! After he had worked about a minute on the fifth and hardest case, my colleague suddenly announced out loud the final answer. Von Neumann was completely perturbed and quickly went back, and at an increased tempo, to his mental calculations. After perhaps another minute he said, 'Yes, that is correct.' Then my colleague fled, and von Neumann spent perhaps another half hour of considerable mental effort trying to understand how anyone could have found a better way to handle the problem. Finally he was let in on the true situation and recovered his aplomb.[67]

Johnny was also deeply interested in current political events, but there our opinions differed sharply. I remember a party we both attended, it must have been sometime in 1947 or 1948, at any rate before the Soviets had their atomic bomb. The discussion turned on US–Soviet relations. I was shocked to hear Johnny proclaim, very calmly, that in his opinion the best thing to do was to annihilate Soviet power right away with atomic bombs. Like other Hungarian-born physicists I have come to know, Johnny was virulently anti-communist.

Von Neumann was one of the rare mathematicians with whom I could talk physics. We physicists use mathematics as a tool and treat it with respect but not always with the same rigor mathematicians do. As is well known in my profession, that often makes exchange of views with mathematicians difficult if not impossible—but not with Johnny. Which explains, incidentally, why during the war he had been such a highly valued consultant at the Los Alamos atomic bomb laboratory.

Back to my own experiences. I once came to him with a mathematics problem that had arisen in my own work and which I could not solve. He listened, then said he did not know the answer either but would think about it. Two weeks later (when meanwhile I had found out by myself how to do it) I received an eight-page letter from him, posted in Los Alamos, in which he gave the solution . . .

At the time I first met von Neumann, his Electronic Computer Project had just got underway.

———————

Computers have a long and venerable history going back 5000 years to the abacus. I limit myself—if for no other reason than that my knowledge of that history is quite skimpy—to mentioning that automated devices had already appeared in the seventeenth century, associated with such famous names as Blaise Pascal and Gottfried Leibnitz, who was the first to construct a machine that could automatically add, subtract, multiply, and divide. In the nineteenth century, Charles Babbage conceived of the first automated digital computer. The earliest prototype of a digital computer that used electronics was constructed shortly before the Second World War. (A digital computer receives data as combinations of 1s and 0s, binary digits, 'bits' for short.) To that last class belong also the ENIAC and EDVAC, mentioned earlier, and the so-called Electronic Computer Project of the Institute for Advanced Study, which became popularly known as the Johnniac.

Records show[68] that von Neumann had already suggested in June 1945 that the Institute build a faster and more flexible electronic computer than existed at that time; and that the concept had been approved the following October.[69] In May 1946 Johnny proposed to house it in a separate building close to the Institute. In a faculty meeting that month,[70] Carl Ludwig Siegel, another distinguished Institute professor of mathematics, commented famously[70] that he did not see the need for such a computer. When he needed a logarithm, he said, he would not even look it up in a table but rather compute it by hand.

Funding for the project was not hard to come by in those years, when financial support for scientific–technological enterprises was plentiful. The Institute trustees pledged $100 000 toward total expenses.[70] Other major funding came from the Office of Naval Research, Army Ordnance, and the Radio Corporation of America (now called RCA) which recently had established offices near Princeton. Staff were recruited for the various aspects of the program: engineering, logical design and programming, mathematics, meteorology. Goldstine was appointed second-in-command of overall activities.

It took six years, twice as long as had been anticipated, until the project was completed. The formal dedication of the computer, a gala affair, did not occur until June 10, 1952.[72] It was followed by a big von Neumann party (which I attended), for which Klari had ordered a model of the computer in ice. By then the machine had already been in use for some time, however. The first large problem—dealing with thermonuclear processes—was run in 1951; it required hundreds of hours of computation. The expectation was that this computer would be a powerful research tool in the investigation of fundamental problems in dynamical meteorology, and would make possible for the first time a direct attack on the problems—which, Johnny once said, were too complex to solve on the back of an envelope—of weather prediction by numerical methods.

The basic ideas on which the Johnniac rests had been worked out in a series of papers by von Neumann and Goldstine, published in the years 1946–48.[73] Binary arithmetic was used internally in order to take advantage of the inherently binary switching nature of the basic elements. Several novelties were incorporated, most notably the principle of stored programs by means of instructions treated as numerals. In later years these ideas have of course evolved and been modified, but the more modern organizations still rest on the pioneering concepts from Princeton.[74]

When the machine was nearing completion, Johnny once said: 'I don't know how really useful this will be. But at any rate it will be possible to get a lot of credit in Tibet by coding "*Om Mane Padme Hum*" [Oh, thou flower of lotus] a hundred million times in an hour. It will far exceed anything prayer wheels can do.'[75] Actually, it did more than that, contributing to such various fields as pure mathematics, statistics, astrophysics, fluid dynamics, atomic and nuclear physics, and numerical meteorology.[76] For details on all these subjects I refer to two excellent monographs, refs 3 and 10.

With the success of a series of numerical experiments, leading to the development of a model in 1953 by which the generation of storms could be predicted, the civil and military forces of the government took over the project in meteorology and the men connected with it left the Institute in 1956. In 1957 the computer was given to Princeton University, where it was used for another three years, then decommissioned. Parts of the computer are now in the National Museum of American History, in Washington, DC. (Its main on–off switch can now be found in an office in building 9 of Microsoft's campus in Redmond, State of Washington.[77])

It is a fitting place for this totally obsolete machine to rest in peace. What was it like, what could it do? It weighed about 1000 pounds, occupied 36 cubic feet, and needed 28 kilowatts of power. Fifteen tons of air-conditioning kept down the heat generated by about 3000 vacuum tubes (used also in radios in those days). It could perform a few thousand multiplications or divisions per second, about 20 times as many additions. Its principal novelty was that it was the first computer capable of storing programs in its innards.

What has happened since? Transistors, which made radio tubes obsolete, had already been discovered in 1948 but did not come on the market until 1959. Next, chips came into use in the late 1960s. The resulting, perhaps most revolutionary, advances in technology of our century have made computers faster, smaller, and cheaper. Example: a young colleague, working a few doors away from me, has standing on his desk a computer that costs less than $10 000 and digests 85 mip = millions of instructions per second . . .

Having now come to the end of my account of Johnny's contributions to mathematics, physics, and technology, I should like to raise the question of how he assessed his own offerings. The best answers I can give are to quote his devoted friend Ulam, with whose opinions I tend to agree, insofar as I can judge:

> As a mathematician, von Neumann was quick, brilliant, efficient, and enormously broad in scientific interests beyond mathematics itself. He knew his technical abilities; his virtuosity in following complicated reasoning and his insights were supreme; yet he lacked absolute self-confidence . . . It is very hard for me to understand this . . . I felt that there was some hesitation on Johnny's part about his own work . . . Only when he found, from time to time, some ingenious, technically elegant trick or a new approach did he seem visibly stimulated or relieved of his own internal doubts . . . He was a master of, but also a little bit a slave to, his own technique . . . He had this habit of considering the line of least resistance. Of course, with his powerful brain he could quickly vanquish all small obstacles and then go on. But if the difficulty was great right from the beginning, he would not knock his head against the wall . . . [but] would switch to another problem. On the whole, in his work habits I would call Johnny more realistic than optimistic.[78]

The final years

The Oppenheimer affair

In the autumn of 1947 Robert Oppenheimer assumed the directorship of the Institute for Advanced Study, after a long, drawn-out selection process for that post. Already a year and a half earlier, Veblen had written to an acquaintance: 'Von Neumann is not as favorable to Oppenheimer as I am, though he has great admiration for him as a scientist.'[79] One senses some ambivalence in Johnny's opinion about Oppenheimer, whom he had known for a long time. 'I think Dr. Oppenheimer and I first met . . . in Goettingen in 1926 . . . We met again in 1943 at which time he told me that he wanted me to join a project which he could not describe at that moment [Los Alamos, of course] . . . Our association has been practically continuous since 1943.'[80]

According to Goldstine:

> [As Institute Director] Oppenheimer was always solidly behind the computer project . . . He fully appreciated its importance . . . He and von Neumann never were

intimate friends, but they deeply appreciated and respected each other . . . von Neumann once remarked to me that the entire Los Alamos venture would in his opinion have been quite impossible without Oppenheimer . . . The two men held quite opposite views on the question of the super or thermonuclear [hydrogen] bomb, but von Neumann never for a moment questioned Oppenheimer's integrity or his loyalty.[81]

One notes again a certain ambivalence—which brings us to the Oppenheimer affair.

From April 12 – May 6, 1954, hearings were held in Washington, DC, before a specially selected security board, to determine whether or not Oppenheimer was a security risk. Forty witnesses testified under oath, including Johnny. From his testimony,[80] which covers fifteen printed pages:

> Q. About the GAC report of 1949 . . . did you agree with the report and its recommendations? [In this report, the GAC, the General Advisory Committee to the US Atomic Energy Commission, of which Oppenheimer was chairman in 1949, had recommended not to build a hydrogen bomb.]
> A. No I was in favor of a very accelerated program . . . My view on that is quite hard-boiled, and that was known.
> Q. Did you consider that the recommendations of the GAC, and in particular of Dr. Oppenheimer, were made in good faith?
> A. Yes. I have no doubt about that.
> Q. Do you have an opinion about Dr. Oppenheimer's loyalty to the United States, his integrity?
> A. I have no doubts about that whatsoever.
> Q. Your opinion, I take it, is quite clear and firm?
> A. Yes, Yes.

After the verdict, which did find Oppenheimer to be a security risk, a formal statement to the press was issued, signed by all Institute professors, in which they expressed their loyal appreciation to him.[82] I vividly remember that von Neumann was the only one who initially declined to add his signature, though eventually he did so. Here Johnny's ambivalence is most striking—very positive testimony about Oppenheimer the scientist/administrator, yet holding reservations about Oppenheimer the man. I have never arrived at a firm opinion regarding the causes of Johnny's attitude but do not believe that their opposite views regarding atomic weapons explains it fully. I cannot shake the idea that reserve on Oppenheimer's side, caused by jealousy, may have contributed, since von Neumann was so much smarter than he.

Automata

In the post-war years, von Neumann became increasingly interested in information as a scientific concept, no doubt a consequence of his involvement with electronic computers. This led him to studies of natural and artificial automata, systems—from the human central nervous system to computers—that process information as part of self-regulating mechanisms. He attacked one of the most complex questions in the field: how to construct self-reproducing machines, a subject that lies in the intermediate area between logic, communication theory, and physiology. His thoughts on these topics are mainly found in lectures, most notably his Silliman lectures at Yale, given in March 1953, published posthumously,[84] and still widely read. Of particular interest is his work on how to design reliable machines using unreliable components.[85] That was the final scientific paper he published while alive. For one last time that one made him cofounder of a new mathematical discipline, of interest to biologists who forever deal with unreliable components. Good reviews of Johnny's ideas on automata are found in ref. 86.

Contemplative writings

It was only in the last few years of his life that Johnny addressed general audiences. I wish he had done more of that. The published papers of this kind show his eloquence and elegant turns of phrase. A few samples follow.

In 1954 he spoke before a conference of Princeton graduate alumni on the role of mathematics in the sciences and in society,[87] raising the questions of how useful mathematics is; how important usefulness is; and whether science should be pursued *per se*, or with relation to use in society. Also what the role of mathematics is in other parts of the sciences.

> A mathematician usually means that a theory is directly useful if it can be used in theoretical physics . . . after which he still has to say that insight in theoretical physics itself is only useful if it is useful in experimental physics. After which you must say that a concept in experimental physics is, by ordinary criteria, useful if it is useful in engineering . . .
>
> The majority of [mathematical concepts] were developed with very little regard to usefulness, and very often without any suspicion that they might become useful later . . . A large part of mathematics which became useful developed with absolutely no desire to be useful . . . This is true for all science. Successes were largely due to . . . refusing things which profit, relying solely on guidance by criteria of intellectual elegance. It was by following this rule that one actually got ahead in the long run, much better than any strictly utilitarian course would have permitted . . . The principle of *laissez faire* has led to strange and wonderful results.

Four more semi-popular articles date from 1955. The first deals with 'Method in the physical sciences.'[88] Von Neumann begins by emphasizing that 'The sciences do not try to explain, they mainly make models . . . mathematical constructs that are expected to work . . . [and] which must be rather simple.' An example he gives is the Newtonian theory, confirmed over a range, on a scale of length, of about 30 powers of 10. Our physical knowledge extends over 10 more powers, but there Newton fails, and relativity theory and quantum theory are the models that help us out further. Even so, there remain 'areas which are not yet properly explained or not yet properly theoretical and controlled . . . we are here in the midst of grave difficulties.' This is the domain of the smallest sizes of things (fundamental particles) studied by man. Now, nearly half a century after Johnny wrote these wise words, those difficulties still remain largely unresolved.

In the second 1955 article, published in *Fortune Magazine*,[89] entitled 'Can we survive technology?', von Neumann attempts to forecast what problems our world will have to cope with 25 years later. 'For the kind of explosiveness that man will be able to contrive by 1980, the world is dangerously small, its political units dangerously unstable . . . Technological evolution is still accelerating . . . their consequences tend to increase instability.' He had not only in mind the fear for atomic weapons, very high in 1955. 'Present awful possibilities of nuclear warfare may give way to others even more awful. After global climate control becomes possible, perhaps all our present involvements will seem simple.' He had in mind that 'It is now possible to wage a new kind of warfare, climate war, in which one country can alter unfavorably the climate in the enemy country.'[63] I found this article particularly interesting because it shows that even a man as wise as von Neumann could not remotely foresee what the world would be like as his century wore on.

In the next article, 'Impact of atomic energy on the physical and chemical sciences,'[90] he makes an observation which few if any of us had thought of before: 'If man and his technology had appeared on the scene several billion years earlier, the separation of uranium 235 [crucial for making bombs] would have been easier. If man had appeared later—say 10 billion years later—the concentration of uranium 235 would have been so low as to make it practically unusable.' Why? Because uranium 235 is radioactively unstable and disintegrates faster than the much more abundant uranium 238. An interesting thought. Johnny also reflects on the new social responsibilities of the scientist: 'He must know something of history, law, economics, government, and public opinion.'

In the last of von Neumann's semi-popular articles of 1955, on 'Defense in atomic war,'[91] he observes: 'It will not be sufficient to know that the enemy has only fifty possible tricks and that we can counter every one of them, but we must be able to counter them at almost the very instant they occur . . . It brings us back to the most powerful weapons of all; namely, the flexible type of human intelligence.'

Commissioner of the AEC

In 1954 von Neumann was invited to become a member of the AEC, at the suggestion of Lewis Strauss, the commission chairman. President Eisenhower supported the appointment, perhaps because it helped to mend fences with the scientific community following the infamous Oppenheimer security hearings.

> Johnny had profound reservations about his acceptance because of the ramifications of the Oppenheimer affair. He knew that the majority of scientists did not like the actions of Admiral Strauss. Some of the more liberal members of the scientific community did not like Johnny's pragmatic and rather pro-military views, nor did they appreciate his association with the atomic energy work . . . But he was flattered and proud that, although foreign born, he would be entrusted with a high governmental position of great potential influence in directing large areas of technology and science. He knew this could be an activity of great national importance . . . Besides, Johnny had a bit of the Teutonic trait of being easily impressed by officialdom.[2]

His five-year appointment was approved by Congress, and on March 15, 1955 he was sworn in as commissioner. My own reaction to his move was puzzlement and worry. Had he not witnessed at first hand how Oppenheimer had been devoured by his desire to enter the corridors of temporal power?

Johnny now took a leave of absence from the Institute in Princeton and moved with his wife to Georgetown, where they had rented a small yellow frame house. His new position had demanded some financial sacrifice because he had to sever a number of lucrative consultant contracts.

Klari has given glimpses of his new lifestyle.

> During the day he works in his offices at the AEC. At night scientists in the many other fields he is interested in come to visit him. Sleep is part of his work. He will go to sleep serenely with an unsolved problem and wake up at three with the answer. Then he goes to his desk and phones his associates. One of his requirements for an associate is that he not mind being awakened in the middle of the night. Johnny will work until morning and then go to his office, as chipper as a lark.[63]

He spent several weeks in Washington each month that the commission was in session and the rest of his time visiting the national laboratories.

The end

Five months after being appointed commissioner, catastrophe struck. Johnny had developed severe pains in his left shoulder and after surgery, performed at the Massachusetts General Hospital in Boston, a small cancerous growth was removed from his clavicle. He seemed to recover fully and afterward went to Los Alamos.

It was to be his last visit there. Surgery had removed only a secondary lesion, the cancer began to spread rapidly and Johnny became increasingly ill. Still he went on. Some committee meetings were now held at his house and later at the Woodner Hotel, to which the von Neumanns had moved so as to be closer to Walter Reed Hospital, where he was undergoing treatment.[93]

Von Neumann's last public appearance was early in 1956 when, in a wheel-chair at the White House, he received the Medal of Freedom from President Eisenhower. It was the second time that a president personally had honored him. In 1947, Truman had handed him the Medal for Merit. In 1956 he also received the Enrico Fermi Prize, awarded by the US Atomic Energy Commission.

In April 1956, Johnny was taken to the Walter Reed Hospital, where he remained to the end. Eisenhower, who had a high regard for him, had arranged for him to have a special room there, where Air Force Colonel Vincent Ford and eight airmen were assigned to him.[94]

Ulam has told the following story of a visit to von Neumann at the hospital.[95]

> I went by mistake to the opposite corner of the hospital but on the same floor, and walked into an antechamber where two military men were sitting. They looked at me in surprise and questioningly. I said I was there to visit a friend and their look turned incredulous. When I added, 'Dr. von Neumann,' they smiled and directed me to the proper rooms. I had entered the Presidential Suite where President Eisenhower at that moment was hospitalized after his heart attack. I told this to Johnny when I regained his room. He enjoyed this. It amused him to be in a location symmetrically opposite to that of the President of the United States.

Lewis Strauss has recalled:

> Until the last, he continued to be a member of the [Atomic Energy] Commission and chairman of an important advisory committee to the Defense Department. On one dramatic occasion near the end, there was a meeting at Walter Reed Hospital where, gathered around his bedside and attentive to his last words of advice and wisdom, were the Secretary of Defense and his Deputies, the Secretaries of the Army, Navy and Air Force, and all the military Chiefs of Staff.[96]

Eugene Wigner has written:

> When von Neumann realized that he was incurably ill, his logic forced him to realize also that he would cease to exist, and hence cease to have thoughts. Yet this is a conclusion the full content of which is incomprehensible to the human intellect and which, therefore, horrified him. It was heart-breaking to watch the frustration of his mind, when all hope was gone, in its struggle with the fate which appeared to him unavoidable but unacceptable.[97]

To ease his deeply disturbed spirits, Johnny sought guidance from a Catholic priest, Father Anselm Strittmatter who, beginning in the spring of 1956, began to see him regularly. I was shocked when I heard this later. He had been completely agnostic for as long as I had known him. As far as I could see this act did not agree with the attitudes and thoughts he had harbored for nearly all his life.

On February 8, 1957, Johnny died in the Hospital, at age 53.

On a sunny but freezing morning late that February, I went to the cemetery on Witherspoon Street in Princeton, to attend the burial of Johnny in a brief Catholic ceremony. Father Strittmatter said a short prayer, followed by a brief eulogy by Admiral Strauss. After the funeral I joined a small gathering at the Princeton house, and hugged Klari.

I never saw Johnny again after he had left Princeton for Washington, nor Klari, except for that day of the funeral. Only much later did I learn what happened to her afterward. After some years she remarried, to Carl Eckart, a physics professor in San Diego. On November 10, 1963 she waded into the Pacific, into the surf off San Diego—a suicide.[98] She is buried in Princeton, near Johnny's grave. Poor dear Klari. It may have been too much for her to miss the stimuli of being with Johnny, always talking in Hungarian with him. This is what she has said about their life together:

> He is complicated, and life is complicated with such a man. But it is intensely rewarding . . . I like the subject matter of our lives. We are like others, we have personal problems, but we talk about them for only a little while, then get on to better things. I am his sounding board. Others would do, but I happen to be the one, and it is fascination itself.[63]

I add a few more of Klari's recollections.

> When we undertake a major project, like buying a house, he is very good. Then his interest lapses . . . He has never touched a hammer or a screwdriver; he does nothing around the house . . .
>
> He loves traffic jams because they present a problem . . . He will twist and maneuver through a crowded street and just make it, delighted that he has calculated correctly . . .
>
> We seldom go to the theatre. We used to go to the movies, but gave it up several years ago. Johnny would sit up happily during the newsreel, then fall asleep during the feature. When I questioned him afterward about the story we'd seen, he would cheerfully make up one to prove he'd been paying attention—very good ones, too, but having nothing to do with what had been on the screen.
>
> Once, von Neumann left in his car from Princeton for New York. A little later I had a phone call from New Brunswick. 'Why am I going to New York?' . . . He forgets things relating to the formal side of life, the non-essentials . . .
>
> I go with him to buy his clothes. Otherwise, out of kindness, he will buy whatever a salesman asks him to buy.
>
> We have a large dog, called Inverse. Johnny walks the dog occasionally, with an air of mild astonishment at finding himself doing so.
>
> He never patronizes children, but talks to them with unsentimental seriousness on their own level, so that they accept him as one of themselves. They even play practical jokes on him that they would not try on another adult.[63]

Von Neumann's reputation and fame have grown steadily since his death. His fantastic brain, and the breadth of his interests and undertakings, have become almost legendary. In his lifetime he had his detractors among some pure mathematicians, however, who, forever defending the virgin purity of mathematics, objected to the fact that he was not a mathematician's mathematician. They could be critical, sharply at times, of his 'outside interests,' from physics to game theory to technology. I do not share these views, even though I too had strong disagreements with him on political matters, from his early warlike position to his later joining the AEC. These, however, have not diminished my overriding feelings of friendship and affection for Johnny's memory.

References

In what follows, N will stand for J. v. Neumann.

1. S. Ulam, *Adventures of a Mathematician*, p. 79, University of California Press, 1979.

2. W. Oncken, *Allgemeine Geschichte in Einzeldarstellungen*, Grote, Berlin, 1884.

3. H. Goldstine, *The Computer*, p. 167, Princeton University Press, 1980.

4. M. Fekete and N., *Jahresbericht, Deutsche Math. Vereinigung*, **31**, 125, 1922.

5. A. Szanton, *The Recollections of Eugene P. Wigner*, p. 57, Plenum Press, New York, 1992.

6. Copies of the report card are in the archives of the Institute for Advanced Study, Princeton.

7. S. Bochner, *Biogr. Mem. Nat. Ac. Sci.* **32**, 438, 1958.

8. N, in 'In the matter of J. Robert Oppenheimer,' transcript of the hearing before a personnel security board, p. 654, MIT Press, Cambridge, MA, 1971.

9. For the relations and collaboration between von Neumann and Wigner, see the essay on Wigner elsewhere in this book.

10. W. Asprey, *John von Neumann and the Origins of Modern Computing*, p. 7, MIT Press, Cambridge, MA, 1990.

11. N, *Math. Zeitschr.* **27**, 669, 1928.

12. C. Reid, *Courant in Göttingen and New York*, p. 336, Springer, New York, 1976.

13. John von Neumann, *Collected Works* (A. H. Taul, Ed.), Pergamon Press, New York, 1961–63. As references to his papers I shall quote these collected works, where in turn one will find references to the original journals in which the articles appeared first.

14. Ref. 13, Vol. 1, no. 3.

15. Ref. 13, Vol. 1, no. 4.

16. Ref. 13, Vol. 1, no. 12.

17. Ref. 13, Vol. 1, no. 16; see further Vol. 1, nos. 13, 14, 15.

18. Ref. 13, Vol. 1, no. 21.

19. K. Gödel, *Monatschr. f. Math. und Phys.* **38**, 173, 1931

20. Ref. 1, p. 80.

21. Ref. 13, Vol. 1, no. 7.

22. Ref. 13, Vol. 1, nos. 9, 10, 11, 25; Vol. 2, nos. 1, 2, 5; Vol. 3, no. 2.

23. N, *Die mathematische Grundlagen der Quantenmechanik*, Springer, New York, 1932; reprinted in Dover Publications, 1943. English translation by R. T. Beyer, Princeton University Press, 1955.

24. Ref. 10, p. 11.

25. N, in *Les Nouvelles théories de la physique*, p. 46, Institut international de coopération intellectuelle, 1939.

26. Ref. 13, Vol. 1, nos. 18, 19, 20, 23, 24; see also Vol. 2, no. 21. See ref. 9 for further details.

27. Ref. 13, Vol. 1, no. 17.

28. Ref. 13, Vol. 1, no. 25; Vol. 2, nos. 12, 13, 14.

29. N. Macrae, *John von Neumann*, p. 24, Pantheon, New York, 1992.

30. Ref. 13, Vol. 6, no. 1. English translation in *Contributions to the Theory of Games*, p. 13, Princeton University Press, 1959.

31. Ref. 10, p. 15.

32. N, *Erg. eines Math. Coll.* **8**, 73, 1937, K. Menger, Ed.

33. E. R. Weintraub, *J. of Econ. Literature* **21**, 1, 1983.

34. N. and O. Morgenstern, *Theory of Games and Economic Behavior*, Princeton University Press, 1944.

35. Ref. 10, p. 16.

36. See ref. 29, chapter 11 for more on the role of von Neumann's work in economics.

37. Ref. 29, p. 256.

38. Ref. 13, Vol. 6, nos. 3, 4, 5, 6, 7, 11.

39. Ref. 1, p. 74.

40. Ref. 29, p. 158.

41. N, at the confirmation hearings for membership of the Atomic Energy Commission, March 8, 1955.

42. Ref. 29, p. 161.

43. Minutes of the Executive Committee, Institute for Advanced Study, January 28, 1933, Institute Archives.

44. Ref. 29, p. 172.

45. J. Dieudonné, *Dictionary of Scientific Biography*, Vol. 14, p. 89, Scribner's, New York, 1976.

46. Ref. 13, Vol. 3, nos. 2, 3, 5.

47. Ref. 13, Vol. 3, nos. 4, 7; Vol. 4, no. 8.

48. Which states that every locally compact group possesses an invariant measure which assigns positive numbers to all operators.

49. Ref. 13, Vol. 2, no. 19.

50. Ref. 13, Vol. 2, no. 22; Vol. 4, no. 6.

51. Ref. 13, Vol. 2, no. 23; Vol. 4, no. 1.

52. Ref. 29, p. 183.

53. A. Turing, *Proc. London Math. Soc.* **42**, 230, 1937.

54. Ref. 13, Vol. 6, no. 37.

55. For more details see ref. 3, p. 178.

56. Ref. 10, p. 25.

57. Ref. 10, p. 26.

58. N and S. Chandrasekhar, ref. 13, Vol. 6, nos. 12, 13; ref. 13, Vol. 6, nos. 14–18.

59. N and E. Fermi, ref. 13, Vol. 6, no. 31.

60. Ref. 1, pp. 230, 231.

61. Ref. 13, Vol. 6, nos. 19, 20, 22–5, 27–9.

62. Ref. 3, p. 167.

63. S. Grafton, interview with Klari, *Good Housekeeping*, September 1956, p. 80.

64. Ref. 3, p. 176.

65. Ref. 1, pp. 78, 79.

66. Ref. 29, p. 153.

67. Ref. 3, p. 181.

68. Minutes of the School of Mathematics, June 2, 1945.

69. *Ibid.*, meeting on October 19, 1945.

70. *Ibid.*, meeting on May 14, 1946.

71. Ref. 3, p. 245.

72. *New York Herald Tribune*, June 11, 1952.

73. Ref. 13, Vol. 5, nos. 1–5. All the rest of Vol. 5 is devoted to work done on and by the computer.

74. See ref. 10, p. 91, for a list of computers built following the IAS design.

75. Ref. 1, p. 230.

76. A detailed table of applications of the IAS computer is found in ref. 10, pp. 156, 157.

77. K. Auletta, *The New Yorker*, May 12, 1997.

78. Ref. 1, pp. 76–8.

79. O. Veblen, letter to L. Strauss, April 12, 1946, quoted in B. Stern, 'A history of the Institute for Advanced Study, 1930–1950,' unpublished manuscript in the Institute Archives.

80. N, testimony in 'In the matter of J. Robert Oppenheimer,' p. 643ff., US Government Printing Office, Washington, 1954; reprinted by MIT Press, Cambridge, MA, 1970.

81. Ref. 3, pp. 317, 318.

82. Described in greater detail in a book on Oppenheimer, in preparation.

83. For the complete text of the statement see A. Pais, *Physics Today* 20, October 1967, p. 35.

84. N, *The Computer and the Brain*, Yale University Press, 1958.

85. Ref. 13, Vol. 5, no. 10.

86. Ref. 10, chapter 8; ref. 3, p. 271ff. See also N in *Theory of Self-reproducing Automata* (A. Burks, Ed.), University of Illinois Press, 1960.

87. Ref. 13, Vol. 6, no. 35.

88. Ref. 13, Vol. 6, no. 36.

89. Ref. 13, Vol. 6, no. 38.

90. Ref. 13, Vol. 6, no. 39.

91. Ref. 13, vol. 6, no. 40.

92. Ref. 1, pp. 237, 238.

93. Ref. 1, pp. 240–1.

94. Ref. 10, p. 335.

95. Ref. 1, p. 243.

96. L. Strauss, *Men and Decisions*, p. 236, Doubleday, New York, 1962.

97. E. Wigner, *Yearbook of the American Philosophical Society 1957*, p. 149; reproduced in *Symmetries and Reflections*, p. 257, Indiana University Press, 1967.

98. *The New York Times*, November 12, 1963.

Wolfgang Pauli in Carlin, Nevada, a whistle stop on his way to Pasadena to announce the discovery of the neutrino, in 1931. (Courtesy of AIP Emilio Segrè Visual Archives, Goudsmit Collection.)

Wolfgang Ernst Pauli

First encounters

Pauli had a far greater influence on the development of my scientific career than I had initially appreciated, as I shall explain shortly. My first contact with Pauli occurred in October 1945, when I received a letter from him. This was the *a propos.*

In June 1945, right after the end of the Second World War, I went to see Léon Rosenfeld, who had been my PhD thesis advisor, to discuss future postdoctoral research opportunities. He made two suggestions: go either to Niels Bohr in Copenhagen, or to Wolfgang Pauli, who was then at the Institute for Advanced Study in Princeton (referred to in the following as the Institute). Since it was not clear what the possibilities would be, he proposed that I send letters of application to both places, which I did.

In the following September I received a cordial letter from Bohr inviting me to spend time at his Institute for theoretical physics. In October the letter from Pauli (just mentioned) came, in which he wrote in part: 'I saw your application for coming into this country . . . I am in favour of it . . . I have received your interesting manuscript on which I just had a look . . . Your work seems very carefully done.'[1] (Here he refers to work I had done during the war years, dealing with quantum field theory.[2]) In December I heard from Princeton that I had been accepted for a one-year stay at the Institute. After consultation with Rosenfeld, I decided to go immediately to Denmark for one year, then go to Princeton.

So it came about that I met Pauli for the first time in Denmark, in early 1946, at a dinner party in Bohr's home. At that time he had already long been recognized as one of the major figures in twentieth-century physics, not only because of his own contributions, but also because of his critical judgments—which could be quite sharp, but nearly always to the point—of others' work. He was known as the conscience of twentieth-century physics, as is reflected in his voluminous correspondence, a very rich source of information concerning the development of physics in the first half of the century, from which I shall quote extensively in what follows. His letters are nearly all in German, which he wrote masterfully.

He was clearly pleased to meet me and was kind enough to invite me for dinner the next evening at Krog's fish restaurant, one of Denmark's finest eateries. In the course of that meal I witnessed for the first time his chassidic mode, a gentle rhythmic to and fro rocking of the upper torso. Something was on his mind. He began to talk of his difficulties in finding a physics problem to work on next, adding 'Perhaps that is because I know too much.' Silence; more rocking. Then: 'Do you know much?' I laughed and said, 'No, I don't know much.' Another silence, while Pauli seriously considered my reply, then: 'No, perhaps you don't know much, perhaps you don't know much.' A moment later: '*Ich weiss mehr*' (I know more). That was said in the Pauli style, without aggression, merely an expression of a statement of fact.

When in September 1946 I arrived at the Institute in Princeton, one of the first things I heard was that Pauli had recently left for Zürich to reassume his professorship there, after having spent the war years in Princeton, from 1940–46. Pauli was gone, a real setback for me, yet even so his temporary presence in Princeton profoundly affected my career—this is what I referred to in my opening lines—since it caused me to spend the next 17 years in Princeton. I was to see much of him later, however, there and elsewhere.

Before continuing my account I give a brief synopsis of what is to follow.

<hr />

Pauli was an infant prodigy. At age 21 he published a review of relativity theory, highly praised by Einstein, still one of the best texts on the subject. He was a recognized expert not only on relativity but also on quantum physics. As we shall see, he enjoyed close personal relations with Einstein, and even closer ones with Niels Bohr. His textbook article (1933) on the principles of wave mechanics is still a classic.

Pauli's most famous original contributions are his exclusion principle, for which in 1945 he received the Nobel Prize, and his neutrino hypothesis. He was the first to recognize that an electron has four degrees of freedom, the fourth soon afterward being understood to be its spin. Less well known is the fact that his doctor's thesis contains the first *quantitative* evidence for the fact that the so-called 'old' quantum theory had reached its limits. Other major contributions are his theory of spin zero quantum fields and his work on the relation between spin and statistics and on the CPT theorem. These and many other of his papers will be discussed in some detail in the sequel.

I shall also deal with aspects of Pauli's personal life, his family background, his two marriages, and his psychoanalysis; this brought him into contact with Carl Jung that lasted from 1932 until shortly before Pauli's death in 1958, and with Marie-Louise von Frantz, Jung's main assistant and his successor as leader of the Jung Institute in Zurich after Jung's death. I shall endeavor to sketch how these contacts led to Pauli's deep involvement with psychological problems, notably with the personality of Johannes Kepler. Pauli's essay on him is a prime example of his far-ranging erudition.

The number of Pauli anecdotes is legion. I mention my favorites. His reply to a young man who asked for an appointment at nine in the morning on a certain day: 'Impossible, that is too late.' His reaction after another young man had explained his ideas to Pauli, who had rapidly made clear to him that these were wrong: 'So young and already so unknown.' The Pauli effect of which he was immensely proud: something would almost inevitably go wrong with experimental equipment when he got near it. The experimentalist Otto Stern, colleague of Pauli in Hamburg, once told me that the two of them would only discuss physics through a closed door leading to Stern's laboratory.

Family background

Jakob Pascheles, Pauli's grandfather, and his wife, Helene née Utitz, ran a bookshop in Prague, a successful business, which enabled them to acquire a house in the Old Town Square in that city. As elder of the congregation of the 'Gypsy's Synagogue,' he had presided over the bar mitzvah of Franz Kafka. On September 11, 1869, a son was born to the couple, who they named Wolfgang Joseph. The boy turned out to be very bright. His education was completed in 1893, when he received the degree Dr Med. from the University of Prague. Initially he practiced as a physician in Vienna, his patients including many prominent society figures. In July 1898 he received permission to change his name to Wolfgang Joseph Pauli. In March 1899 he converted from the Jewish to the Roman Catholic faith. The following May he married Berta Camilla Schütz, the daughter of a writer and editor, herself a correspondent for the influential Viennese *Die neue freie Presse*. On April 25, 1900 their first child was born in Vienna—our Pauli. Before turning to him, let us first round off the picture of his family.

Early on, Pauli's father left pure medicine for chemistry, in which field he became a major pioneering figure. 'Already as a boy he had shown scientific interest in physics and chemistry. In his early student years he spent every free moment in the physics institute of the famous physicist Ernst Mach who became his teacher and model, and who remained his fatherly friend until the end of his [M.'s] life. He [M.] also repeatedly presented brief scientific communications of young Pauli's results to the *Kaiserliche Akademie der Wissenschaften* in Vienna.'[3] Pauli himself has called his contacts with Mach 'the most important event in my intellectual life.'[4]

Our Pauli's middle name, Ernst, was taken after Mach, who was also his godfather. In the Salle Pauli at CERN one finds exhibited, along with a handsome bust of Pauli in his later years, Mach's gift for Pauli's christening, a silver cup with the inscription '31 Mai 1900,' accompanied by a card inscribed in old-fashioned flowery type: 'Dr. E. Mach, *Professor an der Universität Wien*,' as well as a letter by Pauli, dated March 31, 1953, which contains these lines: '[Mach] was a stronger personality than the Catholic priest, and the result seems to be that in this way I am baptized 'antimetaphysical' instead of Catholic.'[5] Mach also gave advice regarding scientific reading for Pauli junior.[6]

In 1898 we already find papa Pauli on the junior faculty of the University of Vienna, rising through the ranks until he became full professor in 1922 and director of the *Institut für medizinische Kolloidchemie*, specially created for him in the medical faculty of the University of Vienna, where he continued his fundamental work on colloids. 'We owe to Pauli the first insights into the exact connections between the constitution, the structure and the stability of colloids, as well as their chemical-physical behavior.'[3] The number of his scientific publications runs into the hundreds, including several books. Which explains why his son published under the name W. Pauli *jun.* until his appointment as full professor at the ETH (Eidgenössische Technische Hochschule) in Zurich, in 1928.

A few additional remarks on Pauli's family. He had a younger sister, Hertha, an author best known for her biography of Bertha von Suttner, an Austrian pacifist. In 1940 she moved to the United States, where she married and became an American citizen. In 1927 Pauli's mother committed suicide. His father remarried in 1928 and moved to Switzerland in 1938, where he died in 1955 in Zurich. A letter from Pauli to Carl Jung gives a glimpse of his relationship with his father:

> On November 4, 1955, my father died at advanced age, from heart weakness. That leads to a considerable change in the subconscious, and I suspect that for me this means a change of the shadow, since for me the shadow had for a long time been projected onto my father. Correspondingly the link to the shadow or devil often appeared projected onto the 'evil stepmother' (who my father now left behind as his much younger second wife.)[6a]

It is known that Pauli had strong ties to his mother . . .

Relativity theory: Pauli and Einstein

Pauli received his early schooling in Vienna. During his high school years at the *Döblingen Gymnasium* he acquainted himself with the mathematics and physics of his day. In his final Gymnasium years, 'he became familiar with Einstein's quite recent papers, which, during boring school hours, he secretly read, hiding them below his desk . . . These studies made a deep impression on him . . . He has told me that it was as if the scales fell from his eyes . . . suddenly he had understood general relativity theory.'[7]

In July 1918 Pauli graduated *mit Auszeichnung* (with distinction). Two months later he submitted his first paper, on general relativity, under the byline 'München, Institut für theoretische Physik,' where he had attended the Ludwig–Maximilian University to study with Arnold Sommerfeld. Soon two more papers followed.[9]

Sommerfeld's admirable courage and faith in Pauli was shown when, in the fourth of the six semesters he (P.) spent with him, he entrusted him with the preparation of a review of relativity theory for the *Encyclopädie der mathematischen Wissenschaften*. It became a 237-page monograph[10] which contains a critical presentation of the mathematical foundations and the physical meaning of the theory, and a complete discussion of the then already voluminous literature. It appeared in 1921, two months after Pauli had received his doctorate.

This work at once received wide acclaim, as is best illustrated by Einstein's review, published in 1922, which contains these lines:

> No one studying this mature, grandly conceived work would believe that the author is a man of twenty-one. One wonders what to admire most, the psychological understanding for the development of ideas, the sureness of mathematical deduction, the profound physical insight, the capacity for lucid, systematical presentation, the knowledge of the literature, the complete treatment of the subject matter, [or] the sureness of critical appraisal.[11]

I would think that never has a physicist so young received such glorious approbation.

Like many others, I learned relativity theory from Pauli's article which, after all these years, I still find the best text. In 1958 an English translation appeared,[12] to which Pauli appended 25 pages of supplementary notes.

Pauli first saw Einstein at the physics meeting at Bad Nauheim (September 16–25, 1920). They probably did not have a personal meeting at that time, for in 1924 Pauli wrote to Bohr: 'I had lengthy discussions with Einstein in Innsbruck [physics meeting September 21–27, 1924]. Now I finally succeeded in meeting him.'[13] Their correspondence had started earlier, however, with a letter by Pauli to Einstein, dealing with quantum physics.[14]

The two men met again in 1927, at the fifth Solvay conference (the first of these which Pauli attended), remembered for the stellar constellation of physicists gathered in Brussels. There Einstein expressed for the first time publicly his critical position regarding quantum mechanics, which had appeared on the scene in 1925. Pauli, who actively participated in discussions, was among those who made comments after Einstein's talk, expressing his disagreement in a restrained way.[15] In 1929 he reported in a letter: 'During the Easter vacation I visited Einstein in Berlin and found his attitude regarding modern quantum physics reactionary.'[16]

Ehrenfest has called Pauli '*die Geissel Gottes*,' the scourge of the Lord.[17] It cannot be emphasized enough that this applies exclusively to his responses to some of his colleagues' scientific efforts. There is no better illustration for this than Pauli's reactions to Einstein's fruitless efforts at constructing a unified field theory: highly caustic, while at the same time very respectful and cordial in his relations to Einstein the man.

In the late twenties, Einstein was deeply immersed in one of his unifying efforts, the so-called theory of distant parallelism.[18] Pauli would have none of that. To one colleague he wrote: '*Jetzt hat Einstein den Bock des Fernparallelismus geschossen*' (now E. has made the boo-boo of distant parallelism).[19] To another he called it '*schrecklichen Quatsch*' (terrible rubbish).[20] To still another: '*Einstein scheint der liebe Gott jetzt völlig verlassen zu haben*' (it appears that E. now has completely abandoned the dear Lord).[21] To Einstein himself he wrote:

> I should like to add something about my position and that of a large part of the younger physics generation regarding this matter . . . It seems to me that your equations hardly show any resemblance with the state of affairs confirmed by experiment . . . I should congratulate you (or should I rather say send condolences?) that you have switched to pure mathematics . . . I will not provoke you to contradict me, in order not to delay the death of [your present] theory.[22]

Einstein replied: 'Your letter is quite amusing but your position seems rather superficial to me . . . say more about it when at least a quarter of a year will have passed.'[23] Pauli in 1932, in a scientific journal: '[Einstein's] never-failing inventiveness as well as his tenacious energy in the pursuit of [unification] guarantees us in recent years, on the average, one theory per annum . . . It is psychologically interesting that for some time the current theory is considered by its author to be the "definitive solution."'[24] Einstein to Pauli, that year: 'So you were right, you rascal.'[25] In 1933 Pauli wrote to Einstein[26] about work *he* had done on unified field theory. It concerns a five-dimensional version known as projective relativity, contained in two papers[27] which he had just sent off for publication. This work, of great mathematical elegance, is not marred by Einstein's visionary concepts, however. Thereafter the two men corresponded but only sparsely.

Finally, in 1943 Einstein and Pauli published a joint paper, not on unified theories but on standard relativity theory. They proved that any everywhere regular and static solution of the source-free gravitational equations which behaves at large distances like a Schwarzschild solution must have a vanishing Schwarzschild mass.[28] This is Pauli's one and only paper on relativity after the three short papers with which he had begun publishing.[8,9]

Pauli's Nobel Prize

On January 13, 1945, Einstein sent the following telegram to the Nobel committee in Stockholm: 'Nominate Wolfgang Pauli for physics prize stop his contributions to modern quantum theory consisting in so-called Pauli or exclusion principle became fundamental part of modern quantum physics being independent from the other basic axioms of that theory stop Albert Einstein.'[29]

On November 15, 1945, the Nobel committee decided to award the physics prize 'to Wolfgang Pauli, for the discovery of the exclusion principle, also named "Pauli principle."'

I briefly digress at this point, to mention nominations for and by Pauli for the prize, making use of documents kindly provided me by Professor Anders Bárány, secretary to the Nobel committee for physics.

The following are the main nominations for Pauli in earlier years: Carl Oseen in 1933, Dirk Coster (1934 and 1940), von Laue, Planck and Léon Brillouin (1935), Schrödinger (1938), Uhlenbeck (1940), Wentzel (1940, 1941, 1943, and 1944). John van Vleck and Kramers were other nominators in 1945. All these colleagues mention the Pauli principle. I am struck by the absence of Bohr on this list.

Nominations by Pauli: Heisenberg (1932), Stern (1938 and 1940), Rabi (1940); possibly more from 1947 onwards, which are still classified at this writing.

———————

Pauli did not go to Sweden in 1945 to receive the prize. On Monday, December 10, the traditional date of the Nobel ceremonies in Stockholm, he was honored instead at a black-tie dinner at the Institute in Princeton. In his address of welcome, Frank Aydelotte, the Institute director, spoke of 'Minds like Newton, Einstein, and Pauli, voyaging through strange seas of thought alone.'[30] In his encomium, Herman Weyl said: 'It is difficult to imagine what the history of physics would have been like without the influence of Pauli during the last twenty-odd years.'[30] Weyl was followed by Einstein, about whose words Pauli wrote in 1955 to Max Born, after Einstein's death:

> A fatherly friend, well-disposed to me, is no more. Never will I forget the speech that he gave about me and for me in Princeton in 1945, after I had received the Nobel prize. It was like a king who abdicates and appoints me as sort of 'son elect' as successor. Unfortunately, no records of this speech of Einstein exist, it was improvised, and a manuscript does not exist either.[31]

Mrs Pauli has told me that Pauli was visibly deeply moved by Einstein's words. Pauli's reply at the dinner consisted of a concise summary of his main work to date.[30] See ref. 32 for a list of others present that evening. On December 13, 1946, Pauli delivered his Nobel lecture in Stockholm, on 'Exclusion principle and quantum mechanics.'[33]

As I have intimated earlier, Pauli's sharpness, in discussion and correspondence, is an expression of his intellectual honesty rather than of personal aggressiveness. I know of no better way to illustrate this than by quoting from his letter to Einstein, written in 1946, after having been 'appointed as his successor':

'It remains my personal conviction—not least because of the negative outcome of your own numerous efforts—that classical field theory is a completely squeezed out lemon from which it is impossible to find something new.'[34] Einstein to Pauli: 'Such efforts appear very promising to me.'[35,36]

In 1949 Pauli sent Einstein congratulations on his seventieth birthday:

> Along with my cordial good wishes I wish to add how strongly I experienced the gift of personal sympathy which you gave me in Princeton at the festivity in December 1945. The human and intellectual attitude toward me which you expressed at that time, will serve me as a reminder to remain forever faithful to the intellectual ideal which binds us.[37]

In that letter he also told Einstein of his contribution to an anniversary volume[38] dealing with Einstein's major contributions to quantum physics in the years 1905–18.

After Einstein's death in April 1955, Pauli wrote an affectionate and thoughtful obituary in a Swiss newspaper,[39] which ends like this: 'His life which points to the future will always remind us of the ideal, threatened in our time, of intellectual, contemplative man, whose thoughts, quietly and inflexibly, stick to the great problems of the structure of the cosmos.'[40]

A conference on relativity in Berne, in 1955, took place only months after Einstein's death. It was presided over by Pauli, who said in his opening remarks: 'This congress . . . should be . . . a farewell to the man,' and who also gave the closing summary.[41]

Old quantum physics: first encounters with Bohr

I return to the autumn of 1918 when, as mentioned, Pauli had started his studies in Munich, with Sommerfeld. It was there that he began work on what was to become his main devotion: quantum physics. His very first paper[42] in this area, completed in June 1920, deals with the magnetic properties of matter, a topic on which later he was to make some of his most famous contributions. He gave a talk on that subject at Bad Nauheim, the first conference he attended.[43]

In July 1925 he received his doctorate with Sommerfeld on a thesis dealing with a model for the ionized hydrogen molecule.[44] In the protocol for Pauli's *examen rigorosum* Sommerfeld praised it as showing 'like his many already published smaller investigations and his large encyclopedia article, the full command of the modern tools of mathematical physics.'[45] In fact, Pauli received his doctorate *summa cum laude*—in spite of the fact that his theoretical results did not agree with experiment! 'This failure made a painful impression on the self-confident young physicist, used to success.'[46]

Sommerfeld's words of praise were nevertheless quite justified. Recall that Pauli finished his thesis during the years of the so-called 'old' quantum theory, which was not a theory at all, but rather was built on a set of *ad hoc* rules superimposed on the classical theory of its time, rules which actually were in conflict with the classical theory. The importance of Pauli's work consisted in fact in providing the *first* firm evidence for showing that the old quantum 'theory' had reached its limits of applicability, this in spite of its major successes which had shown that there were more than germs of truth in what physicists of that time had improvised.

It was Pauli again who has left us with the most complete, authoritative review of the old quantum theory, a handbook article[47] which he completed in October 1925—after the discovery of quantum mechanics, the theory which for the first time put quantum physics on a solid logical footing. This article is no longer pertinent to modern science but indispensable for those interested in the twentieth-century history of atomic structure.

———————— • ————————

Pauli had the greatest respect for Sommerfeld, the only physicist whom he invariably treated with perfect courtesy if not with awe. After Sommerfeld's death in April 1951, the result of an automobile accident, he wrote: 'As is given only to few, Sommerfeld harmoniously combined the qualities of researcher and teacher . . . Mourning him . . . we, his intellectual children, now will continue his labors.'[48]

Sommerfeld was one of two men Pauli met in Munich who have played an important role in his life. The other was the one-and-a-half year younger Werner Heisenberg, who had also become a Sommerfeld student, in 1920, and who has recalled: 'Sommerfeld had introduced me to him (P.) . . . and afterwards said to me that he considered him as one of his most gifted students, from whom I could learn much.'[49] Heisenberg has also told of Pauli's life style those years. 'Wolfgang was a typical night bird. He preferred the town, liked to spend evenings in some café, and would thereafter work on his physics with the highest intensity and great success. To Sommerfeld's dismay he would therefore rarely attend morning lectures and would turn up only around noon time.'[50]

———————— • ————————

In October 1921 Pauli left Munich for Göttingen, to become the assistant of Max Born, who reported that same month to Einstein: 'Pauli is astonishingly wise and very capable. In addition he is humane, quite normal, cheerful, and childlike[51] . . . little Pauli is very stimulating . . . I will never get again such a good assistant . . .'[52] Later: 'I recall that he liked to sleep late and that he missed the eleven o'clock lecture more than once. At ten thirty we sent our maid to him, to be certain that he had gotten up.'[53]

Born and Pauli collaborated on a lengthy article dealing with perturbation methods in quantum theory,[54] and made an unsuccessful attempt at treating the helium atom. In April 1922 Pauli was on the move again, this time to an assistant position in Hamburg. The next June he visited Göttingen, in order to attend a series of lectures given there by Niels Bohr. Of that gathering he said later: 'A new phase of my life began when I met Bohr personally for the first time.'[30]

———————•———————

At the Princeton Nobel Prize party for Pauli he reminisced about those days in Göttingen:

> During these meetings Bohr came to me one day and asked me whether I could come to him in Copenhagen for a year. He needed a collaborator in the editing of his works, which he wanted to publish in German. I was much surprised, and after considering a little while I answered with that certainty of which only a young man is capable: 'I hardly think that the scientific demands which you will make on me will cause me any difficulty, but the learning of a foreign tongue like Danish far exceeds my abilities.' I went to Copenhagen in the fall of 1922, where both of my contentions were shown to be wrong.[30]

In Munich he had already been introduced by Sommerfeld to Bohr's theory of atomic structure with its use of discrete sets of electron orbits, instead of continuous sets demanded by classical theory. 'I was not spared the shock which every physicist, accustomed to the classical way of thinking, experienced when he came to know of Bohr's "Basic postulate of quantum theory" for the first time.'[30,33]

In July 1922 Bohr wrote to Pauli to tell how much he looked forward to the latter's visit.[55] So began the correspondence between the two men which would continue for more than 30 years, and which is one of the richest sources of the history of physics during that period. Also in that July Bohr wrote to Kramers: 'He [P.] is an excellent man in all respects and will most certainly be very helpful.'[56] Pauli arrived in Copenhagen in October 1922 for a stay that would last until September 1923. He returned for numerous shorter visits in later years (every year from 1925 through 1931, 1933, 1936, 1937, 1946, 1947, 1954).

During his first, long Copenhagen stay, Pauli completed three papers. One, with Kramers, on band spectra.[57] Another, on thermal equilibrium between radiation and free electrons,[58] served him as *Habilitationsschrift* (a paper required in order to qualify as university lecturer) in Hamburg, after his return there from Denmark. The third, on the anomalous Zeeman effect,[59] marks the beginning of a series of investigations culminating in Pauli's creative peak in January 1925, his highest I would think.

The exclusion principle

When atoms are excited (by heating, for example), they emit a line spectrum, a discrete set of light frequencies. When exposed to a sufficiently strong magnetic field, each line splits up into several lines. That is the Zeeman effect, so named after its discovery, in 1896, by the Dutch physicist Pieter Zeeman. In 1897 it was shown that the classical theory predicted a splitting into a triplet of lines when observed in the direction perpendicular to the magnetic field. That is called the normal Zeeman effect. In 1898 it was observed, however, that a certain line in the sodium spectrum actually splits up into a quartet of lines. That was the first example of what we now call the anomalous Zeeman effect. The normal effect has since been found to be the exception rather than the rule. The problem Pauli had set himself in Copenhagen was to interpret the anomalous effect on the basis of the old quantum theory.

By then it was known that the anomalous splittings exhibited beautiful and simple regularities, 'but [this] was hardly understandable, since very general assumptions concerning the electron, using classical theory as well as [old] quantum theory, always led to the simple triplet. A closer interpretation of this problem left me with the feeling that it was even more unapproachable.'[30] Pauli to Sommerfeld in June 1923: 'I could not, could not, get agreement. Up till now I have thoroughly gone wrong.'[60] Later he recalled: 'A colleague who met me strolling rather aimlessly in the beautiful streets of Copenhagen said to me in a friendly manner, 'You look very unhappy'; whereupon I answered fiercely, 'How can one look happy when he is thinking about the anomalous Zeeman effect?'[30]

This effect constituted one of the main debacles of the old quantum theory. At that time Pauli himself put it like this: 'How deep seated the failure of the theoretical principles known till now are can be seen most clearly in . . . the anomalous Zeeman effect.'[61]

It is to Pauli's greatest credit that this failure of the theory did not deter him from sticking with the anomalous Zeeman effect. The result was two papers. The first, completed in December 1924, deals with a critique of others' attempts to interpret the effect.[62] The second, completed six weeks later,[63] contains what, in 1926, Dirac was to name Pauli's exclusion principle.[64] These articles contain many technical details which I have reviewed elsewhere.[65] I shall not do so again here, but will confine myself to a brief—admittedly a bit superficial—description of the main lines of thought.

At the time under consideration, it was understood that most electrons in an atom occupy a number of filled, closed shells which together form the *Atomrumpf*, the atomic core. There may be one or more electrons outside the core, so-called valence electrons. These latter generate atomic line spectra upon excitation. In 1923 it had been proposed that the anomalous Zeeman effect is due to a prescribed type of coupling between the angular momenta of the valence electrons and a hypothesized overall angular momentum of the core.[65] In a review article (1925), Goudsmit had written[66] that some of the assumptions of this model were 'completely incomprehensible,' but that, on accepting them, 'one masters completely the extensive and complicated material of the anomalous Zeeman effect.'

Along came Pauli, who analyzed this model for the case of alkali atoms, which have just one valence electron, and showed that for these the idea of a core angular momentum is in serious conflict with other experiments.[62] Paradox: how can it be that the theory is therefore wrong, yet its application to the anomalous Zeeman effect works to an accuracy of about one per cent? Pauli's answer: the core has strictly zero angular momentum, and we have only one option left—ascribe the anomaly to the valence electron. In his words, the explanation is '*due to a peculiar not classically describable two-valuedness [Zweideutigkeit] of the quantum theoretical properties of the valence electron.*'[62]

Today we know well what this peculiarity means: the electron carries a spin, an intrinsic angular momentum, somewhat like the earth spinning around an axis while orbiting the sun; the electron spin is capable of taking on two values only. Many have wondered why Pauli did not take the extra step and discover this himself. I do not fully understand that either but can at least give an important contributing reason.

Four days after his paper on the anomalous Zeeman effect had been received, Pauli wrote to Sommerfeld: 'I have made headway with a few points . . . [regarding] . . . the question of the closure of electron groups in the atom.'[67] He had been deflected from the question: what can the two-valuedness mean? to the question: has the two-valuedness something to do with the closed electron shells in atoms?

In October 1924 Edmund Stoner had proposed[68] the following rule: 'The number of electrons in each completed shell is equal to double the sum of the inner quantum numbers.' I should explain. Imagine what we would call an independent particle model for the atom: each electron moves around the nucleus independently of all the others, and therefore describes a hydrogen-like orbit. Then we can ascribe to *each* electron the following quantum numbers: a principal quantum number n, and the quantum number l which (as known from hydrogen) can take the values $l = 0, 1, . . ., n-1$. Imagine further that these independent electrons are in an external magnetic field. A third quantum number appears: m and each level (n, l) is split into $2l + 1$ levels corresponding to $-l \leq m \leq l$. The number N of levels is:

$$n = 1: l = 0, \qquad\qquad N = 1$$
$$n = 2: l = 0, 1 \qquad\qquad N = 1 + 3 = 4$$
$$n = 3: l = 0, 1, 2 \qquad\quad N = 1 + 3 + 5 = 9, \text{ etc.}$$

Stoner's rule says: a shell corresponds to a fixed n, and the number of electrons in that shell, if completely filled, equals twice N.

Why twice?

Here Pauli takes over.[63] He proposes 'to pursue as far as possible the working hypothesis (about *Zweideutigkeit*] also for atoms other than alkalis,' and goes on to introduce new postulates about two-valuedness: first, it applies to *every* atomic electron; secondly, it is formally expressed by a *two-valued* new quantum number. Thus he is led to introduce *four* quantum numbers for each electron. A doubling of the number of states occurs which, Pauli suggests, accounts for the doubling of N in Stoner's rule. Why can a shell not contain *more* than $2N$ electrons? 'In the atom there can never be two or more equivalent electrons for which the values of all quantum numbers coincide. If there is an electron in the atom for which these quantum numbers have definite values then the state is "occupied."'[63]

This is Pauli's exclusion principle, at which he therefore arrived via the route

Anomalous Zeeman effect → two-valuedness

↓

Stoner's rule → exclusion principle.

He knew well that this was not the end of the story: 'We cannot give a more precise reason for this rule.'[63] True enough—yet the rule as it stands is monumentally important as the crucial ingredient for the understanding of the periodic table of chemical elements.

———————

The discovery of electron spin by Uhlenbeck and Goudsmit, published in October 1925,[69] gave the correct physical interpretation of Pauli's *Zweideutigkeit*. At that time several important details regarding the spin picture remained unresolved, which explains Pauli's comment to Bohr, the next December: '*Die Sache gefällt mir nicht,*' (I do not like this business).[70] By March 1926 Pauli became converted, however.[71] I refer the reader to my essay on Uhlenbeck in this book for the quite complex story of what happened in the intervening months, as well as Pauli's remark on nuclear spin[72] and Uhlenbeck's observations on Pauli's personality.

———————

We have followed Pauli's whereabouts until September 1923, when he left Copenhagen to return to Hamburg, where he was to stay until 1928. On February 24, 1924, he gave his inaugural lecture as *Privatdozent*, on the periodic system of the elements. It was in Hamburg that he completed his papers on the anomalous Zeeman effect and on the exclusion principle.

In 1924 he furthermore completed a lengthy review of the theory of black-body radiation, the publication of which was delayed until 1929,[73] and also became involved in the discussion of the ill-fated Bohr–Kramers–Slater theory of radiation. That last subject I have discussed elsewhere.[74]

'Es wird tag in der quantentheorie'

'Physics is once again at a dead end at this time. For me, at any rate, it is much too difficult and I wish I were a film comedian or something like that and had never heard anything about physics.' So, on May 21, 1925, did Pauli write to a colleague,[75] five months after having finished his paper on the exclusion principle.

Two months after Pauli had written that letter, physics' dead end came to an end when, on July 29, Heisenberg submitted his article[76] which marks the birth of quantum mechanics. That paper, which brought to a close the old quantum theory, with its curious mixture of successes and debacles, augured in what I think is the greatest revolution in twentieth-century science.

As best I know, Pauli was the first to hear of the new theory, when in June Heisenberg wrote to him: 'The principle is: In the calculation of whatever quantity, energy, frequency, etc., only relations may enter between quantities that are in principle observable.'[77] Early in July Heisenberg sent him an advance copy of his paper. Before it had appeared, Pauli wrote to Kramers, for once with unequivocal enthusiasm: 'I have greeted Heisenberg's daring beginnings with jubilation.'[78] And, a few months later, to another colleague: 'Heisenberg's mechanics has restored my zest for life.'[79]

In November 1925, Pauli made his own first contribution[80] to the new mechanics, a *tour de force*: the calculations, with matrix methods, of the discrete spectrum of the hydrogen atom, and of its Stark effect (influence of an external electric field). Both results had also been successfully obtained in the earlier old quantum theory, but in addition Pauli achieved another result where the old theory had failed:[81] the influence of crossed electric and magnetic external fields. Bohr was enthusiastic about these 'wonderful results.'[82] Heisenberg commented: 'I myself had been a bit unhappy that I could not succeed in deriving the hydrogen spectrum from the new theory,'[83] and wrote to Pauli: 'I admire it that you produced this theory so quickly.'[84]

The next fundamental advance in quantum physics occurred in January 1926 when Schrödinger submitted the first of his series of papers on wave mechanics.[85] Pauli was once again deeply impressed, as can be seen from a letter to Jordan: 'I believe that the work counts among the most significant recently written. Read it carefully and with devotion.'[86]

The obvious question now arose: what is the relation between the two theories, both successful, Heisenberg's matrix mechanics and Schrödinger's wave mechanics? It took little time before not one but several physicists showed that the two theories are in fact equivalent. One of them was Pauli, who did not publish this important result because Schrödinger had beaten him to it.[87] He did write to several colleagues, however, that he had arrived independently at the same conclusion (in most detail in ref. 86).

Other memorable events in 1926: Max Born's introduction of probability in the fundamental laws of quantum physics;[88] Pauli's application of this idea to general N-body systems[89]; the first application of quantum mechanics to the physics of molecules, by Pauli;[90] his promotion to professor in Hamburg.[91]

The basic ideas of quantum mechanics as we know it today were completed in 1927. First came Heisenberg's paper on his uncertainty relations.[92] Once again, Pauli was the first to hear of this work, in a long letter from Heisenberg,[93] who has recalled: 'Pauli's reaction was much more positive than I had dared hope . . . [this] encouraged me to write up the contents of these considerations,' and also Pauli's response: '*Es wird Tag in der Quantentheorie*,' (day is dawning in the quantum theory).[83]

Next came Bohr's concept of complementarity, which shows up for the first time in his correspondence in a letter to Pauli, in August 1927.[94] He first spoke publicly about it on September 16, at the Como conference.[95] After the meeting he and Pauli, who was in the audience, spent a week together at Lake Como to rework the manuscript.[96] At about that time the two men changed from the formal *Sie* to the familiar *Du*.[97]

Next came the famous fifth Solvay conference, attended by all the founders of the quantum theory. Then and there began the Bohr–Einstein dialogue on the foundations of quantum physics.[98] 'Pauli and Heisenberg, who were there, did not pay much attention [to Einstein's objections], '*ach was, das stimmt schon, das stimmt schon*' (ah, well, it will be all right, it will be all right).[99]

So far my account of Pauli's activities in 1927 has focussed on his role as comrade-in-arms to Heisenberg and to Bohr. I now turn to his own main contributions of that year.

First, his quantum theory of paramagnetism,[100] of which it has been written: 'It is probably no exaggeration to say that the modern theory of metals was started by Pauli's paper on the paramagnetism of an electron gas.'[101]

This paper is also of historical interest, since it shows that Pauli had not yet understood when to apply which of the two statistics: 'For a material gas Fermi statistics applies and not Einstein-Bose statistics.'[100] In that respect he was in the company of several very distinguished colleagues.[102]

His second important paper of 1927 constitutes his advance over what two years earlier he had called 'not classically describable two-valuedness.' He now introduced 'the intrinsic angular momentum [i.e. the spin] of the electron in a fixed direction as a new variable.'[103] To this end he employed the now so familiar 2 × 2 Pauli matrices. As he emphasized, this theory is nonrelativistic and therefore 'provisional and approximate.'[103]

The year 1928 saw the integration of Pauli's step into a relativistic theory, the celebrated Dirac equation,[104] which was immediately recognized as a great advance, even though it gave rise to serious new problems, not resolved until the proposal and subsequent discovery of the positron had been made.[104]

These early difficulties explain Pauli's initial critical attitude toward Dirac's work, which I illustrate with a story told to me by Uhlenbeck. At Ann Arbor, in the summer of 1931, Pauli attended a lecture on the Dirac equation by Robert Oppenheimer. In the middle of that talk Pauli stood up, marched to the blackboard, and grabbed a piece of chalk. There he stood, facing the board, waving the chalk in his hand, then said: '*Ach nein, das ist ja alles falsch,*' . . . (all that is wrong anyway). Kramers commanded his friend Pauli to hear the speaker out. Pauli walked back and sat down. One still finds some of these reservations in Pauli's splendid 1933 review of the principles of quantum mechanics.[105]

First work on quantum field theory; move to Zurich

The history of quantum physics as applied to the electromagnetic field goes all the way back to the very first papers on the old quantum theory, those by Planck (1900) and by Einstein (1905).[106]

Quantum mechanics was only two months old when we already find it applied to electromagnetism, in a paper by Born and Jordan, in which they introduced what they called 'matrix electrodynamics.'[107, 108] Another two months later their ideas were considerably extended by Born, Heisenberg, and Jordan.[109]

These two important early papers deal with the quantum theory of the pure electromagnetic field, that is, they do not yet include the interaction of that field with matter. The first steps on that long and difficult road were taken in 1927, by Dirac.[110] His work marks the beginning of what we now call quantum electrodynamics (QED).[111] In that same year Pauli began his own research, in quantum field theory (QFT). It became his main concern for the rest of his life.

The first sign of Pauli's new interest that I know of, I found in a letter by Heisenberg to him: 'I quite agree with your program concerning electrodynamics.'[112] A month later, Pauli to Jordan: 'We shall see whether I can get QED done. For the time being I am of good cheer.'[113]

Pauli's first work on QED deals with the relativistic invariance of that theory. The question was this. Up till that time all commutation relations were 'equal time commutators,' the operators commuted refer to the same instant. From the point of view of relativity, this shows an apparently awkward dissymmetry by referring to different points in space, but the same point in time. This is not to say that the relations violate the requirements of relativity, but that their compatibility with relativity needs to be proved.

That was first done by Jordan and Pauli[114] for the case of the free electromagnetic field in which the time dependence of operators is explicitly known so that one can compute explicitly the commutation relations between the various electric and magnetic field components at different space–time points. They verified that all is well with relativity and were the first to generalize the delta function of Dirac to the famous 'invariant delta function.'

* * *

This paper was Pauli's last while professor in Hamburg. On January 10, 1928 he was appointed professor at the ETH in Zurich, effective the following April 1. There he stayed for the rest of his life, with the Second World War causing the only major interruption. Jordan succeeded Pauli in Hamburg.

* * *

In January 1928 Pauli wrote to Weyl of his plans to find a 'quantum theoretical reinterpretation of classical field physics,' including the interaction with matter.'[115] That was the program he now set out to pursue, in close collaboration with Heisenberg. Soon they ran into their first stumbling block: the infiniteness of the electron's self-energy, a difficulty inherent also in the classical theory.[116] More obstacles followed, to such an extent that both men turned to other problems, Pauli to issues in quantum statistical mechanics,[117] and to a draft for a novel 'Gulliver's travels to Urania, a political satire,'[118] which he stopped, and never finished, after hearing from Heisenberg that he (H.) had found a way to resolve their problems. They took up their collaboration again, resulting in their first joint paper: 'On the quantum dynamics of wave fields.'[119] As this title indicates, their main result, the so-called canonical quantization method, has more general application than to QED only. It has become a standard technique in QFT. The hard part of that paper was the proof of the relativistic invariance of the canonical commutation relations, about which Pauli used to say: '*Ich warne Neugierige*' (I warn the curious).[120]

A second joint paper followed,[121] in which they returned to complications noted earlier[119] related to the zero mass of the photon, and improved their treatment by means of gauge invariance arguments. Still the self-energy difficulty remained, causing them to write: 'A definitive formulation of the theory remains remote.'[121] With these papers the first phase of the development of QFT comes to an end.

Pauli's marriages

I have mentioned earlier the suicide in 1927 of Pauli's mother and the remarriage in 1928 of his father with a lady Pauli has referred to as the 'evil stepmother.'[6a] These events can hardly have created the right frame of mind for him to enter into marriage himself—but that is just what he did, on December 23, 1929, with Käthe Margarethe Deppner, in Berlin, where the two had met frequently. There she had studied at the Max Reinhardt School; later she became a performer at the *Danse Schule* Trudi Schopp in Zurich. I do not know whether Pauli's leaving the Catholic church, on the preceding May 6, is in any way related to his relation with Käthe.

Word of his impending betrothal must have spread earlier, for already in the preceding August Pauli had written to Weyl: 'As to me, I must reject the concept 'bride,' because it is too strongly bourgeois.'[122] If you find that rather negative, wait till you see what he wrote to Klein, two months after having been married: 'If my wife would at some point run away, then you, as well as my other friends, will receive a printed announcement.'[123] And a month later, again to Klein, apropos his planned visit to Copenhagen: 'My wife will probably not come along. When I am at all married, then loosely that way!'[124] Nor did Mrs P. accompany her husband on his lengthy voyage (August–September 1930) to the Soviet Union, where he attended the seventh All-Union physics congress in Odessa.

In September 1937 Pauli made a second trip to Russia (his last, I believe) to attend the second All-Union congress on nuclear physics in Moscow, where he gave a talk on the theory of β-decay.[125] Of that visit he has written: 'I got an awful impression of that country. Such terror I have never seen before. Nobody dares to talk and the young people were scared to look me up in my hotel.'[126] By then his marriage had long been over, having ended in divorce in less than a year, in Vienna, on November 29, 1930. In one of his last letters, written two months before his death, Pauli spoke of his 'life-crisis (1930/31).'[127]

In the beginning of the 1930s, Pauli developed serious drinking problems caused, I would guess, by his catastrophic marriage. Whereupon his father suggested that Pauli seek psychiatric help from Carl Jung—which he did. Jung referred him to Erna Rosenbaum, a young assistant with whom, beginning in February 1932, he went through five months of psychoanalysis, which were followed by three months of self-analysis. Thereafter Jung himself took over, and subsequently analyzed 400 of Pauli's dreams, 355 of which occurred outside any contact with him.[127a] After the conclusion of the analysis, the two men remained in steady contact via correspondence (to which I shall return), lasting until very shortly before Pauli's death.

It may meanwhile have raised Pauli's spirits when, on October 1931, he received the Lorentz medal in Amsterdam. In the eulogy, his friend Ehrenfest praised him for 'his penetrating mind, his clarity and honesty, and the exceptional care with which you always acknowledge the credits of other researchers.'[128] There is an entertaining anecdote related to that event. Ehrenfest had ordered Pauli to wear a black suit for the occasion. Pauli replied: 'I have ordered a black suit which I will only wear if you promise to thank me publicly for not having spared the trouble of going to a tailor.'[129] No reference to the suit appears in the published version of the eulogy, but Casimir has remembered that Ehrenfest did mention it. 'I attended the ceremony . . . but do not remember the exact way [of the] one sentence. I do remember Pauli's grin and the approving increase of the amplitude of oscillation of his body.'[130]

When, two years later, Ehrenfest committed suicide, Pauli wrote a moving obituary: 'On September 25 of this year [1933] Paul Ehrenfest carried out his fateful decision to free himself of the burden of life that he could not bear anymore . . . Now we must try to retain the memory . . . and the image of his personality . . . who like a fountain of wit and spirit enters the discussion . . .'[131]

In 1933 Pauli met Franca Bertram at a garden party in Zurich. She was the daughter of a Munich businessman, and lived at that time in Zollikon, a suburb of Zurich. That summer the two of them made an automobile trip to the south of France. Pauli had acquired a car. He had the 'slightly disconcerting habit of saying from time to time: *'Ich fahre Ziemlich gut'* (I'm driving rather well), a statement he underlined by turning around to his passengers and by releasing his hold on the wheel.'[131a] No accidents have been recorded. The next Christmas Pauli introduced Franca to his parents in Vienna. They were married on April 4, 1934, in London. It was Franca who, in Pauli's absence, oversaw the installation of their newly built home at Bergstrasse 35, Zollikon.[131b] Theirs was a good marriage, which lasted until Pauli's death.

Physics in the thirties, mainly about the neutrino

A few rooms had been put at Pauli's disposal in the ETH physics institute, which was then located at Gloriastrasse 35, in old Zurich. 'He gave [three times a week] a course of fairly elementary lectures on theoretical physics . . . These did not enjoy a very good reputation among the students.'[132] In addition, once a week he gave a course on special topics for advanced students. He had very few PhD students. Yet his influence on the younger generation was most important because of what he gave to his assistants (of which he had one at a time), who must be considered as his proper students. During the 1930s these were, in order of appearance[133]: Ralph Kronig, Felix Bloch, Rudolf Peierls, Hendrik

Casimir, Victor Weisskopf, Paul Guttinger, Guido Ludwig, Nicholas Kemmer, and Markus Fierz. All these men went on to make their own names in physics. A typical example of what Pauli expected from his assistants is found in a letter to Kronig, who in May 1928 became his first assistant: 'Every time I say something [you should] contradict me with detailed arguments.'[134] Kronig reported on extracurricular activities: 'Just now we are studying the night life in Zurich and try to improve it by means of a new method due to Pauli.'[135]

The professional appointment of Gregor Wentzel at the University of Zurich was another stimulus to Pauli. The two men got along very well; their weekly joint seminar added to Zurich's rich life in physics. Moreover, a stream of the best young physicists came for visits of various durations, among them Homi Bhabha, Max Delbrück, Lev Landau, Oppenheimer, and Rabi. Thus, while there did not exist a school in Zurich compared to those in Copenhagen, Göttingen, and Munich, one always found a small circle of excellent people there.

———————————

In his early Zurich years, Pauli made one of his most important contributions to physics: his proposal of the neutrino hypothesis, which he described in 1957 in a lecture on the early and later history of the neutrino,[136] and to which he referred in 1958 as 'that foolish [närrisch] child of the crisis of my life.'[127]

While it is difficult, and often impossible, to grasp cause and effect in human endeavor, most particularly in regard to creativity, I tend to regard Pauli's association between his time of personal turmoil and the moment at which he stated his new postulate as highly significant. Revolutionary steps were out of line with his general character. Indeed, he once said of himself, also late in life: 'When I was young I believed myself to be a revolutionary . . . [but] I was a classicist, not a revolutionary.'[137] From personal knowledge I would agree with this self-assessment. In any event, there is a striking confluence of dates. Our first information about the new hypothesis dates from the same week (of November 26, 1930) as Pauli's divorce. December 1: Heisenberg mentions 'your neutrons' in a letter to Pauli.[138] This is not 'our neutron,' discovered only two years later, but the name Pauli initially gave to the neutrino. December 4: Pauli's letter to a group of physicists gathered in Tübingen. One finds this letter reproduced in many places.[139, 140] Here I only state the letter's main points (writing 'neutron' for what we now call neutrino):

> I have come upon a desperate way out regarding the 'wrong' statistics of the nitrogen and the lithium nuclei, as well as the continuous β-spectrum . . . to wit, the possibility that there could exist in the nucleus electrically neutral particles . . . The mass of the 'neutrons' should be . . . not larger than 0.01 times the proton mass . . . For the time being I dare not publish anything about this idea.

Pauli's unwillingness to rush into print should neither be considered a sign of coyness nor of undue reticence. Nor should one consider his use of 'a desperate way out' as overly dramatic. Remember, this was 1930, when only three fundamental particles were known, the electron, the photon, and the proton, and only one of these, the photon, had been predicted on theoretical grounds. As Wigner once told me, his first reaction upon hearing of Pauli's postulate was that this was crazy—but courageous.

Note further that Pauli's mention of 'wrong' statistics refers to paradoxes rampant regarding nuclear spins, magnetic moments, and statistics. (These are discussed in detail in ref. 141.) Thus he hoped that his hypothesis would be a common cure for two ailments. Neither he nor anyone else did, could, anticipate that the two ailments demanded two distinct cures: 'our' neutron and his neutrino.

A letter to Klein, written a week later,[142] shows that Pauli initially, and incorrectly, believed his 'neutron' to be a nuclear constituent: 'Now it matters importantly which forces act on the 'neutron' since they could not stay in the nucleus if there were no such forces or if these were too weak.' That issue was not cleared up until 1934; see below.

In that December month Pauli completed his only other paper of the 1930s dealing with nuclear problems, that one on the hyperfine structure of the lithium spectrum.[143] In May 1931 he left Zurich for his first trip to the United States.

———•———

On June 16 Pauli spoke in Pasadena on 'Problems of hyperfine structure' at a symposium on 'The present status of the problem of nuclear structure' organized jointly by the American Physical Society and the American Association for the Advancement of Science.[144] On that occasion, Pauli has recalled, 'I reported publicly for the first time on my idea of very penetrating neutral particles . . . it seemed to me to be still quite uncertain, however, and I did not have my lecture printed.'[136] The next day Pauli made (as we Americans say) *The New York Times*[145] for the first time: 'A new inhabitant of the heart of the atom was introduced to the world of physics today when Dr. W. Pauli of the Institute of Technology in Zürich, Switzerland, postulated the existence of particles or entities which he christened "neutrons."'[146]

On his way back from California, Pauli stopped at Ann Arbor, where he lectured at the physics summer school, along with Sommerfeld, Kramers, and Oppenheimer. His subject was 'Problems in nuclear physics.' He also gave a colloquium on his new particle. Uhlenbeck told me that there was little discussion afterward. 'I was very impressed but also found it all very strange.' In Ann Arbor 'I fell stupidly enough (in a somewhat tipsy state) down a stairs and broke my shoulder. I must now lie in bed—very boring.'[147]

Shortly after his return to Europe, Pauli attended a nuclear physics conference in Rome (October 11–18). Of that meeting he later recalled two memorable experiences: '*Horribile dictu,* I had to shake hands with Mussolini,' and 'Fermi asked me to talk about my new idea, but I was still cautious and did *not* speak in public . . . only privately.'[148]

Also in 1932, Pauli was clearly still dubious about the neutrino, as is seen from his review of a book by Gamow,[149] the first book ever on *theoretical* nuclear physics. In his review he listed those nuclear physics problems 'which are still from a theoretical classification, such as . . . the continuous β-spectrum.'[150]

The year 1932 is often called the *annus mirabilis* of nuclear physics. 'Our' neutron, the positron, and the deuteron were discovered, and Heisenberg formulated the first quantum mechanical theory of the nucleus. The year 1933 saw the Nazis come to power. Bloch to Bohr: 'I often talk with Pauli and we follow with the greatest regret the developments in Germany.'[151] I found no mention of this upheaval in Pauli's correspondence, however.

It can be said that the neutrino received its first official blessing at the seventh Solvay conference, in October 1933 where, after three years of hesitation, Pauli came for the first time into print with his hypothesis.[152] One of the reasons for this was that, also at that meeting, experimental results were reported which showed that an alternative interpretation of β-radioactivity, proposed by Bohr,[140] which demanded a violation of energy conservation, could be ruled out. '[Bohr's] hypothesis does not seem satisfactory nor even plausible to me.'[152] At that meeting it was also stated for the first time 'that the neutrino has zero intrinsic mass.'[153]

It would be Fermi who, using quantum field theory, showed in 1934 that the picture of the neutrino as a nuclear constituent is incorrect,[154] and who, incidentally, properly baptized the particle. Pauli: 'The italian name [neutrino] is made by Fermi.'[155]

Fermi's theory marks the end of the beginning of neutrino physics.

Most of Pauli's work mentioned so far deals with quantum physics, particularly with particles and fields. More of that is to follow, but it is time to note that his influence has spanned much farther and wider.

I have already recorded that Pauli's one and only article on quantum solid state physics may be considered as the founding paper of that discipline.[100, 101] He did not care at all for that subject, however. '*Ich mag diese Physik des festen Körpers nicht . . . zwar habe ich damit angefangen*' (I don't like this solid state physics . . . I initiated it though).[156] The crude assumptions often necessarily made in this field offended his standards. Nevertheless his influence was enormous. Neither the solid state nor any other state of matter is theoretically amenable without the Pauli principle.

There is another subject on which, at least for a number of years, Pauli's position was decidedly negative: the Dirac equation of the electron, which was considered by nearly everyone to be vindicated after the discovery of the positron in

1932—but not by Pauli, who particularly disliked Dirac's picture of the positron as a hole in an infinite sea of negative energy electrons.[157] In 1933 he wrote to Dirac: 'I do not believe in your perception of "holes" even if the anti-electron is proved.'[158] That theory was the main topic of the correspondence between Pauli and Heisenberg in 1934, the year they wrote more often to each other than before or after: 28 letters by Pauli to Heisenberg, 18 by Heisenberg to Pauli. Sample from Pauli (1934): 'I am quite disgusted with the hole theory.'[159] Heisenberg, too, was critical: 'We know that everything is wrong.'[160] He, however, had the courage to examine in detail various consequences of the Dirac theory, which remained in a rather uncertain state until the late 1940s, as we shall see later.

Pauli spent academic 1935–36 at the Princeton Institute, where he conducted a series of seminars largely devoted to the Dirac theory. As he put it there: 'Success seems to have been on the side of Dirac rather than of logic.'[161] While in Princeton he, together with Morris Rose, published his only early paper on the Dirac theory, dealing with vacuum polarization.[162]

At one of these seminars, Pauli presented what he proudly called 'the anti-Dirac theory.' The first intimations of this theory are found, as usual, in a letter from Pauli to Heisenberg:

> I have hit upon a sort of curiosum . . . The application of our old formalism of field quantization to [the scalar] theory leads *without any further hypotheses* (without the 'hole' idea, without *Limes Akrobatik*, without subtraction physics!) to the existence of positrons and to pair creation processes . . . After field quantization the energy is automatically positive! Everything gauge invariant and relativistically invariant! . . . It has pleased me that once again I could say something nasty about my old enemy the Dirac theory. (*Es hat mich gefreut dass ich meiner alten Feindin . . . wieder eins anhängen konnte*).[163]

Here Pauli referred to what we now call the Pauli–Weisskopf theory,[164] the QFT of charged spinless particles. In the letter just quoted, Pauli further wrote: 'This theory . . . which formally is so very satisfactory . . . has little to do with reality.' Soon after the subsequent discovery of mesons it became clear, however, that this theory had a bright and lasting future.

A brief summary of other topics on which Pauli worked in the 1930s includes: mathematical details regarding the Dirac equation;[164] contributions to unified field theory;[165] contribution to the quantum theory of magnetism.[166] In 1937 he returned to problems in quantum statistical mechanics which had interested him earlier. In 1927 he had been the first to treat Bose and Fermi gases with the help of Gibbs' grand canonical ensemble.[100] In 1928 he had been the first to discuss, within the framework of quantum theory, how a system reaches thermal equilibrium.[117] Now he, together with Fierz, analyzed the H-theorem from the quantum mechanical point of view. [167]

In 1938 Pauli and Fierz undertook a study of the infrared catastrophe.[168] The problem is that the cross section for electron–electron scattering becomes infinite as the relative particle energy tends to zero. The difficulty is removed if one notes that it is impossible to design an experiment which will guarantee that no very low energy photons are emitted in the scattering process.

In 1940 Pauli began his studies[169] of the QFT of particles with arbitrary spin, which he continued after leaving Europe for a lengthy stay in Princeton.

The war years in Princeton

In 1938, Pauli became a German citizen because of Germany's annexation of Austria. He remained officially German all through the Second World War.[170] His comment on this status: 'For me, of course, it is not possible to consider myself as belonging to a single country (that would contradict the whole course of my life). I feel, however, that I am European.'[170]

As the threat of war increased, Pauli wrote to John von Neumann, asking him to change his limited funds in America to a joint Pauli–von Neumann account, as a protection 'against possible measures against German citizens.'[171] Yet three days before the war broke out, he wrote to a colleague: 'Personally I do not believe in war.'[172]

Pauli's situation in Zurich became increasingly precarious after the war had started. It came therefore as a relief to him when in May 1940 he was offered a two-year guest professorship at the Princeton Institute, later extended for another two years, to be financed by a grant from the Rockefeller Foundation at an annual rate of $4000, which amounted to $2950 after taxes.[173] After overcoming a number of obstacles,[174] Pauli and his wife left Switzerland on July 31, 1940, and made a difficult journey to Lisbon, where they boarded ship for America. On August 24, they disembarked in New York, where they were met by von Neumann, who took them by car to Princeton.

Pauli rapidly adjusted to his new surroundings. Characteristically, he went back at once to his physics research.[175] 'I like it very much here. Once again there are visits from elsewhere, congresses and invitations . . . The Chianti is now replaced by a quite serviceable California wine, not too expensive.'[176] The only thing he missed much was his dog, Dixi, who had kept him company while he worked in his study at his Swiss home.[176] (In Princeton he got himself a black poodle named Bessie.)

In November Pauli attended the American Physical Society meeting in Chicago (November 22–23), where he had 'a wonderful time.'[177] A month later he went to a similar meeting in Philadelphia, where he was elected Fellow of the Society.[178] In 1941, he attended Society meetings in Washington (May 1–3) which he found 'very interesting,'[179] in Chicago (November 21–22), and in Princeton (December 29–31), where he gave a talk on QFT.[180] In the summer of

1941 he lectured at the Ann Arbor summer school (June 8 – August 8), where he met Julian Schwinger. From there, he and his wife drove to California in his own new car, visiting Berkeley and Stanford. All of which goes to show how rapidly Pauli had adapted himself to physics on the American scene. His remark, in November 1940: 'In Princeton I have more time than ever before'[177] shows how well he felt.

——————

I turn to Pauli's scientific production during the war. His first paper of that period[181] ranks among his best, it is certainly the best he wrote in those years. It deals with the relations between spin and quantum statistics, a topic that had interested him since the Pauli–Weisskopf paper of 1934. In that year he had written to Heisenberg: 'One cannot quantize the scaler wave equation by the rules of the exclusion principle [that is according to Fermi–Dirac statistics] in such a way that simultaneously: (1) relativistic and gauge invariance hold; (2) the eigenvalues of the energy are positive, while both requirements are satisfied if one quantizes according to Bose statistics.'[182] In 1936 he had remarked that, more generally, the exclusion principle is ruled out for any integer spin.[183] Fierz's paper [184] of 1939 on fields with spin greater than one had been another important step on the way. Out of these preliminaries grew, by and by, the spin-statistics theorem which says, loosely stated, that half-integer (integer) spin fields can only be consistently quantized according to Fermi–Dirac (Bose–Einstein) statistics. More and more the theorem was freed from unnecessary assumptions until, in 1958, it was phrased in the most general way:[185] if a field theory satisfies the conditions: (1) invariance under proper (no space reflections) orthochronous (no time reversal) inhomogeneous (space–time translations included) Lorentz transformations; (2) no states of negative energy; (3) the metric in Hilbert space is positive definite; (4) distinct fields either commute or anti-commute for space-like separations, then no field can have the 'wrong' connection between spin and statistics; and this is true for any spin.

It may be noted here that the conditions just mentioned are also sufficient for the proof of the CPT theorem which states that, given these same conditions, the invariance under the combined CPT symmetry: right ↔ left (P), particle ↔ anti-particle (C), past ↔ future (T) *must* hold. Pauli again played a key role[186] in the evolution of CPT invariance. The most general proof is due to Res Jost.[187]

In 1941, Pauli published a fine review article[188] on relativistic field theories of elementary particles, still very readable today. Here he gives for the first time the interaction describing an anomalous magnetic moment, now known as the 'Pauli term.' This paper was originally meant as a contribution to a Solvay congress planned for 1939 which was never held because of the war.

Other papers about QFT—now of historical interest only—deal with Pauli's comments on others' proposals for eliminating the difficulties (mentioned earlier) caused by the infinities that beset field theory: his work, largely criti-cal,[189] on Wentzel's λ-limiting process,[190] and[191] of Dirac's introduction of photons with negative energy.[192]

————————•————————

In 1935 Hideki Yukawa had proposed that nuclear forces are mediated by a field, the quanta of which are now called mesons. Pauli's initial reaction to this idea was quite skeptical: he referred to it as Yukosis.[193] So it remained until 'In 1941 [when Oppenheimer] pushed me in a direction which was then entirely new to me (meson physics)[194] ... Oppenheimer stimulated my interest in this field in 1941 and I have published [during the war] a number of papers about it with-out definitely solving any problem.'[195] In regard to this last remark he was in good company. In the early 1940s meson physics was in a very confused state, both experimentally and theoretically.

As Pauli began to work on meson theory, he wrote to Oppenheimer: 'Poetry has gone and physics has arrived.'[196] (In Princeton, he did write several poems.[197])

All of Pauli's papers on meson–nucleus interactions were written between 1941 and 1945. They make use of the strong coupling approximation. None of them gave him much satisfaction. The first, on the pseudoscalar case, written together with Sidney Dancoff,[198] gave wrong results for the magnetic moments of proton and neutron, which caused Pauli to be 'alarmed.'[199] The next, jointly with Shirichi Kusaka,[200] on the mixed pseudoscalar-vector theory, gave a wrong result for the magnetic moment of the deuteron and led to unstable nuclei of high charge. The last, together with Ning Hu,[201] on scalar and vector pair theo-ry, gave an incorrect neutron–proton interaction for the deuteron. Pauli's six evening lectures on meson theory and nuclear forces, given at MIT in the fall of 1944, were subsequently published as a small book.[202]

At the end of the war, Pauli had had enough of mesons. As he wrote in 1945: 'I am a bit tired of meson theory.'[203]

————————•————————

In the summer of 1942 Pauli wrote to Wentzel about the reduced activities in pure science all over the world (because of the war), which he 'is facing with sadness.'[204] Yet in 1943 he was considering the possibility of participating in war work himself. Oppenheimer advised him not to:

> Weisskopf was here [in Los Alamos] not long ago and he spoke to us of your uncertainties as to whether you should or not go into research directly connected with the War. It is hard to give an answer to this question that has more than tem-porary validity, but my feeling is that at the present time it would be a waste and an error for you to do that. You are just about the only physicist in the country who can help to keep those principles of science alive which do not seem

immediately relevant to the War, and that is eminently worth doing . . . In this way one may hope that when the War is over there will be at least some people in the country who know what a mesotron is.[205]

Pauli's letter to Rabi,[173] two months later, explains what had given him this idea, so entirely out of character with his usual style: he had been told that, after the expiration of his Rockefeller grant on June 1, 1944, no renewal was possible. Moreover, in December 1942, Aydelotte had told him to look for a job, latest in June 1944, since the Institute was not in a position to replace his stipend. He had made some vain efforts to find a teaching position elsewhere. Therefore, '*the best solution I can see is to do defense work*'[173] (my italics). He did not do so, however. In 1945 he wrote to Oppenheimer: 'Your earlier advice to me to stay with pure science was excellent.'[206]

Pauli's last scientific activity in the Princeton period was the preparation of a Festschrift for Bohr on his sixtieth birthday (October 7, 1945), to appear as an issue of *Reviews of Modern Physics*. In late 1944 he had sent a circular letter[207] to a number of colleagues with the request to send him a contribution to this project. He himself wrote its introductory article,[208] and also published there his paper with Ning Hu.[201]

After the atomic bombs had been dropped on Hiroshima and Nagasaki, Pauli wrote to Klein: 'I feel that our profession will be discredited if this new instrument of murder will not soon be brought under international control.'[209]

After the war, Pauli had a choice of positions. The Institute offered him a professorship as successor to Einstein, at an annual salary of $10 000, raised to $15 000 after he had received the Nobel Prize. That honor may presumably have led to his acquiring American citizenship on January 24, 1946. He also received offers from Columbia University and from Zurich.[210] He was still considering the American option when, in February 1946, he left for Zurich. Only in August did he firmly decide to stay there. 'I was near to accept the Columbia offer.'[211] His decision had been 'awfully hard for myself.'[212]

Jost has recalled:

> It is easy to earn much money in America but difficult to spend it in pleasant ways, Pauli said to me during a joint walk, and looked forward to a glass of red wine and a piece of cheese at our destination . . . Pauli's judgments were independent to the highest degree, and demonstrated the self-assuredness of a man who from childhood on had experienced the respect of his surroundings. He had the self-confidence of a matured child prodigy.[213]

Post-war writings

When, as early as 1938, Pauli had applied for Swiss citizenship, his request had been denied on the grounds that he had not sufficiently mastered the Zurich dialect. (His high German was of course impeccable.) In 1940 he applied once more, again without success. This time he was refused by the Federal Department of Justice and Police in Berne on grounds of insufficient assimilation. A few weeks later the Paulis left for the States . . .[214]

Correspondence between Pauli and ETH authorities during his Princeton years shows that it was not clear whether he would be received with open arms if and when he returned to Zurich. His departure for the US was alleged by some colleagues to show disloyalty to Switzerland and to have weakened his moral authority as a teacher. Pauli reacted indignantly, informing the ETH people that he would bring suit against their institution because of this severe moral censure. This threat of political action caused great consternation among the good Swiss burghers, which increased further when Pauli's public position was strengthened by his Nobel Prize.

Thus grew, from both sides, a willingness to consider reconciliation. After his return to Zurich, the president of the ETH Board was astonished by Pauli's mildness, which he had not expected after their recent correspondence. He found Pauli prepared to continue his activities at the ETH provided the matter of his Swiss citizenship could now be settled in short order.[215]

I do not know exactly when that came to pass, except that it happened before 1949, since in that year the US consul general wrote to Pauli that his Swiss citizenship had automatically annulled his US citizenship.[216]

These experiences caused a change in Pauli's attitude toward the ETH. In spite of his great distaste for bureaucracy, he now increasingly participated in discussions of its management problems. In 1950 he was elected by unanimous vote to a two-year term as chairman of the department of mathematical physics.[217]

By the fall of 1946, Pauli had settled down in his old office on the third floor of the physics building on the Gloriastrasse and began teaching again. Several of his students have said that his lectures were hard to follow, yet were very instructive. A few years later he complained of an overflow of doctoral students.[218] His assistants in those years were Res Jost, 1946/49, Max Schafroth, 1949/53, Armin Thellung, 1953/56, and Charles Enz, from 1956 until Pauli's death in 1958.

Some of Pauli's scientific publications during 1945/58, the last 13 years of his life, have been mentioned earlier: his Nobel lecture of 1946,[33] his papers on spin and statistics[181] and on the CPT theorem,[186] his book on nuclear forces,[202] his contribution to the Festschrift for Bohr.[208] None of these, important though some of them are, can compare with his seminal pre-war work. The same is true for his other publications after the war, to which I now turn.

In 1948, Pauli wrote to Oppenheimer: 'Whereas in 1941 you pushed me in a direction which was then entirely new to me (meson theory), you are not pushing me *further* in a direction to which I had turned recently . . . we are at the beginning of a new development in QED.'[219] Here he referred to the renormalization program, the vastly improved method which originated after the Shelter Island conference (June 1947) for dealing with the QED infinities. His only personal publication[220] on this topic was a mathematical device, now known as regularization, for coping with these infinities, an elaboration of a concept I had introduced some years earlier.[221] Otherwise his contributions to the new program consisted of critical comments on work by others.[222] The most important of these is the long letter[223] he wrote to Schwinger—to whom he referred as 'His Majesty' because of his (S.'s) seminal contributions to the new version of QED. More important than Pauli's own were excellent contributions to the subject by the younger generations of theorists who worked in Zurich under his aegis.[224] Other papers by Pauli on QFT deal with non-local theories,[225] with the Lee model,[226] and two with particle physics.[227]

In this period Pauli wrote, for the first time, on historical questions,[228] and on philosophical issues, particularly on the interpretation of quantum mechanics,[229] which he also discussed in a lively correspondence with Bohr. I shall come back to other aspects of his philosophical ideas in the later section on his relations with Jung.

More personal recollections

In the opening pages of this essay I mentioned Pauli's first letter to me, in 1945, dealing with my work on QFT. That paper had drawn some attention. Pauli mentioned it in a letter to Bohr.[230] Rabi to Pauli: 'Bohr seems rather convinced of the usefulness of Pais' ideas.'[231] I also mentioned earlier my first meeting with Pauli, in Copenhagen in 1946.

In subsequent years I saw Pauli frequently, in Princeton and in Zurich, until shortly before his death in 1958. We also maintained a steady correspondence. I have before me eight letters[232] by Pauli to me, sent during 1947–49. They deal with his comments on my papers on QFT which I had sent to him. Some of these are approving, some not. August 19, 1948: 'This paper seems to be entirely correct but not very interesting. It belongs to the so-called "so what physics." Try to do something better.' He continues with remarks on some of his own work on QED and ends like this: 'In case you see Oppenheimer, please show him this letter so that he may add some ujm-ujm to it.' Here he refers to one of Oppenheimer's verbal peculiarities which I have heard Pauli imitate. He was fond of such imitations, for example in 1931 he wrote to Wentzel of having

made 'a new study of Paul Epstein. I am prepared to give an Epstein perfor-
mance in Zurich.'[233]

Elsewhere, Pauli writes (February 18, 1949) about his long letter to
Schwinger,[223] and about his paper on regularization[220] (April 19 and May 26,
1949) which he had submitted to a Festschrift for Einstein of which I was the
editor.

These letters are cordial, opening with 'lieber Pais,' or 'my dear παις.' On
December 28, 1949 he added a footnote to this last appellation: 'Your [less] intimate friends use your pseudonym "Bram".' 'The word Pais means child in
Greek. The reason why that meaning of the name appealed so much to Pauli has
to do with the appearance of children in his dreams.'[234] Shortly afterward Pauli
adopted the code name μξ in letters to me. According to Mrs Pauli, this name
stems from James Joyce's *Finnegan's Wake* ('The Mookse and the Gripes') and
was given to Pauli by his friend the mathematician Carl Ludwig Siegel.[235]

———————————•———————————

The next time Pauli and I met was in November 1949, when he and his wife
arrived at Idlewild (now JFK) Airport from Zurich for an academic year's stay at
the Institute. Oppenheimer had asked me to pick them up at the airport, using
an Institute station wagon with driver. After cordial greetings we went on our
way to Princeton. In the car I asked Pauli what his plans were. He replied that he
had come to the US to find out what was happening in physics and to lose
weight—he was not impressed with the American cuisine.

In Princeton we saw a good deal of each other. A friendship developed.
Among my fond memories are the times when a small party, including Pauli
and myself, went wood-chopping on the grounds behind the Institute for
Advanced Study. I can still see Pauli, wearing mud boots, a grey sweatshirt, and
a Basque beret, holding a crowbar as if it were a bishop's staff, rocking gently as
he watched others saw down a tree.

We had numerous discussions on physics, often went for long walks, and frequently had lunch together. On such occasions he would often accompany his
words with the characteristic oscillations described before. One day at lunch he
made one of his rather outrageous statements, causing me to burst out laughing
and to say: 'You know, Pauli, there is no one like you.' It was typical for him to
reflect seriously about this banal statement, oscillating along. After a while he
said: '*Ja, es gibt mich nur einmal*,' then a pause, then '*Und das ist vielleicht auch
besser*' (Yes, there is only one like me—and that is perhaps just as well). On
another occasion, during a walk, he stopped, looked at the sky, then said: '*Die
weltfremden Physiker—die Menschen würden sich staunen*' (The unworldly
physicists—people would be surprised). During another walk he said to me: 'I
think we will get along well, because you think slowly, just as I do.'

Yet another time he said that he could not understand why I would permanently settle in the United States, since he perceived me to be so very European in outlook and thought. I truthfully replied that, yes, I was aware of my continued strong ties to Europe but had also developed strong ties to America; and that I had begun to learn how to harmonize those sentiments which, superficially, looked contradictory. This led to interesting discussions about cultural diversity.

Thus our talks were not by any means confined to physics. Another frequent talk was psychoanalysis. I found out that Pauli was an adept of Jung. I am pro-Freud and strongly anti-Jung. The result was an intense debate between Pauli and me, always civilized but occasionally heated.

Pauli never talked to me about his relations with Jung, nor about his first marriage. He would, however, once in a while voice more personal matters. Thus he mentioned several times an extramarital affair he had had with one of his young students. It may have been on one such occasion that he said something to me which I vividly remember: 'When I was young I thought that physics was easy and relations with women difficult. Now it is just the other way around.' Which reminds me of touching lines Pauli had written much earlier: 'It does not work at all between women and myself and it will probably never be otherwise. I will have to resign myself to that, which is not always easy. I am a bit afraid of increasing isolation as I grow older. This eternal talking to myself is so fatiguing.'[233]

Shortly before the Paulis returned to Europe, I invited them and Niels Bohr and his wife for an evening in my apartment with coffee and dessert. I have before me a letter from Franca to me (I always called her Mrs Pauli) dated November 9, 1976. After Pauli's death she and I would occasionally correspond (in German). In that letter she reminisced about the evening just mentioned: 'I recall the unforgettable, unique evening which we, Niels Bohr, Margrethe, you, Wolfgang and I passed in Princeton, when Niels talked about complementarity until dawn. You too were deeply moved and said: "It is like Jesus with his disciples."' The last letter Mrs Pauli wrote to me before her death ends as follows: 'It was during his last three days in the hospital [before his death in 1958] that a visitor, an old acquaintance, asked Pauli whether there was someone he would like to talk with. Pauli answered: Niels Bohr.'

As the end of Pauli's Princeton sojourn drew near, he invited me[234] to come and stay with Franca and him in their home in Switzerland that coming summer. I was happy to accept. Pauli told Bohr of my coming.[236] So it came about that the next July I landed at Zurich airport. Pauli had come to fetch me. We took a taxi to his home, where I was to stay.

Most days Pauli and I would go to the physics institute. I gave a lecture there on nucleon–nucleon scattering.[237] Evenings were spent with the Paulis at home. I had met Franca a number of times before, but now I got to know her much better and could observe how she dealt with her husband—not the easiest of customers—with affection, but firmly. Margrethe Bohr has told the following story of the two. When Pauli came home in the afternoon he would always ask Franca what was new. (He never read newspapers.) She prepared herself for this questioning, but one day had nothing to tell. When she so informed Pauli, he said: '*Nah ja, man kann sich auch langweilen*' (Oh well, one can also be bored).

While staying with Pauli, he gave me a novel to read: *Le grand Meaulnes*, by Henri Alain-Fournier, which he liked very much. So, in the event, did I. When the time came to leave, Pauli handed me a present. It was volume 7 of Jung's *Psychologische Abhandlungen*, which had just appeared.[238] Pauli had inscribed it: '*Seinem jüngeren Freund Pais als Gegenwicht gegen Freud, zur Erinnerung an dem Sommer 1950 in Zürich*' (to his younger friend Pais as counterweight to Freud, in memory of the summer of 1950 in Zurich). I was moved by this gesture of friendship. The book still stands on my shelves in New York.

————————●————————

Our correspondence continued after my return. In August 1950, Pauli wrote to me at length about his views on Jung[239] (to which I shall return) and on politics, quoting Schopenhauer: 'Every nation criticizes every other one—and they are *all* correct.' In 1951 he wrote from Sicily, where he was reading Plato.[240] In August of that year: 'The only news from the U.S. is that you are in good spirits. The only gossip from Europe is why you didn't come here this summer.'[241] In April 1952 he writes about the death of Kramers.[242] 'So ends a long friendship which began with Kramers' regular "Pauli, fetch milk" in Copenhagen (1922) . . . That is now of the past for both of us. Now we turn again to the future. At any rate, I am pleased that younger ones, like you, are represented among my closer acquaintances.' One month later: 'Au revoir in Copenhagen.'[243] A few weeks thereafter: 'I look forward very much to see you in Copenhagen, so that we can *not* discuss your recent papers on mesons.'[244] Of that encounter I remember animated discussions during a walk through old Copenhagen. Pauli participated in the conference discussions[245] but did not give a talk.

————————●————————

I saw Pauli again in June 1953, in Leiden this time, at a conference to commemorate the centennial of the births of two of Holland's great physicists, Hendrik Lorentz, and Heike Kamerlingh Onnes. I had been invited to give a talk there and had chosen to report on recent work dealing with my proposal[246] for introducing a new quantum number to account for the behavior of the strange particles, specifically to do so[247] by enlarging the long-known isospin group $SU(2)$ for non-strange particles to a bigger group, a way of thinking which has since been pervasive in particle physics. I was of course very pleased with comments afterward by Heisenberg: 'I think the most useful attempt will be of the kind presented by Pais,'[248] and by Pauli: 'I am very much in favor of the general principle to bring empirical conservation laws and invariance properties in connection with mathematical groups of transformations of the laws of nature.'[249]

At that meeting Pauli also raised a technical question related to my work: 'I would like to ask . . . whether the transformation group with constant phases can be amplified in a way analogous to the gauge group for the electromagnetic field in such a way that the meson–nucleon interaction is connected with the amplified group.'[249] This is the first time I heard of an idea out of which would grow a major new chapter in theoretical physics: non-Abelian gauge theories. Like most of my contemporaries, I was unaware at that time of related work by Klein[250] which, however, was obscured by his remarks on the Kaluza–Klein theory.[251]

Pauli kept pondering his question. Right after the Leiden conference he wrote to me[252] about a possible answer in terms of what he called a *geometrization* of the meson–nucleon forces, following up on my idea that 'the element of space–time is not a point but a manifold' (which I called ω-space).[247] I was unaware at that time that I was talking about a fiber bundle of the most trivial kind. What Pauli had proposed was to make an analogy with electromagnetic gauge transformations, where one distinguishes between (a) global gauge invariance, phase transformations with constant phase—which corresponds to my trivial fiber bundle, and (b) local gauge invariance, phase transformations which are space–time dependent. '*Something like this I had of course in mind* (his italics) when I made my discussion remark[249] after Pais' lecture.'[252] Letters to Klein and to Fierz[253] show how deeply this idea preoccupied him.[254]

On July 25, Pauli sent me a manuscript[254] entitled 'Meson–nucleon interactions and differential geometry,' that begins: 'Written down July 21–25 to see how it is looking.' In these pages he introduces an isotriplet of gauge field potentials, and finds as his 'main result' the correct expression for the corresponding field strengths, which today we call non-Abelian gauge fields. He did not, however, write down the associated dynamical field equations.

In his covering letter to me,[254] Pauli wrote: 'The whole note is of course written to drive you further into real *Neuland* (virgin country). You have, I think, quite a good chance to go on where we old ones have left the problem.' Correspondence with Klein[255] and with Oppenheimer[256] shows his continued preoccupation with my work. In November 1953 he gave two seminars on the subject, also attended by Klein.[257]

Late in 1953 Pauli's enthusiasm began to wane. 'If one tries to formulate field equations . . . one will always obtain *vector mesons with rest mass zero* [his italics]. One could try to get other meson fields—pseudoscalars with positive rest mass . . . But I feel that is too artificial.'[258]

My final comments on this subject brings me to the spring term of 1954, when two important seminars were given at the Institute for Advanced Study. One, on February 23, was by Chen Ning ('Frank') Yang, a brilliant young Chinese physicist who in 1949 had been appointed to a five-year Institute membership. (In 1955 he was promoted to professor.) It was the first talk in which Frank reported on his work with Robert Mills dealing with non-Abelian gauge fields, which came to be known more popularly as 'Yang–Mills fields.' They published their work in two short fine papers[259] in which they founded modern gauge theory.

Two weeks earlier, on February 10, Pauli (back for that term) had given a talk on the same subject! This work is very little known because he never published it. Notes of his two November 1953 lectures on this subject later appeared in print, however.[260]

Yang had not been present when Pauli gave his seminar. He has recalled:

> Oppenheimer invited me to return to Princeton *for a few days in late February* [my italics] to give a seminar on our work . . . Soon after my seminar began Pauli asked, 'What is the mass of this field?' I said we did not know. Then I resumed my presentation, but soon Pauli asked the same question again. I said something to the effect that that was a very complicated problem, we had worked on it and had come to no definite conclusion. I still remember his repartee: 'That is not sufficient excuse.' I was so taken aback that I decided, after a few moments' hesitation, to sit down. There was general embarrassment. Finally Oppenheimer said, 'We should let Frank proceed.' I then resumed, and Pauli did not ask any more questions during the seminar.
>
> I don't remember what happened at the end of the seminar. But the next day I found the following message:
>
> February 24
>
> Dear Yang,
> I regret that you made it almost impossible for me to talk with you after the seminar.
> All good wishes,
>
> Sincerely yours,
W. Pauli.[261]

I, too, was at Yang's seminar and well recall Pauli's critical and negative reaction. He was not the only one to respond that way. Indeed, the Yang–Mills theory was initially received with skepticism, to put it mildly. The reason was that the quanta of the new fields appeared to have zero mass, *as Pauli had already noted in his December 1953 letter to me.*[258] In their first paper on that subject,[259] a piece of chutzpah for that time, Yang and Mills simply stated that they had 'no satisfactory answer' to that difficulty.

The mass problem caused the theory to be almost completely forgotten until about 20 years later, when it was resolved. Since then, Yang–Mills fields have become crucially important for the description of the weak as well as the strong interactions. This development is as profound as were Maxwell's nineteenth-century equations for electromagnetism.

As to Pauli, chutzpah never was one of his strong suits. Had he had the temerity to publish in 1953, he would now have been remembered for his most important post-war contribution to physics, as one of the founding fathers of modern gauge theory . . .

Pauli and Jung

Pauli was interested and widely read in philosophy from an early age. For example, at age 22 he wrote to a philosopher on his views regarding positivism.[262] A few of his early papers touch on philosophical issues, such as the one of 1936 on space, time, and causality in modern physics. This article is found not only in his collected scientific papers[263] but also in a very good collection, all translated in English where necessary, of his writings on physics related to philosophy.[264]

The paper just mentioned is closer to physics than to philosophy. The same is true of some of Pauli's later writings which nevertheless are properly considered to have a philosophical touch, such as his papers on 'Matter'[265], on the historical evolution of the notions of space and time,[266] on complementarity,[267] on relativity,[268] and on probability in physics.[269]

None of this work does yet touch on what Pauli has called 'my larger spiritual transformation in later years,'[270] about which he has said: 'To give philosophers their bearings, I may say at once that I am not myself an adherent of any particular philosophical trend with a name ending in "ism." I am moreover opposed to associating particular "isms" with particular physical theories,'[271] and also: 'My own philosophical background is a blend of Schopenhauer, Lao Tse, and Niels Bohr.'[272]

The origins of Pauli's spiritual transformation are twofold.

First were his reflections on Bohr's concept of complementarity. His correspondence with Bohr[273] yields glimpses of the depth of Pauli's understanding of Bohr's ideas which was perhaps greater than that of any other physicist. If he disagreed with Bohr, it was only on details of formulation which need not concern us here.

Second, there were Pauli's 'extensive and essential discussions with C. G. Jung on the psychological aspect of the concept formation in the natural sciences and their archetypal foundations.'[274]

The 25-year-older Jung was unquestionably the non-physicist who had the greatest influence on Pauli. In turn, Jung also profited from discussions with Pauli: 'Thanks to the kind interest which Professor Pauli has shown in my research I was in the advantageous position of discussions with a qualified physicist who appreciated my psychological arguments.'[275]

Jung has briefly appeared earlier in this essay. I need now to enlarge considerably on the contacts between the two men, which began in 1932 as the result of Pauli's psychoanalysis by one of Jung's assistants.

———•———

Jung himself never treated Pauli but followed closely the dream material which Pauli produced in writing, about which he (J.) has written extensively. By 1936 he had already published 59 of them, without revealing the dreamer's identity, however:

> My material consists of more than 1000 dreams and visual impressions of a scien-
> tifically gifted younger man . . . We owe it to the care and meticulosity of the
> dreamer to have been able to follow step by step the labors of his unconscious . . .
> It was impossible [to include] dreams which deal with the intimate details of his
> personal life . . . These must be withheld from publication . . . It is a special plea-
> sure to thank the 'author' for his service to knowledge.[276]

Jung's fascination with this material stemmed mainly from Pauli's use of what he (J.) saw as mandala symbolism. (Mandala is Sanskrit for circle or magic cir-
cle.) Lack of space and, more crucially, of knowledge makes it impossible for this writer to enter into details. I feel nevertheless obliged to include some brief comments on this aspect of Pauli the man, since without these my account would be lamentably incomplete.

A further source is the collection of 80 letters exchanged between Pauli and Jung and the latter's coworkers, published by Pauli's friend Carl Alfred Meier.[270] These date from 1932 until October 1958—two months before Pauli's death. From them we learn that Pauli kept sending Jung accounts of his dreams until as late as 1957.[277] Also, in Vol. 4, part 1, of the Pauli correspondence one finds 114 letters exchanged between him and the Jung group.

I should note that all this material came to my notice only long after Pauli's death. While he and I had frequent discussions about his relations with Jung, I was never in a position to discuss his dreams with him. I have, however, a letter by him to me,[278] in which he expressed his opinions about Jung:

> I consider his idea of the collective unconscious in general and the interpretation
> of the mandalas as essentially correct. Not, of course, because the great Jung has
> said so (after all I am not a woman [!] and belief in authority has not been sung at
> my cradle) but because the idea in itself is plausible to me . . . It cannot be denied,
> however, that there exists an extraordinarily strong inbreeding in Jung's circle, the
> result of a complete lack of creativity and talent among his intimates . . . In detail I
> disagree on many points . . . I do not want to have anything to do with horoscopes
> . . . and with his theology.[279]

Regarding the content's of Pauli's dreams, I shall restrict myself to mentioning only one theme: his recurrent preoccupation[280] with the numbers 3 and 4, which had mystic–symbolic significance for him. About this he has commented: 'My road to the exclusion principle had to do with the difficult transition from 3 to 4, with the necessity to assign to the electron a further *fourth* degree of freedom [spin] in addition to the *three* for translations [his italics].'[281]

More important (I would think) than Pauli's dreams is his preoccupation with Jung's ideas of deep connections between physical and psychological phenomena. '*It is my personal opinion that in the science of the future reality will neither be "psychic" nor "physical" but somehow both and somehow neither*'[278] (my italics).

This brings us to Pauli's central idea regarding psychology. Going beyond Jung, he assumed the relation between the conscious and the unconscious to be a complementary one in the sense of Bohr. He hoped that in this way the unified world picture of the seventeenth century, which since had disintegrated into a rational and a mystical–religious branch, could be restored by overcoming their antitheses. He saw 'correspondences between psychological and quantum mechanical concepts,'[281] has called the unconscious 'a secret laboratory,'[282] and has characterized the relation between mysticism and rationalism like this: 'In my opinion it is a narrow path to truth which leads between the Scylla of a blue haze of mysticism and the Charybdis of a sterile rationalism. This path will always be full of traps and one can plunge into the abyss in both directions.'[283] He considered the process of understanding nature and the happiness which man experiences when he becomes aware of new understanding 'a coincidence of preexisting inner images . . . with external objects.'[284]

Pauli published on psychological issues only after the Second World War. In his paper in honor of Jung's eightieth birthday, he wrote:

> Since the unconscious is not quantitatively measurable, and therefore not capable of mathematical description and since every extension of unconsciousness ('bringing into consciousness') must by reaction alter the unconscious, we may expect a 'problem of observation' in relation to the unconscious, which, while it presents analogies with that in atomic physics, nevertheless involves considerably greater difficulties . . . [I] expect that the further development of the ideas of the unconscious will not take place within the narrow framework of their therapeutic applications, but will be determined by their assimilation to the main stream of natural science as applied to vital phenomena.[285]

Pauli's most important contribution to psychology is his long paper on the writings of Johann Kepler.[274] It was Pauli's deep interest in the contrasts between mysticism and rationalism which led him to Kepler, whose work marks the beginnings of the split between these two modes of thought. On the one hand, Kepler's three laws of planetary motion made him the founder of modern astronomy; on the other, he believed that the celestial harmonies stem from a sentient soul animating the sun as the solitary auditor, and also that our earth was a live being with a soul, the *anima terrae*. The studies of this work resulted in Pauli's paper[286] about Kepler's influence on archetypal imagery in the formation of physical theories. (The term archetype, which means primordial image, and was used by Kepler, goes back at least to Cicero.)

Because of Pauli's fascination with the numbers 3 and 4, mentioned earlier, his paper on Kepler treats at length the latter's controversy with his contemporary, the mystical philosopher Robert Fludd. Whereas Kepler considered the number 3 to be magical—for example, he linked the Christian Trinity with the three-dimensionality of space—the number 4 was divine to Fludd, who saw it revealed in the tetragram of God's name (Jahveh is spelled with 4 consonants in Hebrew), in the fourness of the seasons, of geometry (point–line–surface–body), and of nature (substance–quality–quantity– motion). Pauli sided with Kepler, yet also had a certain sympathy for Fludd. His paper[274] reveals aspects of his personality and erudition (he quotes Plotinus at length) which are familiar to few physicists only.

I was present when, in March 1950, Pauli gave a lecture on Kepler at the Princeton home of his friend Erik Kahler. The only thing I remember of that event was that Einstein, also present, fell asleep during the talk.

The final years

I continued to stay in contact with Pauli during his last years, though never again as intensely as in 1953. We saw a good deal of each other during his final two stays at the Institute, in the springs of 1954 and 1956. Our continued correspondence includes a letter by me to Pauli ('Dear $\mu\xi$')[287] on time reversal, the only letter from me to him that has survived. Letters by Pauli to me[288] deal with strong coupling, the subject he had worked on during the war years.

In these years he also traveled a good deal, notably to India where, in the winter of 1952–53, he lectured at the Tata Institute in Bombay, fulfilling his long-held desire to get better acquainted with India's culture.

Pauli's writings in this final period include articles on QFT, mentioned earlier,[289] one on the hidden variable version of quantum mechanics, on which he had dim views,[290] those on philosophical issues, also mentioned before, and a few papers on historical questions,[228] including, most importantly, on the history of the neutrino (1957)[291] and on parity violation (1958).[292]

Pauli lived just long enough to see the experimental verification of his neutrino hypothesis. He first heard the news via a telegram, sent to him from Los Alamos, on June 14, 1956, by Frederick Reines and Clyde Cowan, which reads: 'We are happy to inform you that we have definitely detected neutrinos from fission fragments by observing inverse beta decay of protons. Observed cross section agrees well with expected six times ten to minus forty-four square centimeters.'[293]

A week after that telegram was sent, Tsung Dao Lee and Frank Yang submitted a paper to the *Physical Review*[294] in which they noted that the conservation of parity had never yet been verified in β-decay, and proposed experiments to do so. Pauli reacted like this: 'I am prepared to bet that experiment will turn out to favor reflection invariance [parity conservation], since—in spite of Lee and Yang—I do not believe that God is a "weak left-hander."'[295]

In the closing days of 1956 it turned out that Pauli's belief was incorrect. A few weeks later he wrote in a letter:

> Now the first shock is over and I begin to collect myself again . . . It is good that I did not make a bet. It would have resulted in a heavy loss of money (which I cannot afford); I did make a fool of myself, however (which I think I can afford to do)—incidentally, only in letters or orally and not in anything that was printed. But the others now have the right to laugh at me.
>
> What shocks me is not the fact that 'God is just left-handed' but the fact that in spite of this He exhibits Himself as left/right symmetric when He expresses Himself strongly. In short, the real problem now is why the strong interactions are left/right symmetric.[296]

It still is.

A letter in Pauli's handwriting, appended to his article on parity violation,[297] reads as follows:

> It is our sad duty to make known that our dear *Freundin* [female friend] of many years
>
> PARITY
>
> has gently passed away on January 19, 1957, following a brief suffering caused by experimental treatment. On behalf of the bereaved,
>
> e, μ, υ

The last two years of Pauli's life, on which I must now report, were not a good episode.

Firstly there was his break with Res Jost, his junior colleague in Zurich, described elsewhere in this book.[298] Secondly there was his final collaboration with Heisenberg, which led nowhere. Both events strongly indicate Pauli's emotional instability in his last years.

In the mid-1950s, Heisenberg had suggested that a certain non-linear equation could describe all properties of all fundamental particles.[299] He has described Pauli's response to his idea:

> In the late autumn of 1957 . . . I informed Wolfgang of the latest development . . . [He] was extremely excited as well . . . We decided that both of us would look into the question . . .
>
> With every step Wolfgang took in this direction he became more enthusiastic—never before or after have I seen him so excited about physics . . . He became

firmly convinced that our equation . . . must be the right starting point for the unified field theory of elementary particles.[300]

Heisenberg quotes[300] from a letter by Pauli to him with New Year's wishes for 1958: 'Everything is in flux . . . It's all bound to turn out magnificently . . . This is powerful stuff . . . Let us march toward it. It's a long way to Tipperary, it's a long way to go.'

A few weeks later Pauli left for a three-month lecture tour in the United States. Heisenberg: 'I did not like the idea of this encounter between Wolfgang in his present mood of great exaltation and the sober American pragmatists, and tried to stop him from going. Unfortunately, his plans could no longer be changed.'[300]

Pauli's first stop was New York. He had requested to be allowed to give a 'secret' seminar on his recent work with Heisenberg at Columbia University, by invitation only. Actually he spoke in the overfilled large lecture hall in Pupin Laboratory. I was present and vividly recall my reaction: this was not the Pauli I had known for so many years. He spoke hesitantly. Afterward, a few people, including Niels Bohr and myself, gathered around him. Pauli said to Bohr: 'You may well think that all this is crazy.' To which Bohr replied: 'Yes, but unfortunately it is not crazy enough.'

Pauli's journey ended up in Berkeley. From there he sent a letter to Landau, with copies to other colleagues, including me, in which he wrote of 'my present attitude to a new situation, which is far from being final, but on the contrary is always changing.'[301] Heisenberg again: 'Then we were divided by the Atlantic and Wolfgang's letters came at greater and greater intervals . . . Then, quite suddenly, he wrote me a somewhat brusque letter in which he informed me of his decision to withdraw from both the work and the publication.'[300]

Heisenberg and Pauli were both present at an international conference at CERN (June 30 – July 5, 1958). Heisenberg has remembered: 'I was due to give a report on the current state of research into the disputed field equation, and Wolfgang's attitude to me was almost hostile.'[300] Pauli's critical attitude is expressed in the conference proceedings.[302] Shortly after the conference Pauli said to Heisenberg: 'Perhaps all our hopes will be fulfilled, and your optimism will be rewarded. As for me, I have had to drop out. I just haven't the strength.'[300]

As to Heisenberg, he was not swayed.[303] His later work has not been influential in the long run, however.

———•———

On December 5, 1958, Pauli had to abruptly interrupt his class because of severe pains and took a taxi home. The next day he was brought to the Rote Kreuz Hospital in Zurich. It disturbed him that the number of his hospital room was 137, a reminder of the number 1/137, the fine structure constant, which his teacher Sommerfeld had introduced into physics, one of Pauli's links to the 'magic–symbolic' world with which he was so familiar. A pancreatic carcinoma was diagnosed. On December 13 he was operated upon. On December 15 he died, at age 58.

On December 20 a memorial service was held in the Fraumünster church in Zurich, although Pauli was not religious. Friends and colleagues, including Niels Bohr, spoke in his memory. His ETH colleague Paul Scherrer characterized him as follows: 'It was difficult to get to know Pauli the man. Humanly he was understanding and gentle but was severe and unyielding in scientific discussions. Yet it was just this merciless demand for honesty which one learned to appreciate most especially in the long run'[304]—to which I should like to add what Ehrenfest had said 25 years earlier[128] on the occasion of Pauli's receiving the Lorentz medal: '[You are esteemed] because of your sagacity, your clarity

A stamp issued by Austria to commemorate the 25th anniversary of Pauli's death.

and honesty, and the extraordinary care with which you always acknowledged the merits of other researchers.'

After the service Mrs Pauli held a reception in the Guild Hall Zur Meise. On January 2, 1959, she wrote to me: 'I was deeply moved by the expression of your sympathy.' One day in 1963 I sat next to her at a dinner given by Mrs Bohr. I have jotted down what she said to me about her late husband at that time: 'He was very easily hurt and therefore would let down a curtain. He tried to live without admitting reality. And his unworldliness stemmed precisely from his belief that that was possible.'

Postscript

My most precious material link to the past masters of physics is the opening page of the galley proof of Appendix II, 'Generalized theory of gravitation,' which appeared first in the 1950 edition of Einstein's *The Meaning of Relativity*. On that page the following words are written in the 70-year-old Einstein's slightly shaky handwriting:

Pauli (after perusal please give to Pais!)

References

Abbreviations used in the following:
P: W. Pauli
CSP: *Collected Scientific Papers by Wolfgang Pauli* (R. Kronig and V. Weisskopf, Eds), Wiley, New York, 1964
SC: *Wolfgang Pauli, Scientific Correspondence*, several volumes, those used here edited by K. von Meyenn, Springer, New York, 1979 and later years.

1. Letter by P to Pais, October 23, 1945, SC Vol. 3, p. 324.
2. A. Pais, *Trans. Kon. Ak. Wet. Amsterdam* **19**, 1, 1947; briefly summarized in A. Pais, *Phys. Rev.* **68**, 227, 1945.
3. A. Chwala, *Monatshefte f. Chemie* **81**, 3, 1950.
4. W. J. Pauli, letter to E. Mach, February 17, 1913, quoted in W. Pauli, *Physik und Erkenntnistheorie* (K. von Meyenn, Ed.), p. VIII, Vieweg, Braunschweig, 1984.
5. Letter reproduced by C. P. Enz, in 'W. Pauli's scientific work,' in *The Physicist's Conception of Nature* (J. Mehra, Ed.), p. 766, Reidel, Boston, 1973.
6. SC, Vol. 1, p. 11.
6a. P, in letter to C. Jung, October 23, 1956, reprinted in C. A. Meier, *Pauli-Jung Briefwechsel*, p. 150, Springer, New York, 1992.

7. M. Fierz, 'Wolfgang Pauli,' in *Dictionary of Scientific Biography* (C. Gillispie, Ed.), Vol. 10, p. 422, Scribner's, New York, 1974.

8. P, *Phys. Zeitschr.* **20**, 25, 1919, CSP, Vol. 2, p. 1.

9. P, *Phys. Zeitschr.* **20**, 457, 1919; *Verh. Deutsch. Phys. Ges.* **21**, 742, 1919; CSP, Vol. 2, pp. 10, 13.

10. P, *Encyclopädie der mathematischen Wissenschaften*, Vol. 5, part 2, Teubner, Leipzig, 1921; CSP, Vol. 1, p. 1.

11. A. Einstein, *Naturw.* **10**, 184, 1922.

12. P, *Theory of Relativity*, Pergamon, New York 1958.

13. P, letter to N. Bohr, October 2, 1924, SC, Vol. 1, p. 163.

14. P, letter to A. Einstein, November 10, 1923, SC, Vol. 1, p. 128.

15. P in *Électrons et photons*, p. 256, Gauthier-Villars, Paris, 1928.

16. P, letter to H. Weyl, July 1, 1929, SC, Vol. 1, p. 505.

17. P. Ehrenfest, letter to P, November 26, 1928, SC, Vol. 1, p. 477.

18. For details see A. Pais, *Subtle is the Lord*, pp. 344–6, Oxford University Press, Oxford and New York, 1982.

19. P, letter to H. Weyl, August 26, 1929, SC, Vol. 1, p. 518.

20. P, letter to P. Jordan, November 30, 1929, SC, Vol. 1, p. 525.

21. P, letter to P. Ehrenfest, September 29, 1929, SC, Vol. 1, p. 522.

22. P, letter to A. Einstein, December 19, 1929, SC, Vol. 1, p. 526.

23. A. Einstein, letter to P, December 24, 1929, SC, Vol. 1, p. 528.

24. P, *Naturw.* **20**, 186, 1932, CSP, Vol. 2, p. 1399.

25. A. Einstein, letter to P, January 22, 1932, SC, Vol. 2, p. 109.

26. P, letter to A. Einstein, July 16, 1933, SC, Vol. 2, p. 189.

27. P, *Ann. d. Phys.* **18**, 305, 337, 1933, CSP, Vol. 2, p. 630.

28. A. Einstein and P, *Ann. Math.* **44**, 131, 1943, CSP, Vol. 2, p. 994.

29. Copy in Einstein archives.

30. *Science*, **103**, 213, 1946; CSP, Vol. 2, p. 1073.

31. P, letter to M. Born, April 24, 1955, SC to be published.

32. SC, Vol. 3, p. 328.

33. P, in *Les Prix Nobel*, p. 131, Norstedt, Stockholm, 1948, CSP, Vol. 2, p. 1080.

34. P, letter to A. Einstein, September 19, 1946, SC, Vol. 3, p. 383.

35. A. Einstein, letter to P, April 1, 1948, SC, Vol. 3, p. 518.

36. Other letters: P to A. Einstein, September 6, 1938, SC, Vol. 2, p. 598; January 6, 1944, SC, Vol. 3, p. 213; April 21, 1948, SC, Vol. 3, p. 520; Einstein to P: September 1938, SC, Vol. 2, p. 600; May 2, 1948, SC, Vol. 3, p. 524.

37. P, letter to A. Einstein, March 7, 1949, SC, Vol. 3, p. 643.

38. P, in *Albert Einstein: Philosopher–Scientist* (P. Schilpp, Ed.), Tudor, New York, 1949.

39. P, in *Neue Zürcher Zeitung*, August 22, 1955, CSP, Vol. 2, p. 1237.

40. See also P in *Neue Zürcher Zeitung*, January 12, 1958, CSP, Vol. 2, p. 1362.

41. P, in 'Fünfzig Jahre Relativitäts theorie,' *Helv. Phys. Acta*, Supplement 4, 27, pp. 261, 282, 1956; CSP, Vol. 2, p. 1299.

42. P, *Zeitschr. f. Physik* **2**, 201, 1920, CSP, Vol. 2, p. 24.

43. P, *Phys. Zeitschr.* **21**, 615, 1920, CSP, Vol. 2, p. 36.

44. P, *Ann. der Phys.* **68**, 177, 1922, CSP, Vol. 2, p. 70.

45. SC, Vol. 1, p. 32.

46. K. von Meyenn, *Die grossen Physiker*, Vol. 2, p. 319, Beck, Munich, 1957.

47. P, 'Quantentheorie,' in *Handbuch der Physik*, Vol. 23, Springer, Berlin, 1926, CSP, Vol. 1, p. 269.

48. P, *Z. f. Naturf.* **6a**, 468, 1951; CSP, Vol. 2, p. 1159.

49. W. Heisenberg, *Der Teil und das Ganze*, p. 41, Piper, Munich, 1969.

50. Ref. 49, p. 45.

51. M. Born, letter to A. Einstein, October 21, 1921, in *Albert Einstein und Max Born, Briefwechsel*, p. 88, Nymphenburg, Munich, 1969.

52. M. Born, letter to A. Einstein, November 29, 1921, ref. 51, p. 93.

53. M. Born, ref. 51, p. 95.

54. M. Born and P, *Zeitschr. f. Physik* **10**, 137, 1922, CSP, Vol. 2, 48.

55. N. Bohr, letter to P, July 3, 1922, SC, Vol. 1, p. 60.

56. N. Bohr, letter to H. A. Kramers, July 15, 1922, reprinted in *Niels Bohr, Collected Works* (J. R. Nielsen, Ed.), Vol. 3, p. 658, North-Holland, New York, 1976.

57. H. A. Kramers and P, *Zeitschr. f. Physik* **13**, 351, 1923, CSP, Vol. 2, p. 134.

58. P, *Zeitschr. f. Physik* **18**, 272, 1923; CSP, Vol. 2, p. 161.

59. P, *Zeitschr. f. Physik* **16**, 155, 1923; CSP, Vol. 2, p. 151.

60. P, letter to A. Sommerfeld, June 6, 1923, SC, Vol. 1, p. 94.

61. Ref. 47, p. 437.

62. P, *Zeitschr. f. Physik* **31**, 373, 1925; CSP, Vol. 2, p. 201.

63. P, *Zeitschr. f. Physik* **31**, 765, 1925; CSP, Vol. 2, p. 214.

64. P. A. M. Dirac, *Proc. Roy. Soc.* **A112**, 661, 1926.

65. A. Pais, *Inward Bound*, chapter 13, section (b), Oxford University Press, 1986.

66. S. Goudsmit, *Physica* **5**, 281, 1925.

67. P, letter to A. Sommerfeld, December 6, 1924, SC, Vol. 1, p. 182.

68. E. Stoner, *Phil. Mag.* **48**, 719, 1924.

69. G. E. Uhlenbeck and S. Goudsmit, *Naturw.* **13**, 953, 1925.

70. P, letter to N. Bohr, December 30, 1925, SC, Vol. 1, p. 274.

71. See the Pauli correspondence in February–March 1926, SC, Vol. 1, pp. 296–312.

72. P, *Naturw.* **12**, 741, 1924, CSP, Vol. 2, p. 198.

73. P, chapter 27 in Müller-Pouillet's *Lehrbuch der Physik*, Vol. 2, p. 1483, Vieweg, Braunschweig; CSP, Vol. 1, p. 565.

74. See ref. 18, chapter 22, p. 417ff; and my *Niels Bohr's Times*, chapter 11, p. 235ff, Oxford University Press, 1991.

75. P, letter to R. Kronig, May 21, 1925, SC, Vol. 1, p. 214.

76. W. Heisenberg, *Zeitschr. f. Physik* **33**, 879, 1925.

77. W. Heisenberg, letter to P, June 24, 1925, SC, Vol. 1, p. 225.

78. P, letter to H. A. Kramers, July 27, 1925, SC, Vol. 1, p. 232.

79. P, letter to R. Kronig, October 9, 1925, SC, Vol. 1, p. 315.

80. P, *Zeitschr. f. Physik* **36**, 336, 1926; CSP, Vol. 2, p. 252.

81. For this failure see my essay on O. Klein in this book.

82. N. Bohr, letter to P, November 25, 1925, SC, Vol. 1, p. 268.

83. W. Heisenberg, in *Theoretical Physics in the Twentieth Century*, p. 40, Interscience, New York, 1960.

84. W. Heisenberg, letter to P, November 3, 1925, SC, Vol. 1, p. 252.

85. E. Schrödinger, *Ann. d. Phys.* **79**, 361, 1926.

86. P, letter to P. Jordan, April 12, 1926, SC, Vol. 1, p. 315.

87. E. Schrödinger, *Ann. d. Phys.* **79**, 734, 1936.

88. See the essay on Born in this book.

89. P, *Zeitschr. f. Physik* **41**, 81, 1927; CSP, Vol. 2, p. 284.

90. L. Mensing and P, *Phys. Z.* **27**, 509, 1926; CSP, Vol. 2, p. 280.

91. W. Heisenberg, letter to P, July 28, 1926, SC, Vol. 1, p. 337.

92. W. Heisenberg, *Zeitschr. f. Physik* **43**, 172, 1927.

93. W. Heisenberg, letter to P, February 23, 1927, SC, Vol. 1, p. 376.

94. N. Bohr, letter to P, August 13, 1927, SC, Vol. 1, p. 407.

95. For details of this episode, see my *Niels Bohr's Times*, ref. 74, chapter 14, section (e).

96. P, letter to N. Bohr, October 17, 1927, SC, Vol. 1, p. 411.

97. N. Bohr, letter to P, May 14, 1928, SC, Vol. 1, p. 456; P, letter to N. Bohr, June 16, 1928, SC, Vol. 1, p. 462..

98. For details see ref. 18, chapter 25, section (a); ref. 95, chapter 14, section (f).

99. Account by Otto Stern, taped on December 2, 1961, by Res Jost.

100. P, *Zeitschr. f. Physik* **41**, 81, 1927; CSP, Vol. 2, p. 284.

101. R. Peierls, *Memoirs Members F. R. S.* **5**, 175, 1959.

102. Ref. 65, chapter 13, section (d).

103. P, *Zeitschr. f. Physik* **43**, 601, 1927; CSP, Vol. 2, p. 306.

104. P. A. M. Dirac, *Proc. Roy. Soc.* **A117**, 610, 1928; **118**, 351, 1928. See further, ref. 65, chapter 13, section (e); also the essay on Dirac in this book.

105. P, *Handbuch der Physik*, Vol. 24, part 1, Springer, Berlin, 1933; CSP Vol. 1, p. 771.

106. For the role of these and other contributions dating from the old quantum theory, see ref. 18, chapters 19, 21, and 22.

107. M. Born and P. Jordan, *Zeitschr. f. Physik* **34**, 858, 1925.

108. English translation. of ref. 107 in B. L. van der Waerden, *Sources of Quantum Mechanics*, Dover, New York, 1968.

109. M. Born, W. Heisenberg, and P. Jordan, *Zeitschr. f. Physik* **35**, 557, 1925, English translation in ref. 108.

110. P. A. M. Dirac, *Proc. Roy. Soc.* **A114**, 243, 710, 1927.

111. All papers mentioned so far are reviewed in ref. 65, chapter 15.

112. W. Heisenberg, letter to P, February 23, 1927, SC, Vol. 1, p. 376.

113. P, letter to P. Jordan, March 12, 1927, SC, Vol. 1, p. 385.

114. P. Jordan and P, *Zeitschr. f. Physik* **47**, 151, 1928; CSP, Vol. 2, p. 331.

115. P, letter to H. Weyl, January 29, 1928, SC, Vol. 1, p. 427.

116. P, letter to H. A. Kramers, February 7, 1928, SC, Vol. 1, p. 432.

117. P, in anniversary volume for A. Sommerfeld, p. 30, Hirzel Verlag, Leipzig, 1928; CSP, Vol. 1, p. 549.

118. P, letter to O. Klein, February 18, 1929, SC, Vol. 1, p. 488.

119. W. Heisenberg and P, *Zeitschr. f. Physik* **56**, 1, 1929; CSP, Vol. 2, p. 354.

120. G. Wentzel, in ref. 83, p. 51. This paper gives a good synopsis of ref. 119.

121. W. Heisenberg and P, *Zeitschr. f. Physik* **59**, 168, 1930; CSP, Vol. 2, p. 415.

122. P, letter to H. Weyl, August 26, 1929, SC, Vol. 1, p. 518.

123. P, letter to O. Klein, February 10, 1930, SC, Vol. 2, p. 2.

124. P, letter to O. Klein, March 10, 1930, SC, Vol. 2, p. 2.

125. P, *Izv. Akad. Nauk SSSR*, 1938, p. 149; CSP, Vol. 2, p. 843.

126. P, letter to P. Epstein, December 10, 1937, SC, Vol. 2, p. 541. For more details on P's visits to the USSR, see V. Frenkel, in, *Wolfgang Pauli* (C. P. Enz and K. von Meyenn, Eds), p. 56, Vieweg, Braunschweig, 1988.

127. P, letter to M. Delbrück, October 6, 1958. See SC, Vol. 2, p. 38.

127a. C. Jung, *Psychology and Alchemy*, section 45, Gesammelte Werke, Vol. 12, Walter Verlag, Otten, Switzerland, 1972.

128. P. Ehrenfest, *Collected Scientific Papers* (M. Klein, Ed.), p. 617, North-Holland, Amsterdam, 1959.

129. P, letter to P. Ehrenfest, October 26, 1931, SC, Vol. 2, p. 96.

130. H. B. G. Casimir, *Haphazard Reality*, p. 86, Harper and Row, New York, 1983.

131. P, *Naturw.* **21**, 841, 1933; CSP, Vol. 2, p. 698; See also P, letter to W. Heisenberg, September 30, 1933, SC, Vol. 2, p. 215.

131a. Ref. 130, p. 144.

131b. P, letter to W. Heisenberg, March 10, 1938, SC, Vol. 2, p. 556.

132. Ref. 130, p. 137.

133. See SC, Vol. 2, p. VII for much detail.

134. P, letter to R. Kronig, November 22, 1927, SC, Vol. 1, p. 415.

135. R. Kronig, letter to P. Jordan, June 4, 1928, SC, Vol. 1, p. 458.

136. P, CSP, Vol. 2, p. 1313.

137. Statement by P to R. Jost (Jost, private communication).

138. W. Heisenberg, letter to P, December 1, 1930, SC, Vol. 2, p. 37.

139. P, letter to L. Meitner and others, December 4, 1930, SC, Vol. 2, p. 39; also ref. 136.

140. See ref. 65, chapter 14, section (d), for an English translation as well as a detailed history of the surrounding events.

141. Ref. 65, chapter 14, section (b).

142. P, letter to O. Klein, December 12, 1930, SC, Vol. 2, p. 43.

143. P. Güttinger and P, *Zeitschr. f. Physik* **67**, 743, 1931; CSP, Vol. 2, p. 438.

144. P, *Phys. Rev.* **38**, 579, 1931.

145. *The New York Times*, June 17, 1931.

146. See also *Science* **74**, 111, 1931.

147. P, letter to R. Peierls, July 1, 1931, SC, Vol. 2, p. 88.

148. P, letter to F. Rasetti, October 6, 1956, copy in Niels Bohr Archive, Copenhagen.

149. G. Gamow, *The Constitution of Atomic Nuclei and Radioactivity*, Oxford University Press, 1931.

150. P, *Naturw.* **20**, 582, 1932; CSP, Vol. 2, p. 1400.

151. F. Bloch, letter to N. Bohr, April 6, 1933, copy in Niels Bohr Archive, Copenhagen.

152. P, in *Structure et propriétés des noyaux atomiques*, p. 324, Gauthier-Villars, Paris, 1934.

153. F. Perrin, ref. 152, p. 327.

154. E. Fermi, *Nuov. Cim.* **11**, 1, 1934; *Zeitschr. f. Physik* **88**, 161, 1934.

155. P, letter to P. M. S. Blackett, April 19, 1933, SC, Vol. 2, p. 158.

156. Quoted in ref. 83, p. 137. See also R. Peierls, ref. 101, p. 140.

157. Described in more detail in my essay on Dirac in this book.

158. P, letter to Dirac, May 1, 1933, SC, Vol. 2, p. 159.

159. P, letter to W. Heisenberg, February 6, 1934, SC, Vol. 2, p. 274.

160. W. Heisenberg, letter to P, April 25, 1935, SC, Vol. 2, p. 386.

161. 'The theory of the positron and related topics,' notes by B. Hoffmann, Institute for Advanced Study, 1935–36, mimeographed notes.

162. P and M. Rose, *Phys. Rev.* **49**, 462, 1936; CSP, Vol. 2, p. 749.

163. P, letter to W. Heisenberg, June 14, 1934, SC, Vol. 2, p. 327.

164. P, *Helv. Phys. Acta* **5**, 179, 1932; CSP, Vol. 2, p. 481; in *Pieter Zeeman, Verhandelingen*, p. 31, Nÿhoff, The Hague, 1935; CSP, Vol. 2, p. 724; *Helv. Phys. Acta*, **12**, 147, 1939; CSP, Vol. 2, p. 847.

165. Ref. 27, and also P and J. Solomon, *J. Phys. Radium* **7**, 452, 582, 1934, CSP, Vol. 2, p. 461.

166. 'Le magnetisme,' *Proceedings of the 6th Solvay conference*, 1930, pp. 175, 250, CSP, Vol. 2, p. 502.

167. P and M. Fierz, *Zeitschr. f. Physik* **106**, 582, 1937; CSP, Vol. 2, p. 797. For a review see M. Fierz, ref. 83, p. 161.

168. P and M. Fierz, *Nuov. Cim.* **15**, 167, 1938; SC, Vol. 2, p. 812.

169. P and F. J. Belinfante, *Physica* **7**, 177, 1940; SC, Vol. 2, p. 895.

170. P, letter to H. B. G. Casimir, October 11, 1945, SC, Vol. 3, p. 320.

171. P, letter to J. von Neumann, April 19, 1939, SC, Vol. 3, p. xxvii.

172. P, letter to N. Kemmer, August 29, 1939, SC, Vol. 2, p. 674.

173. P, letter to I. Rabi, July 10, 1943, SC, Vol. 3, p. 186.

174. SC, Vol. 3, p. XXIX.

175. P, letter to M. Fierz, September 3, 1940, SC, Vol. 3, p. 35.

176. P, letter to H. Hopf, October 15, 1940, SC, Vol. 3, p. 46.

177. P, letter to V. Weisskopf, November 28, 1940, SC, Vol. 3, p. 53.

178. P, letter to V. Weisskopf, December 30, 1940, SC, Vol. 3, p. 57.

179. P, letter to J. M. Jauch, May 11, 1941, SC, Vol. 3, p. 98.

180. P, letter to G. Wentzel, December 30, 1941, SC, Vol. 3, p. 116.

181. P, *Phys. Rev.* **58**, 716, 1940, CSP, Vol. 2, p. 918; see also P, *Progr. Theor. Phys.* **5**, 526, 1950, CSP, Vol. 2, p. 1131.

182. P, letter to W. Heisenberg, June 28, 1934, SC, Vol. 2, p. 334.

183. P, *Ann. Inst. Poincaré* **6**, 137, 1936; CSP, Vol. 2, p. 781.

184. M. Fierz, *Helv. Phys. Acta* **12**, 3, 1939.

185. N. Burgoyne, *Nuov. Cim.* **8**, 607, 1958; see also the review by R. Jost in ref. 83, p. 107.

186. P, in *Niels Bohr and the Development of Physics*, p. 30, McGraw-Hill, New York, 1955.

187. R. Jost, *Helv. Phys. Acta* **30**, 409, 1957 and ref. 83, p. 107. For a review of the CPT theorem see R. F. Streater and A. Wightman, PCT, *Spin and Statistics and All That*, Benjamin, New York, 1964.

188. P, *Rev. Mod. Phys.* **13**, 203, 1941; CSP, Vol. 2, p. 923.

189. P, *Phys. Rev.* **64**, 332, 1943; CSP, Vol. 2, p. 1034.

190. G. Wentzel, *Zeitschr. f. Physik.* **86**, 479, 1933; **87**, 726, 1934, reviewed in his *Quantum Theory of Fields and Particles*, Interscience, New York, 1948.

191. P, Rev. Mod. Phys. **15**, 175, 1943; also *Phys. Rev.* **65**, 255, 1944; *Helv. Phys. Acta* **19**, 254, 1946; reprinted in CSP, Vol. 2, pp. 1001, 1047, 1076, respectively.

192. P. A. M. Dirac, *Ann. Inst. Poincaré* **9**, 13, 1939; *Proc. Roy. Soc.* **A180**, 1, 1942; *Comm. Dublin Inst. Adv. Study* **A1**, 1942.

193. P, letter to G. Breit, December 18, 1937, quoted in SC, Vol. 3, p. xxii.

194. P, letter to R. Oppenheimer, January 6, 1948, SC, Vol. 3, p. 493.

195. P, letter to H. B. G. Casimir, October 11, 1945, SC, Vol. 3, p. 320.

196. P, letter to R. Oppenheimer, October 4, 1941, SC, Vol. 3, p. 109.

197. See SC, Vol. 3, p. 997; also P, letter to R. Oppenheimer, April 9, 1945, SC, Vol. 3, p. 265.

198. P and S. Dancoff, *Phys. Rev.* **62**, 85, 1942; CSP, Vol. 2, p. 953.

199. P, letter to R. Oppenheimer, April 9, 1942, SC, Vol. 3, p. 134.

200. P and S. Kusaka, *Phys. Rev.* **63**, 400, 1943; CSP, Vol. 2, p. 977.

201. P and Ning Hu, *Rev. Mod. Phys.* **17**, 267, 1945; CSP, Vol. 2, p. 1053.

202. P, Meson *Theory of Nuclear Forces,'* Interscience, New York, 1948, CSP, Vol. 1, p. 939.

203. P, letter to L. Rosenfeld, July 20, 1945, SC, Vol. 3, p. 295.

204. P, letter to G. Wentzel, July 20, 1942, SC, Vol. 3, p. 149.

205. J. R. Oppenheimer, letter to P, May 20, 1943, SC, Vol. 3, p. 181.

206. P, letter to J. R. Oppenheimer, April 9, 1945, SC, Vol. 3, p. 265.

207. For example, P, letter to M. Delbrück, December 1, 1944, SC, Vol. 3, p. 251.

208. P, *Rev. Mod. Phys.* **17**, 97, 1945; CSP, Vol. 2, p. 1048.

209. P, letter to O. Klein, August 31, 1945, SC, Vol. 3, p. 308.

210. SC, Vol. 3, p. XLVIII.

211. P, letter to J. R. Oppenheimer, September 8, 1946, SC, Vol. 3, p. 380.

212. P, letter to I. Rabi, August 12, 1946, SC, Vol. 3, p. 375.

213. R. Jost, *Phys. Bl.* **40**, 178, 1984.

214. SC, Vol. 4, part 1, pp. 2, 3.

215. Ref. 214, pp. 4–8.

216. See footnote 2 in P, letter to M. Fierz, September 1, 1949, SC, Vol. 3, p. 696.

217. Ref. 214, p. XXX.

218. P, letter to M. Fierz, June 2, 1949, SC, Vol. 3, p. 657.

219. P, letter to J. R. Oppenheimer, January 6, 1948, SC, Vol. 3, p. 493.

220. P and F. Villars, *Rev. Mod. Phys.* **21**, 434, 1949; CSP, Vol. 2, p. 1116.

221. A. Pais, *Phys. Rev.* **68**, 227, 1945.

222. For example, P, in *Physical Society of Cambridge Conference*, 1946, Report p. 5; CSP, Vol. 2, p. 1097, and in *Proceedings of the 8th Solvay Conference*, 1948, p. 287; CSP, Vol. 2, p. 1127.

223. P, letter to J. Schwinger, January 24, 1949, SC, Vol. 3, p. 609. See also P, letters to H. Bethe, May 15, 1948; January 25, 1949, SC, Vol. 3, pp. 528, 619, respectively.

224. See the essay on Jost in this book.

225. P, *Nuov. Cim.* **10**, 648, 1953; CSP, Vol. 2, p. 1176.

226. G. Källen and P, *Kgl. Danske Vid. Selsk. Mat.-Fys. Medd.* **30**, 3, 1953, CSP, Vol. 2, p. 1261.

227. P, *Nuov. Cim.* **6**, 204, 1957; **14**, 205, 1959; CSP, Vol. 2, pp. 1338, 1383, respectively.

228. P, *Vierteljahresschr. Naturf. Ges. Zurich* **97**, 137, 1952; *Proceedings of the Rydberg Conference on Atomic Spectroscopy*, Lund 1954, p. 22; CSP, Vol. 2, 1160, 1231, respectively.

229. P, *Experientia* **6**, 72, 1950; CSP, Vol. 2, p. 1149; *Verh. Schweitz. Naturf. Ges.* p. 76, 1952; CSP, Vol. 2, p. 1196; *Dialectica* **6**, 141, 1952; **8**, 112, 1954; **11**, 36, 1957; CSP, Vol. 2, pp. 1163, 1199, 1350, respectively.

230. P, letter to Bohr, October 29, 1946, SC, Vol. **3**, p. 394.

231. I. Rabi, letter to P, October 2, 1946, SC, Vol. 3, p. 385.

232. P, letters to A. Pais, November 17, 1947; August 19, December 26, 1948; February 18, April 1, April 19, May 26, December 28, 1949, SC, Vol. 3, pp. 477, 566, 585, 633, 647, 650, 654, 728, respectively.

233. P, letter to G. Wentzel, September 7, 1931, SC, Vol. 3, p. 751.

234. See footnote 1 to P, letter to A. Pais, June 6, 1950, SC, Vol. 4, part 1, p. 113.

235. See footnote 3 to P, letter to A. Pais, July 3, 1953, SC, Vol. 4, part 2.

236. P, letter to N. Bohr, June 6, 1950, SC, Vol. 4, part 1, p. 110.

237. P, letter to M. Fierz, July 5, 1950, SC, Vol. 4, part 1, p. 139.

238. C. G. Jung, *Gestaltungen des Unbewussten*, Rascher Verlag, Zurich, 1950.

239. P, letter to A. Pais, August 17, 1950, SC, Vol. 4, part 1, p. 151.

240. P, postcard to A. Pais, April 9, 1951, SC, Vol. 4, part 1, p. 287.

241. P, postcard to A. Pais, August 22, 1951, SC, Vol. 4, part 1, p. 356.

242. P, letter to A. Pais, April 28, 1952, SC, Vol. 4, part 1, p. 617.

243. P, letter to A. Pais, May 7, 1952, SC, Vol. 4, part 1, p. 626.

244. P, letter to A. Pais, May 20, 1952, SC, Vol. 4, part 1, p. 632.

245. P, in mimeographed Report International Physics Conference, Copenhagen, June 1952, p. 51.

246. A. Pais, *Phys. Rev.* **86**, 663, 1952.

247. A. Pais, *Physica* **19**, 869, 1953.

248. W. Heisenberg, *Physica* **19**, 905, 1953.

249. P, *Physica* **19**, 887, 1953.

250. O. Klein, in *New Theories in Physics* (Warsaw Conference, May 30 – June 3, 1938), p. 77, Nÿhoff, The Hague, 1939.

251. For more on this see my essay on Klein in this book.

252. P, letter to A. Pais, July 3, 1953, SC, Vol. 4, part 2.

253. P, letters to O. Klein, July 14, 1953, and to M. Fierz, July 3, 22, 25, 1953, SC, Vol. 4, part 2.

254. P, letter to A. Pais, July 25, 1953, SC, Vol. 4, part 2.

255. P, letters to O. Klein, August 25, September 30, October 23, 1953, SC, Vol. 4, part 2.

256. P, letters to R. Oppenheimer, September 3, October 23, 1953, Vol. 4, part 2.

257. P, letters to M. Fierz, October 5, 1953, and to R. Schafroth, November 17, 1953, SC, Vol. 4, part 2.

258. P, letter to A. Pais, December 6, 1953, SC, Vol. 4, part 2.

259. C. N. Yang and R. Mills, *Phys. Rev.* **95**, 631; **96**, 191, 1954.

260. P. Gulmanelli, *Su una teoria dello spin isotopico*, Publicazioni sezione di Milano dell' Istituto Nazionale di Fysica Nucleare, Casa Editrice Pleion, Milan, undated.

261. C. N. Yang, *Selected Papers 1945–1980*, p. 19, Freeman, San Francisco 1983.

262. P, letter to M. Schlick, August 21, 1922, SC, Vol. 2, p. 692.

263. P, *Scientia* **59**, 65, 1936; CSP, Vol. 2, p. 737.

264. Pauli, *Writings on Physics and Philosophy* (C. P. Enz and K. von Meyenn, Eds), Springer, New York, 1994.

265. P, CSP, Vol. 1, p. 1125, ref. 264, p. 27.

266. P, CSP, Vol. 2, p. 1290, ref. 264, p. 137.

267. P, *Experientia* **6**, 72, 1950; CSP, Vol. 2, p. 1149, ref. 264, p. 35.

268. P, *Helv. Phys. Acta* supplement 4, 282, 1956; CSP, Vol. 2, p. 1299, ref. 264, p. 107.

269. P, *Dialectica* **8**, 112, 1954; CSP, Vol. 2, p. 1199, ref. 264, p. 43.

270. P, letter to C. G. Jung, March 31, 1953, reprinted in *Wolfgang Pauli und C. G. Jung* (C. A. Meier, Ed.), p. 103, Springer, New York, 1992.

271. P, *Dialectica* **11**, 36, 1957; CSP, Vol. 2, p. 1350, ref. 264, p. 127.

272. P, letter to V. Weisskopf, February 23, 1954, SC.

273. See especially P, letters to N. Bohr, February 15 and March 11, 1955; N. Bohr, letters to W. Pauli, March 2 and 25, 1955, SC.

274. P and C. G. Jung, *Naturerklärung and Psyche*, p. 167, Rascher Verlag, Zurich, 1952.

275. Ref. 274, p. 101.

276. C. G. Jung, 'Traumsymbole des Individuationsprozesses,' p. 13, in *Eranos Jahrbuch 1935*, Rhein Verlag, Zurich, 1936. The quoted lines are found on pp. 14, 15, 126. This work was brought to my attention by my late friend Res Jost. More on Pauli's dreams is found in C. G. Jung, 'Psychologie und Alchemie,' and 'Psychologie und Religion,' *Collected Works* (H. Read *et al.* Eds), Vols 11, 12.

277. See ref. 270, pp. 34, 133, 159.

278. P, letter to A. Pais, August 17, 1950, SC, Vol. 4, part 1, p. 151.

279. See also P, letter to C. G. Jung, February 27, 1952, SC, Vol. 4, part 1, p. 557.

280. See, for example, ref. 276, letters No. 3, 4, 15, 55, 56, 59, and ref. 270, letters No. 23, 42, 44, 55, 69.

281. P, letter to M. Fierz, October 3, 1951, SC, Vol. 4, part 1, p. 375.

282. P, letter to M. L. von Franz, July 18, 1954, SC.

283. P, letter to V. Weisskopf, February 8, 1954, SC.

284. P, letter to M. Fierz, January 7, 1948, SC, Vol. 3, p. 495.

285. P, *Dialectica* **8**, 283, 1954; CSP, Vol. 2, p. 1212, ref. 264, p. 149.

286. P, ref. 274, p. 109; translation in ref. 264, p. 219.

287. A. Pais, letter to P, April 20, 1954, SC.

288. P, letters to A Pais, December 27, 1954; December 9, 1956, SC.

289. See refs. 189 and 225–7, 229.

290. P, in *L. de Broglie, Physicien et Penseur*, p. 33, A. George, Paris, 1953; CSP, Vol. 1, p. 1115.

291. P, CSP, Vol. 2, p. 1313, extended version in ref. 264, p. 193.

292. P, *Experientia* **14**, 1, 1958; CSP, Vol. 1, p. 1368, ref. 264, p. 183.

293. Reprinted in F. Reines, *J. de Physique*, Colloque C8, December 1982, pp. C8–237.

294. T. D. Lee and C. N. Yang, *Phys. Rev.* **104**, 254, 1956.

295. P, letter to R. Schafroth, December 22, 1956, SC.

296. P, letter to V. Weisskopf, January 27, 1957, CSP, Vol. 1, p. xvii.

297. Ref. 264, p. 192.

298. See the essay on Res Jost.

299. See, for example, W. Heisenberg, *Rev. Mod. Phys.* **29**, 267, 1957.

300. W. Heisenberg, *Physics and Beyond*, chapter 19, Harper and Row, New York, 1971.

301. P, letter to L. D. Landau, March 11, 1958.

302. P, in *Proceedings of the 1958 Conference at Cern* (B. Ferretti, Ed.), p. 122, CERN, Geneva, 1958.

303. See his papers on the subject in W. Heisenberg, *Collected Works*, Series B, Springer, New York, 1984, especially his 1966 review on p. 677.

304. P. Scherrer, *Phys. Bl.* **15**, 34, 1959.

I. I. Rabi in the 1960s. (Courtesy of Mrs I. I. Rabi.)

Isidor I. Rabi

In September 1946 I left my native Holland by ship, bound on my first journey to America. After ten days on the Atlantic I arrived in New York harbor on a miserably hot and humid Indian summer evening.

I had been invited to give a paper at a meeting of the American Physical Society to be held in New York, starting on September 19. During my war years in hiding in Holland I had done work on quantum electrodynamics (QED) that had been well received, also in the US; it was the subject of my paper.

On the evening of the 20th, a conference dinner was held at the Men's Faculty Club of Columbia University. I was seated well, together with Patrick Blackett from Manchester, Dean George Pegram of Columbia, Oliver Buckley, president of Bell Laboratories, and Isidor Rabi, Columbia's most renowned physicist.

It was my first meeting with Raab—as his friends used to call him—who, after a few pleasantries, fired this question at me: 'Do you think that the polarization of the vacuum can be measured?' I recall my astonishment at being in a new land where experimentalists would know, let alone bother, about vacuum polarization. For the present story it is of no relevance to explain what vacuum polarization is. Suffice it to say that at that time it was a subject considered esoteric even by most theoretical physicists.

I liked Rabi from the start. He invited me to a party at his home the following evening. There I met his wife Helen, a kind yet formidable lady.

A few days later I met Rabi again, this time in Princeton. We were both participants in a conference on 'The future of nuclear science,' one of a series of topical conferences held from September 23–25, to celebrate the university's bicentennial. Rabi was one of the speakers, his topic: 'The relations of research in universities to government and commercial laboratories.'[1] In his address he said:

> My opinions on this subject come from a five year war experience . . . In the subject of physics . . . enormous amounts of money are available for the support of research . . . Should the universities become more like the commercial and the government laboratories? I think not . . . We should not endanger the existence of the little oasis that is free and not under the direct necessity of continually justifying itself in the material sense.

These words clearly indicate that a new phase in Rabi's career had begun. At that time he was still active in research—as I will show in a moment—but had also begun engagement in a quite important new phase of his career, that of statesman of science. For example, earlier in 1946 he, together with his student (later Nobel laureate) Norman Ramsey, had taken the initiative of proposing the formation of the first consortium of universities for the purpose of jointly managing costly physics research enterprises, to be funded by the US government. This led to the creation of Brookhaven National Laboratory on Long Island.[2] In a similar spirit, it was Rabi again who, at a UNESCO conference held in the Palazzo Vecchio in Florence, in June 1950, submitted a resolution (adopted by unanimous vote) proposing the establishment of a European joint laboratory, out of which grew CERN, the European Center for Nuclear Research.[3]

I return to the Princeton conference of 1946. During one of the conference breaks Rabi came up to me and asked if I might consider spending the second semester of that academic year as guest lecturer at Columbia. I replied that I felt honored by his suggestion but could not accept, since I did not wish to break up my current one-year fellowship at the Institute for Advanced Study.

Shortly after these events, I began to receive approaches by several universities regarding academic positions. One of these came from Rabi, who in November called me from New York with an offer of a visiting professorship at Columbia, giving me time to think that over. I told him that I would seriously consider his proposal. So I did, until early 1947, when negotiations had begun for a long-term appointment at the Institute for Advanced Study. This led me to call Rabi, in April, to thank him once more for his offer but declining it. His reply was gracious.

A few months later we met once more, being both part of a group of about 20 physicists who gathered, from June 1–3, 1947, at a conference on the foundations of quantum mechanics, held at Shelter Island (a small island off Long Island). In the years since I have found comments in letters by, and interviews with, participants, to the effect that this meeting may well have been the most important event of its kind in their entire scientific career—also my opinion. Robert Oppenheimer, the unofficial leader of the pack, summarized, fittingly I think, the response of all participants: 'The three days were a joy to us and perhaps rather unexpectedly fruitful . . . [we] came away a good deal more certain of the directions in which progress may lie.'[4] This comment refers first and foremost to the conference contributions by Rabi and junior members of his Columbia school, dealing with experiments bearing on QED.

Even the very first presentation, by Rabi's colleague Willis Lamb brought spectacular news. It dealt with his refined experiment on the spectrum of atomic hydrogen. His result: a small but definitive deviation, since known as the

Lamb shift, from then current predictions.[5] Here was the answer to the question about vacuum polarization that Rabi had put to me at our first encounter—except that the answer was of opposite sign and about 40 times larger than what vacuum polarization had predicted.

The next paper, by Rabi himself, was no less impressive. He told of other experimental results[6] that can be expressed by saying that the electron's magnetic moment—a measure for the fact that this particle acts like a tiny magnet—was not exactly as predicted from the theory then known. It was at once clear to all present that both experiments reported that morning were so fundamentally new that they would probably lead to Nobel prizes—as indeed they did, in 1955.

Rabi and I were also present at a meeting, the sequel to Shelter Island, held from March 30 to April 2, 1948, at Pocono Manor, a large inn in Pennsylvania's Pocono Mountains. By that time, the first steps toward an understanding of the new effects were well underway, causing Rabi to make this memorable comment: 'What the hell should I measure now?'

The preceding was an account of my early encounters with Rabi. Before turning to our meetings in later years, I give a sketch of his life and career, treated by others in much greater detail than given here.[7,8,9]

———— ■ ————

Rabi was born on July 29, 1898, in Rymanow, a small town in Galicia, then a province of the Austro-Hungarian Empire, now in Poland. David, his father, and Sheindl, his mother, were deeply religious orthodox Jews. He had a five-year younger sister, Gertrude.

The first language Raab learned was Yiddish, 'which I spoke very well.'[7] He was still an infant when his father emigrated to the United States, not as a refugee from persecution but to make a better living. Within months after David's arrival he had the money to send for his wife and son. Of his early life, Rabi has recalled: 'I never had any envy of rich people. They were just richer, we were just poor.'[7]

Rabi's education began at age three, in Hebrew school, where he quickly learned to read Yiddish. Next came a public school on New York's Lower East Side. When his mother was asked his name on enrolling him, she replied 'Izzy,' which is short for Israel—his parents had named him Israel Isaac. The school official thought that Izzy was short for Isidore and put that name down. The mistake was never corrected but Rabi dropped the 'e', and so he has since been known by one and all as Isidor Rabi.

The boy did well at that school, 'though I was no prodigy.'[7] He once told me how, coming home from school, his mother would greet him with: 'Did you ask any good questions today?'

In 1907 the family moved to the Brownsville section of Brooklyn, where Rabi discovered the Carnegie Library, the local branch of the Public Library, especially its science books. Reading those 'has determined my life more than anything else.'[7] He learned about electricity, particularly telegraphy, built his own telegraph station at home, learned Morse code, and obtained a license.[10] So began his career in experimental physics. He spent his high school years at the Manual Training High School in Brooklyn, graduating in 1916. None of his schools had impressed or taught him much. He was very largely self-educated.

One last item about those early years. In 1911 Raab became bar mitzvah, the ritual marking his initiation in manhood at age 13. Normally this is celebrated in a synagogue, but Rabi refused to do so. 'What could [my parents] do? I was a bastard of a kind not to worry about them. As I look back now it horrifies me.' In the end he did become bar mitzvah but on his own terms, giving a speech at home, in Yiddish, on 'How electric light works.'[10]

I do not know exactly when Rabi lost religion but do know how. As he once told me, it happened one Sabbath morning, he was a young boy, as he was attending a synagogue service during which at one moment the Cohanim (those men named Cohen or Kohn, which means priest) gather at one area in the synagogue to say a benediction over the congregation while their heads are covered with their prayer shawls. This is done because at that time God's blinding light is shining on them. For that same reason all others present look down to the ground. So did Rabi that morning when the thought came to him: what would come to pass if I look up—but with one eye only? Nothing happened, and that was the end of that.

———————

In 1916 Rabi enrolled in Cornell, supported by two scholarships. He began as a student in electrical engineering, found that too dull, then switched to chemistry. He loved qualitative analysis: one is given an unknown substance and has to determine what chemical it contains. 'I thought it was wonderful—like research.'[7] In 1919 he graduated with a major in chemistry, then started looking for a job, but 'Jews didn't get jobs in chemical companies or in universities. It was really terrible.'[7] After three years of holding odd jobs, he returned to Cornell for graduate work in chemistry. It was then that he found his niche: 'I realized that the part of chemistry I liked was called physics.'[7] A year later, in 1923, he switched to Columbia University, mainly because he had met Helen Newmark, a young woman who was a student at Hunter College in New York. There he supported himself with a job at City College that demanded 16 hours a week of teaching and paid $800 a year. On August 16, 1926, he sent in his doctoral dissertation, on experimental studies of magnetism in crystals. The next day Helen and he were married. They were to have two daughters, Nancy (b. 1929), now a lawyer, and Margaret (b. 1934) now a psychologist, and four grandchildren.

One of the century's vintage years for getting the Doctor's degree in physics was 1926. Quantum mechanics had just been discovered, wide new vistas for research lay open. Rabi devoured the papers on this revolutionary new subject as soon as they arrived from Europe. He has told me how he began looking through books on classical mechanics for a nice problem to solve by the methods published only months earlier by Erwin Schrödinger, found the symmetric top, then went to see Ralph Kronig, another young Columbia PhD, and said 'Let's do it.' They did.[12]

Eager to visit the source of all this novelty, Rabi applied for and received a Barnard fellowship from Columbia, enabling him and Helen to travel to Europe, living as sparsely as possible. He left in July 1927 and spent time with Schrödinger in Zurich, then with Arnold Sommerfeld in Munich, then with Bohr in Copenhagen (of whom he saw little), showing up unannounced at these places, simply appearing and saying something like 'My name is Rabi; I've come to work here.' Then he went to Hamburg, 'The most formative experience I had.'[7] There he met Wolfgang Pauli, the theoretician, and Otto Stern, the experimentalist, both men of great stature. Stern was to have the decisive influence on Rabi's career.

Stern had done pioneering work on the behavior of molecular beams as they pass through a magnetic field. In a discussion with Stern, Rabi casually mentioned a theoretical suggestion on how to improve the accuracy and simplicity of Stern's method. To his surprise he was asked to do the experiment himself. 'So I did—my first with molecular beams.'[7] A year's painstaking work produced splendid results.[13]

Next Rabi resumed his theoretical studies, now financed by a fellowship of the International Education Board, part of the Rockefeller philanthropic empire, which provided $182 for living expenses. From Hamburg he went to Leipzig, to study with Werner Heisenberg, then again to Pauli, who meanwhile had moved to Zurich. There, in 1929, he received a telegram from Columbia's Dean Peagram: 'Offer lectureship here next year three thousand salary write.' 'This was beyond the dreams of avarice.'[7] As far as he knew, he was the first Jewish member of the physics department.

When, the next August, Rabi returned to New York, his apprenticeship in physics was over. He had learned plenty from the masters of quantum theory but his success in Hamburg had taught him that his future lay with experiment. His experiences with and knowledge of theory would, however, became important to him in developing a style that is not unique yet fairly rare: he liked to find his own problems to experiment on and to interpret. As he liked to say, he was not one of those who would go to a theorist to ask: 'Now what shall I do?' and, after having finished, would come back to ask: 'What have I done?' 'I have always taken physics personally. It's my own physics, within my powers. It's between me and Nature.'[7] Also, among his scientific papers, some 50 in all—not a large number but of fine if not outstanding quality—one finds a handful of purely theoretical articles.[14]

At the time, 1929, of Rabi's return to the States, American physics was just about to begin its rise from second rank status—with notable exceptions of some illustrious individuals—to preeminent scientific power in the world. 'From the viewpoint of 1930, it is astonishing that by 1940 we had enough first rate scientists to man the laboratories for microwave radar, atomic energy, and all the rest.'[7] Already, on May 11, 1935, *The New York Times* had quoted the French Nobel laureate Louis de Broglie as saying: 'Today scientific publications from the United States are awaited with an impatience and curiosity inspired by those of no other country.'

These changes were due, first and foremost, to the return from Europe of a handful of young Americans ready and able to spread the word of the new physics, Rabi among them. In Europe, 'The general contempt for physics in the United States [had been] a bit hard to take.'[7]

Rabi, forever deeply imbued with a love not only for physics but also for America, was confident—he always was—that he could play a part in improving that situation. At Columbia he taught the most advanced courses and started a weekly theoretical seminar, at that time the only seminar of its kind in New York. 'I was the life of the place, students were flocking around, and I was in correspondence with other physicists who were well known.'[7] His classes were something else, however. As he has said publicly: '[I gave] bad courses and bad grades,'[1] an opinion frequently confirmed by his best students, who all the same found them inspiring.

Nevertheless his efforts were appreciated. Starting as a lecturer in 1929, he was promoted to assistant professor the next year even though he had not published anything. Further promotions followed apace: associate professor 1935–37, full professor 1937–64, university professor 1964–67, after which he retired but remained active in the department, where he kept an office till his death.

———————

Soon after having begun his career at Columbia, Rabi decided to make molecular beam experiments his main topic of research, and started his own school of bright young physicists. Going around New York, he scrounged together his equipment at good prices. Remember, it was the beginning of the great Depression, when finances for research were severely strained. By 1931 he had his own molecular beam laboratory in order. It continued operations without interruption until the fall of 1940.

Those were the years during which Rabi did his greatest physics. For an understanding of Rabi the man, it is almost more important to know what drove him than the results he obtained. A leading theme in his scientific thinking was to challenge quantum mechanics, to see whether its principles might be found wanting. 'I was very skeptical about quantum mechanics. I could use it and know it but it is a *strange* theory. I had to satisfy myself. It's hard for me to describe the pleasure and joy we had in these experiments . . . half philosophy, half craftsmanship.'[15] To the end of his life he never was fully persuaded that the current interpretation of quantum mechanics would remain.

The experimental program of Rabi's laboratory was largely set by major advances in nuclear physics: in 1932 a new particle had been discovered, the neutron, the neutral partner of the proton, the nucleus of hydrogen. Almost at once it now became clear that all atomic nuclei are composites of neutrons and protons, the simplest of these being the deuteron, discovered in 1931, consisting of one neutron plus one proton. The Rabi group now had its work cut out for it: to apply Stern's methods and variants thereof for *atoms* to the determination of magnetic moments and spins of *nuclei*. (Loosely speaking, we say that a particle has spin if it performs gyrations around an intrinsic axis.)

I shall refrain from giving a detailed survey of the progress in instrumentation and of the results obtained in the Rabi lab during the 1930s. For these I refer to detailed technical reports and also to a good popular account.[16] Here I mention only the highlights.

In the early 1930s the theme of Rabi's experiments was, in his words, 'to play the changes on the original Stern setup.'[7] Spins and magnetic moments were determined for a variety of elements, later experiments on the same element being executed with ever improving accuracy.[17] From the theoretical point of view, the most important results of that period concerned the magnetic moments of the proton and the deuteron. These had first been measured by Stern and coworkers, that of the deuteron only roughly.[18] The Rabi group repeated these two experiments with much better precision.[19]

Then, in 1936, Rabi had the greatest idea of his career. In a paper published in 1937 he proposed[20] to place between the uniform magnetic fields of the Stern arrangement an additional magnetic field that oscillates periodically in time, with a frequency that can be varied with high precision. Leaving out all details (for which see ref. 16), I note that this new arrangement has made possible considerable improvement in the accuracy of magnetic moment measurements, the first application already by an order of magnitude. When (as mentioned earlier) Rabi reported on the magnetic moment of the electron at Shelter Island, his method had made it possible to determine that quantity to six significant figures—a precision unheard of till then.

In 1937 it could not have been foreseen how far-reaching this so-called magnetic resonance method would become, not only in physics, but also in chemistry, biology, and medicine. Scientists and laymen alike have heard of the NMR (Nuclear Magnetic Resonance) equipment used in hospitals—an application of Rabi's ideas.

Armed with their new techniques, the Rabi group revisited earlier magnetic moment measurements, repeating them with improved precision. In the course of their work they made a discovery of fundamental importance for the theory of nuclear forces, those acting between neutrons and protons inside the nucleus. They found that the deuteron's shape was not a perfect little sphere—as had been assumed till then for all nuclei—but was ellipsoidal, like an American football; in technical terms the deuteron possessed an electric quadrupole moment.[21]

A coworker has given a picture of Rabi's role in all these experiments.

> Rabi was very active on the ideas for the experiments, but was completely uninterested in details. In other words, he really was the stimulating and guiding force . . . When there were leaks in the apparatus he just disappeared . . . He didn't contribute to the manual work . . . He contributed very importantly to the concepts of the experiment and of the apparatus and to the interpretation of the results.[22]

Another has said: 'We wouldn't let him touch the apparatus.'[23] It has also been said of him that he was lazy, bored, and irresponsible in the face of routine.[24]

However that may be, 'many were aware of Rabi's ability to hit the jackpot in his physics,'[24] as was fittingly recognized in 1944 when, one day in November, he received a call from a newspaper man that went like this:[25]

Reporter. Hello, I am Mr. Johnson. I represent a Swedish newspaper.

Rabi. Yes, Mr. Johnson?

Reporter. I suppose you can guess what I am calling about?

Rabi. Yes, Mr. Johnson.

Reporter. Have you heard anything?

Rabi. No, Mr. Johnson.

Reporter. Neither have I.

The next day, Rabi received word that he had been awarded the physics Nobel prize for 1944, 'for his resonance method of recording the magnetic properties of atomic nuclei.' That same day Stern was told that he had received the delayed prize for 1943. Circumstance of war made it impossible to travel to Stockholm to receive the honors. So it came about that the ceremony took place in New York City, for the only time in history. According to *The New York Times* of April 12, 1945, the day before, Nicholas Murray Butler, president of Columbia, and himself a Nobel laureate (for peace, in 1931), presented Rabi with the medal and diploma—which had been put in his care by the Swedish ambassador—at a reception at the Men's Faculty Club on 117th Street.

A postscript to this event has been recorded by Rabi's biographer.[26] 'Many years later, in 1982, Rabi was informed by Abraham Pais that Einstein had also nominated him for the Nobel prize. "Are you serious?" asked Rabi. Pais had seen the letter [in the course of preparing Einstein's biography]. "Isn't that marvelous?" Rabi said.'

The only first rate experiment in which Rabi participated after his Prize was the one he reported in Shelter Island. Thereafter he published some more research papers—I have counted about ten of those—but these were more routine in character. The Nobel Prize had diminished his ardent pursuit of pure science—a phenomenon one finds rather frequently among those so honored. 'Unless you are very competitive you aren't likely to function with the same vigor afterward. It's like the lady from Boston who said, "Why should I travel when I'm already there?" The prize also attracts you away from your field because other avenues open up.'[7]

Rabi's other avenue was determined by the outbreak of the Second World War. 'I really felt I ought to do something. And later, with the fall of France, I became desperate to get into the war.'[7]

And so, in November 1940, he left New York and headed for Cambridge, Massachusetts, to go to war. There he found the radar project that was just starting up. He became the deputy director of that enterprise, which became known as the Radiation Laboratory, or Rad Lab for short. 'He was the forward-looking director of research. He was invaluable.'[27] It has been said that 'The atomic bomb ended the war, but radar won the war.'[28] Combining these two comments, one sees the manifest importance of Rabi's contribution. (I only know some bare details of that work.)

Moreover, Raab also became an advisor to the Los Alamos Laboratory, the center of the atomic bomb project. In December 1943, Robert Oppenheimer, its director, offered Rabi, whose experience and know-how he was eager to get, the associate directorship of that laboratory. The two men had known each other since 1928, when they studied in Leipzig with Heisenberg; in 1929 they both had gone to Zurich to work with Pauli. 'We got along very well. We were friends until his last day. I enjoyed the things about him that some people disliked.'[7] Rabi rejected Oppenheimer's offer, but agreed to become his non-paid personal advisor, 'chiefly as his troubleshooter.'[29] So it came about that he was present at the successful atomic bomb test on July 16, 1945, near Alamogordo in New Mexico. 'A few minutes after the explosion I had goose pimples all over me when I realized what this meant for the future of humanity.'[7]

Oppenheimer said later that, right after the blast, some lines of the *Bhagavad Gita* went through his mind: I am become Death, the destroyer of worlds. Perhaps so, though to me it sounds like one of his priestly exaggerations. More relevant to me is an observation of Rabi as the group of witnesses to the test walked back to their cars afterward. 'Something in Oppenheimer's bearing brought Rabi's gooseflesh back again. The man moved like a confident stranger, darkly glittering, at ease, in tune with the thing. "I'll never forget his walk," says Rabi. "I'll never forget the way he stepped out of the car."[30]

A few months after the war had been won, Rabi wrote: 'The physicist has been placed in an embarrassing position . . . [He] now is hailed as the messiah who will bring us a new world . . . new industries, an expanding economy, and jobs for all . . . Industry, with considerable success, is trying to lure the physicist from his academic hide-out with glittering pieces of silver.'[31] Physicists were now listened to with respect, if not with awe, by the world at large. As one *Life* reporter put it, they now seemed to wear 'the tunic of Superman.'[32]

Done with war work, Rabi wanted to go back to Columbia. As a result of war events, 'We had gone from being one of the best departments in the world to almost nothing.'[7] He therefore set as a condition for his return that he would become department chairman, the best position for recruiting new strength. This was accepted and so he was chairman from 1945 to 1949. His efforts at attracting senior men led nowhere, however; those had already been appointed elsewhere at high salaries. 'I decided that we would have to begin by developing our own young people and bringing in other young people'[7]—which explains the offers I received from him, as mentioned earlier. That approach was largely successful; three of the young people he managed to attract became Nobel laureates, Lamb, Polykarp Kusoh, and Charles Townes, discoverer of the laser.

Rabi was also instrumental in getting a cyclotron built for Columbia, which for a few months was the most powerful machine of its kind in the world. He never used this accelerator for his own research, however. 'Big physics,' done by groups, never held appeal for him. He was quite enthusiastic, however, about what others achieved that way in the essentially new post-war branch of physics that deals with the structure of matter in its finest details, now known as particle physics. 'To me that is the most exciting in the whole world of science. To me that's No. 1 . . . In particle physics you have something entirely new—tremendously new and mysterious.'[7]

I noted earlier that in 1946 Raab's role as statesman of science was on its way, giving as two examples his promotion of collaboration between American universities and of an international laboratory in Europe, ideas clearly tied to pure science. I now turn to his activities in the realm of 'pure' politics—if you pardon the expression.

Late in 1945, Rabi and Oppenheimer got together to discuss the issue of control of atomic energy in the United States. They composed a proposal on how to handle this important problem. That led to the so-called Baruch plan, which never got anywhere. In 1946 Rabi received presidential appointment to the

General Advisory Committee (GAC) of the US Atomic Energy Commission, which held its first meeting on December 9, 1946. From then until 1952, Oppenheimer was its chairman, after which he was succeeded by Rabi, who held that post until 1956.

The most important issue ever to come up on the GAC agenda was whether the US should develop the 'Super,' the hydrogen bomb, which their group debated in their meeting of October 29–30, 1949. Their report, in which the committee unanimously advised against the Super, contains a minority addendum, dated October 30, 1959, signed by Enrico Fermi and Rabi, which goes much further, in that it emphasizes future consequences: 'The use of such a weapon cannot be justified on any ethical ground . . . it would put the United States in a bad moral position . . . would leave unresolvable enmities for generations . . . an evil thing considered in any light . . .'[33]

The advice against the Super, which was ignored, as we all know, was a contributing factor that led to the hearings in Washington of April 1954, in which the question at stake was whether or not Oppenheimer was a security risk: Rabi, one of the many who testified, spoke forcefully and at length in support of Oppenheimer. In his testimony, which fills 23 pages of the government report,[34] he said: 'It didn't seem the sort of thing that called for this kind of proceeding . . . against a man who has accomplished what Dr. Oppenheimer has accomplished [in the framework of the U.S. weapons program] . . . What more do you want, mermaids?'

The outcome of the hearings, a vote against Oppenheimer, angered Rabi, not just because of that verdict but also because Oppenheimer's defense had been very poor, as is generally agreed. As Raab once said to me: 'He could have become the guru of science, with great influence in the corridors of power, but he blew it himself. A terrible loss for us all.'

None of that detracted from Rabi's strong affection for the man, however. At the same time he could see right through him, so to say, regarding his personal foibles, and would not hesitate to say so. I recall a day, a year after the hearings, when Edward Murrow came to the Institute for Advanced Study in Princeton to interview Oppenheimer for one of his celebrated programs 'See it Now.' That afternoon somebody knocked at my office door. It was Rabi, who had come to see Oppenheimer but was told to wait until the interview was over, and so came to me for a chat meanwhile. After some time he became impatient and said 'let's go down', which we did. Quietly we entered Oppenheimer's office and sat down, watching the interview. When Murrow had finished and had left, Rabi turned to Oppenheimer and said: 'Robert, you're a ham'—which, I felt, was quite deserved but did not enthuse Robert, who did not reply.

It was typical for Rabi to make pronouncements like this, straight to the point. I remember that in a conversation I had with him years after

Oppenheimer's death, I asked how he would characterize him. Another characteristic Rabi dictum: 'Oppenheimer? A rich spoiled Jewish brat from New York.' Yet the finest, most sensitive eulogy of him is from Rabi's hand. I shall quote just one line from it: 'In Oppenheimer the element of earthiness was feeble.'[35]

To continue with Rabi's political activities; these were much influenced by the cordial rapport he developed with Dwight Eisenhower during the years 1948–52 when the latter was president of Columbia University, after which he became President of the United States. It was Rabi who urged him to appoint a special assistant to the President for science and technology. 'I told him that he should pick a person he liked and could get along with, who could be his confidant'[7]— which came about in 1957. That year Rabi himself became the first chairman of PSAC, the President's Science Advisory Committee, on which he served until 1968.

In Rabi's own opinion, the most important political event in which he played a leading role was the organization of the first International Conference on the Peaceful Uses of Atomic Energy. That was an outgrowth of Eisenhower's speech on December 8, 1953 before the United Nations, in which he had proposed that fissionable material should be made available to serve the peaceful pursuits of all mankind. 'My whole purpose was not just to get *people* together but to get the *governments* together.'[7] In the course of helping prepare the conference, Rabi became friends with Dag Hammarskjöld, then the Secretary General of the UN. The conference took place in Geneva, from August 8–20, 1953. Hammarskjöld has said about that meeting: 'It was the greatest political event of the decade.'

Rabi served as vice president, as he would do again for similar conferences held in 1958 and 1964. It was most fitting that in 1968 he would receive the American Atoms for Peace Award. In April 1985 the US National Academy of Sciences arranged a symposium 'The atom and Rabi,' to commemorate the thirtieth anniversary of the Geneva conference and Rabi's role in organizing that meeting.

In 1964 Columbia named Rabi as university professor, the first to hold this high academic post. It allowed him to teach on any subject in any department.

When, in 1967, he retired, a 'Rabi Day' was organized, where former associates and students gave scientific talks. A formal dinner that evening was followed by more personal remarks. All talks were collected in a small book,[36] presented to him a year later, on his seventieth birthday.

Earlier and later Rabi received many honors, including the US Medal for Merit, Britain's King's Medal, France's Legion of Honor, election to numerous learned societies at home and abroad, and, by my count, 15 honorary degrees. In 1985, Columbia established a professorship in his name.

Rabi has written a short recollection of his life and times as a physicist[37] and, in the 1980s, sat for a full life oral history memoir (in 41 sessions) for the Oral History program at Columbia University.[9] In later years he would express his views on general subjects at banquets, on television, in print. Just a few small samples. On the humanities: 'However much I enjoy the humanities, and I do so, vastly, I do not think they are universal.'[7] On science and religion: 'It is only in science that we can get outside ourselves. I have the same feeling, but only to a certain degree, about some religious expressions, such as the opening verses of the Bible, and the story of the Creation.'[7]

A student of the history of Columbia University has said to me that, of all the outstanding persons who have served on its faculty throughout its history, Rabi was the most prominent, in view of his combined accomplishments in science and in public affairs.

———————— • ————————

One day, in December 1987, a colleague came into my office in the Rockefeller University, to inform me that he had just seen Rabi, who had told him that he wanted to talk with me. I knew where Raab was: across the street, in Memorial Sloan-Kettering's hospital, and why: he was terminally ill with cancer. I went there at once, suspecting that he had some final message to convey to me. There he was in remarkably good humor. What did he want to talk about? The foundations of quantum mechanics, which, as told, had troubled him for decades and, in these last weeks, were still on his mind. We argued for maybe half an hour, then I said good-bye to him, forever. On January 11, 1988, Rabi died.

On February 11, 1988, family and friends of Rabi gathered at St Paul's Chapel, Columbia University, for a memorial service, fittingly called 'A Celebration.' I remember that event as sober, yet joyous. Of the addresses given that day (which have been published[38]), I shall only quote a few of the words by the university president: 'He is absolutely irreplaceable . . . He had a healthy appreciation of his own abilities and achievements, neither grandiose nor self-deprecating, but clear and true.'

On a day in October 1996, I went to Pupin Laboratory for a preview of what was being done to Room 813, Rabi's office for many decades, where he and I had sat together quite a few times to talk of subjects of common interest, physics, the Jews, politics. It had been made into the 'Rabi memorial room.' A wall is covered with photographs of significant moments in Raab's life. It was officially inaugurated on December 13, 1996.

———————— • ————————

What do I remember best of Raab? His lack of sentimentality which incompletely masked deep feelings. His pugnacious utterances, his infectious, high-pitched laughter. His pride in being an American. His deep, non-religious, Jewishness. His deep love of and devotion to science.

In the address by Columbia's president, just mentioned, he also said: 'I believe Rabi was aware of the respect and love that so many of us felt for him.' I am one of those many.

Notes and references

In what follows R will stand for I. I. Rabi.

1. R, in 'Physical Science and Human Values' (E. P. Wigner, Ed.), p. 28, Princeton University Press, 1947.

2. For the history of these events, see N. F. Ramsey, Report BNL 992, T-421, 1966.

3. For R's role in the creation of CERN, see History of CERN (A. Hermann et al., Eds), Vol. 1, p. 82ff., North-Holland, New York, 1987.

4. J. R. Oppenheimer, letter to F. B. Jewett, June 4, 1947, copy in the Rockefeller University Archives.

5. W. E. Lamb and R. C. Retherford, Phys. Rev. 72, 241, 1947.

6. J. E. Nafe, E. B. Nelson, and I. I. Rabi, Phys. Rev. 71, 914, 1947; P. Kusch and H. M. Foley, ibid. 72, 1256, 1947.

7. J. Bernstein, The New Yorker, issues of October 13 and 20, 1975.

8. I. I. Rabi, oral history, Columbia University.

9. J. S. Rigden, Rabi, Scientist and Citizen, Basic Books, New York, 1987.

10. Ref. 9, pp. 26, 27.

11. R, Phys. Rev. 29, 174, 1927.

12. O. K. Kronig and R, Phys. Rev. 29, 262, 1927.

13. R, Nature 123, 1929; Zeitschr. f. Physik 54, 190, 1929.

14. Ref. 12 and, with G. Breit, Phys. Rev. 38, 2082, 1931; Phys. Rev. 49, 324, 1936; ibid. 51, 652, 1937; with F. Bloch, Rev. Mod. Phys. 17, 237, 1945.

15. Ref. 9, p. 118.

16. Technical: N. F. Ramsey, Molecular Beams, Oxford University Press, 1985. Popular: ref. 9, chapters 6–8.

17. R with V. Cohen, Phys. Rev. 43, 582, 1933; ibid. 46, 707, 1934 (for Na); with S. Millman and R. Fox, ibid. 46, 320, 1934 (K); with M. Fox, ibid. 48, 746, 1935 (Li, K, Na); with S. Millman and J. R. Zacharias, ibid. 53, 384, 1938 (In); with J. R. Zacharias, S. Millman and P. Kusch, ibid. 53, 495, 1938 (Li, F); with S. Millman and P. Kusch, ibid. 54, 968, 1938 (N); with S. Millman and P. Kusch, ibid. 55, 526, 1939 (Li, F); with S. Millman and P. Kusch, ibid. 55, 666, 1939 (Be); with same ibid. 55, 1176, 1939 (N, Na, K, Cs); with same ibid. 56, 165, 1939 (B).

18. O. R. Frisch and O. Stern, Zeitschr. f. Physik 84, 4, 1933; I. Estermann and O. Stern, Zeitschr. f. Physik 85, 17, 1933; 86, 132, 1933.

19. R and J. M. Kellogg and J. R. Zacharias, Phys. Rev. 46, 157, 163, 1934.

20. R, Phys. Rev. 51, 652, 1937.

21. R with J. M. Kellogg, N. F. Ramsey, and J. R. Zacharias, Phys. Rev. 55, 318, 1939.

22. N. F. Ramsey, quoted in ref. 9, p. 116.

23. J. R. Zacharias, quoted in ref. 9, p. 116.

24. Ref. 9, p. 117.

25. Ref. 9, p. 169.

26. Ref. 9, p. 177.

27. Lee DuBridge, director of the Rad Lab, quoted in ref. 9, p. 140.

28. Lee DuBridge, interview with J. S. Rigden, ref. 9, p. 164.

29. Ref. 9, p. 154.

30. N. P. Davis, *Lawrence and Oppenheimer*, p. 242, Simon and Schuster, New York, 1968.

31. R, in *The Atlantic*, October 1945.

32. *Life Magazine*, August 20, 1945.

33. Full text in H. York, *The Advisors*, p. 158, Freeman, San Francisco, 1976.

34. R in *In the Matter of J. Robert Oppenheimer*, pp. 451–73, United States Government Printing Office, Washington, 1954. The quotation given from R's testimony is found on p. 468. This report has been reprinted by MIT Press, 1971.

35. R in *Oppenheimer*, p. 3, Scribner's, New York, 1969.

36. *A Tribute to Professor I. I. Rabi*, Department of Physics, Columbia University, 1970.

37. R, *My Life and Times as a Physicist*, Claremont College, Claremont, CA, 1960.

38. *A Celebration of Thanksgiving for the Life of I. I. Rabi*, published privately by the Rabi family.

Serber lecturing in Berkeley, early 1950s. (Courtesy of Professor Robert Crease.)

Robert Serber*

Serber is one of the unsung heroes of twentieth-century physics, in which he played an important role, in peace as well as war. It is a reflection of his personality that this is not as widely known as it should be: he always spoke softly, both literally and figuratively, never sought the limelight, and often did not much care for publishing his scientific results.

———————

Robert was born in 1909, in Philadelphia, the oldest of the three children of David Serber, a lawyer, and Rose, née Frankel. His paternal grandfather had been a Russian immigrant. He received his early education in his native city, and did his undergraduate work at Lehigh University in Bethlehem, Pennsylvania. In those years he held various picturesque summer jobs, such as oilman on a tanker. In 1930 he went to the University of Wisconsin in Madison for graduate studies. In 1933 he married Charlotte Leof (b. 1911), whom he had known since his Philadelphia years.

Robert had published six papers before he got his PhD. A typical Serber story: at his final exam he could not remember which one of these papers he had submitted for his Doctor's degree. Thereafter he and his wife took off for Princeton, where he intended to spend the National Research Council Fellowship he had been awarded, one of five given out nationwide that year in theoretical physics. It carried a stipend of $1200, not a royal but still a princely sum for that time. (Robert and Charlotte paid $25 a month for their room in Madison.) On the way they stopped off in Ann Arbor, to attend one of the famous summer schools. There they met Robert Oppenheimer for the first time—which changed the course of their lives. Deeply impressed, Serber decided to change the venue of his NRC Fellowship to Berkeley, where he arrived in the autumn of 1934.

———————

After Oppenheimer had returned in 1929 to the US from Europe, he had started a school of theoretical physics at Berkeley and CalTech, which became the

* Address given at a memorial meeting in honor of Serber, held at the Physics Department, Columbia University, on April 30, 1988.

centers where quantum field theory in America was founded. Serber at once contributed to this subject with two papers,[1] in the first of which he introduced a concept which is now part of the physics language: to *renormalize* the polarization of the vacuum. He also participated in other lively work at the physics frontiers, notably in nuclear physics, an area that became one of his life-long interests. Thus he and Oppenheimer were the first, I believe, to note (1938) that isospin is conserved in nuclear reactions.[2] In 1947 he introduced[3] the 'Serber forces' which act between nucleon pairs with even orbital angular momentum only. His last research paper (1976) deals with a simple nuclear model.[4] Back to the Berkeley days, a paper[5] of 1937, together with Oppenheimer, appears to be the first in which Yukawa's meson theory is mentioned in a Western publication. He also published on theories of cosmic rays and of stellar constitution. Of Oppenheimer's contributions in those years, Serber has recalled: 'His physics was good but his arithmetic awful.'[6] On his personal relations with him he has said that there was 'from the beginning a very special rapport between us.'[7]

Much as he liked Berkeley, Serber nevertheless accepted in the spring of 1938 an offer for an assistant professor position at the University of Illinois in Urbana. Jobs were scarce at that time, especially for young Jews. He kept in steady touch with Oppenheimer, however, who 'would write to me every Sunday.'[8] Both Serbers also continued their earlier summer visits to Oppenheimer's ranch in New Mexico. Serber's most memorable work in Urbana was his paper[9] with Donald Kerst on theoretical aspects of the betatron, a new type of accelerator, 'the most useful thing I did for particle physics.'[6]

———————

Around Christmas 1941, just after Pearl Harbor, Serber received a call from Oppenheimer, who wanted to come to Urbana to discuss a delicate matter. On a walk in the corn fields he told him that he would be appointed head of the atomic bomb project and asked Serber to be his assistant. So it came about that Robert and Charlotte were the first after Oppenheimer to arrive in Los Alamos.

One of Serber's early tasks was to give a series of lectures on what physics was known about the project. This resulted in *Los Alamos Report Number 1: The Los Alamos Primer*.[10] He became the group leader assigned to overseeing the design of the uranium 235 bomb and the gun assembly (its detonation device)—the Hiroshima bomb. He was present at the Trinity test of that gadget on July 16, 1945. On that same day a cruiser left San Francisco harbor with Little Boy, the Hiroshima bomb, on board, bound for Tinian in the Mariana Islands in the Pacific, where also Fat Man, the plutonium bomb destined for Nagasaki, was delivered.

Serber was flown out to Tinian, with the field rank of colonel, to participate in the gun assembly. While there he was asked by Colonel Tibbets, commander of the *Enola Gay*, the plane that was to make the Hiroshima drop, to calculate

The Bomb Materials

URANIUM-235

A great deal was already known about this fission material.

The Critical Mass: It had recently been estimated that 15 kilograms would be the critical mass, though some new figures just in from Madison and Minneapolis indicated that an even larger amount might be needed.

Preparation: The main hope lay in electromagnetic and gas diffusion methods. Both were expensive to industrialise and they were still far from certain to succeed.

The Explosion Mechanism: Two important facts were still unknown about uranium-235. Were sufficient neutrons released from each fission to allow the chain reaction to multiply quickly enough? This still needed checking.

Was the time between the absorption of the neutron and the release of the energy and the new neutrons fast enough? If it was not, then the fissioning mass could blow apart before the reaction was fully underway throughout the metal. Both these questions had to be answered.

PLUTONIUM

In April 1943 it was still not proved for certain that this element existed. Yet the construction of a whole industrial plant sited at Hanford, Washington employing thousands of people was planned to start within two months.

The Critical Mass: This had been calculated at 5 kilograms of plutonium, a good deal less than uranium. It was hoped that once Hanford began production, it would be more readily available than uranium-235.

Preparation: To be made in atomic piles, the prototype of which, designed by Fermi's team, went critical only four months earlier in Chicago.

Explosion Mechanism: No details known.

The Bomb Mechanism

The mechanism most favoured for the mechanism was the so-called 'gun method;

The main problem foreseen at this stage was pre-detonation. If the two subcritical pieces were not brought together quickly enough, the bomb would blow apart before the fission chain reaction had properly started. This would happen because of stray neutrons which initiate just enough fission to produce the energy to simply blow the bomb itself apart but no more.

These stray neutrons are produced by the interaction of particles in the metal with certain impurities also present.

Thus there were two courses of action:
1: Purification of the Metal
2: Develop techniques for almost instant assembly.

In April 1943, it was hoped the so-called gun method would be fast enough.

The status of knowledge about atomic weapons in April 1943. From Serber's *The Los Alamos Primer.*[10]

whether his flight plan would make his plane survive the blast. Serber did so and could assure the colonel that he would be perfectly safe.

Two stories about the Nagasaki drop. First, Serber, Luis Alvarez, and Phil Morrison had written a letter to Ryokichi Sagane, a Japanese physicist whom they knew from the time he had worked with Ernest Lawrence in Berkeley, in which they implored him to urge his government to stop the war in order to avoid further destruction. This letter, which was dropped on August 9, together with the Nagasaki bomb, reached Sagane, who eventually returned it to Alvarez.

Second story. Serber was supposed to run the camera that would take pictures of the Nagasaki drop, but was thrown off the accompanying plane because he had no parachute.

When it was all over, Serber was made head of mission to inspect on-site the results of the two atom bombings and so, in September 1945, was among the first Americans to enter Japan. He returned to Los Alamos on October 15.

In January 1946 Serber was back in Berkeley, now as full professor. His first task was to give a series of lectures on high energy processes, which were later published under the title *Serber Says*.[11] His research in the late 1940s includes papers on the workings of new Berkeley accelerators.[12]

I first met Bob (as everyone called Serber) at the 'Shelter Island' conference in 1947, where he reported on first results obtained with the 184-inch Berkeley cyclotron—the first high energy experiments. I met him again during the sequels to this meeting, the 'Pocono' conference in 1948, and the 'Old Stone' conference in 1949, where he described the first experiments with artificially produced π-mesons. Of these early encounters I recall that he spoke softly, and with a slight stutter, but that *what* he said showed him to be a true professional. I also saw Bob in Princeton, in October 1949. I did not know at that time that he was there to attend a meeting on the fate of the hydrogen bomb project.[13]

Meanwhile Bob had run into some political problems. In 1948 he had been the subject of investigations into his 'character, associations, and loyalty,' not pleasant but causing him no harm in the event. In 1950 the regents of the University of California demanded that all faculty members take an oath of loyalty to the United States. 'I was unhappy but I didn't take it so seriously that I wouldn't sign.'[14] He was much offended, however, when colleagues were fired for refusing to sign. Even more unpleasant for him was to be caught in the middle of political controversies between Lawrence, the conservative, and Oppenheimer, the liberal, a situation so uncomfortable that Bob felt he had better leave Berkeley. In 1951 he did so, starting his professorship at Columbia University.

I, too, was at Columbia, in academic 1954–55, on a sabbatical from the

Institute for Advanced Study in Princeton. It was in that year that I got to know Bob really well and that our friendship began. We collaborated on several papers, one[15] on the interaction of K-mesons with atomic nuclei, and two[16] on strong coupling theory. I got to like his dry sense of humor. Two examples. A story Bob liked to tell. He dreamt that he had died and gone to heaven. Saint Peter leads him into the presence of God, who says to him: 'You won't remember me but I took your quantum mechanics course in Berkeley in 1946.' Another story about a discussion we once had. I told him how much I liked the beautiful designs on wings of butterflies. Bob's reply: he much liked the design on the back of a turtle on which was written: Greetings from Atlantic City.

That year began our joint trips by car to Brookhaven National Laboratory, where both of us were consultants. (At some time or other Bob was also consultant for Fermi Laboratory, SLAC, and Los Alamos.) That was before the Sunrise Highway and the Long Island Expressway had been constructed, so the ride was still fairly lengthy but nevertheless enjoyable, not least because at that time Bob had a Jaguar XKE, the sexiest car I have ever driven in.

We have also frequently been in touch with each other in later years but never as closely as during my time at Columbia University.

I conclude with brief remarks on Bob's later years.

In the late 1960s, Charlotte was diagnosed as suffering from Parkinson's disease. In 1967 she committed suicide by taking an overdose of sleeping pills. I have been told that Bob stopped stuttering after her death.

In 1970 Bob served as president of the American Physical Society.

After Oppenheimer's death in 1967, Bob had become intimate with Kitty, his widow. In 1972 he and Kitty planned to cross the Pacific by sailboat, which also had a motor on board, helped by a crew of four. They did not get further than the Panama Canal, when Kitty had to be put into a Panama City hospital, suffering from an embolism, of which she died. Bob saw to it that her ashes were scattered in the sea, near Carvel Rock on St John, Virgin Islands, where also Oppenheimer's ashes had been dispersed.

From 1975 until his retirement in 1978 Bob was chairman of the Physics Department, Columbia University.

In 1976 Bob met Fiona St Clair, daughter of old-time residents of St John. They married in 1979. Fiona brought along Zacharias (then aged 4), her son by an earlier marriage. In 1980 Bob and Fiona's son William was born.

In 1983, Bob was one of three physicists who presented to the secretary general of the United Nations a petition signed by about 10 000 physicists, asking for an end to the testing and production of nuclear weapons.

In 1993 Bob gave the keynote address at the 50th anniversary celebration of Los Alamos. The meeting was classified, armed guards standing at the door.

In 1997 Bob underwent surgery to remove a brain tumor. He never fully recovered from that operation, and died on June 1, 1997, at age 88.

Honored be his memory.

Added Note. On the day I gave this address, Robert Crease was so kind as to present me with a copy of the memoir on Serber, the result of interviews with him, which had just come out.[7] I have used this very readable book to add here some biographical details about Bob's life and work.

References

1. R. Serber, *Phys. Rev.* **48**, 49, 1935; **49**, 545, 1936.

2. R. Oppenheimer and R. Serber, *Phys. Rev.* **53**, 636, 1938.

3. R. Serber, *Phys. Rev.* **72**, 1114, 1947.

4. R. Serber, *Phys. Rev.* **C14**, 718, 1976.

5. R. Oppenheimer and R. Serber, *Phys. Rev.* **51**, 1113, 1937.

6. R. Serber, in *The Birth of Particle Physics* (L. Brown and L. Hoddeson, Eds), p. 206, Cambridge University Press, 1983.

7. R. Serber with R. Crease, *Peace and War*, p. 29, Columbia University Press, New York, 1998.

8. Ref. 7, p. 57.

9. D. W. Kerst and R. Serber, *Phys. Rev.* **60**, 53, 1941.

10. Published in 1992 by the California University Press.

11. R. Serber, *Serber Says*, World Scientific, Singapore, 1987.

12. R. Serber, *Phys. Rev.* **70**, 434, 1946; **71**, 449; **72**, 740, 748, 1114, 1947.

13. R. G. Hewlett and F. Duncan, *Atomic Shield*, p. 381, University of California Press, 1990.

14. Ref. 7, p. 17.

15. A. Pais and R. Serber, *Phys. Rev.* **99**, 1551, 1955.

16. A. Pais and R. Serber, *Phys. Rev.* **105**, 1636, 1957; **113**, 955, 1959.

George Uhlenbeck in his office at the Rockefeller University, about 1970. (Courtesy of Emilio Segrè Visual Archives, Uhlenbeck Collection.)

George Eugene Uhlenbeck*

During my career I have known physicists who were at least as distinguished as Uhlenbeck. I have never, however, met anyone who could lecture better on science than he. His calmness, his style—systematic without a trace of pedantry—compelled me not to miss a word he said. He was the best teacher I have had. Later we became colleagues and friends and published together. I shall turn presently to my personal contacts with George.

Descent. Early years

The owl depicted on the signet ring George Uhlenbeck used to wear—'Uhlenbeck' in German means 'owl's brook'—derives from his family's coat of arms. The shield reads, in the language of heraldry: azure, on a tree trunk proper rising from water argent, an owl contourné, head affronty. In plain language, it depicts an owl with its head turned toward you, sitting on a tree trunk in natural color, which rises up out of a silvery brook. (I owe the transcription of the Dutch blazon into English heraldry to Michael Maclagan, the Richmond Herald in the College of Arms, in London.)

The Uhlenbeck ancestry can be traced to German roots. Records for the years 1634 and 1656 kept at the Staatsarchiv in Düsseldorf, at one time the capital of the duchy of Berg, mention that at those times a Jan in der Ulenbeck was the proprietor of the estate Üllenbeck, situated near the township of Velbert in the district of Angermund. The next four generations of George's ancestors were born and raised on that same estate. A great-great-grandson of Jan in der Ulenbeck, Johannes Wilhelmus Uhlenbeck, went into military service under King Frederick II—'the Great'—of Prussia. On account of a duel he had to flee the country. In 1768 he entered the military service of the Dutch East India Company on the island of Ceylon, a Dutch colony from 1658 until 1796. He was the first of the Dutch branch of the Uhlenbeck family.

* Part of this essay is taken from the lecture I gave at the Uhlenbeck Memorial Symposium of the American Physical Society, held in Baltimore on May 3, 1989, printed in *Physics Today*, December 1989 issue, p. 34; also in the Yearbook 1989 of the American Philosophical Society, p. 327. Japanese translation in *Parity*, June 1990, p. 24.

Eugenius Marius Uhlenbeck, a great-great-grandson of Johannes Wilhelmus, born in 1863 in Bondowoso on the island of Java in the Dutch East Indies (now Indonesia), served with the Dutch East Indian Army, eventually as lieutenant colonel. Two of his uncles also served as officers in that army. Their lives came to a tragic end on June 9, 1848, during the war against Bali. 'The two Uhlenbeck brothers were mortally wounded. One of them took his own life in order not to fall alive into the hands of the enemy.'[1]

In 1893, Eugenius Marius married Anne Marie Beeger, who was born in 1874 in Solok on Sumatra, the daughter of a Dutch major general. They had six children, two of whom died very young in the Indies, of malaria. Of the survivors, the oldest was a daughter, Annie who got a degree in biology with the right to teach that subject in high school. Five years later came George, always called Broer, Dutch for Brother, by his family, born in Batavia (now Jakarta) on December 6, 1900. After him came two more sons, first Willem Jan, who became inspector of the Dutch railways, and finally Eugenius Marius ('Bob'), who became a distinguished linguist, specializing in Javanese, and a professor at the University of Leiden. 'I think that one of the disappointments of my parents was that none of their sons went to military schools.'[2]

Military duties caused the family to move about a good deal. Thus it happened that George received his first schooling at a kindergarten in Padangpandjang, on Sumatra.

Early interest in physics

'One year in the Indies counted as two years' [military] service, so after twenty years my father retired although he was only forty-two, and he did it mainly for the education of the children.'[2] So in 1907 the family moved permanently to Holland and settled in The Hague. '[There] I went all through elementary and high school [a HBS, a higher burgher school, now called an atheneum]. I was a very dutiful student, *very* dutiful. I always worked very regularly and I was always very good in class. I was certainly not clear until the last years in high school what I was going to do.'[2]

Then he knew. 'The physics in high school was quite good. My teacher was quite a good physicist. He had a Ph.D. and had also published things ... He partially determined my direction.'[3] The teacher (his name was A. H. Borgesius) discussed science with George and gave him books from which to study differential and integral calculus. Eager to learn more, George would bicycle to the Royal Library in The Hague to seek further information. There he absorbed Hendrik Lorentz's *Lessen over de Natuurkunde* (Lectures on Physics), an undergraduate university text. Uhlenbeck's particular interest in kinetic gas theory dates from those early days.

In July 1918 Uhlenbeck passed his final high school examination. He could not enter a Dutch university, however, because his school had not provided training in Greek and Latin, at that time a prerequisite by law for university study in any discipline. (Johannes van der Waals and Jacobus van't Hoff, in similar positions at earlier times, had been able to enter a university only by special governmental dispensation.) In September 1918 he therefore entered the *Technische Hogeschool* (Institute of Technology) in Delft, intent on studying chemical engineering. 'I was very unhappy in Delft, mainly because it was such a mechanical sort of business, all these many lectures which one had to go to and chemical laboratories which one had to take and at which I was not very good at all. I didn't like that.'[2] George's youngest brother has written to me that his family considered him (G.) quite clumsy as a young man.[4]

Almost immediately after Uhlenbeck had arrived in Delft, a new law was enacted—known in Holland as the *Wet* (which means law) Limburg—which dispensed with the Greek and Latin requirements for university training in the sciences. As a result George left Delft in January 1919 and enrolled in the University of Leiden to study physics and mathematics. At that time the physics professors in Leiden were Paul Ehrenfest, Heike Kamerlingh Onnes, and J. P. Kuenen. Every Monday Hendrik Antoon Lorentz, Ehrenfest's predecessor, would come from Haarlem to give a physics lecture.

All through his undergraduate years, Uhlenbeck commuted, by train between Leiden and his family's home on the Lübeckstraat in The Hague. His mother would pack his lunch and give him a *kwartje* (25 cents) for coffee. He saved the money until one day he spent it on a secondhand copy of Boltzmann's *Vorlesungen über Gastheorie* (Lectures on Gas Theory), lecture notes that he found hard to grasp. Not long thereafter his brother-in-law, a chemist, introduced him to Paul and Tatiana Ehrenfest's encyclopedia article on statistical mechanics.[5] 'That was a revelation. I began to see what Boltzmann was up to.' (Quotations without attribution are from private conversations with Uhlenbeck.) The Leiden style suited Uhlenbeck perfectly.

> With regard to the education, I found it quite heavenly. Mainly because there were practically no lectures, you had nothing to do. There were only lectures in mathematics, analytic geometry and calculus and analysis and so, and they were only about four hours a week altogether. Two hours geometry, two hours analysis. Then there was physics. There was the big lecture with demonstration, which I thought was quite dull and I didn't go to that. I didn't have to. I mean there was no attendance, nobody took any kind of responsibility for the student . . . There were problems in class, but never assigned problems . . . And that was, of course, what I liked. They treated us completely as grown-ups. You could take the responsibility. You made your own problems . . . There was one man who gave a special course on the foundations of analysis. And that I thought was marvelous . . . because it was so rigorous.[3]

George wanted to become a theoretical physicist, but that demanded that he do some experimental work as well.

> Then you had to do this practical, set up experiments. But since I was a first-year student, I was allowed to do that only one afternoon a week, which was just fine for me. Just one afternoon, there was no more. So I had an enormous amount of free time. There was this library which Ehrenfest had started. I didn't get in touch with Ehrenfest at all. But I studied for myself Boltzmann's gas theory, I remember, and mechanics as much as I needed. It was quite heaven . . .
>
> The second year you had to work at least two or even three afternoons to get ready, because there was an assigned number of these experiments which you had to do before your exam. You had to give reports on them, written reports on the results. These experiments were quite interesting for me, mainly because there were lots of formulas in them. You had to check and see whether you could put in experimental values and it would come out. All about diffraction, and all kinds of things. I learned a lot for myself at those times. You had to do, I think, about forty experiments in which for each of them there was written out a little syllabus in which all the formulas and so on which one had to use were mentioned. Then you had to write a little report for each thing, and those I took enormously seriously because, as I said, I was very dutiful. I derived all these formulas; I wanted to derive them all. That's one of the reasons I did this Maxwell theory. And I wrote it all at length. That made for me personally a good impression because Kuenen got so impressed by that; he saw those things, and as a result, the third year, through the efforts of Kuenen, I got what you call a fellowship, which was quite exceptional in those days. It was a state fellowship, which meant, on the one hand, that you didn't need to pay the tuition, and that was a godsend for my parents.[3]

About examinations:

> You see, the whole method of education consisted of doing two exams. One was called 'Candidates,' which you did after two or three years. And then again two or three years later you did the doctorandus examination. In between there was never any examination, never! And also no attendance, in courses or anything. Of course one knew what one had to know, because that was essentially the content of the lectures. Whether you had gone there or not gone there, there was always someone who took notes.
>
> I did my Candidates towards the end of the second year, and that was terrible for me. The examination consisted only of oral examinations. All separate topics. On analysis you went to the professor, made an appointment, and talked for half an hour while he asked questions. Same in geometry. Same in physics, for this general course and thermodynamics. So that was a little bit of the pressure, when one was under pressure. Because then one has to know everything at the same time . . . It was just this kind of cramming I thought was very disgusting . . . I took the exam on time [in December 1920], but afterwards I was a little bit overworked; I was very tired.[2,3]

Ehrenfest

Now a graduate, Uhlenbeck partially supported himself by teaching ten hours a week at a high school in Leiden. The flirtatious young girls there contributed greatly to his difficulties in keeping order in his classes. 'Mainly I did it for money, because I kind of hated it . . . For the first time I now lived in Leiden. Then I had the money to have a room.'[3]

Those teaching activities did not cause George to interrupt his graduate studies, however. He attended courses by Ehrenfest and Lorentz and also the celebrated Wednesday evening 'Ehrenfest colloquium,' which one could attend by invitation only, but to which one had to go once admitted. Ehrenfest even took attendance.

Ehrenfest was by far the most important scientific figure in Uhlenbeck's life. In all the years I knew Uhlenbeck, in Utrecht, in Ann Arbor, and in New York, a single picture always stood on his office desk; a small photograph of a warmly smiling Ehrenfest. In 1956, upon receiving the Oersted Medal from the American Association of Physics Teachers, Uhlenbeck publicly expressed[6] his veneration for his respected and beloved teacher, whose life had long since come to a tragic end. In his acceptance lecture he recalled some characteristic Ehrenfest sayings:

'*Was ist der Witz* . . .? [Do you say that to make a point, or only because it happens to be true?] *Weshalb habe ich solche gute Studenten? Weil ich so dumm bin.* [Why do I have such good students? Because I am so stupid.]'

Uhlenbeck also described some typical traits of Ehrenfest's style of lecturing and conducting seminars:

First the assertion, then the proof. . . . His famous clarity, not to be confused with rigor . . . He never gave or made problems; he did not believe in them; in his opinion the only problems worth considering were those you proposed yourself . . . He worked essentially with only one student at a time, and that practically every afternoon during the week . . . In the beginning, at the end of the afternoon one was dead tired.

In later years, George added more comments on Ehrenfest:

I think it was extremely healthy for me that I got in contact with Ehrenfest who did *not* want to do anything learned; if you couldn't say it simply, if you couldn't be to the point, then he didn't want to hear it, and anything which was, so to speak, long-winded and learned, he made immediate fun of. And as a result, and since he was finally the man who certainly had the *most* influence on me, this counteracted this thing of mine considerably. You see, in mathematics for instance, in the old days, I was the one who wanted to have it *absolutely* rigorous; now, after Ehrenfest, I think it is bad when it is very rigorous! So it was very good for me when Ehrenfest really took me in hand in that respect. He also used his assistants sometimes to read papers which he wanted to know. Then we had to tell him about them from notes we made and so on, and then, of course, if I didn't say the point—Jesus!—or if I hadn't understood the point![2]

Ehrenfest was a man who always had to get it out of his toes. He had, somehow, no technique. Nothing was in his fingers. He always had to think it out completely from the beginning. Although he knew mathematics it was not simple for him. He was not a computer. He could not compute. That's the one thing I never learned from him. I had to learn it all by myself later on.[7]

'When he got older it got more and more difficult for him to get it out of his toes, to learn it all.'[7] The advent of quantum mechanics, in 1925, caused Ehrenfest problems.

I think he always hated it. Oh, and then there was this whole generation which came with it. All these youngsters, who had, with great facility, made these calculations because it was, so to say, a technique which was given you, and you didn't have to understand much. You just computed and you did this and you did that and everything came out. Ehrenfest said '*Diese Klugscheisser*!' [Those smartalecks] 'Always so clever they were! And nobody understood anything.' Which was partially true and partially wrong of course. There was, therefore, a mathematical apparatus built with Hilbert's basis, with operators, which had a sort of abstractness. It was so against his creed that I am sure that he suffered from it . . . Well, he understood it all right. He said he was just too old. It was against his creed to really take part in it. We, in those later years, did all these calculations.[7]

It is not so uncommon that inability to keep up with developments causes depression. That, however, explains only in part Ehrenfest's somber mood in the last years of his life. All along he had suffered from a sense of inadequacy, the high esteem in which he was held by the best of physicists notwithstanding. In 1932 he sat down and wrote a letter to friends, part of which follows.

'I absolutely do not know any more how to carry further during the next few months the burden of my life which has become unbearable. I cannot stand it any longer to let my professorship here [in Leiden] go down the drain. I MUST vacate my position here . . . I have no other 'practical' possibility than suicide.'[8]

On September 25, 1933, Ehrenfest took his own life. I have never discussed that tragedy with Uhlenbeck, since it seemed too delicate a matter.[9]

———————

Let us return to the early 1920s. Ehrenfest's graduate lectures consisted of a two-year course: Maxwell theory, ending with the theory of electrons and some relativity, one year; and statistical mechanics, ending with atomic structure and quantum theory, the other. Uhlenbeck attended these lectures and took additional instruction in mathematics. One day toward the end of his second graduate year, Ehrenfest asked in class whether anyone might be interested in a teaching position in Rome. Uhlenbeck raised his hand. So it came to pass that from September 1922 until June 1925 he became the private tutor in mathematics, physics, chemistry, Dutch, German, and Dutch history of the younger son of the Dutch ambassador J. H. van Royen.

The summers were spent in Holland, however, and in September 1923 Uhlenbeck obtained the degree of 'doctorandus,' the equivalent of a Master's degree.

> The exam was then divided into two parts. One of them was very short, an hour at the most, in which one was formally quizzed a little bit. Then you have to get to what they call 'scriptions.' It was not quite a problem. You had to write part of it as a problem and part of it as an essay. I got one in mathematics and one in physics . . . You were simply given a problem and told you had three days to write it. And you could have access to books, and even friends of course. It was very important that you have! Everybody helped, you see, everybody helped! . . . And then you wrote it out—the physics. Mathematics—it was a tough problem that even with my friends we only solved half. And the mathematician Kluyver, who had his doubts about me, let it go at that. But he was not quite content, really. Ehrenfest gave me for a scription something on which I had talked in the colloquium, so I wrote it out a little bit further. I still remember what it was. It was on the dynamical theory of X-ray reflection which I had studied a little bit at that time. And that was perfectly okay.
>
> Then the second half of the exam was a short discussion of these scriptions, and then it was through! I got my diploma . . . which was required by law for anyone who wanted to teach in high schools. I was allowed to teach physics, mathematics, and theoretical mechanics, which were always separate subjects, even in high schools.[3]

The Roman episode. Fermi

For about a year right after his arrival in Rome, Uhlenbeck took Italian language lessons at the Berlitz school. Thereafter he continued his Italian studies by taking private tuition two hours a week, eventually reading Dante's *Divina Commedia* with his teacher. He reread Dante in later years. I can still hear him declaiming: *Lasciate ogni speranza . . .*, from Book 3 of the *Inferno*. By the fall of 1923 he had mastered the language sufficiently to attend mathematics courses taught at the University of Rome by Federigo Enriques, Tullio Levi-Civita, and Vito Volterra. He also made contact with Roman physicists. When Uhlenbeck was in Holland during the summer of 1923, Ehrenfest told him of a young Italian physicist by the name of Enrico Fermi who had written a paper on the ergodic theorem. Ehrenfest had not understood Fermi's reasoning and asked Uhlenbeck to carry a letter to Rome with questions for Fermi. Thus it came about that Uhlenbeck and Fermi, who was nearly a year younger, met for the first time in the autumn of 1923. Their acquaintance grew into a friendship that lasted throughout Fermi's life. Together with a few other young Italian physicists they organized a small colloquium. 'Fermi was the born leader and did most of the talking.'

George and Enrico also

> talked about all kinds of things and also about the Italian situation, with which he was not happy. There was so little future for him at that time, you see. On the other hand, of course, one must remember that this was the revolutionary period in Italy. I mean I saw the march through Rome. I was there. And I listened to Mussolini's first speeches in Rome. And I saw all these blackshirts in the streets of Rome . . . It was very exciting, those revolutionary times.[3]

George thoroughly disliked fascism, however.

Fermi wrote his paper on the ergodic theorem in 1923 during his stay in Göttingen, Germany, a visit that adversely affected his self-confidence. The learned Göttingen style did not agree with him. At Uhlenbeck's urgings, Fermi went to Leiden for three months in 1924; he even published a paper in Dutch. One of Uhlenbeck's contributions to physics lies in initiating the personal contact between Ehrenfest and Fermi, which helped greatly to restore Fermi's self-confidence. That it was the Dutchman Uhlenbeck who introduced Fermi, born and raised a Roman, to Michelangelo's Moses in the church of San Pietro in Vincoli says something about the personalities of the two physicists.

In the 1930s, when Uhlenbeck had become a professor in Ann Arbor, Michigan, and had become a leader in organizing its famous summer schools, he saw to it that Fermi came to lecture there, four times in fact. His 1930 lectures[10] on quantum electrodynamics, edited by Uhlenbeck, played an important role in the early spreading of quantum field theory. George has told me that Fermi had prepared himself for lecturing in English by taking a course at a Berlitz school in Rome, thus acquiring fluency which, however, was not quite accent-free. 'Finite' became 'feeneetay.' When a lecturer asked about something being infinite, Fermi did not understand and Uhlenbeck had to explain. 'Ah,' Fermi smiled, 'infeeneetay.' At another summer school, the two men collaborated on a study of one-quantum annihilation, $e^+ + e^- \rightarrow \gamma$, if the electron is bound to a nucleus.[11]

Let us return to Rome. Uhlenbeck's contacts with Fermi caused him to stay in touch with the sciences during his Italian period. Yet they receded from the center of his attention. He became deeply involved in history, especially cultural history. He became a regular visitor of the Nederlandsch Historisch Instituut in Rome; befriended a Dutch contemporary, Johan Quiryn van Regteren Altena (who later became a professor of art history in Amsterdam, and was the first Erasmus professor at Harvard); and studied the works of Johan Huizinga, a professor in Leiden, and other cultural historians. The first article Uhlenbeck ever published is historical and is written in Dutch.[12] It deals with the Dutchman Johannes Heckius, one of the four cofounders of the Academia dei Lincei in Rome, in 1603.

Later, Uhlenbeck has said about his digression into history:

> I got *completely* dissociated from physics; I didn't do any physics at all because I didn't know anything. The second year at Rome I still had contact with Fermi but not later and the people I saw were all of another direction. So somehow the study of physics disappeared and I didn't do anything for a whole year, no reading. I, of course, had my job to do which was relatively simple but I read all kinds of Jacob Burckhardt and Theodor Mommsen and history of art—I had a very good friend who was an art historian with whom I went around—and all kinds of things for a whole year, you see. So at the end I didn't know if I should do it at all? Thank God, the one thing that kept me back was that I didn't know Latin and Greek and it was clear that if I wanted to do history—which I wanted at that moment mainly through the influence of the books of Huizinga which I then thought were so magnificent that that was really the thing to do—I had to learn that.[2]

When Uhlenbeck left Rome for good to return to Holland, in mid-June 1925, he was seriously considering giving up physics to become a historian. He called on Huizinga in Leiden, who gave him a friendly reception; and he discussed the matter with his uncle, the distinguished linguist Christianus Cornelius Uhlenbeck, a professor of Sanskrit and comparative linguistics at Leiden, and an expert on Eskimo and Blackfoot Indian languages.

> I still remember that I talked with my uncle [he was actually a cousin of his father] about it; he thought very highly of Huizinga and was a colleague of his at Leiden. He said, 'Ja, that is very fine; of course, that is very profound stuff, but you have to learn Latin and Greek.' So I started to learn Latin; I took lessons in it as soon as I came back but my uncle said, 'Try anyway also to see whether you can still get a PhD in physics because that sounds, so to speak, more practical.' And that's why I went to Ehrenfest and Ehrenfest said, 'All right.'[2]

Ehrenfest responded benevolently to George's history projects but suggested that he first find out what was currently happening in physics. He proposed that Uhlenbeck work with him for a while, and also that he learn from Goudsmit what was going on in *Spektralzoologie*, as Pauli used to call the study of spectra. Uhlenbeck accepted both suggestions, at the same time arranging for lessons in Latin from a friend in The Hague. His work with Ehrenfest on wave equations in multidimensional spaces (with special emphasis on the differences between odd and even numbers of spatial dimensions) led to a mathematical paper,[13] followed by a joint paper with Ehrenfest.[14] Uhlenbeck enjoyed this collaboration. So did Ehrenfest, who in the fall of 1925 appointed him to succeed the mathematician Dirk Struik as his assistant, a post he was to hold for two years.

Throughout the summer of 1925 Goudsmit came to the Lübeckstraat in The Hague, in the house where George's parents were living, to educate Uhlenbeck in spectra. In his later years Uhlenbeck would refer to this period as the 'Goudsmit summer.' 'In that fall I still started to learn Latin, but very soon it was far too difficult for me and I had so many things to do that I never even went over the hump with Latin, and the whole thing disappeared.'[2]

The main reason for that change of mind was that, in mid-September 1925, doctorandus Uhlenbeck and graduate student Goudsmit discovered spin. Gone were Uhlenbeck's aspirations to become a historian.

The discovery of spin

Samuel Abraham Goudsmit—'Sem' to his friends—was born in 1902 in The Hague, the son of a prosperous wholesale dealer in bathroom fixtures. His mother owned a fashionable hat shop. He got his first taste of physics at the age of 11 when browsing through an elementary physics text; he was particularly struck by a passage explaining how spectroscopy shows that stars are composed of the same elements as the Earth. As Goudsmit recalled, 'Hydrogen in the sun and iron in the Big Dipper made Heaven seem cozy and attainable.'[15] After finishing high school in one year less than the usual time, he became a physics student in Leiden, where Ehrenfest turned his interest into devotion. It soon became evident that he had a bent for intuitive, rather than analytical, thinking, starting from empirical hunches. Uhlenbeck later said of Goudsmit: 'Sem was never a conspicuously reflective man, but he had an amazing talent for taking random data and giving them direction. He's a wizard at cryptograms.'[15] I. I. Rabi said: 'He thinks like a detective. He is a detective.'[15] In fact, Goudsmit once took an eight-month course in detective work, in which he learned to identify fingerprints, forgeries, and bloodstains. A two-year university course taught him to decipher hieroglyphics. In physics the decoding of spectra became his passion. At age 19 he completed his first paper, on alkali doublets.[16] Uhlenbeck called it 'a most presumptuous display of self-confidence but . . . highly creditable.'[15]

> Sem was not a dutiful student. He never could do exams. He had not even done his doctorandus exam, which I had done already a few years ago. This was because he was so afraid of the professor in mechanics. That's a very interesting sidelight. Finally we had to push him through his doctorandus exam. Ehrenfest was only finally able to do that by letting him drop mathematics or, rather, mechanics as a minor. But he had to have two minors, so he took experimental physics and astrophysics as his two minors. This was of course at that time very strange, because as a result he was not allowed to teach mechanics or mathematics in the Dutch high schools. Of course as soon as he was in Ann Arbor, he was the one who always gave the course in theoretical mechanics . . . He did it always with great pleasure. I

always kidded him that he had no right to teach it. According to the Dutch law he was not allowed to teach mechanics. Anyway, he had already published several papers. He knew Heisenberg and Hund, and he knew all the spectroscopy of course very well . . . That was his specialty. Especially this kind of formal business, this looking with the help of numbers through the experimental material, and getting some regularities out. In that he was really a past master.[17]

On Sem's first visit to Copenhagen, Niels Bohr took him to the collection of Egyptian sculpture at the Glyptotek museum. As Bohr started to translate the Danish labels, Sem quietly told him that this was not necessary; he could read the inscribed hieroglyphics.

In August 1925 the two men started their regular meetings in The Hague. However, 'Goudsmit was not with me all the time that fall. I was assistant of Ehrenfest, Goudsmit was assistant of Pieter Zeeman in Amsterdam. He was three days of the week in Amsterdam, and then he always came to Leiden for the colloquium and stayed also a few days in Leiden.'[17] Their collaboration continued, meanwhile. George was the more analytic one, better versed in theoretical physics, a greenhorn in physics research and an aspiring historian with a paper on Heckius to his credit. Sem was the detective, thoroughly at home with spectra (on which he had already published several papers), and known in the physics community. In almost no time Sem's tutelage of George turned into joint research and publication, and their relationship into a close and lasting friendship. I know, more from my own later personal friendships with both than from their writings,[18, 19, 20, 21] how each remained forever beholden to the other for his share of the work during those months. There was no politesse, but deep appreciation.

Among the topics that Sem taught George that summer was Alfred Landé's theory of the anomalous Zeeman effect, those splittings of spectral lines that do not follow the patterns predicted much earlier by Lorentz on the basis of classical theory. In 1921 Landé had found it possible to explain those anomalies by the new and quite daring assumption that angular momentum quantum numbers can take on half-integer values. Sem went on to tell the story: how Werner Heisenberg, in his first published paper, had gone further by proposing that in alkalis the valence electron and the residual atomic *Rumpf*, the core, each have angular momentum ½ (in units of $h/2\pi$). How Landé then deduced from this that g, the gyromagnetic ratio, should have the value 2 for the core instead of 1, the classical prediction. How next Pauli had shown that the core had to have zero angular momentum. How he, Sem, had written that Landé's $g = 2$ is 'completely incomprehensible' but that, using this assumption, one nevertheless 'masters completely the extensive and complicated material of the anomalous Zeeman effect.'[22] How Pauli thereupon—we are now in January 1925—had proposed to assign a new, a fourth, half-integer-valued quantum number, not to the core but to the electron itself. And how Pauli was thereby led to the discovery of the exclusion principle.

Another subject Sem taught George was Arnold Sommerfeld's formula for the fine structure of the hydrogen spectrum: how it worked very well, how there was no problem with the Zeeman effect that experimentally appeared to be (but of course was not) normal at that time.

George was unhappy. 'He knew nothing; he asked all those questions which I never asked,' Goudsmit would later recall.[18] Why two distinct models if the alkalis and hydrogen were so much alike? Why not try the half-integer quantum numbers on hydrogen as well? When I once asked Uhlenbeck what on earth possessed him in thinking so at that time, he replied that they were just guessing, and reminded me that playing with half-integer values for quantum numbers had been done earlier, for the Zeeman effect. He also told me that Ehrenfest looked dubious when they told him about this idea but suggested that they write a little note—which they did. It was their first joint paper,[23] an excellent contribution but little known because it was written in Dutch. In it they modified the quantum number assignments Sommerfeld had given earlier and reported an improved treatment of the He^+ fine structure. Uhlenbeck called it the August paper.

Goudsmit wrote about what happened next: 'Our luck was that the idea [of spin] arose just at the moment when we were saturated with a thorough knowledge of the structure of atomic spectra, had grasped the meaning of relativistic doublets, and just after we had arrived at the correct interpretation of the hydrogen atom.'[19] Uhlenbeck recalled: 'It was then that it occurred to me that, since (as I had learned) each quantum number corresponds to a degree of freedom of the electron, Pauli's fourth quantum number must mean that the electron had an additional degree of freedom—in other words the electron must be rotating!'[20]

Everything fell into place. The electron had spin ½. Landé's $g = 2$ does not apply to the core but to the electron itself!

Sem asked whether this g value could be given a physical meaning.[20] Following a hint by Ehrenfest, George found in an old article by Max Abraham[24] that an electron considered as a rigid sphere with only surface charge does have $g = 2$. All this was written up in a short note[25] that includes the Abraham model, but with a caveat: if that model were the explanation of $g = 2$, then the peripheral rotational velocity should be much larger than the velocity of light, assuming the electron to be an extended object with 'classical radius' e^2/mc^2.

That last comment is quite important. It makes clear that the discovery of spin, made after Heisenberg had already published the first paper on quantum mechanics, is an advance in the spirit of the *old* quantum theory, that wonderfully bizarre mixture of classical reasoning supplemented by *ad hoc* quantum rules.

At the Kamerlingh Onnes Laboratory in Leiden, 1926. Uhlenbeck is at the far left. Goudsmit is at the far right, next to Kramers. Ehrenfest is at the right, rear, next to his wife. Paul Dirac is the one in the dark coat at the left. (Courtesy of American Institute of Physics, Niels Bohr Library, Uhlenbeck Collection.)

The discovery was published with Uhlenbeck as first author and Goudsmit as second because (George told me) Ehrenfest suggested that this order would avoid the impression that George was only Sem's student, while Sem himself preferred to come second because it was George who had first thought of spin.

The discovery note is dated October 17, 1925. One day earlier Ehrenfest had written to Lorentz asking him for an opportunity to have 'his judgment and advice on a *very* witty idea of Uhlenbeck about spectra.'[26]

> Lorentz was retired already. He was in charge of the Teyler Institute in Haarlem which was a kind of retirement job . . . He lived in Haarlem, but he came every Monday to Leiden and he gave a lecture from 11 to 12 Monday morning. It was the Monday morning lecture of Lorentz. There you had to go. Ehrenfest simply drove you to it. People came from all over. Lorentz there talked always about his recent work or recent literature. They were always very beautiful, beautiful lectures. Anyway, that was why he came to Leiden.
>
> One of these Monday mornings then we saw Lorentz and told him about this idea. Lorentz was not discouraging. He was a little bit reticent. He said that it was interesting and that he would think about it. He immediately, of course, knew about Abraham, and he also then thought he should do some calculations about it. And he did. It was so typical of Lorentz, that he immediately made very extensive calculations on the classical theory of rotating electrons. I think already the next week, but maybe two weeks later, he gave me such a stack of papers with long calculations. Large white paper, I still remember. He tried to explain it to us—to me, but it was so learned for us that I—by the way, he published these things. It was the last thing Lorentz published. It was his contribution to the Como Congress, in September 1927.[27]
>
> The only thing which was clear out of his explanation, the only thing I really remember, is that he pointed out this famous difficulty, that the magnetic energy would be too large. Lorentz' point was that the spinning electron should have a magnetic energy on the order of μ^2/r^3, where μ is its magnetic moment and r its radius. Equate this energy to mc^2. Then r would be on the order of 10^{-12} cm, too big to make sense. [The weak point in this argument was to be revealed years later by the positron theory.]
>
> And so we told it to Ehrenfest, and that I still very well remember. We told it to Ehrenfest. Lorentz was, of course, the god nearly, also for Ehrenfest, and certainly for everyone in Holland—the absolute authority. 'Lorentz has shown us that this is nonsense.' And so we said to Ehrenfest, 'We'd better not publish that note.' And then Ehrenfest said 'I have sent it away already weeks ago and it will appear next week!' And then he said to us—I don't know whether Sem remembers, but I remember—'Well, *Sie beide sind jung; Sie können sich eine Dummheit leisten!*' [You are both young, you can afford a stupidity.[17]]

No sooner had George and Sem's note appeared when Goudsmit received a letter from Heisenberg congratulating him on his '*mutige Note* [brave note]' and inquiring '*wie Sie den Faktor 2 losgeworden sind* [how you have got rid of the factor 2]' in the formula for the fine-structure splitting in hydrogen as derived from a semiclassical treatment of spin precession.[28] The young Leideners had not even thought of calculating this splitting. After some struggle they found that Heisenberg was right: the fine structure came out too large by a factor of 2. That puzzle was still unresolved when, in December 1925, Niels Bohr arrived in Leiden to attend the festivities for the golden jubilee of Lorentz' doctorate. 'Bohr came and he always stayed at Ehrenfest's house.'[17] Late one evening in 1946, Bohr told me in his home in Gamle Carlsberg what happened to him on that trip.

Bohr's train trip

Bohr's train to Leiden made a stop in Hamburg, where he was met by Wolfgang Pauli and Otto Stern, who had come to the station to ask him what he thought about spin. Bohr must have said that it was very interesting (his favorite way of expressing his belief that something was wrong) but he could not see how an electron moving in the electric field of the nucleus could experience the magnetic field necessary for producing fine structure. (As Uhlenbeck admitted later, 'I must say in retrospect that Sem and I in our euphoria had not really appreciated [this] basic difficulty.'[20]) On his arrival in Leiden, Bohr was met at the train by Ehrenfest and Albert Einstein, who asked him what he thought about spin. Bohr must have said that it was very, very interesting but what about the magnetic field? Ehrenfest replied that Einstein had resolved that. The electron in its rest frame sees a rotating electric field; hence by elementary relativity it also sees a magnetic field. The net result is an effective spin–orbit coupling.

Bohr was at once convinced.

> We talked then with Bohr really very long—whole mornings . . . I remember that I talked with him about what Lorentz had said. He said: 'This is of course not classical, and so one has not to think of it in those terms! He was, of course, worried. He always worried about difficulties, but he had such a feeling that that was the answer to many of these difficulties . . . We also told him about Heisenberg's calculation and the factor two and so on.[17]

Bohr urged Sem and George to write a more detailed note on their work. They did, in a Letter to *Nature*[29] to which Bohr added an approving comment. 'I think with regard to the *Nature* Letter, in my memory, he essentially wrote it . . . We did very little with it . . . but the style of that Letter is essentially Bohr. My memory is that I certainly didn't write one word of that Letter.'[17]

After Leiden, Bohr traveled to Göttingen. There he was met at the station by Heisenberg and Pascual Jordan, who asked what he thought about spin. Bohr replied that it was a great advance and explained about the spin–orbit coupling. Heisenberg remarked that he had heard this remark before but that he could not remember who made it and when. (I will return to this point shortly.) On

Bohr's way home the train stopped at Berlin, where he was met at the station by Pauli, who had made the trip from Hamburg for the sole purpose of asking Bohr what he now thought about spin. Bohr said it was a great advance, to which Pauli replied, '*Eine neue Kopenhagener Irrlehre*' (a new Copenhagen heresy). After his return home Bohr wrote to Ehrenfest that he had become 'a prophet of the electron magnet gospel.'[30]

I conclude the spin story with a few scattered comments.

1   'At the Lorentz Jubilee a Lorentz fellowship was created, and Sem was one of the first Lorentz fellows. [He went to Copenhagen] and there he worked, unfortunately not successfully, with Bohr, on the helium spectrum . . . But at that time, when he was there Thomas was also in Copenhagen. Thomas had this factor two. That paper of his was so learned at that time. He was also such a remarkable man—he gave, then, a speech about it in Leiden. I still remember it very well, because he couldn't write on the blackboard. It was just physically impossible for him to write on the blackboard. Everything came out so large. It was very remarkable. Kramers then also tried to simplify it very much. Anyway, we were able to simplify it sufficiently—Sem and me. Then we wrote our third paper on the spin, which is not very well known . . . That paper[31] appeared again in Dutch.'[17]

It was Llewellyn Hilleth Thomas who in February 1926 supplied[32] the mysterious factor 2, which has since been known as the Thomas factor. Thomas noted that earlier calculations of the precession of the electron's spin had been performed in the rest frame of the electron, without taking into account the precession of the electron's orbit around its normal. Inclusion of this relativistic effect reduced the angular velocity of the electron (as seen by the nucleus) by the needed factor of 2. 'Even the cognoscenti of the relativity theory (Einstein included!) were quite surprised.'[20] On February 20, 1926, Bohr wrote[33] almost identical letters to Heisenberg and Pauli. 'We have felt it as a minor triumph . . . that at least the difficulties with the much discussed factor two seem to be only apparent . . . Thomas, a young Englishman who has been here the last six months . . . has discovered that the calculations made so far probably contain an error.'

2   Concerning precursors. Already in 1900, FitzGerald had raised the question of whether magnetism is due to rotation of electrons.[34] In 1921 Arthur Compton had a similar idea: 'It is the electron rotating about its axis which is responsible for the ferromagnetism . . . The electron itself, spinning like a tiny gyroscope, is probably the ultimate magnetic particle.'[35] The same proposal was made in 1922 by Kennard,[36] who made a calculation identical to Abraham's[24] (of which he was unaware) to show that an electron could have $g = 2$. In all these instances electrons were pictured as rotating rigid bodies of finite extent, in Compton's case with quantized angular momentum.

3   In August 1924 (before the fourth quantum number and the exclusion principle) Pauli had proposed[37] an explanation of hyperfine structure: 'The nucleus possesses

in general a non-vanishing angular momentum . . . In the future one might hope to learn something [from this hypothesis] about the structure of nuclei.' I have heard it said that this was the first suggestion of spin. With all appreciation for this nice paper by Pauli, I cannot agree. Pauli himself said later about this paper: 'Already in 1924 before the electron spin was discovered I proposed to use the assumption of nuclear spin . . . [which] influenced Goudsmit and Uhlenbeck in their claim of an electron spin.'[38] It seems to me that Pauli's use of the term nuclear spin is but one of untold many examples of an adaptation of language to later usage. As to the influence on the discovery of electron spin, Goudsmit has written: 'We were not aware of this paper till five years later.'[39] For a more detailed discussion of the issue see ref. 40.

4   In March 1926 Kramers received a letter from America written[41] by Ralph Kronig, a young Columbia University PhD who had spent two years studying in Europe, including a stay in Copenhagen from January to November 1925. Kronig reminded Kramers that, prior to Goudsmit and Uhlenbeck, he, Kronig, already had the idea of spin, though he too was missing the factor 2 in the fine structure; and that he and Kramers had discussed these matters in Copenhagen. Heisenberg's hazy recollection, mentioned a few lines earlier, of having heard part of the spin story before must refer to a discussion with Kronig. Returning to Kronig's letter, he told Kramers that he had not published because 'Pauli ridiculed the idea, saying "that is indeed very clever but of course has nothing to do with reality."' And added: 'In the future I shall trust my own judgment more and that of others less.'

After Kramers had told this story to Bohr, the latter wrote to Kronig, expressing his 'consternation and deep regret.'[42] Kronig replied: 'I should not have mentioned the matter at all [to Kramers] if it were not to take a fling at the physicists of the preaching variety, who are always so damned sure of, and inflated with, the correctness of their own opinion.'[43] He asked Bohr to refrain from public reference to the affair since 'Goudsmit and Uhlenbeck would hardly be very happy about it.' Kronig was an eminent physicist and a gentleman. So was Uhlenbeck who has written: 'There is no doubt that Ralph Kronig anticipated what certainly was the main part of our ideas.'[20] It is certain that it was because of this episode that no Nobel Prize for spin was ever awarded.[44] I like Thomas' comment to Goudsmit[18] on Pauli's role in this affair: '[It] goes to show that the infallibility of the Deity does not extend to his self-styled vicar on earth.'

On the evening in Carlsberg, when Bohr reminisced about his train trip in 1925, he also told me this Kronig story. I recall well how I said to Bohr that I felt great pity for Kronig. I have never forgotten Bohr's reply, which came as a shock to me at that time. He said, verbatim: 'No, Kronig was a fool,' explaining that in his opinion one should publish when one is convinced of one's ideas, never mind what anybody else says. I have never recorded publicly Bohr's statement, out of consideration for Kronig, who has recently passed away, however. I now believe that I should speak up about Bohr's comment, since it has certainly been a lesson for me and may be likewise for others. It has become my own belief that in the final analysis only the published record should decide.

It has happened before and will happen again that destinies will be affected by the choice between submitting to authority and going one's own way. It has happened before and will happen again that debates will arise about priorities of unpublished material. In the case of spin it should be added that others also had the idea without publishing: Harold Urey for the electron,[45] Bose (in 1924) for the photon.

First meetings with Pauli, Klein, Oppenheimer

The Uhlenbeck–Goudsmit paper on spin was submitted in October 1925, three months after Heisenberg's first paper on quantum mechanics (July 1925), and three months before Schrödinger's first paper on wave mechanics. At the time spin appeared,

> We knew about the first Heisenberg paper but [his use of matrices] was complete-ly—at least to me—completely strange . . . [But] everything which Heisenberg did had to be taken seriously, because Heisenberg, Pauli, and, of course, Bohr, were the gods. They were the people who knew everything . . . And that changed with Schrödinger[3] . . . In the spring of 1926, Ehrenfest and I worked extremely hard on the Schrödinger equation.[46]

George has told me: 'The Schrödinger equation came as a great relief, now we did not any longer have to learn the strange mathematics of matrices.'

In the spring of 1926, Uhlenbeck made his first wave mechanics calculation, 'but I made a mistake . . . Ehrenfest couldn't see what the error was. He said "You write it all down, nicely," and I wrote it all out. And Ehrenfest sent it off to Pauli with a little footnote: "*Bitte, behandle die Tiere sanft*,"[7] (please treat the animals gently). Which Pauli indeed did.[47]

George's reminiscences in later years about Pauli give us glimpses about the per-sonalities of both men:

> He was really at the bottom a very friendly fellow. He was a man who in his early days always—and it *was* always clear, at least to me—tried to see whether a person had an area of sensitivity. If he found it, then he pushed, certainly. If he didn't find it, well, then he looked at you. He always said something, and then he looked at you to see whether that hit something or not. I always had to laugh because I saw that he wanted to do that. I remember in Ann Arbor when I told him, 'ja,' I was working on Brownian motion. Pauli remarked: 'Desperation physics! Typical des-peration physics!' Then he looked at me. I said, '*Es ist schon wahr, es ist schon wahr*' [It is no doubt true]. Then he saw that I was completely untouched by it because I realized that it was so. So afterwards he said to [my wife], 'Ja, ja, that Uhlenbeck, such a *Starken*' [tough one], because he couldn't get my goat. He was a charming man.[7]

Until Pauli's death, the two men continued to have great respect for each other.[48] In the 1930s they corresponded on scientific issues.[49]

Then—that was very important—Oskar Klein came to Leiden on a Lorentz fellowship.'[3] Klein was a Swedish physicist, then in his early thirties. 'We stayed in the same rooming house . . . We had, all the time, these discussions with Klein. Every afternoon . . . He had written down what now is called the Klein-Gordon wave equation . . . Then he had also these ideas about five-dimensional relativity,[50] and we discussed about that. It was very interesting . . . I wrote a paper with Ehrenfest on this five-dimensional stuff[14] . . . and I still remember one time after these discussions . . . Klein told how out of that quantum conditions could come. You see, from the periodicity conditions in the fifth dimension you got the quantum conditions. And I was so excited. I told them, 'Very soon we [will have] the world formalized. We will know everything!' Well, it was a beautiful exaggeration . . . Ehrenfest was much more skeptical than I was . . . The feeling that one knew everything that of course I'm sure he didn't have. I mean that was more the younger generation which got this feeling.[3]

The time had now come for Uhlenbeck to write his Doctor's dissertation.

It was clear that I would never write a dissertation if I stayed in Leiden. And then he sent me off with a Lorentz fellowship. He said now you go to Copenhagen and there you write your dissertation. And Sem was there then too, and then for two months we did essentially nothing else but writing. That was all. It was high pressure. Boy was it high pressure, writing this dissertation. And the last day of the academic year—it was already all arranged, Ehrenfest had made the dates fixed, so it had to be printed, and a correction had to be read, and the whole book had to be read—well, it all came through.[46]

The records of Bohr's Institute show that he was in Copenhagen from April till June 1927. I shall turn presently to the contents of George's PhD thesis.

'I was in Göttingen [we are still in 1927] after I wrote my dissertation.'[7] It was there that Uhlenbeck heard of the first attempt, by Pauli, to build spin into quantum mechanics, by means of introducing 'the intrinsic angular momentum [i.e. the spin] of the electron in a fixed direction as a new variable.'[51]

It was very profound really, because it was a big step to go from the scalar [one-component] wave function to the two-component wave function. I remember that I studied that paper very hard, and it was very clearly written. Except that it was so full of these transformations of these wave functions—the Cayley parameters as I remember, which, of course Pauli knew. It sounded profound to me, and difficult too. Although again, it was that it was so clear that afterwards you could use it. Many people did of course . . . Pauli told me that he never thought that that was such an important paper, afterwards. But he says: 'Ja, es war viel wichtiger als ich dachte' [It was much more important than I thought.] He has told me that.[7]

Also in Göttingen, George met Robert Oppenheimer for the first time.

He was, so to say, clearly a center of all the younger students. In the early Oppenheimer period he was really a kind of oracle. He knew very much. He was very difficult to understand, but very quick, and with a whole group of admirers. Robert was really one of the leaders there among the younger students. He had done, I think, his degree with Born, maybe half a year before. Again the one that appreciated it immediately was Pauli. He was the only one who understood it. I doubt that Born understood it properly because it was really very complicated.[7]

After Göttingen, both Uhlenbeck and Oppenheimer went to Leiden.

I stayed in Leiden for about a month together with Oppenheimer. He was, for a while, assistant to Ehrenfest . . . Oppenheimer liked Ehrenfest, and he was very patient, very patient. Ehrenfest didn't understand Oppenheimer at all well, but he at least was willing to try. He was very patient. Only the people who were so clever and didn't want to talk further about it or try to make it clear were of the type that Ehrenfest couldn't stand. Robert wasn't like that, although he was certainly not always patient with people. Then he was. Yes. That's why he had so many students. The impatient Oppenheimer was the post-War Oppenheimer. He was quite different before the War.[7]

On July 7, 1927, Uhlenbeck received his Doctor's degree on a thesis dealing with issues in statistical mechanics.[52] One hour later, Goudsmit also received his degree, on topics in atomic spectra.

We got the degree the same day. Ehrenfest wanted that. He said, you must do it on the same day, because at the dissertation the professor is always supposed to give a speech about the students. And he says he did not want to give two speeches. He wanted to modulate it a little bit, first the one and then the other. This was also not quite kosher for the Dutch tradition. They didn't like it. Ehrenfest, of course, was so un-Dutch in many respects. And I remember that our dissertations—the dissertation is always defense of thesis . . . You have always these assertions, at the end. That's typical Dutch method. And that gives really maybe something to talk about. And that lasts only about half an hour or forty minutes . . . Then, the faculty goes out and afterwards they come in again. It is given to you with the speech. So I think Sem was the first. No, I was the first. And then Ehrenfest said, 'You go out, you go out, and we take Sem.' And then at the end, I still see us sitting next to each other in front of this whole row of professors. And then Ehrenfest made the speech to both of us.[3]

On that promotion day, both young men already knew that instructorships were waiting for them in Ann Arbor, Michigan.

That was already settled, that was settled in the spring . . . Ehrenfest was responsible that we got it. That was marvelous, because as a result we didn't have to do high school teaching. You see we had immediately a place where there was at least a university. The way that came about—I still remember. Walter Colby, from Ann Arbor, was then in Europe, looking around really for people for Ann Arbor to succeed Oskar Klein, who was also two years in Ann Arbor, I think. There he discovered the wave equation. Colby came to Ehrenfest, and we were also present. Ehrenfest gave him an impassioned speech, in which he said that this was a very bad idea, to try to get one man to Ann Arbor. Because that was—nobody there—that was just wilderness—you must at least have two, he says, otherwise they have nobody to talk to. Even better, more than two. And he was very serious. He could talk so seriously about how science develops. He made an enormous impression on Colby. We walked home with him, and he says 'Yes, he's a great man. He's really a great man.' As a result, two or three weeks later, we got both an appointment to Michigan as an instructor. And we both accepted.[3]

On August 23, 1927, George married Else Ophorst, a chemistry student in Leiden. In 1942 their son, Olke Cornelis ('Okkie') was born. He is now a distinguished biochemist, a member of the US National Academy of Sciences.

On one of the last days of that August, George and Else, as well as Sem and his wife, boarded the *S. S. Baltic*.

> On arrival in New York, Oppenheimer [who had returned to the United States in mid-July] was at the dock, with his father's car and uniformed chauffeur, to welcome them. He took the Uhlenbecks to their hotel—the Brevoort on lower Fifth Avenue, because he thought they would like its European atmosphere—and to dinner at a hotel in Brooklyn from which they could see the lighted Manhattan skyline. Robert persuaded the Uhlenbecks to delay their departure for Ann Arbor in order to meet his parents at tea the next day. Having encountered one novelty in the form of New York stoplights, Else Uhlenbeck had another surprise when they reached Oppenheimer's Riverside Drive apartment. 'What a very large house,' she thought as they went up in the elevator, for tall apartment houses were unknown in Holland. Because her English was still poor, her impressions of this first, but by no means last, experience of Oppenheimer hospitality were largely visual—the beautifully furnished living room, the Van Gogh and other paintings.[53]

In September 1927, Uhlenbeck and Goudsmit arrived in Ann Arbor, to start their academic careers.

Goudsmit's later years

Sem has so far appeared as a main character in this story. He will also return briefly on the scene later, but more as a member of the supporting cast. It seems fitting, therefore, to give at this point a very brief sketch of his later years. I am sure that this would have pleased George. The two men remained warm friends until Sem's death.[54]

In Ann Arbor, Sem produced some fine PhD students. He published two books in those years, one[55] (together with Robert Bacher, a student), another[56] with Linus Pauling. During the Second World War he was detailed to the army on a scientific intelligence mission, code named Alsos (Greek for Groves, the name of the military commander of Los Alamos), to find out how far the Germans had progressed with producing atomic bombs, about which he wrote a widely read book.[57] In 1948 he came to Brookhaven National Laboratory, where he remained until his retirement in 1970. From 1952 to 1960 he was chairman of its physics department, from 1951 to 1974 editor-in-chief of the American Physical Society's publications. In 1958 he founded the since renowned *Physical Review Letters*, about which he had many good stories, such as the case of a manuscript received which was followed by a telegram: 'I am worried about equation two.'

During Sem's tenure at Brookhaven, I spent many six-week summer periods there as a visiting physicist. It was during those times that I came to know Sem really well and got some insights into his complex personality. I found him riddled with a sense of inferiority and insecurity. It is my guess that this was due to the fact that he never felt he knew enough theoretical physics—remember, he was more like a 'detective' in physics. None of which has ever detracted from my respect and warm feelings of friendship for him. He did receive his share of honors, however. For example, I was with George and Sem in Düsseldorf when, in 1965, the two men received the Max Planck Medal of the German Physical Society.

In 1974 Sem was appointed distinguished visiting professor at the University of Nevada, in Reno. It was there that, on December 4, 1978, he died on campus. The request in his will that no memorial service be held for him was typical of his self-effacing ways.

Uhlenbeck and statistical mechanics

About half the number of George's publications, nearly 100 in all, deal with statistical physics, the relation between the atomic world and the macroscopic world. In his oration, spoken when, in 1955, he became the Lorentz professor in Leiden—the first to hold this honorary short-term position—we read what had drawn him to that subject: 'The majority of the lacunae in physics is made up out of unsolved problems in statistical physics . . . To me the great charms of statistical physics lies in its connection with parts of mathematics with which otherwise one comes rarely in contact.'[58]

I find statistical mechanics one of the most fascinating areas in physics. I am not an expert in that field, however, though George and I once, in 1959, wrote a joint paper on that subject (on the quantum theory of the third virial coefficient[59]) of which I am rather proud. I have been fortunate, however, to have, down the hall from my office in the Rockefeller University, an expert, good friend, and one-time coworker of George on statistical problems, E. G. D. Cohen, whom I have consulted and of whose biographical sketch 'George Uhlenbeck and statistical mechanics'[60] I have made grateful use.

'Already from my early days my main interest was kinetic theory and statistical mechanics,' Uhlenbeck has recalled.[3] His first contribution to those subjects was his Doctor's thesis.[52] For this he was at the right place: Ehrenfest was a recognized expert in statistical physics; and at the right time: in 1927, the year in which he completed his thesis, quantum statistics was in its infancy, as is illustrated by a phrase from his thesis—'For a real gas it is completely uncertain which [quantum] statistics should be preferred.'[61]

At the Einstein centennial conference in Princeton, in 1979, George has recalled[62] the most interesting issue raised in his thesis:

> I started to study in the beginning of 1927 the paper of Einstein in which he claims that an ideal gas like helium would show a condensation phenomena as a consequence of the Bose statistics.[63] This seemed very paradoxical, and to my surprise I came to the conclusion that Einstein was wrong! In my opinion his error was to replace the partition function over the discrete energy levels of the particles by an integral; that was not allowed near the condensation point. The exact formula did not show any kind of singularity, so that, for instance, the equation of state would be quite smooth. I was of course quite excited, especially because Ehrenfest was convinced that I was right when I told him my reasoning. I know that he lectured about it at a few places and also that he wrote a letter to Einstein [which contains the phrase]: When kings are building, then the sewer cleaners have work to do.
>
> In retrospect I think one should say that, although I was technically right, Einstein had somehow intuitively understood that a phase transition like the Bose condensation can occur only for large systems and is a kind of limit property. This should justify the replacement of sums by integrals. Of course Einstein did not prove this! In fact I know from a later conversation with him, in the thirties, that he agreed with my criticism.

The point is that a sharp phase transition can only occur in the so-called thermodynamic limit in which the number N of particles as well as the volume V tend to infinity but such that N/V remains fixed. This view emerged in a morning-long debate that took place during the van der Waals centenary conference in Amsterdam in November 1937. The issue was, does the partition function contain the information necessary to describe a sharp phase transition? The transition implies the existence of analytically distinct parts of isotherms. It was not clear how this could come about. The debate was inconclusive, and Kramers, the chairman, put the question to a vote. Uhlenbeck recalls that the ayes and nays were about evenly divided. However, Kramers' suggestion to go to the thermodynamic limit was eventually realized to be the correct answer. Shortly afterwards, Uhlenbeck withdrew his objections to Einstein's result, in a joint paper with his gifted student Boris Kahn.[64]

The problem of Bose–Einstein (BE) condensation stayed with George all his life. In the 1970s it led to papers on superfluid helium.[65] He did not live long enough to witness the experimental verification[66] of BE condensation, in 1995.

A full account of George's further labors in statistical physics could easily fill a book, modest in size perhaps, but rich in content. I shall content myself here with a brief synopsis.

Brownian motion. This includes one of the two papers Uhlenbeck and Goudsmit co-authored in the post-Leiden years,[67] and the classic paper with Ornstein, another Dutchman.[68] See ref. 69 for his seminal review of 1945. Twenty-five years later he came back to this subject.[70]

The classical theory of condensation, began with his work together with Kahn,[71] continued through the following 20 years,[72] and led him to detailed studies of the mathematics of linear graphs.[73] This line of study came to an end with his beautiful papers on the van der Waals equation of state,[74] the subject of his inaugural address in 1964 as the van der Waals guest professor—again the first—in Amsterdam.[75] Another example of his work in classical physics is the paper on heat conductivity.[76]

Of his later work in quantum statistics I mention his work on the second[77] and third[59] virial coefficient; on the quantum theory of transport phenomena;[78] and on quantized vortices in helium II.[79] George was also a master in applying statistical methods to areas outside conventional statistical mechanics: to the calculation of the density of nuclear energy levels;[80] to fluctuations of cosmic ray showers;[81] to the dispersion of sound in helium;[82] to shockwaves.[83] He also co-authored a book on threshold signals.[84]

This incomplete summary, meant to illustrate Uhlenbeck's versatility in dealing with statistical physics, does not yet convey, however, his deepest interest, which concerned the fundamental issues of statistical mechanics. These are most particularly the mathematical and logical problems that arise in the study of the connection between the reversible (in time) atomic and the irreversible macroscopic phenomena. He coined the term 'Zeroth law of thermodynamics' to denote that a closed macroscopic system will always tend to equilibrium and stay there. To him, the *approach* to equilibrium rather than equilibrium itself was the central problem of statistical mechanics. Several papers and lecture notes deal with his work and views on this question.[85]

When, more recently, important new concepts bearing on statistical physics were developed, such as renormalization group methods, scaling laws, universality classes, Uhlenbeck did not participate, in fact he tended to reject them. Cohen has written:

> He was one of those great examples of a man caught on the verge of a transition of one age to a new one . . . He felt not only the heir but the guardian of a tradition [which] he jealously guarded, setting, in doing so, an inimitable standard of probity in statistical mechanics . . . He educated several generations of physicists

in statistical mechanics in a style rare in this century . . . [His papers] were of a classic nobility.[60]

With the exception of his thesis, all of Uhlenbeck's work in statistics and mechanics was done after he had left Leiden. It is therefore time to catch up with his peregrinations.

Ann Arbor to Utrecht and back. My first encounters

Ehrenfest had urged George and Sem to go to Ann Arbor.

> He said: 'Of course you should go there; all the younger people who are really good should go away, and then you should afterwards come back if they want to make you professors somewhere.' That was, so to speak, another theme of Ehrenfest's; he thought you should send them all away and then you could call them back, but the last one didn't happen, of course.[2]

George's early impressions about Ann Arbor:

> Well, we were on the outskirts, we were in the provinces, that was very clear. In one respect it was very nice because you were *not* in a center—nowhere in America, not only in Ann Arbor. The only feeling of being in the center again was during the summer schools because of all the people who came.'[2] Be it remembered that Ann Arbor was the first place in America, perhaps anywhere, to have a physics summer school. 'Randall [Harrison Randall, at one time head of the physics department] started it and there also was a summer school before we came, but as soon as we came, then it became really quite a center of activity of the department. Of course, Ehrenfest came, and Fermi, Kramers, Pauli, Sommerfeld, Dirac, and everybody came; then, of course, the summers were extremely busy and you worked very hard because you went to the lectures, too, but at the same time, you had to *give* lectures because that was, so to speak, the way it was set up. Then, of course, during the fall you started to digest what happened during the summer.[2]

The summer schools have continued. I lectured there (on quantum field theory) in 1950. That time I met Mark Kac, a distinguished mathematician, friend and collaborator of Uhlenbeck. George has told me a story of the 1931 school, when Pauli attended a lecture by Oppenheimer on the still rather controversial Dirac equation. In the middle of that talk Pauli stood up, marched to the blackboard, and grabbed a piece of chalk. There he stood, facing the board, waving the chalk in his hand, then said: '*Ach nein, das ist ja alles falsch,*' . . . all that is wrong anyway. Kramers commanded his friend Pauli to hear the speaker out. Pauli walked back and sat down.

———————

In Uhlenbeck's early Michigan years, 'The center was still Europe. That's also why Randall said we had to go to Europe every two years and he convinced the administration of that: that's what I also did. Then really the shift came when I

Uhlenbeck with Hendrik Kramers and Goudsmit in Ann Arbor, Michigan, around 1928.
(Courtesy of American Institute of Physics, Goudsmit Collection.)

went back to Europe because all of the people like Bethe and so on came slowly to this country and, of course, nuclear physics started.'[2]

During the next 20 years George himself contributed some ten articles to this then young branch of physics, beginning in 1934 with two papers, one on bombardment of lithium by protons and deuterons,[86] the other[87] with the challenging title: 'Spontaneous disintegration of proton or neutron according to the Fermi theory,' which shows, first that it was still under debate which of the two is heavier, proton or neutron, secondly, that Uhlenbeck was among the first (perhaps the very first) to apply the Fermi theory of β-radioactivity, published only a few months earlier.[88] Other work includes studies of the role of γ-rays in nuclear physics,[89] on the law of Sargent[90] which relates the decay rate of β-radioactivity to the nuclear charge and the maximum energy released in the process, and on the stability of nuclear isomers.[91] In 1950 he was the first to publish on directional correlations of successive nuclear radiations[92] and on β–γ correlations.[93] I remember Uhlenbeck telling me that, after these papers had come out, experimentalists told him that no such correlations existed but that, stimulated by his work, they soon found them all over the place. I may note here that, in 1952, George wrote his only paper on particle physics, on μ-mesons.[94]

The greatest stir caused by Uhlenbeck's writings on nuclear physics was his 1935 paper[95] jointly with Emil Konopinski, commonly referred to as the KU theory. It deals with a modification of Fermi's theory of β-radioactivity.[88]

That theory gives a prediction for the relative number of electrons emitted as a function of their energy. Fermi had already noted that his proposal gave too few slow electrons. The KU modification, on the other hand, fitted the current data very well, and for the next five years was widely accepted. Uhlenbeck has told me what happened next. Jim Lawson, a young experimentalist, came to see him to tell that all the β-spectra measurements to date were wrong, they had been distorted by secondary effects, in particular by absorption and scattering within the source itself and within its support material. Lawson had shown[96] that thinning the source improved the agreement with the Fermi theory. As a result, the KU theory vanished from the scene.

It has happened before and later that, as in this case, a theoretical idea has been worked out flawlessly but is nevertheless wrong because Nature does not like it. It was typical of George that he accepted reality without regret. In fact, a few years later he and Konopinski wrote a pioneering paper on β-theory, dealing with the classification into allowed and forbidden transitions.[97]

In 1938, when I first met Professor Uhlenbeck, the KU theory was still going strong, however.

In 1933, the year of Ehrenfest's suicide (mentioned earlier), Hendrik Kramers was professor of theoretical physics in Utrecht and the natural choice as successor for the now vacant Leiden chair, which he indeed took over in 1934. Now there was an opening in Utrecht. Uhlenbeck has recalled what happened next: 'After about a year of interregnum in which nobody was [in Utrecht] it was finally offered to me . . . after a long discussion with Kramers . . . who, so to speak, pulled the "duty racket" on me. He said it was my duty to come back to the fatherland in 1935 and I did, although I didn't want to at all.'[2] On March 23, 1936 he gave his inaugural address.[98]

In my undergraduate years in my native Amsterdam I began taking courses in physics, chemistry, and mathematics, in a rather unfocussed way. Then in the winter of 1938 Uhlenbeck came for a visit and gave two lectures on beta decay. I did not understand much. I had not yet heard about neutrinos. Nevertheless, listening to those talks given in a calm yet ever so compelling way I knew, I just knew: that is what I want to do—and I want to do my graduate work with Uhlenbeck.

In February 1938 I obtained my Bachelor degree, after which I wrote right away to Uhlenbeck, asking for an interview. I received a reply, inviting me to come over on a specific day. When the time had come, I took a train to Utrecht and walked from the station to Bÿlhouwerstraat, where the physics laboratory was then situated (it has since moved to other quarters). Uhlenbeck shared one room there with his assistant. I knocked at the door of room 220, went in, was invited to sit down, then told Uhlenbeck of my hopes to become a graduate student in theoretical physics under his guidance.

Uhlenbeck's response was unexpected. 'If you like physics,' he asked, 'why don't you consider becoming an experimentalist? Or if you like the mathematical aspects of theoretical physics, why not become a mathematician?' In explanation he noted that the practical future for a theoretical physicist in the Netherlands was extremely limited, while experimental physics as well as mathematics opened many more possibilities, for example in industry. Furthermore, he added, theoretical physics is very difficult, it would be a life of toil with many frustrations and disappointments.

I was quite taken aback and mumbled, 'But I like theoretical physics so much.' Uhlenbeck's reaction was again unexpected. 'If that is really true,' he said, 'then by all means become a theorist; it is the most wonderful subject you can imagine.' As he later told me, his preliminary attempts at dissuasion were exactly like those he himself had been exposed to when he wanted to start his own graduate studies, adding that he used the same routine whenever anyone applied to study with him.

Having gone through these preliminaries, Uhlenbeck said next that he wanted to tell me about his current research. The subject was cosmic rays, radiations of photons and various other species of particles that come from outer space and are detectable on earth. He outlined the theoretical treatment on the blackboard, while I sat and listened, occasionally asking for more explanations or information, which he patiently provided. Some mathematical tools were new to me, so I had to keep my wits together, following not only the physical reasoning but also the mathematical analysis. I did not do all that badly, but after an hour became tired of the intense discussion. Uhlenbeck imperturbably went on, however. After another hour I was dazed but told myself to hang in there, boy, this is trial by fire. This went on still a bit longer, then the professor stopped, gave me the reference to the paper we had been discussing, told me to study it and come back in two weeks. I sort of staggered out of the room, unable to concentrate on anything but getting back to the train station.

Years later I told Uhlenbeck how that first afternoon with him had affected me. He told me with a smile that he had gone through the very same treatment, had the very same reactions, when he had visited Ehrenfest for the first time. Ehrenfest in turn had received the same treatment from the great Ludwig Boltzmann in Vienna. This tradition is part of teaching in the grand old style, concentrating on but very few students. In my time I was the only student

Uhlenbeck had taken on. Because of that privilege I may count myself as a spiritual great-grandson of Boltzmann. Meanwhile the old style has gone forever, I think, because of the large number of students now clamoring for higher education.

All through the spring term of 1938 I paid regular visits to Uhlenbeck. Then there came a time when he told me that the following term he was taking a leave of absence to become a visiting professor at Columbia University in New York— a disappointment for me.

When Uhlenbeck returned from America, he brought the news about the recently discovered nuclear fission. We had long discussions on this brand-new branch of nuclear physics. He told me of a meeting in Washington he had attended, where Bohr and Fermi had for the first time made public the news about fission, and how American newspapers had immediately picked this up as a piece of sensational news.[99] He also told me of sharing an office at Columbia University's Pupin Laboratory with Fermi, who had just escaped from Italy with his family. (The reason for his flight was that Mussolini's government had recently enacted anti-Semitic laws—and Fermi's wife was of Jewish extraction.) One day, he said, Fermi and he had been discussing fission. Fermi got up, walked to the window, looked out, and said something like: 'Do you realize, George, that fission may make possible the construction of bombs so powerful that just a few of them can destroy this whole big city?' Which goes to show that there was nothing secret about atomic weapons: the issue was obvious to the physicists, and even I, a youngster, at once understood the import.

———————————

Among my assignments for obtaining the Master's degree was giving a few theoretical seminars. My first one was on fission. I was well prepared, I thought, and began my talk, writing formulas on the blackboard as I went along. Uhlenbeck interrupted almost at once: 'First tell us what the problem is,' he said, 'then state your conclusions at once. Only thereafter should you go into details of the derivations.' I followed instructions, but still the professor interrupted me several times with comments like: 'You must explain in simple language, not show how smart you are.' It was a most instructive and illuminating experience, and I have taken it to heart ever since. Uhlenbeck also taught blackboard techniques which, he later told me, he had learned from Ehrenfest, one of the best physics teachers in the early parts of the twentieth century: 'Start on the top left corner, prepare your written comments so that by the end of your talk you are at the right bottom corner. Never, never erase anything while making your presentation.' Such advice may seem simple, almost trivial, but it is crucial for keeping your audience's attention, for not distracting them, as many otherwise good physicists do by holding a piece of chalk in one hand and an eraser in the other while they lecture. Among the debts of gratitude I owe to this great teacher is this style of presentation.

Then the time came for Uhlenbeck's departure. I vividly remember our last encounter on Dutch soil. I thanked him for all I had learned from him. His final words to me were: 'We shall meet again.' That remark gave me added courage during the subsequent dark war years. He left by boat in August 1939, only weeks before the outbreak of the Second World War. The next time we were to meet was in September 1946—in New York.

The later years

What I have told earlier about Uhlenbeck's work, in both statistical mechanics and nuclear physics, includes nearly all I have to say about his post-war scientific contributions. The remainder of this essay deals therefore almost entirely with personal aspects of the later years.

First about his war work. From 1943 to 1945 he was at the Massachusetts Institute of Technology's radiation laboratory, the brain center for American radar development, working as group leader in charge of developing wave guide theory. I have no information about his scientific activities there, but am aware that 'radar won the war.'[100] I do know an interesting story of that period, however: Uhlenbeck's influence on Julian Schwinger, one of the great theorists of my generation. This episode began during Uhlenbeck's leave from Utrecht, in the autumn of 1938.

> I was in Columbia in '38 and Schwinger was in trouble; he couldn't get his PhD because he didn't go to lectures of the mathematicians and he didn't have enough credits. So Rabi had told Schwinger that he *had* to go to my lectures at Columbia; of course, he didn't because it was early in the morning, and I asked Rabi, 'what shall I do?' because I was, of course, perfectly willing to give him an 'A' on that because he needed the credits . . . He clearly knew just as much as I did . . . We talked as complete equals . . . Rabi said, 'no, that you shouldn't do; you give him an exam and you make it a tough one.' So I did, we made an appointment, and, of course, he knew everything; he had somehow gotten the notes! I also cleaned up a couple of derivations which I had had done a little bit sloppily and which he had done much better and again it was so that he knew everything, so I said, 'fine, I will tell Mr Rabi.' I could now with good conscience give him an 'A' and that helped him in getting his degree.
>
> I was always involved in saving Schwinger somehow; even during the war I was involved in it because then he was at the radiation laboratory. He was at Chicago with the atomic energy business but he didn't like that, so, typically Julian, he just hopped in a car and went to Boston. He didn't tell anybody—he just went! He came to Rabi, who was then at the radiation lab and Rabi said, 'well, all right, of course, you can work here.' And that he liked; he was in my group and he did all these mathematical problems on wave guides which was very good, of course . . . He was a real computer, really remarkable. He was mathematically and technically really remarkably good.[2]

Schwinger did most of his work in the night, so that

> the experimentalists finally only came to him in the evening at about 4 o'clock. I finally got him to give a seminar at 4.30. Julian was always out of breath when he came in, but then I had a certain influence on him so he did it and very conscientiously. But then the people in Chicago got mad that he had left and through channels it was told that Schwinger should be sent back to Chicago, that he was needed there, and that especially I should be reprimanded for having taken him away. So I was brought to Lee Du Bridge [the director of the radiation lab], and he said, 'well, they tell me you have seduced Schwinger into working at the radiation lab.' I said, 'nothing of the kind! He just came. I had nothing to do with it; he just wants to do it.' 'Well,' he said, 'people are very mad and you've got to go to Chicago and put the thing right.' So I had to go and spend a day or so in Chicago talking to Eugene Wigner and all these guys; I just told them how it happened and, thank God, they weren't mad anymore and dropped the thing. I was complimented by Lee Du Bridge for my great diplomatic efforts in dealing with Schwinger, who didn't even know about it; he was just sitting there! So I had to save him from going to atomic energy work which he just somehow didn't like[2]

In the fall of 1945, Uhlenbeck returned to Ann Arbor, where, in 1954, he was named Henry Cahart professor of physics.

My first experience on arriving in America, in September 1946, was attending a meeting of the American Physical Society in New York. There I met Professor Uhlenbeck again, for the first time since the summer of 1939. I was touched by the warmth of his greeting. During a break, he invited me to lunch together with his dear friend Goudsmit, whom I had never met before but who knew who I was. We talked. As a well-bred Dutchman, I answered Uhlenbeck's questions with yes professor, no professor. After a while he peered at me, then said: 'Why don't you call me George?' I may well have blushed. In any event, that question marked a rite of passage for me.

The next time we met was in June 1947, at the Shelter Island conference. It was there that the foundations were laid for what soon came to be known as the renormalization program in quantum field theory.

Even more important to me was George's presence, during academic 1948–49, at the Institute for Advanced Study in Princeton, where I was then a staff member. At that time we started our first collaboration, which produced some new results in renormalization theory.[101] Then we turned to another investigation, which would take us a year to complete. At issue was a critical examination of several recent attempts at eliminating the QED infinities, not by introducing an additional field (as I had tried), but by modifying the equations of the electromagnetic field itself by making the action nonlocal, that is, changing—in a variety of ways—the Maxwell equations by introducing higher derivatives. Our work led us to introduce some new mathematical techniques and to discover that these attempts led to unexpected other kinds of inadmissible results. This solid piece of work is still being used and quoted.[102]

That year Uhlenbeck did something marvelous for me; he introduced me to the game of squash. Twice a week we made our way to the university's Dillon Gym, which housed 15 courts. Though he was almost 20 years older, George consistently kept beating me that year. He would position himself at the favored central position and from there hit the ball now in one corner, then in the other, so that I had to run my little ass off. In due course I realized that players must not only be physically fit but also mentally quick.

I spent the Christmas vacation of 1949 in Ann Arbor as guest of the Uhlenbecks, to put the final touches to our paper.[102] There I got to know and grow fond of Else, George's wife, and of their young son Olke. Above all, those years marked the beginning of George's and my deep friendship, which was to last until his death. I now developed a better understanding of his personality, especially of what I would call his purity. As Kramers once put it to me, George was 'once-born' (using a term coined by William James). In my files I found a letter which I cosigned,[103] in which we urged colleagues to join us in nominating George for the presidency of the American Physical Society. We succeeded, he was president for the year 1959. (I have already mentioned other honors: the Lorentz professorate in 1955, the Oersted Medal in 1956.)

Uhlenbeck spent one more year at the Princeton Institute, in 1958–59. During that time we wrote another joint paper, referred to earlier.[59] The final phase of that collaboration brought both of us to Brookhaven National Laboratory in the summer of 1959, where I had an unusual experience. On one morning when we were to meet in my office there, a hurricane passed nearby, sparing the laboratory, but drenching it with torrential rains. We were both so soaked when we met that we had to take off most of our clothes. This resulted in a scene that may well be unique in the annals of science: two physicists in their underwear arguing in front of a blackboard.

In 1960 Uhlenbeck left Ann Arbor, when he joined the Rockefeller Institute for Medical Research in New York (now the Rockefeller University) as a professor. I visited him frequently there from nearby Princeton, where I had long since been an Institute professor. Since I liked the quiet and intimacy of the Rockefeller, and since I had had enough of the Institute, I asked George one day if he would be interested in having me join him in New York. I remember his enthusiastic response. So it came about in 1963 that I, too, became a Rockefeller professor. I could now thoroughly enjoy many years of almost daily discussions with him.

In 1971 George became emeritus but remained active, continuing to come regularly to his office. In those later years many more honors came his way: the

Planck Medal (1965), the Lorentz Medal of the Royal Dutch Academy of Sciences (1970), the National Medal of Science, the highest scientific honor the United States can bestow (1977), the Woolf Prize (1979), for honorary doctorates. In 1977, the year of his and Sem's golden Doctor's Jubilee, the Queen of the Netherlands named both men to the quite high rank of Commander of the Order of Oranje Nassau.

––––––––––

So George's life went on peacefully, as he continued to meditate on the foundations of statistical mechanics—until one day in 1984, shortly whereafter I received a phone call. He had had a stroke and had been brought to nearby New York Hospital. It took some time before I was permitted to visit him there. I was struck by his haggard looks. While no expert, I had the distinct impression that his days were numbered. Remarkably, he recovered, however, and after some weeks returned to his New York apartment.

Else, and Ockie, his devoted son who had come over, decided, and George agreed, that New York city was no longer the best place for him to live. Accordingly, in early 1985 the whole family moved to Urbana-Champaign, where Ockie was a professor of microbiology. From there, George sent a letter[104] to us, his Rockefeller physics colleagues, still in his handsome writing which looks like calligraphy. It reads in part:

> First let me tell you of my state of health. It is much better! I walk around as usual and have gained weight (20 lbs!). But . . . my sight and hearing have become worse . . . I cannot read the papers, nor the Physical Review Letters . . . My memory is awful. As a result I really cannot do any sensible physics which would satisfy me and perhaps be of help to the younger generation. So I thought, it is time to quit . . . Well, fellows, this is all for today! . . . Your old friend George U.

When in 1986 Ockie was appointed professor at the University of Colorado in Boulder, the family moved there. George's health now went through a slow, lengthy decline. There, on October 31, 1988, he died of a stroke, at age 87.

In my office stands a memento of him: his favorite Eames chair.

––––––––––

When George started his Lorentz professorship in Leiden with an oration,[58] on April 1, 1955, he had said:

> One of the principal qualities a researcher should have is courage. Ehrenfest's method is the only way I know how to instill that in a young student . . . This necessitates the ideal ratio between the number of professors and students, to wit one-on-one, which seems to belong more and more to the past.

I shall always remember my beloved one-on-one teacher who has given me much of the courage I have been able to muster.

References

1. A. Gerlach, *Fastes militaires des Indes-Orientales Néerlandaises*, p. 571, Joh. Noman et Fils, Zalt-Bommel, 1859.

2. G. E. Uhlenbeck, interview by T. S. Kuhn, December 9, 1963, transcript in Niels Bohr Archive (NBA), Copenhagen.

3. Ref. 2, interview on April 5, 1962.

4. E. M. Uhlenbeck, letter to A. Pais, November 20, 1990.

5. P. Ehrenfest, T. Ehrenfest, in *Enzyklopädie der Mathematischen Wissenschaften* Vol. 4, part 2, Teubner, Leipzig, 1911. English translation by M. J. Moravcsik, in *The Conceptual Foundations of the Statistical Approach in Mechanics*, Cornell University Press, Ithaca, NY, 1959.

6. G. E. Uhlenbeck, *Am. J. Phys.* **24**, 431, 1956.

7. Ref. 2, interview on March 30, 1962.

8. P. Ehrenfest, letter to N. Bohr, A. Einstein, J. Franck, G. Herglotz, A. Joffe, Ph. Kohnstamm, and R. Tolman, August 14, 1932, copy in NBA.

9. For reactions of some colleagues, see A. Pais, *Niels Bohr's Times*, pp. 408–10, Oxford University Press, 1991.

10. E. Fermi, *Rev. Mod. Phys.* **4**, 87, 1932.

11. E. Fermi and G. E. Uhlenbeck, *Phys. Rev.* **44**, 510, 1933.

12. G. E. Uhlenbeck, *Commun. Dutch Hist. Inst. Rome*, **4**, 217, 1924.

13. G. E. Uhlenbeck, *Physica* **5**, 423, 1925.

14. P. Ehrenfest and G. E. Uhlenbeck, *Proc. Kon. Akad. Wetensch.* **29**, 1280, 1926.

15. D. Lang, *The New Yorker*, November 7, 1953, p. 47; November 14, 1953, p. 45.

16. S. Goudsmit, *Naturwissenschaften* **9**, 995, 1921.

17. Ref. 2, interview on March 31, 1962.

18. S. Goudsmit, *Ned. Tÿdschr. Natuurk* **37**, 386, 1971. English translation in *Delta*, Summer 1972, p. 77.

19. S. Goudsmit, *Physica* B1, **21**, 445, 1946.

20. G. E. Uhlenbeck, *Physics Today*, June 1976, p. 43.

21. S. Goudsmit, *Physics Today*, June 1976, p. 40.

22. S. Goudsmit, *Physica* **5**, 281, 1925.

23. S. Goudsmit and G. E. Uhlenbeck, *Physica* **5**, 266, 1925.

24. M. Abraham, *Ann. der Phys.* **10**, 105, 1903, section 11.

25. G. E. Uhlenbeck and S. Goudsmit, *Naturwissenschaften* **13**, 953, 1925.

26. P. Ehrenfest, letter to H. A. Lorentz, October 16, 1925, Lorentz Archives, University of Leiden.

27. *H. A. Lorentz, Collected Works*, Vol. 7, p. 179, Nÿhoff, The Hague, 1936.

28. W. Heisenberg, letter to S. Goudsmit, November 21, 1925; reproduced in ref. 18.

29. S. Goudsmit and G. E. Uhlenbeck, *Nature* **117**, 264, 1926.

30. N. Bohr, letter to P. Ehrenfest, December 22, 1925, copy in NBA.

31. S. Goudsmit and G. E. Uhlenbeck, *Physica* **6**, 273, 1926.

32. L. H. Thomas, *Nature* **117**, 514, 1926; *Phil. Mag.* **3**, 1, 1927.

33. N. Bohr, letters to W. Heisenberg and to W. Pauli, February 20, 1926, copies in NBA.

34. G. F. FitzGerald, *Nature* **62**, 564, 1900.

35. A. H. Compton, *J. Franklin Inst.* **192**, 145, 1921.

36. E. H. Kennard, *Phys. Rev.* **19**, 420, 1922.

37. W. Pauli, Naturw. **12**, 741, 1924.

38. W. Pauli, Nobel lecture 1946; reprinted in his *Collected Scientific Papers by Wolfgang Pauli* (R. Kronig and V. Weisskopf, Eds), Vol. 2, p. 1080, Wiley, New York, 1964.

39. S. Goudsmit, *Physics Today* **18**, June 1961, p. 21.

40. L. Belloni, *Am. J. Phys.* **50**, 461, 1982.

41. R. Kronig, letter to H. A. Kramers, March 6, 1926, copy in NBA.

42. N. Bohr, letter to R. Kronig, March 26, 1926, copy in NBA.

43. R. Kronig, letter to N. Bohr, April 8, 1926, copy in NBA.

44. See my essay on Oskar Klein elsewhere in this book.

45. F. R. Bichowski and H. Urey, *Proc. Nat. Ac. Sci.* **12**, 801, 1926.

46. Ref. 2, interview on May 10, 1962.

47. W. Pauli, letter to G. E. Uhlenbeck, June 9, 1926; reprinted in *Wolfgang Pauli, Scientific Correspondence* (A. Hermann *et al.*, Eds), Vol. 1, p. 329, Springer, New York, 1979.

48. See the essay on Pauli in this book for more comments by Uhlenbeck on Pauli.

49. W. Pauli, letter to G. Uhlenbeck, June 4, 1937; reprinted in ref. 47, Vol. 2, p. 521; Pauli to Uhlenbeck, July 9, 1938, *ibid.*, p. 583; Uhlenbeck to Pauli, July 1938, *ibid.*, p. 590; Pauli to Uhlenbeck, July 27, 1938, *ibid.*, p. 591.

50. These ideas on five-dimensional relativity are discussed in my essay on Klein elsewhere in this book.

51. W. Pauli, *Zeitschr. f. Physik* **43**, 601, 1927.

52. G. E. Uhlenbeck, *Over statistische methoden in de theorie der quanta*, Nÿhoff, The Hague, 1927.

53. A. K. Smith and C. Weiner, *Robert Oppenheimer*, p. 107, Harvard University Press, 1980.

54. The comments on Goudsmit were much helped by an obituary of him, M. Goldhaber, *Physics Today*, April 1979, p. 71.

55. R. Bacher and S. Goudsmit, *Atomic Energy States*, McGraw-Hill, New York, 1932.

56. S. Goudsmit and L. Pauling, *The Structure of Line Spectra*, McGraw-Hill, New York, 1930.

57. S. Goudsmit, *Alsos*, Schuman, New York, 1947.

58. G. E. Uhlenbeck, *Oude en nieuwe vragen der natuurkunde*, North-Holland, Amsterdam, 1955.

59. A. Pais and G. E. Uhlenbeck, *Phys. Rev.* **116**, 250, 1959.

60. E. G. D. Cohen, *Am. J. of Phys.* **58**, 618, 1990.

61. Ref. 52, p. 93. For details on the early years of quantum statistics see A. Pais, *Subtle is the Lord*, chapter 23, Oxford University Press, Oxford and New York, 1982.

62. G. E. Uhlenbeck, in *Some Strangeness in the Proportion* (H. Woolf, Ed.), p. 524, Addison-Wesley, Reading, MA, 1980.

63. A. Einstein, *Berl. Ber.* 1925, p. 3.

64. B. Kahn and G. E. Uhlenbeck, *Physica* **5**, 399, 1938.

65. S. Putterman and G. E. Uhlenbeck, *Phys. Fluids* **12**, 2299, 1969; the same and M. Kac, *Phys. Rev.* **29**, 546, 1972.

66. M. H. Anderson *et al.*, *Science* **269**, 198, 1995; C. C. Bradley *et al.*, *Phys. Rev. Lett.* **75**, 1687, 1995; K. B. Davis *et al.*, *ibid.*, **75**, 3969, 1995.

67. G. E. Uhlenbeck and S. Goudsmit, *Phys. Rev.* **34**, 145, 1929. The other paper is found in the *Pieter Zeeman Jubilee Volume*, p. 201, Nÿhoff, The Hague, 1935.

68. G. E. Uhlenbeck and L. S. Ornstein, *Phys. Rev.* **36**, 823, 1930.

69. M. C. Wang and G. E. Uhlenbeck, *Rev. Mod. Phys.* **17**, 323, 1945.

70. R. Fox and G. E. Uhlenbeck, *Phys. Fluids*, **13**, 1893, 2881, 1970.

71. B. Kahn and G. E. Uhlenbeck, *Physica* **4**, 1155, 1937, and ref. 64.

72. R. Riddell and G. E. Uhlenbeck, *J. Chem. Phys.* **21**, 2056, 1953.

73. See the review by G. E. Uhlenbeck and G. W. Ford, in *Studies in Statistical Mechanics* (J. de Boer and G. E. Uhlenbeck, Eds), Vol. 1, p. 119, North-Holland, Amsterdam, 1962.

74. P. Hemmer, M. Kac, and G. E. Uhlenbeck, *J. Math. Phys.* **4**, 216, 229, 1963; **5**, 60, 1974.

75. G. E. Uhlenbeck, *Van der Waals Revisited*, North-Holland, Amsterdam, 1964.

76. C. S. Wang and G. E. Uhlenbeck, in ref. 73, Vol. 2, p. 743, 1964.

77. G. E. Uhlenbeck and E. Beth, *Physica*, **3**, 729, 1936; **4**, 915, 1937. See also G. E. Uhlenbeck and L. Gropper, *Phys. Rev.* **41**, 79, 1932.

78. E. Uehling and G. E. Uhlenbeck, *Phys. Rev.* **43**, 552, 1933; **46**, 917, 1934.

79. S. Putterman, M. Kac, and G. E. Uhlenbeck, *Phys. Rev. Lett.* **29**, 546, 1972.

80. G. E. Uhlenbeck and C. van Lier, *Physica* **4**, 1155, 1937.

81. A. Nordsieck, W. Lamb, and G. E. Uhlenbeck, *Physica* **7**, 344, 1940; W. Scott and G. E. Uhlenbeck, *Phys. Rev.* **62**, 497, 1942.

82. W. Chang and G. E. Uhlenbeck, in ref. 73, Vol. 5, 17, 1970.

83. W. Chang and G. E. Uhlenbeck, in ref. 73, Vol. 5, 27, 1970.

84. J. L. Lawson and G. E. Uhlenbeck, *Threshold Signals*, McGraw-Hill, New York, 1950.

85. Samples: G. E. Uhlenbeck, in *Proceedings of the International Congress of Mathematics*, p. 256, 1958; *Phys. Today* **13**, 16, 1960; *Fundamental Problems in Statistical Mechanics*, Vol. 2, p. 1, North-Holland, 1968; same title, Lectures at Ames, Iowa, 1968.

86. G. E. Uhlenbeck and T. Y. Wu, *Phys. Rev.* **45**, 553, 1934.

87. G. E. Uhlenbeck and H. Wolfe, *Phys. Rev.* **46**, 237, 1934.

88. E. Fermi, *Ric. Scient.* **4**, 491, 1934; *Nuov. Cim.* **11**, 1, 1934; *Zeitschr. f. Physik* **88**, 161, 1934.

89. M. Rose and G. E. Uhlenbeck, *Phys. Rev.* **48**, 211, 1935; J. Knipp and G. E. Uhlenbeck, *Physica* **3**, 425, 1936.

90. G. E. Uhlenbeck and H. Kuiper, *Physica* **4**, 601, 1937.

91. M. Hebb and G. E. Uhlenbeck, *Physica* **5**, 605, 1938.

92. D. Falkoff and G. E. Uhlenbeck, *Phys. Rev.* **79**, 323, 1950.

93. D. Falkoff and G. E. Uhlenbeck, *Phys. Rev.* **79**, 340, 1950.

94. C. S. Wang Chang and G. E. Uhlenbeck, *Phys. Rev.* **85**, 684, 1952.

95. E. Konopinski and G. E. Uhlenbeck, *Phys. Rev.* **48**, 7, 1935.

96. J. Lawson and J. Cork, *Phys. Rev.* **57**, 982, 1940. See also C. S. Wu, *Rev. Mod. Phys.* **22**, 386, 1950.

97. E. Konopinski and G. E. Uhlenbeck, *Phys. Rev.* **60**, 308, 1941.

98. G. E. Uhlenbeck, *Het principe van behoud van energie*, Nÿhoff, The Hague, 1936.

99. For example *The New York Times*, January 29, 1939.

100. Quoted in J. S. Rigden, *Rabi*, p. 164, Basic Books, New York, 1987.

101. A. Pais and G. E. Uhlenbeck, *Phys. Rev.* **75**, 1321, 1949.

102. A. Pais and G. E. Uhlenbeck, *Phys. Rev.* **79**, 145, 1950.

103. Circulatory letter, dated February 14, 1957, signed by K. M. Case, A. Pais, and C. N. Yang.

104. G. E. Uhlenbeck, letter to his Rockefeller University colleagues, May 6, 1985.

Victor Weisskopf, about 1970. (Courtesy of AIP Emilio Segrè Visual Archives, *Physics Today* Collection.)

Victor Weisskopf*

'All knowledge and wonder (which is the seed of knowledge) is an impression of pleasure itself.' This comment by Francis Bacon not only was the inspiration for the title of Weisskopf's *Knowledge and Wonder*, a book which leaves impressions of pleasure on non-scientists and scientists alike, but also conveys its author's two main urges: the pursuit of knowledge and the installment of wonder in others.

Victor Friedrich Weisskopf was born in Vienna in 1908, a son of Emil, a lawyer, and Martha, née Gut. He hailed from a well-to-do assimilated Jewish family (who celebrated Christmas in their home). He received his elementary and high school and the beginning of his university education in his native city. Early on his main interests became evident, ranging from science, the arts, and classical music to social and political affairs. At age eight he began taking piano lessons, became accomplished on that instrument, and in later years enjoyed participating in chamber music. In his high school years he joined the socialist youth movement. From that time dates the beginning of his warm friendship with Bruno Kreisky, who in 1970 became chancellor of Austria.

Viki (as all his friends call him) had a favorite quotation for expressing his range of interests from science to the arts: in the morning I turn from mystery to reality, in the evening I return from reality to mystery.

In 1928, after two years at the University of Vienna, Weisskopf went to Göttingen, where in 1931 he received his doctorate with Max Born. Shortly afterward he went for his first visit to the Soviet Union. The next six years he worked with Schrödinger in Berlin, then with Bohr in Copenhagen, then with Pauli in Zurich. While in Denmark he married Ellen Tvede, in 1934. It was a harmonious union. They had a son who became an economist and a daughter who became an educator. Their happy marriage lasted until Ellen's death in 1989. A few years later he married Dascha Schmid. In 1937 the Weisskopfs went to the United States, where Viki held an assistant professorship at Rochester University from 1937 to 1943. In 1942 he became a US citizen.

I mention next some of Weisskopf's main scientific contributions: the theory

* On presenting Weisskopf for the degree of Doctor *honoris causa* in the Rockefeller University, June 2, 1982.

of the width and collision broadening of spectral lines and of resonance fluorescence; the quantization of spinless wave fields; a series of fundamental papers on quantum electrodynamics; and numerous important articles on the theory of the atomic nucleus as well as a textbook on that subject.

As was the case with so many distinguished physicists, the Second World War changed Weisskopf's destiny. In 1943 he joined Los Alamos, where, as the head of group T-3 of the Theory Division, he participated in the inevitable construction of the atomic bomb. In 1945 he was present at the test bomb explosion, baptized Trinity, on a nearby site.

Immediately upon war's end Weisskopf was among the first scientists to warn of the gruesome dangers of the new weapons. As the chairman of the Town Council of Los Alamos, he chaired the first town meeting ever held anywhere on these issues. That was in December 1945, in the Anthropological Museum in Santa Fe. In 1946 he joined the eight-member Emergency Committee of Atomic Scientists, chaired by Einstein. He was a cofounder of the Federation of Atomic Scientists. As chairman of its committee on visa questions he testified on international scientific contacts before Congressional committees. To this day he has not ceased working for nuclear sanity.

It was in 1946 that I first met Weisskopf, at a physics meeting in New York. We got along famously from the start and have been good friends ever since. One of our joint specialties is multilingual jokes, such as the one in French, German, and Yiddish about the dog, the cat, the castle, success, and the bird, which, alas, we cannot share with others.

The preceding account of Viki's early post-war activities marks only the beginnings of his later specialty: to make excellent use of his combined talents for dealing with science and with people. Here is more of the same:

From 1961 to 1965 he was director general of CERN, the joint European laboratory for high energy physics near Geneva. During that period he bought a house in Vesancy, a village on the slope of the French Juras, which he kept afterwards as a summer residence. He was pleased to be named (1972) *pompier honoraire* (honorary fireman) of Vesancy, and there has proudly shown me his fireman's helmet and diploma.

In 1966 he was elected the first chairman of HEPAP (the high energy advisory panel) which advised government agencies on matters of distribution of funds.

From 1976 to 1979 he was president of the American Academy of Arts and Sciences.

Thus Viki is a Renaissance man, at home on two continents, and familiar with the three forms of intelligence: human intelligence, animal intelligence, and military intelligence.

Weisskopf has received many honors. He has been awarded the French *Légion d'Honneur* and the German order *Pour le Mérite*. He is probably unique in having received the combined distinctions of the National Medal of Science of the

United States, honorary membership in the Academy of Sciences of the Soviet Union, and membership in the Pontifical Academy. This last distinction he cherishes highly. I recall a long telephone conversation with him on the delicate question of how to explain the big bang creation of the universe to the Holy Father. On various occasions Viki has advised John Paul II on nuclear disarmament, and was sent by him to President Reagan to convey the Pope's concern in these grave matters. On being asked after that event whether he was in fact responsible for interesting the Pope in arms control problems, Viki replied: 'The Pope gets his inspiration from God, not from a Viennese Jew,' which goes to show that even theoretical physicists are capable of humility.

His has been and continues to be a rich life. We honor him today as creative scientist, as an author, and as a statesman of science who uses his wisdom *pro bono humani generis*.

Added Note. I have extended my 1982 presentation by including some biographical details found later in Weisskopf's autobiography, *The Joy of Insight*, Basic Books, New York, 1991.

Eugene Wigner, about 1950. (Courtesy of AIP Emilio Segrè Visual Archives, *Physics Today* Collection.)

Eugene Wigner

My first contact with Wigner occurred in the spring of 1946, when I received a letter from him and John Wheeler—while I was a postdoc in Copenhagen—asking me to give an invited paper at the American Physical Society meeting in New York, to be held the coming September 19–21. I replied that I was pleased to accept. That meeting was to be followed by academic festivities in Princeton, from September 23–25, to celebrate the university's bicentennial, to which I had also been invited.

So, on September 22, I made my first trip to Princeton, in the company of a few other physicists whom I had met at the New York meeting. Local colleagues were present to greet us at Princeton's railway station, all new faces to me. One of them was Wigner.

During the next half century I have met Eugene—as I soon was to call him—quite frequently. I have had untold discussions with him in those years, some at 8 Ober Road, his home, and have read quite a number of his papers. As a result I have grown to be in awe of his scientific oeuvre, of its depth as well as its range, from pure mathematics to engineering, from philosophical reflections to patents. His collected works, over 500 articles, fill eight volumes, containing almost 5000 pages.[1] I cannot claim sufficient familiarity with all parts of this immense output, but will have comments to make on a variety of topics Wigner has dealt with. First, however, I shall turn to a biographical sketch, largely helped by his published recollections[2] and interviews with him.[6]

Jenö Pal—later Americanized to Eugene Paul—Wigner was born on November 17, 1902, in Pest, the eastern part of Budapest, Hungary's capital, in an upper middle class family. Antal ('Toni'), his father, was of German–Jewish descent, the only child of a leather-tanning family. Eugene has told me that the family name is a derivative of the German Wiegner, which means cradle maker. Erzsébet ('Elsa'), Eugene's mother, was devoted to managing the home and arranging the social life of her husband and their three children, Bertha ('Biri'), one year older than Eugene, and Margit ('Manci'), two years younger. 'She knew the special weaknesses of the family: that I needed a great deal of sleep; that Biri could be too kind for her own good; and that Manci did not always like to play by the rules.'[3]

Both parents were nominally Jewish, but Judaism was not practiced in their home. 'We had a little Seder [Passover celebration] when I was a child, and I was prepared for the Bar Mitzvah [Jewish ritual of transition to manhood, at age 13], but [that event] had no religious meaning to me and my family.'[4]

In Wigner's high school years, a local priest and a rabbi were brought in to give religious instruction. The rabbi led the Jewish boys firmly through Bible readings in both Hebrew and Hungarian, and taught Hebrew grammar and vocabulary until they could read some fine Hebrew texts. Wigner never spoke formal Hebrew with any skill, however.[5]

'The population of Budapest was about twenty-five percent Jewish . . . I never thought of wondering "Is [this or that person] Jewish or not Jewish?" It just did-n't enter my mind.'[6] Wigner was in his late teens when the family converted to Lutheranism. 'I have never missed Judaism . . . Today [said in his eighties] I am only mildly religious, and I know few Jewish people well.'[7]

Wigner's education began with years of private teaching at home between the ages of five and ten, whereafter he entered the third grade of an elementary school. He was awkward at sports, since he was small and wore eye glasses. At the time of his graduation from high school, 'I cut an unimpressive figure at 5 feet 6 and 120 pounds.'[8] At age of about 11 he was diagnosed to have tuberculo-sis and was sent to a sanitarium in Breitenstein, in Austria. His earliest recollec-tion of working on a mathematics problem dates from the time he spent there. 'I had to lie on a deck chair for days on end, and I worked terribly hard on con-structing a triangle if the three altitudes are given.'[9] After six weeks the doctors decided that the tuberculosis diagnosis had been mistaken, and Eugene happily went home again.

Wigner always spoke warmly about his high school years, at a Lutheran Gimnázium, which he entered in 1915. There he received solid grounding in Latin, Hungarian language and literature, mathematics, history, and religion. In these years his love for mathematics kept growing. All through his life he would refer to his mathematics teacher with great admiration and respect. 'Science was taught less seriously, and that irked me. Physics and chemistry were hardly treated more seriously than geography or art. We had just one year of chemistry and two of physics.'[10] He used to speak well of his teacher in physics, however, a subject to which he was increasingly becoming attached. At a student colloqui-um at the Gimnázium, he once lectured on relativity theory. In all he ranked among the top students of his class.

Wigner was about 13 when, for the first time, he met Jancsi ('Johnny') von Neumann, who was one grade below him in his school, and whose brilliance in mathematics had already been recognized even at that early age. 'I never felt I knew von Neumann well at Gimnázium. Perhaps no one did; he always kept a bit apart.'[11] They would become good friends in later years, however, as we shall see.

Wigner's high school years were interrupted in 1919, when in March the Hungarian government fell to the communists. This led him and his family to move to Austria until November, when that régime was overthrown, and they returned to Budapest. Wigner's rabid anti-communism dates from that period.

In 1920 Eugene graduated from his high school, as one of the top students in his class. Already he was widely read in physics and mathematics. It had become his ambition to be a physicist. Prospects for an academic position in Hungary were dim, however. At that time there were only three physics professorships in the country, two in Budapest, one in Szeged. Moreover, those of Jewish descent were at a distinct disadvantage in regard to the pursuit of an academic career. Whereupon his father, who, in the tradition of his family, was part owner of a leather tannery, though aware that physics was his son's true love, proposed that Eugene would be much better off in practice if he would study chemical engineering, in preparation for joining him in the tannery business. Wigner accepted that suggestion, though it was never his devotion.

So began Eugene's university studies in chemistry, first one year at the Technical Institute in Budapest. In 1921, at age 18, he moved to the Technische Hochschule in Berlin. There, 'I went to practically no classes [attendance was not required so long as one passed the examination] . . . but worked extremely hard in the laboratory. I loved inorganic chemistry.'[9] Those activities consumed him for two years, six days a week.

Meanwhile, Wigner continued to study physics and mathematics on his own. Of other readings he has remembered being very impressed by Freud's *The Interpretation of Dreams*. 'Freudian psychology is an artful creation which I have admired all my life.'[12]

During those years, Wigner also became a regular attendant of the Thursday afternoon colloquia at the University of Berlin, located quite near to his Hochschule. The meetings were held in a sizable classroom, filled with three rows of wooden chairs. Up front sat great men: Einstein, Max Planck, Max von Laue, Walther Nernst. Among youngsters, Wigner first met Edward Teller and Leo Szilard at the colloquium. Wolfgang Pauli and Werner Heisenberg also attended occasionally. 'I was too young to see the historic meaning of these colloquia.'[13] Of Einstein, Wigner has recalled listening to his report on a recent paper by Satyendra Bose[9]—which led to the 'Bose–Einstein statistics'[14]—and remembers that Einstein never encouraged young people to do one piece of research or another.

In his third year at the Technische Hochschule, Wigner arranged to work about 18 hours a week at the Kaiser Wilhelm Institute in Dahlem, a suburb of Berlin. There he met Herman Mark, together with whom he published a paper on the lattice structure of rhombic sulfur.[15] Even more important was his first encounter there with the physical chemist Michael Polanyi, another native of Budapest, a man who decisively marked Wigner's thinking, not just about physics, but also about philosophy and politics. (Years later I met Polanyi in Princeton, in Wigner's company.)

When Eugene had chosen the topic for his doctoral dissertation, chemical reaction rates, he found Polanyi willing to be his thesis advisor for a degree in chemical engineering. That work led to a joint publication[16] by Polanyi and Wigner, submitted in June 1925. Twenty years later, Wigner wrote: 'It is characteristic of Polanyi's modesty that it required considerable persuasion to induce him to have his name associated with the article.'[17]

The thesis, which contains the first theory of the rates of association and dissociation of molecules, is based on a set of assumptions which I find altogether remarkable. For example, 'It postulated that the excited states of the molecule obtained by the association have a finite energy spread $\Delta\varepsilon$ [first assumption] and that $\Delta\varepsilon$ is related to the average life time $\Delta\tau$ of that molecule by the relation $\Delta\varepsilon\Delta\tau = h$, that is, Planck's constant [second assumption]'[17]—a relation that is almost (not quite) identical with the uncertainty relation *derived* by Heisenberg two years later.[18] Note also that the thesis was submitted one month before Heisenberg's very first paper on quantum mechanics![19] Much later Wigner has written, rather laconically, of his assumptions: '[They] appeared drastic at that time but . . . subsequently proved to be correct.'[17]

After thus having completed his university studies, the 22-year-old Doctor Wigner returned to Budapest, to join his father in the tannery. However, 'I did not get along very well in the tannery . . . I did not feel at home there . . . I did not feel that this was my life.'[9] Meanwhile he kept up his reading in physics, especially the early papers on quantum mechanics. Then, one day in 1926, there came a surprise.

> I received a letter from a crystallographer at the Kaiser Wilhelm Institute, [saying] that he wanted an assistant . . . to find out why the atoms occupy positions in the crystal lattices which correspond to symmetry axes . . . He also told me that this had to do with group theory and that I should read a book on group theory and then work it out and tell him.[9]

Wigner learned soon thereafter that this offer was the work of Polanyi, with whom he wrote another joint paper two years later.[20] He was happy when his father advised him to accept the offer. 'When I reached Berlin I vowed that from here on the study of physics would be my permanent occupation.'[21]

And so it went, starting off right away with a bang. Indeed, before the year 1926 was over, Wigner had launched the beginnings of what would become his main contribution to theoretical physics.

'That was to a considerable extent due to Heisenberg,'[6] Wigner has said. I should enlarge. In the spring of 1926, Heisenberg had written a paper[22] on quantum states of two identical electrically charged oscillators symmetrically coupled to each other. These, he found, separate into two sets of states, one symmetric, the other antisymmetric, under exchange of the oscillator coordinates. He further discovered that radiative transitions can occur only between states within each set, never between one set and the other. He went on to conjecture that non-combining sets should likewise exist if the number of identical particles is larger than two, but had not yet found a proof.[23] Six weeks later, this work led Heisenberg to give the theory of a famous, yet unsolved two-electron problem, the spectrum of the helium atom.[24]

Wigner, who had read these papers soon after his return to Berlin, had become interested in this more-than-two n- identical particle problem. He rapidly mastered[25] the case $n = 3$ (without spin). His methods were rather laborious; for example he had to solve a (reducible) equation of degree six. It would be pretty awful to go on this way to higher n. So he went to consult the mathematician Johnny von Neumann. In the late 1950s Wigner explained to me what happened next, when I came to consult him on another many-body problem (dealing with multi-π meson systems) I was then working on.

When he posed his question to von Neumann—Wigner told me—Johnny walked to a corner of the room, faced the wall, and started mumbling to himself. After a while he turned around and said: 'You need the theory of group characters.' At that moment Eugene had no idea what that theory was about. Whereupon von Neumann went to Issai Schur, obtained reprints of two of his papers,[26] and gave them to Wigner.

> [Those were] so easy to read, and of course it was clear that that was the solution.'[6] Within weeks, he had completed a second paper, now for the general n-particle problem.[27] It contains these lines: 'It is clear that one can hardly apply these elementary methods [he had used for $n = 3$] to the case of 4 electrons, since the computational difficulties get to be too large. There exists, however, a well-developed mathematical theory which one can use here: . . . group theory . . . Herr von Neumann has kindly directed me to the relevant literature . . . When I told Herr von Neumann the result of the calculations for n = 3, he correctly predicted the general result.

A few years later he applied group theory to the vibration of molecules and to the quantum physics of crystals.[27]

Thus did group theory enter quantum mechanics.

Wigner has said later: 'I had a bad conscience because I felt that I should have published [that] second paper together with von Neumann.'[6] Joint publications did follow soon, however, three papers[28] on atomic spectra which take account of the spin of the electron; and two papers[29] on eigenvalue problems. Also in later years they produced joint work, of a mathematical nature.[30]

I need to return briefly to my own consultation with Wigner. He told me that I, too, needed the theory of group characters for my own work. Like Eugene in 1926, I did not know that theory then. He advised me to study that subject in the book he himself had written on group theory,[31] where one finds recorded such fine contributions as the Wigner $3j$-symbols, and the Wigner–Eckart theorem. The original German version had come out in 1931; I used a later English translation. I had tried earlier to read that book but without getting far—I had no motivation then, but had one now. I read through the whole book as if it were a detective story, picking up clues for what I needed on the way. When I had finished, I was ready to attack my own problem.[32]

Wigner's book on applications of group theory to quantum mechanics was actually the second to appear on that subject. Herman Weyl had published two editions of another one of his own before him.[33] That sequence of event angered Eugene throughout his life. 'Both Johnny [von N.] and I felt that that was a very unfair thing . . . Weyl had before [my] article [ref. 27] no knowledge of it . . . We both felt that it was . . . deeply incorrect.'[6] Wigner's is still the ideal introductory text. Weyl is much harder going but well worth the effort.

The use of group theory in physics met with initial distaste.

> There was, first of all, a certain enmity to group theory . . . There was a word, '*die Gruppenpest*' (the group pest) and you have to chase away the *Gruppenpest* . . . Most people thought 'Oh, that's a nuisance. Why should I learn group theory? It is not physical and has nothing to do with it' . . . I remember how Schroedinger told me: 'This is the first way to derive the root of spectroscopy, but surely nobody will do it in this way in five years.'[6]

For us, the modern physicists, group theory has become a crucial, inevitable tool, as was foreseen by Wigner when he wrote in his book:

> It seems to me that the deliberate utilization of elementary symmetry properties is bound to correspond more closely to physical intuition than the more computational treatment.

Eugene spent academic 1927–28 in Göttingen, where he had been appointed assistant to David Hilbert. That contact, with one of the greatest mathematicians of the early twentieth century, turned out to be less than fruitful. Wigner saw Hilbert only five times.[6] 'I found him painfully withdrawn . . . His enormous fatigue was plain . . . [He was suffering from pernicious anemia. He] seemed quite old . . . I decided: If I could not work for Hilbert, I would work for physics.'[34]

Which he did, producing another pair of major papers. One, together with Pascual Jordan, introduces a new technique[35] (often referred to as second quantization) for dealing with many-electron systems. Their method would turn out to be indispensable for the development of a systematic description of electrons together with positrons. In his other paper, entitled: 'On the conservation laws in quantum mechanics,'[36] Wigner introduced a new concept in physics: parity.

At issue here was the age-old notion that the laws of physics are the same in one world as compared with another world obtained from ours by spatial reflection, in other words, that our world and its mirror image obey the same laws. Wigner's fundamental discovery was that in quantum mechanics this mirroring operation can be described by associating a number with each quantum state, called the parity quantum number, P, or parity for short, which can only take on one of two possible values: +1 or −1; and that *parity is conserved* in reactions, for example in the reaction A + B → C + D the parity of the initial state A + B has the same value as that for the final state C + D. This property is commonly denoted as *P*-conservation or *P*-invariance. (Initially parity was given the name 'signature,' used by Weyl[33] and by Pauli.[37] The name 'parity' is found[38] in 1935. I do not know whose invention that name was.)

Now Wigner makes this very important observation: '[*Parity*] *has no analog in classical mechanics*'[36] (my italics). That is to say, invariance under spatial reflections, while well defined (and used classically, as in the classification of crystal types), yields the associated concepts of parity and its conservation only in quantum mechanics. Wigner's comment: 'Only rarely will one be able to use [parity], since it only has two eigenvalues [that is, ±1] and has therefore too little predictive power'[36] has turned out to be far off the mark, however. In a later paper,[39] Wigner and coworkers have given a detailed analysis of the measurability of parity.

A few years later, Wigner scored another important first: the quantum mechanical treatment of invariance under time reversal, the relation between the movement forward in time of a system to the movement backward, that is, to the movement in which all velocities (and spins) are reversed. Again the laws of physics are the same for a given motion and its time reversed one but here, Wigner explained, there does not exist an associated new quantum, as for spatial reflection.[40]

I regard Wigner's contributions described up to this point, all of them (also parity and time reversal) dealing with symmetry principles in quantum mechanics, as the most important of his career, as is also emphasized in the citation for his Nobel Prize, received in 1963: 'For his contributions to the theory of atomic nuclei and elementary particles, especially for the discovery of fundamental symmetry principles.' I recommend the reading of Wigner's Nobel Prize lecture: 'Events, laws of nature, and invariance principles,'[41] for a survey of his contributions to group theory, not only those first mentioned but also later ones, on applications in nuclear physics (which I shall mention shortly) and to relativity theory.[42]

The citation just mentioned also makes clear that Eugene had been active in parts of physics on which I have not yet touched—but on which I shall do shortly.

———————

In late 1928 Wigner returned to Berlin. '[There] I was a *Privatdozent* and I gave a class on quantum mechanics. I had a good number of students.'[43] He also worked on his book[31] and continued his researches.

During this Berlin period, Wigner had a relation with a lady who bore him a daughter out of wedlock. I met the daughter, Erika Zimmerman, in Princeton during the 1980s. She was also present at the memorial service for Wigner in the Princeton University Chapel, held in early 1995, and got along very well with Eugene's widow. She is mentioned in Eugene's will as 'my friend.'

Then, in October 1930, Eugene was startled to receive a cable from Princeton University, offering him a one-term lectureship at a salary of $700 per month. 'I had never seen so much money in one heap'[44]—his monthly salary in Berlin was about $80.

Wigner accepted, and off he went on his 11-day voyage to the New World. On arrival in Princeton he found quarters in the university's graduate college. The culture shock of the transition was lessened by the company of von Neumann, who had received a similar offer from Princeton. The appointments to both men were extended. From 1930–33 the two of them oscillated between Princeton and Europe—until the rise of nazism brought those trips to an end. In 1935–36, Eugene became a full-time teacher at the university, adding substantially to the local level of physics, which was then quite rudimentary. (Meanwhile von Neumann had received appointment as professor at the newly founded Institute for Advanced Study in Princeton.)

In those years, also later, Wigner saw a good deal of Einstein, who had settled in Princeton in 1933. 'I was one of the few people near [him] who loved much the same physics as he did. I treasured Einstein's faith in my favorite symmetry and invariance principles . . . We often walked together.'[45] Eugene has told me that on many of these walks they discussed Einstein's never-ending reservations about quantum mechanics, and that in particular they returned to an old idea of his (E.) from 1926: that the wave fields in Schrödinger's wave mechanics could serve as *Führungsfelder*, guiding fields, for light quanta or other particles, one for each particle. 'Einstein, though in a way he was fond of [this idea] never published it,'[46] since one field per particle was incompatible with strict energy conservation. It was fitting that Wigner would be one of the speakers at the symposium in Princeton on March 19, 1949, on the occasion of Einstein's seventieth birthday,[47] and again at the Einstein centennial celebrations in 1979.[46]

Wigner's first paper published in America deals with the impact of quantum mechanics on thermodynamics.[48] It was what in the movie industry is called a sleeper, widely ignored for half a century, whereafter it has become a major topic in the study of quantum chaos. This paper is a first example of a marked change in Wigner's oeuvre: all of his papers produced in America deal with subjects he had not addressed hitherto.

Eugene's main research in his early Princeton years concerned the then young branch of solid state physics. In these efforts 'I had brilliant luck with my own graduate students,'[49] three of whom were to rise to great eminence: Frederick Seitz; John Bardeen, the first man ever to be awarded two Nobel Prizes in a single field; and Conyers Herring. Seitz, his first student, has remembered: 'I spent much of our spare time discussing what [W.] referred to as the "customs of your country,"'[50] and has told me that Eugene did not fit easily into the Princeton style in those early years.

This solid state work began with Wigner and Seitz's landmark papers on sodium,[51] which aimed to explain what holds a metal together, followed by a paper by Wigner alone,[52] on properties of a dense electron gas. In 1935 he wrote with Bardeen on monovalent metals.[53]

In the autumn of 1934 Eugene received a visit from his sister Manci, who was then still living in Budapest. Paul Dirac, the Lucasian professor from Cambridge, England, also was in Princeton for academic 1934–35, as visitor to the Institute for Advanced Study. Manci and Paul met, fell in love, and were married in January 1937. From then on Wigner would invariably refer to Dirac as 'my famous brother-in-law.'

'In 1936 came a shock . . . Princeton dismissed me . . . they never explained why . . . I could not help feeling angry.'[54] That statement puzzled me. After all, Wigner had been quite productive and had delivered excellent PhD students during the preceding Princeton years. Upon consulting with my friend Arthur Wightman, another physics professor at Princeton, I learned that Eugene's recollections on this point are in fact incorrect. Going through university files, Arthur had found out that the authorities had actually proposed to reappoint Wigner, who, however, was resentful because he was not given the promotion he had set his eyes on. All of which resulted in Eugene taking a leave of absence from Princeton to go to the University of Wisconsin at Madison, where his colleague Gregory Breit had successfully persuaded the authorities to offer Eugene an acting professorship. Wigner accepted, arrived in Madison in the fall of 1936 and stayed there for two years. On January 8, 1937, he became a US citizen in Trenton, New Jersey.

Theoretical nuclear physics could only begin in earnest after the discovery of the neutron in 1932 and the subsequent insight that atomic nuclei are built up out of two basic constituents: protons and neutrons. Eugene had made interesting contributions to this new area of theoretical study already in his first Princeton period, 1930–36, notably his early study of nuclear forces. Four types of these can be distinguished, depending on whether they do or do not allow for exchange of spin and/or of electric charge between protons and neutrons. The type in which neither exchange occurs is now known as the Wigner force.[55]

Wigner had met Breit in Princeton, when the latter had spent some time at the Institute for Advanced Study. They had published two papers on nuclear physics.[56] In the second of these they proposed the famous Breit–Wigner formula for the reaction cross section of a resonance reaction, still a standard tool in the arsenal of theorists. In Wisconsin they published another joint nuclear physics paper.[57]

In the most important article Eugene wrote in Madison, he applied once again his mastery of group theory, this time to nuclear forces.[58] In this so-called supermultiplet theory, a group, code named SU(4), appears in a different role than in previous work. There, groups were universally applicable, here SU(4) holds only under restricted circumstances. First, it refers to nuclear forces *only*, no longer when one includes electromagnetic forces. Secondly, supermultiplet theory is valid only for low-lying nuclear energy levels. Approximately valid symmetry groups have gone on to play an ever more important role, especially in the physics of fundamental particles, where Wigner's SU(4) has provided the guide to another important development.[59] In addition, Wigner produced another half dozen articles while in Wisconsin.

In Madison, Eugene and Amelia Frank, a young Jewish physics student, fell in love. On December 23, 1936 he, at age almost 34, and Amelia were married in Princeton University's Chapel. Within a few months thereafter she fell seriously ill with cancer. She died on August 16, 1937. 'My grief was long and intense.'[60]

In 1938, 'Princeton invited me back to nearly the same job they had dropped me from two years before . . . the invitation was a kind of apology.'[61] Eugene was now appointed Thomas D. Jones professor of mathematical physics—the position he had hoped for in 1936. During the next few years he continued to be productive in nuclear physics.[62]

A new chapter in nuclear physics, in fact in world history, began in January 1939 with the advent of nuclear fission. To physicists it became almost at once clear that this discovery could well make possible the creation of bombs vastly more powerful than any then in existence—a prospect that was all the more grim because a world war was threatening.

Wigner, deeply concerned about these implications, discussed this possibility over and over again with a close friend of his, the physicist Leo Szilard, another Jewish native of Budapest, whom he had known since his Berlin days and who had also emigrated to the United States. Eugene once said to me: 'Szilard was more interested in personal power than in science.' Szilard's greatest disappointment must have been that he never achieved his ultimate aim: to be a political leader.

Both Wigner and Szilard came to the conclusion that it would be most important to inform the US government of the military threats posed by fission. They decided to enlist Einstein's help. On June 16, 1939 they called on him at his summer place in Peconic, Long Island. They found him quite receptive. The three men concluded that President Roosevelt should be informed. Einstein dictated a letter in German to Wigner, who has kindly provided me with a photocopy of his handwritten draft. Thereupon Wigner produced a translation into English which Einstein signed on August 2. This document was brought to Dr Alexander Sachs, an economist and unofficial advisor to the President, who handed the document to Roosevelt on October 3, 1939. Allegations sometimes made that this letter was the initial stimulus for the US atomic bomb project are without substance.[63] Commenting on the government's lukewarm response to the letter, Wigner wrote after the war that he and his colleagues felt as if they were 'swimming in syrup.'[64] And, still later: 'It is quite possible that the course of events would have been very much the same without the Einstein letter.'[65]

Wigner became one of the leading figures in the US atomic bomb effort. In April 1942, he took a formal leave of absence from Princeton to go to work at the metallurgical laboratory of the University of Chicago.

He went there with his second wife. In the summer of 1940 Eugene had met Mary Annette Wheeler, a physics teacher at Vassar College. They got along from the start and on June 4, 1941 were married. They had two children, David and Martha.

Eugene arrived in Chicago well in time to be one of the about 50 people present, on the afternoon of December 2, 1942, in the large hall (actually a squash court) underneath the University's Stagg Field stadium, when the first man-made nuclear chain reaction was initiated, after which Wigner presented a bottle of Chianti to Enrico Fermi, the leader of the project. Those present signed their names on the bottle's label, the only written record of that historic event.

From 1942 to 1945, Eugene's place of work was the fourth floor of Eckart Hall on the university's campus, as leader of about 20 theoretical physicists. The group had to do a great number of engineering calculations, so Wigner's engineering background stood him in good stead. Their studies included chain reactions, the effect of γ-rays and neutrons on matter, and help with the planning and evaluation of experimental work.[66] Their main task was the design of a reactor for plutonium production to be erected at Hanford in the state of Washington. The Du Pont Corporation had been assigned the construction of that reactor. Eugene's contacts with that corporation caused him unhappy moments but also pleasure. He continued to have contact with Du Pont for many years.

During his Chicago years, Wigner invented many of the techniques that are now taught in textbooks of reactor design. Among his numerous contributions was his anticipation of what came to be known as 'the Wigner disease,' a term Eugene has always disliked: intense neutron bombardment of graphite in a reactor causes its crystal lattice to swell and occlude the reactor fuel elements—a continuing concern of reactor engineers. As a result of all these activities Eugene came to hold or co-hold 37 US patents on nuclear reactors, filed between 1944 and 1953.[67]

Eugene's concern with the issue of civil defense against atomic bomb attacks on the US began during the Second World War, and from then on lasted for the rest of his life. In the 1950s and 1960s he tried 'to expose the foolishness of mutual assured destruction,'[68] the American government's declared position in this matter. He was the director of the Harbor Project, a six-week study of civil defense conducted by 62 scientists, engineers, and statesmen, held in the summer of 1963 under the auspices of the National Academy of Sciences.[69] His participation in several Pugwash meetings gave him yet other opportunities to express his views. In the preface of a book on civil defense, published in 1969, of which he was editor and contributor, he wrote of 'the possibility of a nuclear attack, which is undeniable.'[70] He was an outspoken supporter of the Vietnam War. In the 1980s he supported the Strategic Defense Initiative ('Star Wars'). A whole chapter of his autobiography is devoted to civil defense.[71] I find it remarkable that there one does not find a change of mind about the need for civil defense, although the book was written after the collapse of the Soviet Union.

The reaction of colleagues to Wigner's unceasing hammering on civil defense was, in his own words: 'I kept trying to arouse my colleagues about civil defense. But when I made my case, most of them said: "Oh, Eugene. Not again . . . Please leave me alone."'[72]—exactly my own sentiment. I would guess that Eugene's obsession with this issue was a consequence of his exposure to communism in 1919.

During academic 1945–46 Wigner, back in Princeton, resumed his activities in pure science. The first topic he addressed was a much-needed, more rigorous formulation of the Breit–Wigner theory.[56] These studies eventually led to a series of papers, spanning a decade, containing his so-called R-matrix theory,[73] which has since developed into a major tool for resonance analysis. Much of this work is summarized in a book he published in 1958.[74] Pursuing resonance theory further in later years, Eugene created a new field of research: the study of random matrices.[75] Quite a different area of research to which Wigner contributed after the war was relativistic quantum mechanics.[76]

In 1946, Wigner took another leave from Princeton to accept appointment as director of research and development at the Clinton Laboratory in Tennessee, long since known as Oak Ridge National Laboratory. At that time the laboratory was designing a uranium research reactor as a step toward producing atomic energy for peaceful purposes. The position was for an indefinite length of time, but after one year Eugene had had enough; he could not stand the bureaucracy of the place and returned to Princeton. He was succeeded by his devoted friend Alvin Weinberg, another distinguished reactor physicist, together with whom, some years later, he wrote a textbook on reactor physics.[77] For many years he remained a consultant for Oak Ridge.

———

Here my story of Wigner's physics comes to an end. There is ever so much more that can be told about his scientific oeuvre, but a complete account is not my purpose. For that I refer to his collected papers.[1] I hope, however, that the preceding has made it sufficiently clear why I spoke at the beginning of this essay of my awe for the depth and range of Eugene's contributions.

This is a natural place for mentioning the recognition Wigner has received for his work in physics. The principal honors bestowed on him are: the US Medal for Merit (1946), the Franklin Medal (1950), the Fermi Prize (1958), the Atoms for Peace Award (1960), the Planck Medal (1961), and, as already mentioned, the Nobel Prize (1963). By my count he has received 20 honorary doctorates. He was president of the American Physical Society for 1956, member of the General Advisory Committee for the US Atomic Energy Commission from 1952 to 1957 and 1959 to 1964, and has served on many panels of the President's Scientific Advisory Committee.

I turn next to a few remarks about Wigner's writings on subjects other than physics in the technical sense.

———

'Old men have a weakness for generality and a desire to see structures as a whole. That is why old scientists so often become philosophers ... I was becoming one too.'[78]

To me, the best access to Wigner's thinking about subjects at the limits of physics and beyond is his collection of essays, *Symmetries and Reflections*,[41] which, however, deals in part with physics itself. The most suitable account I can give about this extended range of Eugene's thoughts is to reprint next [with permission] the first book review I ever published, which deals with this volume of essays.

> From epistemological questions concerning quantum mechanics to disarmament; from time reversal invariance to consciousness; from existence proofs of biological systems to the economy of nuclear power; such is the range of topics discussed in this collection of papers and essays by one of today's foremost physicists. The contributions appeared originally in a variety of publications, including *Reviews of Modern Physics*, the *Proceedings of the American Philosophical Society*, and *The New York Times Magazine*, to name a few.

> Thus Wigner has written about many kinds of problems and for diverse audiences. He raises questions that are stimulating, and sometimes disquieting. One need not agree with all his answers to recognize this as an important book. The author takes care, in text and in footnote, to disclaim authority whenever he believes that the reader should be so cautioned. The reading, rarely light, is strongly thought-provoking. This volume deserves an audience far wider than that of physicists only.

> The book has a coherence of principal themes much greater than one would expect from a glance at the two dozen titles of the separate papers. Three of these themes which to this reviewer seem uncommonly challenging are selected here.

> *Are there biotonic laws?* A biotonic law (a term coined by Walter Elsasser) is a law of nature which cannot be contained in the laws of physics. The question arises in the discussion of the probability for the existence of self-reproducing states. Under carefully stated assumptions (notably that interaction between a 'living' state and a suitable nutrient always leads to multiplication) the author gives a simple quantum mechanical argument which yields zero for this probability. This reminds one of Charcot's dictum: *La théorie c'est bon, mais ça n'empêche pas d'exister*. In any event, Wigner says that his argument is not conclusive. At the same time, he does not exclude the possibility that, in the realm of biological phenomena, biotonic laws do come into play. In fact, he does believe in the existence of biotonic laws, but on other grounds: his 'firm conviction in the existence of biotonic laws stems from the overwhelming phenomenon of consciousness.'

> *Consciousness as a subject of scientific inquiry.* For most scientists this is a question at most worthy of discussion after the day's labor is done. Not so for Wigner. One finds a strong preoccupation with this problem in various parts of this book. At the core of Wigner's convictions lies his distinction between two kinds of reality or existence: 'the existence of my consciousness and the reality or existence of everything else.'

> *Epistemology and quantum mechanics.* Concerning the type of information which we can acquire and possess about the external inanimate world, according to quantum mechanics, Wigner subscribes to the 'orthodox' theory of measurement—with two main reservations. First, he states a formal alternative, namely 'that the superposition principle will have to be abandoned.' Second, he does not at all exclude the possibility of an effect of consciousness on physical phenomena.

Clearly Wigner's unease about the epistemology of quantum mechanics is not of the 'hidden variable' variety. Nor should parapsychologists now feel encouraged to descend on his roof. The spirit in which the author deals with these three inter-connected themes is one neither of apodictic statement nor of novel prediction, but of earnest concern about the possible need to extend the scope of scientific inquiry to domains now most often considered scientifically tabu. A further study of the relevant chapters (12 and 13) is recommended to all (including this review-er). However, better bone up on your density matrix theory first.

In deciding to review this book from the end to the beginning, as is done here, I have had more in mind the spectrum of readers of this journal than the generic lines of development of the author's ideas. For, evidently, most of the author's ventures into other fields are strongly rooted in his activities as a physicist. In fact, the very title of this volume is a physicist's delight. The papers devoted to physics are reflections of Wigner's interests and major contributions in the following fields: invariance principles; nuclear theory, as well as a great deal of nuclear practice; and solid-state theory.

Wigner is a master of symmetry. The opening paper of this volume, on invari-ance in physics, was first presented at Einstein's 70th birthday celebration in the Palmer Laboratory at Princeton. It is a classic. In this and subsequent papers, we are reminded of the physicist's task of finding out what is irrelevant in the initial conditions in his experiments, the minimality of relevant initial conditions being a necessary condition for maximal theoretical insight.

We read again of the relations between invariance and conservation principles; of the lack of clarity concerning the conservation law of electric charge; and of the vastly more important role of invariance in quantum as compared to classical the-ory. And we think of two short papers by the author, tucked away in the *Göttinger Nachrichten*, where the concept of parity was first introduced and the principle of time reversal invariance in quantum theory was first fully stated. We are led from the first laws of physics, invariance under space displacement and under time dis-placement, via more recondite principles such as the covariance called crossing symmetry, to the very deep, difficult, and dark question of how to put general rel-ativity on speaking terms with quantum mechanics. Every physics student should read all of this, but preferably after a few years of graduate work.

The main nuclear physics in this book is Wigner's Richtmyer lecture on the compound nucleus. Other physics contributions include a short exposé of the four classes of lattices met in solid bodies; a discussion of effects called radiation damage (in solids); a 'burner versus breeder' argument from the longer-range view of applying nuclear energy; and historical notes on the first pile and on the plutonium project.

Amidst all this beautiful physics there is one remark in this book which, it seems to me, is not true to Wigner's style. It is this one. 'It is true that many of the young men are attracted by the big machines of big science and that it is difficult to resist the easy success which these machines promise.' Surely, some of Wigner's brilliant younger Princeton colleagues in experimental physics would have no difficulty in conveying to the author that the success-to-heartbreak ratio in big-machine work is not so much different from what it is in other parts of physics and that no big-machine experimentalist who respects himself and his students will promise them easy going.

The book contains two moving biographical notes with noble passages on the struggle of von Neumann and the stoicism of Fermi in the face of death.

'The promise of future science is to furnish a unifying goal to mankind rather than merely the means to an easy life, to provide some of what the human soul needs in addition to bread alone,' the author says. With this volume he has provided.[79]

In June 1971, Eugene retired from the Princeton faculty, at age 68, after which he was for a year a visiting professor at Louisiana State University in Baton Rouge. Thereafter he returned to Princeton where, apart from some travel, he remained for the rest of his life.

In those last 25 years of his life, Eugene kept publishing, indeed copiously, about 250 papers, the last one at age 87. Only about ten of these deal with physics. The rest treats of his other interests, philosophy, civil defense, reminiscences, obituaries. Many of them make for worthwhile reading, yet do not add substantially to my preceding account.

It is easier to give a picture of Wigner the scientist and philosopher—as I have done so far—than of Wigner the man. It has been said of him: 'It sometimes appears that there are communications barriers between Wigner and other physicists, but there seems no barrier at all between Wigner and physics.'[80] Which reminds me of what Pauli once wrote to him: 'We have very different ways of thinking and I find it difficult, especially in personal discussions, to understand what you mean.'[81] I also recall being present at a seminar which Eugene gave in Copenhagen, where the lack of communication between him and Bohr was striking.

As to myself, I never felt that I fully understood who he was, and so it has been with colleagues of mine with whom I have discussed his personality. While his autobiographical sketch[2] does not really lift the communication barrier between Wigner and the world, it gives nevertheless one very important clue, where Eugene says: 'After 60 years in the United States I am still more Hungarian than American . . . much of the [American] culture escapes me.' I believe that accounts for the fact that I have not been able to grasp the personalities not only of Wigner but also of Szilard and Teller. That I am European born—Dutch— has not helped me one bit to get closer to Hungarian attitudes. My relations with Eugene have always been quite cordial, yet I could not characterize them as a friendship. That would demand at least a modicum of intimacy which we simply did not share.

One Wigner trait familiar to all who knew him was his politeness—which I also ascribe to his Hungarian descent—which could be excessive. Many of us have struggled with him about who should go through a door first. I found a solution to that problem when I said to him: 'Eugene, let us introduce a new rule between us. He who goes through a door last is the impolite one.' It worked. My good friend Sam Treiman hit upon another stratagem. 'I asked him outright [to go first] so that I could win a bet.'[82]

One way one could see through Wigner's surface-thin veneer of modesty was when he would introduce himself to people he knew damned well knew who he was—a quite frequent ploy of his. One example, again by Treiman:

> [He, Treiman] was beginning his appointment to a junior post in Princeton, and on his first day on the job he spotted Wigner in a corridor of the laboratory. He had met Wigner when he was being interviewed for the appointment, but he was not sure whether to presume on this slight acquaintance, which Wigner might not remember. He thus did not know if he should attempt a greeting. The problem was resolved for him when Wigner came up to him and said, 'Good morning, Dr. Treiman, I am so glad to see you here. You may not remember me; we met at the interviewing board. I am Wigner!'[83]

On other occasions he would show his unique ability of blending politeness with biting sharpness. Examples: Once I was talking with Wigner when a young man passed us by, whereupon Eugene turned to me and said: 'Excuse me, but is this man a fool?' Or when he said: 'Go to hell, please,' to a mechanic who did not handle his car to his satisfaction.

The preceding observations on Wigner's personality are anecdotal scraps rather than a fleshed-out picture. The few scattered remarks to follow may help a bit more but still do not add up to a rounded picture of the man.

In 1933 Wigner appealed to American colleagues for help in providing financial support and positions for German physicists dismissed by the Nazis.[84]

In 1954 Eugene, although politically conservative, tried to intercede on Oppenheimer's behalf in the infamous case against him.[85]

Wigner on Richard Feynman: 'He is a second Dirac, only this time more human.'[86]

Once, in the 1970s, Manci, Eugene's sister, said to me: 'Bram, Eugene is meshugge. Can't you talk to him?' That was in reference to Wigner's participation in conferences sponsored by the Unification Church of the Reverend Sun Myung Moon, an organization with a bad, perhaps criminal, reputation. I replied to Manci that I, too, thought that this showed pretty awful judgment on her brother's part but that I could not see how I could influence him to desist. Wigner's own comment on this affair does little to clarify his position.[87]

Family. Around 1939, Eugene brought his parents, then in their sixties, over to the United States, first to Princeton, later to rural New York State. He did his best to make them comfortable but did not succeed. 'I had hoped that they could come to an adored land where they could live without suppression, but they could not. They spent their time wishing that Hitler had never existed.'[88]

I have had many occasions to observe how happy the union was of Eugene and Mary, his second wife. As told, they were married in 1941. Mary was well liked and respected by all who knew her, including me. She died of cancer in 1977.

At about that same time, Donald Hamilton, a distinguished physics professor in Princeton, also passed away. In 1979, Eugene married Don's widow, Eileen, known to all as Pat, whom he has called 'a lovely woman, a lovely trusted companion, a constant helper and friend.'[89] Princeton friends, including me, are fond of her.

Eugene also survived a number of colleagues he was fond of and respected, Fermi (d. 1954), Einstein (1955), von Neumann (1957), Szilard (1964), and Polanyi (1976).

———— —————

Toward the end of his life, Eugene once said: 'That I will die hardly bothers me . . . We are all guests in this life, and our culture commits a crime when it persuades us to think otherwise . . . As a scientist, I must say that we have no heavenly data. So I am afraid that after death we merely cease to exist.'[90]

In his last years, Wigner showed clear signs of senility. Martha, his daughter, has told me: 'A few days before he died he still knew me and, I believe, he knew Pat. He was terribly tired and had a very hard time talking, but was loving, kind, and concerned to the very end.' He died on the first of January, 1995.

He was a very strange man and one of the giants of twentieth-century physics.

Notes and references

1. E. P. Wigner, *The Collected Works*, A. S. Wightman, Ed. for Vols. 1–5, J. Mehra, Ed. for Vols. 6–8, Springer, New York, 1992–1997.

2. *The Recollections of Eugene P. Wigner, as Told to Andrew Szanton*, Plenum Press, New York, 1992. I am indebted to Martha Wigner Upton, Eugene's daughter, for pointing out to me several errors in this book.

3. Ref. 2, p. 26.

4. Ref. 2, pp. 33–4.

5. Ref. 2, p. 47.

6. E. Wigner, interview by T. S. Kuhn, December 3, 1963, transcript in Niels Bohr Archive.

7. Ref. 2, p. 39.

8. Ref. 2, p. 60.

9. Ref. 6, interview, November 21, 1963.

10. Ref. 2, p. 54.

11. Ref. 2, p. 57.

12. Ref. 2, p. 67.

13. Ref. 2, p. 71.

14. For this episode, see A. Pais, *Subtle is the Lord*, chapter 23, Oxford University Press, Oxford and New York, 1982.

15. H. Mark and E. Wigner, *Zeitschr. f. Physik Chemie* **111**, 398, 1924.

16. M. Polanyi and E. Wigner, *Zeitschr. f. Physik* **33**, 429, 1925.

17. E. Wigner, obituary of Polanyi, in *Obit. Not. Fell. Roy. Soc.* **23**, 413, 1977.

18. W. Heisenberg, *Zeitschr. f. Physik* **43**, 172, 1927.

19. W. Heisenberg, *Zeitschr. f. Physik* **33**, 879, 1925.

20. M. Polanyi and E. Wigner, *Zeitschr. f. Physik Chemie* A. **139**, 439, 1928.

21. Ref. 2, p. 103.

22. W. Heisenberg, *Zeitschr. f. Physik* **38**, 411, 1926.

23. Ref. 22, p. 425.

24. W. Heisenberg, *Zeitschr. f. Physik* **39**, 499, 1926.

25. E. Wigner, *Zeitschr. f. Physik* **40**, 492, 1927.

26. I. Schur, Berl. Ber. 1905, p. 406; 1908, p. 664.

27. E. Wigner, *Zeitschr. f. Physik* **40**, 883, 1927. Application to molecules: *Gött. Nachr. 1930*, p. 133; to crystals: Wigner *et al.*, *Phys. Rev.* **50**, 58, 1936.

28. J. von Neumann and E. Wigner, *Zeitschr. f. Physik* **47**, 203, 1928; **49**, 73, 1928; **51**, 844, 1928.

29. J. von Neumann and E. Wigner, *Phys. Z.* **30**, 465, 467, 1929.

30. J. von Neumann, P. Jordan, and E. Wigner, *Ann. Math.* **35**, 29, 1934 (on the possible use of non-associative algebras in quantum mechanics); J. v. Neumann and E. Wigner, *Ann. Math.* **41**, 746, 1940; **59**, 418, 1954.

31. E. Wigner, *Gruppentheorie und ihre Anwendung auf die Quantenmechanik der Atomspektren*, Vieweg, Braunschweig, 1931. English translation *Group Theory and its Application to the Quantum Mechanics of Atomic Spectra*, Academic Press, New York, 1959.

32. A. Pais, *Ann. of Phys.* **9**, 548, 1960; **22**, 274, 1963.

33. H. Weyl, *Gruppentheorie und Quantenmechanik*, Hirzel, Leipzig, 1928, 1931. In English: *The Theory of Groups and Quantum Mechanics* (H. P. Robertson, Transl.), Dover, New York, 1949.

34. Ref. 2, pp. 109, 112.

35. P. Jordan and E. Wigner, *Zeitschr. f. Physik* **47**, 631, 1928.

36. E. Wigner, *Goett. Nachr. 1927*, p. 375.

37. W. Pauli, in *Handbuch d. Phys.* 24/1, p. 185, Springer, Berlin, 1935.

38. E. U. Condon and G. H. Shortley, *The Theory of Atomic Spectra*, MacMillan, New York, 1935.

39. G. C. Wick, A. Wightman, and E. Wigner, *Phys. Rev.* **88**, 101, 1952.

40. E. Wigner, *Goett. Nachr. 1932*, p. 546.

41. E. Wigner, *Symmetries and Reflections*, p. 38, Indiana University Press, 1967.

42. E. Wigner, *Ann. of Math.* **40**, 149, 1939, *Zeitschr. f. Physik* **124**, 665, 1948; *Rev. Mod. Phys.* **29**, 255, 1957; with V. Bergmann, *Proc. Nat. Ac. Sci.* **34**, 211, 1948; with E. Inonü, *Il Nuov Cim.* **9**, August 1, 1952; *Proc. Nat. Ac. Sci.* **39**, 510, 1953.

43. Ref. 6, interview on December 4, 1963.

44. Ref. 2, p. 117.

45. Ref. 2, p. 169.

46. E. Wigner, in *Some Strangeness in the Proportions* (H. Woolf, Ed.), p. 461, Addison-Wesley, Reading, MA, 1980.

47. E. Wigner, *Proc. Am. Philos. Soc.* Vol. 93, December 1949 issue.

48. E. Wigner, *Phys. Rev.* **40**, 749, 1932.

49. Ref. 2, p. 166.

50. F. Seitz, *On the Frontier*, p. 59, American Institute of Physics, 1994.

51. F. Seitz and E. Wigner, *Phys. Rev.* **43**, 804, 1933; **46**, 509, 1934.

52. E. Wigner, *Phys. Rev.* **46**, 1002, 1934; see further E. Wigner, *Sci. Monthly* **42**, 40, 1936; Transactions *Faraday Soc.* **34**, 678, 1938.

53. E. Wigner and J. Bardeen, *Phys. Rev.* **48**, 84, 1935.

54. Ref. 2, pp. 171–3.

55. E. Wigner, *Phys. Rev.* **43**, 252, 1933; *Zeitschr. f. Physik* **83**, 253, 1933.

56. G. Breit and E. Wigner, *Phys. Rev.* **48**, 918, 1935; *ibid.* **49**, 519, 1936.

57. G. Breit and E. Wigner, *Phys. Rev.* **53**, 998, 1938.

58. E. Wigner, *Phys. Rev.* **51**, 106, 1937.

59. To wit, the SU(6)-symmetry, reviewed in A. Pais, *Rev. Mod. Phys.* **38**, 215, 1966.

60. Ref. 2, p. 178.

61. Ref. 2, p. 179.

62. Including Wigner with C. Critchfield and E. Teller, *Phys. Rev.* **56**, 530, 1939; with L. Eisenbud, *Phys. Rev.* **56**, 214, 1939; *Proc. Nat. Ac. Sci.* **27**, 281, 1941; with H. Margenau, *Phys. Rev.* **58**, 103, 1940; with C. Critchfield, *Phys. Rev.* **60**, 412, 1941.

63. For the origins of this project see A. Pais, *Niels Bohr's Times*, pp. 492–4, Oxford University Press, 1991.

64. E. Wigner, *Saturday Review of Literature*, November 17, 1945, p. 28.

65. E. Wigner, letter to A. B. Lerner, September 19, 1967; reprinted in A. B. Lerner, *Einstein and Newton*, p. 215, Lerner, Minneapolis, 1973.

66. For a summary of these activities see E. Wigner, ref. 41, p. 113ff.; p. 126ff. For much greater detail see ref. 1, Vol. 5.

67. These patents are listed in ref. 1, Vol. 5, part 4.

68. Ref. 2, p. 290.

69. *Civil Defense: Project Harbor Summary Report*, National Research Council, National Academy of Sciences, 1964.

70. *Survival and the Bomb* (E. Wigner, Ed.), Indiana University Press, 1969. The quotation is found on p. viii. See also *Who speaks for Civil Defense* (E. Wigner, Ed.), Scribner's, New York, 1968.

71. Ref. 2, chapter 17.

72. Ref. 2, p. 295.

73. E. Wigner, *Phys. Rev.* **70**, 15, 606, 1946; **73**, 1002, 1948; **98**, 145, 1955; *Proc. Am. Philos. Soc.* **90**, 25, 1945; with L. Eisenbud, *Phys. Rev.* **72**, 29, 1947.

74. L. Eisenbud and E. Wigner, *Nuclear Structure*, Princeton University Press, 1958.

75. For a summary see E. Wigner in *Statistical Properties of Nuclei* (J. Garg, Ed.), p. 7, Plenum Press, 1972.

76. For example E. Wigner, *Zeitschr. f. Physik* **124**, 665, 1958; *Phys. Rev.* **77**, 711, 1950; *Helv. Phys. Acta* supplement IV, 210, 1956; *Rev. Mod. Phys.* **29**, 255, 1957.

77. A. Weinberg and E. Wigner, *The Physical Theory of Neutron Chain Reactors*, University of Chicago Press, 1958.

78. Ref. 2, p. 307.

79. A. Pais, *Science* **157**, 911, 1967.

80. V. Bargmann *et al. Rev. Mod. Phys.* **34**, 587, 1962.

81. W. Pauli, letter to E. Wigner, December 30, 1935; reprinted in *Wolfgang Pauli, Scientific Correspondence* (K. von Meyenn, Ed.), Vol. 3, p. 779, Springer, New York, 1993.

82. S. B. Treiman, *Ann. Rev. Nucl. Sci.* **46**, 1, 1996.

83. Quoted in R. Peierls, *Bird of Passage*, Princeton University Press, 1985.

84. A. Kimball Smith and Ch. Weiner, *Robert Oppenheimer*, p. 173, Harvard University Press, 1980.

85. R. Rhodes, *Dark Sun*, p. 540, Simon and Schuster, New York, 1995.

86. Quoted in ref. 84, p. 269.

87. Ref. 2, p. 261.

88. Ref. 2, p. 186.

89. Ref. 2, p. 304.

90. Ref. 2, pp. 317–18.

Onomasticon